WHERE MUSIC HELPS: COMM
THERAPY IN ACTION AND R

Where Music Helps:
Community Music Therapy in Action and Reflection

BRYNJULF STIGE,
University of Bergen, Norway
Uni Health, GAMUT, Norway

GARY ANSDELL
Nordoff-Robbins Music Therapy, UK

COCHAVIT ELEFANT
University of Bergen, Norway

MERCÉDÈS PAVLICEVIC
Nordoff-Robbins Music Therapy, UK
University of Pretoria, South Africa

ASHGATE

Published by
Ashgate Publishing Limited
Wey Court East
Union Road
Farnham
Surrey, GU9 7PT
England

Ashgate Publishing Company
Suite 420
101 Cherry Street
Burlington
VT 05401-4405
USA

www.ashgate.com

British Library Cataloguing in Publication Data
Where music helps: community music therapy in action and reflection. – (Ashgate popular and folk music series)
1. Music therapy. 2. Music – Social aspects.
I. Series II. Stige, Brynjulf.
615.8'5154–dc22

Library of Congress Cataloging-in-Publication Data
Stige, Brynjulf.
   Where music helps: community music therapy in action and reflection / Brynjulf Stige,
   Gary Ansdell, Cochavit Elefant, and Mercédès Pavlicevic.
      p. cm. – (Ashgate popular and folk music series)
   Includes bibliographical references and index.
   ISBN 978-0-7546-6850-3 (hardcover: alk. paper)
   1. Music therapy. 2. Music – Social aspects. I. Ansdell, Gary. II. Elefant, Cochavit. III.
   Pavlicevic, Mercédès. IV. Title.
   ML3920.S82 2009
   615.8'5154–dc22

                                                                                    2009016836

ISBN 9780754668503 (hbk)
ISBN 9781409410102 (pbk)

Printed and bound in Great Britain by
MPG Books Group, UK

Contents

PART X
Brynjulf Stige, Gary Ansdell, Cochavit Elefant and Mercédès Pavlicevic

List of Figures

General Editor's Preface

The upheaval that occurred in musicology during the last two decades of the twentieth century has created a new urgency for the study of popular music alongside the development of new critical and theoretical models. A relativistic outlook has replaced the universal perspective of modernism (the international ambitions of the 12-note style); the grand narrative of the evolution and dissolution of tonality has been challenged, and emphasis has shifted to cultural context, reception and subject position. Together, these have conspired to eat away at the status of canonical composers and categories of high and low in music. A need has arisen, also, to recognize and address the emergence of crossovers, mixed and new genres, to engage in debates concerning the vexed problem of what constitutes authenticity in music and to offer a critique of musical practice as the product of free, individual expression.

Popular musicology is now a vital and exciting area of scholarship, and the *Ashgate Popular and Folk Music Series* presents some of the best research in the field. Authors are concerned with locating musical practices, values and meanings in cultural context, and may draw upon methodologies and theories developed in cultural studies, semiotics, poststructuralism, psychology and sociology. The series focuses on popular musics of the twentieth and twenty-first centuries. It is designed to embrace the world's popular musics from Acid Jazz to Zydeco, whether high tech or low tech, commercial or non-commercial, contemporary or traditional.

Derek B. Scott
Professor of Critical Musicology
University of Leeds, UK

Acknowledgments

This book presents and discusses results from an international research project on Community Music Therapy, funded by the Research Council of Norway and performed over a period of four years (2004–2008). The study has been part of a larger research project "Music and Health in Late Modernity: Resource-oriented Music Therapy and Community Music Therapy," which was initiated by Sogn og Fjordane University College. The project has been hosted by this university college, the last two years in collaboration with GAMUT, the Grieg Academy Music Therapy Research Centre at the University of Bergen. The other parts of the larger project (not discussed in this book) include an explorative study of resource-oriented music therapy in mental health care, meta-analysis of existing quantitative research on the effects of music therapy, and a multi-center RCT on the effects of resource-oriented music therapy. Co-researchers in the larger umbrella project have been Leif Edvard Aarø, Christian Gold, and Randi Rolvsjord, and we want to thank you warmly for your contributions and helpful feedback to our project. We also want to thank the Research Council of Norway for making this collaboration possible and the University of Bergen for supporting the publication of this book.

The research project that is the basis for this book has been developed as a series of case studies in four different national contexts; Norway, Israel, South Africa, and England. We have therefore, somewhat self-indulgently probably, created an acronym from the first letters of these countries and called our group the NISE Research Group. Much of the communication in the group has of course been through e-mails, but in the project period we also had the pleasure of coming together for a week or so twice a year, in nice places such as Bergen, Brandal, London, Pretoria, and Sandane. We want to thank the various hosting institutions for generously helping us in realizing this; Sogn og Fjordane University College and the University of Bergen in Norway, the Nordoff-Robbins Music Therapy Centre in United Kingdom and the University of Pretoria in South Africa.

We have now been given the possibility of communicating what we have learnt in the process, and special thanks go to the music therapists and the participants and co-workers in the eight Community Music Therapy projects that we have tracked:

Gary says: I want to thank *Musical Minds* (and their host organization *Together Tower Hamlets* and facilitator Sarah Wilson) and the *Scrap Metal Project* (and its facilitator Stuart Wood) for allowing me to witness their process and performance events. Sarah and Stuart have also most generously shared with me their many thoughts about the challenges and rewards of performing within these contexts.

Cochavit says: Thanks to Beit Issie Shapiro, Raanana, who let me step out of my conventional music therapy role in order to take the children to new arenas.

Thanks also to the courageous Bilu elementary school that joined the project. And: special thanks to the amazing group of children, staff and parents. Without their belief, trust and hard work, a successful inclusion and community change would not have happened. I also want to thank Rina Stadler, the music therapist who courageously invited me to enter her arena in order to find new directions for her choirs. And: Thanks to *Idud* choir and a special thanks to *Renanim* choir who deeply moved and transformed me with their courage of letting their voices be heard!

Mercédès says: Thank you to the *Music Therapy Community Clinic* in the Western Cape: Kerryn Torrance, Sunelle Fouché, (indirectly) Cerri Newdigate, and those wonderful Heideveld children, whose generosity of time and spirited enthusiasm left me endlessly admiring of their tenacity and dedication. I also want to thank Carol Lotter, at *Youth Development Outreach* in Eersterust, for being available to my many and ongoing demands, and for doing such brilliant work in often trying circumstances.

Brynjulf says: Thanks to the music therapists, the participants, and the volunteers in NFU (a Norwegian organization for individuals with intellectual disabilities and their families), who over the years have developed the *Cultural Festival* in Sogn og Fjordane (Western Norway) into a celebration of participatory possibilities. And; thanks to Solgunn Knardal and the members of the *Senior Choir* in Sandane, for your musicality and hospitality.

Finally: Thanks to all who have nurtured our thinking over the last few years, through support and critique. You are too many to be listed here, but we want to make an exception for Even Ruud (University of Oslo) and Tia DeNora (University of Exeter), whose scholarly work on music, health, and everyday life has been an immense inspiration for our efforts in exploring where and how music helps. Lastly we want to express our thanks to music therapists Randi Rolvsjord and Katrina McFerran and psychologist Signe Stige who have read earlier versions of the manuscript and gave us valuable food for thought.

PART I

Chapter 1

Introduction
Music and Health in Community

Brynjulf Stige

Listening to *Musical Minds*

"The arts are not drugs," wrote the British novelist E. M. Forster; "they are not guaranteed to act when taken."[1] We have experienced how popular opinion often associates music therapy with the systematic application of specific music for specific purposes, such as relaxing people. This may sound proper and scientific in many people's ears, but it leaves little space for personal participation. We could say that it is an idea based upon a mechanical metaphor, reducing music to a "pill" and focusing upon the effect of musical stimuli on the human organism. Within the discipline of music therapy critique of this idea has been quite common. In music therapy there is an interest in human interaction through music and not just in the organism's reaction to music. Music therapy practice therefore often focuses upon human expression and communication.

We acknowledge the importance of this critique. Still, this book is based upon a critique of the critique, claiming that it has not been radical enough. Human interaction through music requires *space* and *place*, and it is therefore not enough to critique ideas based upon mechanical metaphors. The implications of *contextual* or *ecological* metaphors must also be taken into consideration. Music is a socio-cultural phenomenon and musical activity involves social action, as the projects described in this book will illuminate in various ways.

In this book you will hear about:

- A singing group called *Musical Minds* who meet weekly in a deprived area of East London. They meet under the auspices of an organization that helps adults with long-term mental health problems, and music and singing are for the group unique ways of finding meaning and a sense of *belonging* in a difficult environment.
- Two diverse groups of young children who attended schools in separate parts of the town Raanana in Israel; one group in an elementary school and the other in a center for special education. Through participation in collaborative musical activities involving an intricate *intergroup process*

---

[1] Quoted in Oliver Sacks's book *Musicophilia* (2007, p. 299).

these children gradually became connected. The story of this process illuminates how the children creatively performed their own solutions to social problems.

- The *Music for Life* programme in Western Cape, South Africa, where two music therapists have set up a traveling service with the aim of working with and within local communities rather than providing a music therapy place that others come to. The programme includes the Heideveld Children's Choir, which prepares for the annual Heideveld Community Concert, and this event illuminates the traveling music therapy service's contribution to the *musical and social life* of Heideveld as well as Heideveld's contribution and support for the work.

- The *Cultural Festival* for adults with intellectual disabilities in Sogn og Fjordane, Western Norway. The association organizing this festival stresses its function as an inclusive arena for musical and social *participation* and it turns out that the participants indeed are involved in many different ways, ranging from the most silent and careful partaking to adventurous and eccentric acts that challenge established procedures and role relationships.

- A unique *performance* project in rural South of England for adults with neurological disabilities, which was called *Scrap Metal*. Beginning from a conventional music therapy program, the project evolved into a complex socio-cultural collaboration where participants (both able and disabled) used scrap metal to build instruments, workshop musical idioms and perform a one-off concert in a church to a local audience.

- *Renanim*, a choir of adults with physical disability and normal cognition living in the Israeli town of Natanya. *Giving voice* to this choir was the idea behind a performance in collaboration with another choir, but this gave a contradictory outcome. *Renanim* felt that their voices were not heard, in spite of the good intentions of the music therapist. An adjusted Participatory Action Research project follows the development of the choir in their communication and exploration towards the discovery of how they could achieve their shared concern – claiming their voice.

- A music project in Eersterust, close to Pretoria in South Africa, where a music therapist works at *Youth Development Outreach*, a community-based organization that caters for young people in trouble with the law. Through group singing, drumming, and dancing young people who are used to conflict, violence, and mistrust in their daily lives develop skills in listening to one another, co-operating, and supporting one another, and also consider what these experiences mean in terms of their daily lives.

- The *Senior Choir* in Sandane, rural Western Norway, with members who eagerly participate in choir rehearsals and performances in spite of various constraints. The rehearsals mean hard work on "getting the music right" and include challenging negotiations on values that shape their culture and everyday life, but the overall atmosphere is still one of warmth, hospitality, and *mutual care*.

All these groups and projects are being facilitated by music therapists but are not necessarily identified formally as music therapy groups and projects. They exemplify a movement within contemporary music therapy that has been labeled *Community Music Therapy*. As practices these projects are characterized by collaborative and context-sensitive music-making and they focus upon giving voice to the relatively disadvantaged in each context. The participants' interest in and love for music is essential, but the shared music-making also relates to concerns for health, human development, and equity. Community Music Therapy therefore involves what we could call *health musicing*[2] (Stige, 2002), as it focuses on the relationships between individual experiences and the possible creation of *musical community* (Pavlicevic and Ansdell, 2004).

Community Music Therapy is controversial in some music therapy circles, since it may involve some substantial rethinking of music therapy theory and practice. In our view it fills a need in a range of contexts and also contributes to further development of music therapy as discipline and profession. We consider Community Music Therapy as one voice in a broader multi-disciplinary dialogue on the relationships between the musical and the social in human life. This book is therefore written to the music therapist as well as to any student of music, health, and social life. Our ambition has been to document and analyze practices that have been underreported in the literature so far, so that we can listen to and learn from groups such as *Musical Minds*, who remind us about how our musical minds are embodied and embedded in real world situations.

Music and Music Therapy as Social and Situated Activity

Music therapy was established as university discipline and professional practice in the US in the 1940s and was pioneered in Europe, South America, and Australia a decade or two later. Currently music therapy is growing in all continents and is in the process of being instituted in an increasing number of countries. In the 1960s and 1970s, formative years for attempts by modern music therapy to link music and health in theory and practice, most musicologists concentrated on Western music history or the analysis of works of the Western classical canon and thus did not have much to say about ordinary people in contemporary real world situations (whether in the West or anywhere else). Their scholarly work was thus not of much use for music therapists, who either developed a quite pragmatic approach with little consideration of theory or concentrated on cultivating relationships to theories in medicine, special education, psychology, and psychotherapy.

The recent emergence of Community Music Therapy implies that theories from fields such as systems theory, anthropology, sociology, and community psychology are taken into consideration as well. Particularly, we suggest that it implies that music studies become more important for music therapy, and possibly vice versa.

---

[2] The term *musicing* will be explained in more detail below.

Recently, music therapists have had to ask themselves questions like: "What has the New Musicology to say to music therapy?" (Ansdell, 1997) and "Musicology: misunderstood guest at the music therapy feast?" (Ansdell, 2001). One of the reasons why there is need for more sophisticated music thinking in music therapy is that most theories in disciplines such as medicine and psychology have had little to say about music. Also, musicology has changed and become more relevant for music therapy, by focusing more upon music as social and situated activity.

The work of music therapy theorist Even Ruud illustrates quite well how relationships between music therapy and other branches of music studies have been strengthened lately. In one of his most important early works, *Music Therapy and its Relationship to Current Treatment Theories* (Ruud, 1980a), the focus is almost entirely on relationships to theories of medicine, psychology, and sociology, even though various concepts of music in different music therapy theories are discussed. In an introduction to music therapy published about the same time, Ruud (1980b) indicates that music therapy is interesting and important for musical reasons also, for instance in relation to handicapped people's right to music. A few years later this trend is more explicit; Ruud (1987/1990) locates music therapy in the humanities and argues that relationships between music therapy and musicology would be mutually beneficial. Some of Ruud's later work, such as his studies of music and values (Ruud, 1996) and of music and identity (Ruud, 1997b), is quite explicit in its ambition to bridge various approaches to music studies, including music therapy. In other words; there has been more and more of an integration of Ruud's work as a music therapy theorist and a musicologist. We propose that Community Music Therapy may contribute to integration of music therapy and music studies more generally.

An openness to interdisciplinary perspectives linked to an interest in the relationships between music, culture, and society is quite characteristic of the development of music studies in the last two decades. The story of how and why this happened has been told many times, in many different ways. Some have focused upon the emergence of a "new musicology" with integration of critical and cultural perspectives, as developed by e.g. Gary Tomlinson and Susan McClary and pioneered by Joseph Kerman (1985) and others. Some have focused upon developments in ethnomusicology, which after the "cultural turn" proposed by Alan Merriam (1964) worked out perspectives of broader relevance for the understanding of music in any culture (as has been demonstrated by researchers such as John Blacking and Steven Feld). Others again have focused upon the emergence of a culturally informed music sociology (as developed by e.g. Howard Becker and Tia DeNora). The importance of the new area of popular music studies (with scholars such as Simon Frith and Philip Tagg) has also been underscored. Richard Middleton (2003) describes these developments as "distinctive but often mutually affecting routes" toward a position against pure musical autonomy:

> "Music is more than *notes*" represents the bottom line, an idea whose seeming banality today perhaps signals its triumph. (Middleton, 2003, p. 2)

For a lay person who conceivably thinks of music in terms such as emotion, energy, and engagement in everyday life activities it would probably be somewhat surprising that a range of scholars have had to work hard for years to show that music is "more than notes." Part of the scholarly context is of course that musicology had established itself quite firmly as the study of the works of the great masters (of Western art music). We could say that the idea of music as autonomous art belonging to a "special sphere" separated from e.g. the market and other social circumstances had insulated musicology from taking interest in how most people use and experience music. The abovementioned change in music studies could thus be described in various ways; as a cultural turn; as a critique of an elitist and ethnocentric heritage, and as the merging of musicology, ethnomusicology, music sociology, and popular music studies.[3]

In more straightforward language we could say that students of music increasingly have realized that there is no clear dividing line between classical music and popular music or between music of the West and music of "the rest." The cultural, contextual, and interpretive turn in music studies thus also could be described as a move in the direction of a musicology with people in it, a "populated musicology," which suggests that dialogues between music therapy and other fields of music studies become more relevant and interesting than used to be the case. Most scholars would agree that a "populated musicology" could not take interest in the construction of geniuses only. It could thus be described as a democratization of music studies. This change in perspective has implications for the conception of *musicality*, which no longer could be thought of as a gift for the happy few but rather as a shared capacity of the human species (a capacity which unfolds and develops in ways that depend on the life history and cultural context of the individual).[4]

If music is acknowledged as a situated activity not only reflecting but also performing human relationships, then it is not just legitimate but in fact highly relevant to study *how people actually use music. Use* is an important asset of human interaction with the world and could not be reduced to instrumental purposes in the narrow and negative sense of that term.[5] In the flow of texts on this theme the term

---

[3]   For overviews and discussions of these interdisciplinary shifts, see e.g. (Leppert and McClary, 1987; Cook, 1998; Cook and Everist, 1999; Scott, 2000; Clayton, Herbert and Middleton, 2003; Martin, 2006).

[4]   The inclusion of biological and evolutionary perspectives in music studies was supported by the influential work of John Blacking (1973) and has been developed considerably the last few years. See e.g. (Trevarthen and Malloch, 2000; Wallin, Merker and Brown, 2000; Cross, 2003). See also (Stige, 2002) for a discussion linked to music therapy theory.

[5]   Contributions that have paved the way for a serious rethinking of *use* as human activity and condition include Heidegger's (1927/1962) discussion of use as a sort of knowledge, Wittgenstein's (1953/1967) discussion of collaborative use as a human way of meaning-making, and Gibson's (1979/1986) description of affordance.

musicing has been appropriated by a variety of authors. The books of David Elliott (1995) and especially Christopher Small (1998) discuss this notion in detail, and Small most carefully underscores how the idea of music as an activity is linked to a contextual and relational understanding of human life.[6] The idea of musicing, then, goes far beyond the simple point of suggesting that music could be treated as a verb and not just as a noun; it suggests awareness about how music affords and requires human interaction and collaboration in any given context.[7]

Perhaps in the margins of these cultural and disciplinary shifts, music therapists have developed their practice with a wide range of people in a wide range of contexts. An interest in how and where people use music is one of the places where music therapy thinking and newer music thinking could meet. While traditional musicology could privilege very specific uses (such as contemplation) and disparage others (such as distraction and entertainment), contemporary music studies would examine how such value attribution is linked to social interests and cultural values in broader contexts.

At the time Ansdell (2001) asked if musicology was a "misunderstood guest at the music therapy feast" it would probably also have been relevant to ask if music therapy was a misunderstood guest in various music studies contexts. Integration of music therapy perspectives has not been too common in music studies. There are signs, however, suggesting that things are in the process of changing: Increasingly, music therapy is part of broader multidisciplinary discourses on music, in relation to themes such as the origins of music (Grinde, 2000; Merker, 2000; Kennair, 2001; Dissanayake, 2001), communicative musicality (Trevarthen and Malloch, 2000; Malloch and Trevarthen, 2009; Wigram and Elefant, 2009; Pavlicevic and Ansdell, 2009), music and communication (Ansdell, 2005b; Thaut, 2005), music and emotion (Bunt and Pavlicevic, 2001), and music in everyday life (Berkaak and Ruud, 1992, 1994; DeNora, 2000). The above examples are in no way meant to be comprehensive but illuminate a higher degree of interdisciplinary exchange than used to be the case just a few years ago.

One of the reasons why music therapy contributes to the broader field of music studies is that music therapists often engage with users that conventionally have been excluded, not only from music studies but even from any kind of musical engagement and experience. There are inequities in access to the resources required for musical participation, inequities that in various ways may be linked

---

[6]   Even though the work of Small has been especially important for our understanding, we prefer Elliot's (1995) straightforward spelling of "musicing" instead of Small's (1998) more archaic-looking "musicking."

[7]   Musicing is of course no new "thing" or activity, only a relatively new term. The idea of music as social and situated activity has been developed in music sociology and ethnomusicology for decades and it has been quite well established in music therapy theory also, for instance in the work of Even Ruud (1987/1990, 1998). What Small (1998) has achieved, is to produce an articulation of this perspective that has been read and found useful by a comparatively large and multidisciplinary group of music scholars and students.

to gender, class, ethnicity, and handicap. In music therapy there is a strong tradition for countering inequities due to handicap, for instance through musically flexible forms of improvisation where the music therapists use their interpersonal and musical skills in ways that enable participation for individuals who in other situations would have been deemed to be too handicapped or have too limited skills to be included in any type of musical activity. The limitation of this tradition is that it mainly has been developed within the confines of the four walls of the music therapy room, or more precisely within the confines of professional and institutionalized care. The movement of Community Music Therapy addresses mechanisms of exclusion and inclusion in broader contexts and requires a more socially engaged practice.

In these and other ways, it is probable that Community Music Therapy may illuminate and problematize the interplay of what is usually described as musical issues and extra-musical issues. Community Music Therapy exemplifies that music as a social phenomenon is a very common thing and potentially also a very special thing. Community Music Therapy projects are often related to ordinary everyday contexts and practices where people engage in music regularly. But Community Music Therapy sometimes also involves extraordinary processes creating unique events and experiences. Examples in this book include adolescents recreating their identity from criminal band members to musical band members, adults with mental health problems collaborating through music in ways they could not manage together without music, or elderly people participating competently in choir singing in spite of problems that make participation in almost any other activity impossible.

Two caveats are important in relation to the suggestion that Community Music Therapy could be seen in relation to a broader interdisciplinary discourse on music as social and cultural phenomenon. First, the interest for music as a sociocultural phenomenon does *not* suggest that individuality is irrelevant and only communal processes of interest. Music may be perceived as constitutive for and expressive of both individuality and community. Whether these dimensions complement each other or compete is an issue that needs to be examined in context. Second, for Community Music Therapy it is not adequate to take interest in music as social and cultural participation if this is not seen in relation to health, human development, and social change in some way or another. We claim this even though we also claim that "more music" and "music for all" could be important and legitimate objectives in the development of Community Music Therapy practices. How these two claims could be made compatible will be clarified in the various case studies of this book and discussed specifically in Part X.

Studying Community Music Therapy

The pioneering decades of modern music therapy were characterized by a post-war optimism on the value of health and education for all. This may represent one of the contexts explaining the inclusive character of the work of many music therapy pioneers. Take the central pioneers in the British context as examples: Juliette Alvin, Nordoff and Robbins, and Mary Priestley all developed forms of practice that later have been cultivated largely as one-on-one traditions of therapy in clinical settings, but these pioneers also experimented with much more public practices in the service of health promotion, such as ensembles, music clubs, and musical performances. As music therapy gradually became more professionalized in the 1980s and 90s, these latter activities often were put in the background, with clinical work within more conventional therapeutic boundaries in the foreground. Music therapy more and more came to mean special music for special people in special places. The discipline and profession of music therapy became affiliated with medicine, special education, and psychotherapy and the main bulk of literature documenting the processes and outcomes of music therapy practice focused upon the effect of music in relation to individual pathology and symptomatology.

There have been many sub-currents leading in other directions, so the above brief is admittedly oversimplified, but it should give a reasonable foundation for reflecting upon why there is need for a movement such as Community Music Therapy. Before explaining this, we want to clarify that we think of Community Music Therapy as something more than and different from music therapy in community settings. Historically, deinstitutionalization of care for populations such as psychiatric patients certainly has stimulated reflections on relationships between music therapy and community. The pioneering work of the American music therapist Florence Tyson who established what she called a Community Music Therapy Center in New York in the 1960s is a good example of this. But while Tyson's (1968) work was adjusted to a new context of practice it was still to a high degree informed by a medical and psychotherapeutic frame of thinking, so that the primacy of individual therapeutic work in discrete settings would not be challenged substantially.

The current (post 2000) international Community Music Therapy movement is different. It goes beyond conceptions of music therapy in community settings to also embrace music therapy *as* community and music therapy *for* community development. For decades there have been community-oriented music therapy practices in several countries (see Stige, 2003), but an international scholarly discourse on Community Music Therapy is a quite recent phenomenon. Community Music Therapy was a burning topic of debate in the 10th World Congress of Music Therapy in Oxford in 2002, preceded and accompanied by some of the first international texts specifically discussing a contemporary concept of Community Music Therapy (Ansdell, 2002; Kenny and Stige, 2002; Stige, 2002). Two years later the first chapter book providing case examples from several national contexts was published (Pavlicevic and Ansdell, 2004).

As Norwegian music therapy theorist Even Ruud (2004a) has argued, it may be time for music therapy to go beyond its relatively marginal position (in the clinic and in society) in order to engage more directly with problems and possibilities of music and health in society. In this Introduction we have positioned the emergent movement of Community Music Therapy in relation to developments within the modern discipline and profession of music therapy and suggested that this movement may operate as a "cultural critique" informed by sociocultural processes of change both in society at large and in the academic discourse on music. Our goal with this book is to offer a range of case studies that may explore localized processes of health musicing and suggest concepts and perspectives that may clarify possibilities and limitations of musical community in the service of health.

Community Music Therapy projects are concerned with the challenge of making music possible in contexts where the helpful appropriation of music is challenged, be that in the clinic, in a community center, or in other everyday settings. The studies to be presented in this book are related to a discipline and a profession which for historical reasons is labeled *music therapy*. This does not mean that the projects and activities themselves always could or should be labeled therapy. Alternative labels for some of these projects could be prevention, health promotion, non-medical care, community development, or just music.[8] Many of the music groups and projects that are described in this book have given themselves proper names, such as *Musical Minds*, *Music for Life*, *Scrap Metal*, and *Renamim*, reflecting how the participants identity themselves as music-makers. They are still concerned, however, with how music may afford therapeutic experiences and processes of change, the main idea shared being that through collaborative musicing it is possible to mobilize resources for the benefit of individuals and communities.

Writing *Where Music Helps*

In suggesting a social and ecological understanding of human problems and resources, Community Music Therapy may challenge some established assumptions on the relationships between music and human wellbeing. In preparation for one of the seminars we arranged in the process of developing the collaborative research project that this book documents, Gary Ansdell made the following reflective note:

> To use a metaphor from Wittgenstein we could say that music therapy has been "held captive by a picture" for a generation or more (in what I call the "consensus model") – a picture of …

---

[8]   An implication of this is that various terms are used for description of the non-professional participants. In some examples Community Music Therapy projects grow out of medical contexts where there is tradition for use of the term *patient*. In other contexts, such as mental health care, the term *client* is much more common. In many Community Music Therapy projects focusing upon empowerment and participation in non-clinical contexts, terms such as *participant* or *musician* are more useful.

- Self-contained individuals relatively unrelated to social, cultural or political contexts, with an emphasis on authenticity, essential self, self-responsibility (the "capsule self").
- Music as reflective of intra-psychic life (or at most of intersubjective relatedness), and representative of clients' pathological aspects.
- Therapy as engagement with pathology, problems and adjustment and as a process of traveling *in-and-down* with the patient by ensuring privacy and containment.

    This overall "picture" accorded badly with my practical experience as a music therapist, of "following where people and music led." The "picture" I was "shown" instead was of musicing leading towards a closer integration (and travel between) intra- and inter-personal, cultural and communal realms of experience. The picture was not just the opposite of the "consensus model" of music therapy but a finer-drawn inter-relationship between: illness/health; autonomy/community; culture/context, privacy/public witness, containment/-performance … (Ansdell, note written in 2005)

This note reveals that in music therapy there are clearly several different discourses on music, human health, and therapy. There is no one paradigm or perspective that dominates the field and there are few reasons to expect or hope that such domination will be achieved. This could be seen as a resource if we want to acknowledge and explore multifaceted phenomena such as music and human health (see e.g. Ruud, 1980a). So maybe Community Music Therapy is just one more specialty, one more flower in the colorful bouquet that we call music therapy? The fact that some music therapists have responded to Community Music Therapy as if it was an unwanted weed and used terms such as "professional suicide" suggests that this image might grasp only one aspect of what is going on. We think that Community Music Therapy could also be thought of as a "cultural critique" addressing pertinent questions on what the mission of music therapy in current societies could or should be. In relation to this we want to clarify two points: First, the relationship between "mainstream" music therapy and Community Music Therapy varies from country to country. Second, in no context will Community Music Therapy represent a complete break from more established professional traditions; there is always a dialectics of tradition and innovation involved.

The first point is exemplified by the four national contexts selected for this study. In the UK, community-oriented practices were integral to the work of many of the pioneers of the 1960s and 1970s but then gradually were overshadowed by more clinically oriented work. In consequence, the post 2000 re-emergence of Community Music Therapy has been quite controversial in this country. The situation is very different in Norway, where community-oriented work has been acknowledged as an integral part of mainstream music therapy from the 1970s and to this day. In Israel and South Africa the situation is quite different again. In Israel, Community Music Therapy is a relatively new idea and still quite marginal. It is also new in South Africa, but so is the whole idea of modern music therapy in that country, and Community Music Therapy is currently establishing itself as the central approach to professional music therapy, more culturally and socially appropriate than individualized approaches to music therapy would have been.

The second point could be illuminated by some thoughts on the idea of Community Music Therapy as cultural critique. As indicated above, it is probably correct to suggest that there have always been elements of cultural critique in modern music therapy. Music therapists have been able to develop sensitive ways of communicating musically with people in need, even with people with the most serious and multiple handicaps. Music therapy therefore has challenged restricted notions about what music is and about who could and should participate in music. In this way, music therapists have contributed to a better understanding of how music may link to human values such as dignity, respect, and quality of life. Also, music therapists to some degree have challenged common notions of therapy, by developing practices that are strengths-based and appealing even to clients that typically are not motivated for therapy engagement. Community Music Therapy could be seen as an expansion of this tradition of critique, by providing even more radical challenges to established notions of music and therapy – within and without the discipline and profession of music therapy. Community Music Therapy, then, represents a different way of thinking about music therapy, but this difference should be understood both as a continuation of and a contrast to pre-existing music therapy discourse and practice.

This book communicates the main findings produced in a collaborative research project funded by The Research Council of Norway. This project has enabled us to track eight Community Music Therapy projects in four different countries; England, Israel, South Africa, and Norway. Our accounts will necessarily be partial; they will be both incomplete and predisposed in certain ways. Eight case studies and four countries do not cover the range of intriguing contexts and projects in contemporary Community Music Therapy. Furthermore, the complexity of each of the eight projects that we have studied goes far beyond what is possible to communicate in this book. We also acknowledge that our accounts are colored by our relationships to this field of study as well as to the specific projects studied. We cannot deny that we have interest in the development of Community Music Therapy and also we all had various relationships to the music projects we have studied, before we started tracking them for this book. In some cases some of us have been engaged in establishing or developing the projects themselves, in other cases we have previously trained the music therapists that are engaged in the projects, or the music therapists that we have studied have been colleagues who we know well.

We do suggest, however, that partiality may be tolerable, maybe even a quality, if it is acknowledged and managed in ways that warrant the description "self-conscious serious partiality" (Clifford, 1986). We cannot offer objective facts produced by neutral observers. What we can offer are careful descriptions and interpretations based upon prolonged experience and engagement with the projects tracked, combined with clarifications of our own positions and perspectives.

In order to approach this, we have chosen to employ more than one text genre when writing this book. Our personal experience of each project is presented in *narratives* under the heading "Action," preceding each research-based *essay* under the heading "Reflection." An initial presentation of each author and the four national contexts is given in Chapter 2 after this introduction. The narratives and essays of the book are also framed by two dialogues; an initial dialogue that clarifies some of the hopes and ambitions that the four authors had before writing the book and then some inconclusive thoughts at the end. This should at least provide the reader with some tools for appraisal of our partiality.

The development of the texts for this book is informed by a few broad questions such as: "How can Community Music Therapy processes be described in relation to their specific social and cultural contexts?" "How do clients/participants participate in and experience Community Music Therapy projects?" "In what ways can Community Music Therapy promote health and change? Does it offer other cultural benefits?" In the work with each case study, more specific questions were developed, as they emerged from the analysis of empirical material, engagement with the literature, and discussions in the research group. The case studies presented all focus upon a theme that was suggested by the analysis of the material. The themes include *belonging*, *intergroup processes*, *collaborative musicing*, *participation*, *performance*, *participatory change processes*, *social activism*, and *mutual care*. Each theme could be considered a "handle" that could be used when opening the complexities of each case, or a "prism" for the reading of it. We do not claim that the handle or prism that we offer is all there is to each case or that a theme that is discussed in one essay is of relevance only to this particular case, but we have chosen this way of dealing with the complexities of the projects that we have studied.[9]

Our goal has been to write in ways that enable us to acknowledge the important pioneering work in many current Community Music Therapy projects around the world. We try to communicate this intention in the subtitle of the book: *Community Music Therapy in Action and Reflection.* The case studies focus upon Community

---

[9]   Our research methodology could be described as ethnographically informed qualitative case studies. Our approach has been interpretive, we have tried to draw on an epistemological position that avoids polarization of empiricist and constructionist positions. Both views build on assumptions on the nature of language that we find problematic. The correspondence theory on truth, typical of empiricist positions, assumes that language mirrors reality without or with minimal distortion, while a radical constructionist position leads to "disconnection" of language and the phenomenon under scrutiny. The Danish ethnographer Kirsten Hastrup (1999) has, with reference to Charles Taylor (1985), suggested an alternative or middle ground that we find helpful. Theories and concepts need not to be limited to either a designative function or to be left for "free" construction; they may be *expressive of relationships*. Instead of picturing the world "as it is" the descriptions and concepts that we will develop in this book attempt to articulate *specific and contextualized aspects* of the projects that we have studied, aspects that would not otherwise have found an expression.

Music Therapy as human *action* and *interaction* in context. What the book offers to the reader is a reflection of these practices as well as our *reflections* upon them. These reflections are grounded in the case studies but also informed by our values and our theoretical understanding. We therefore acknowledge that our reflections are also *actions* in relation to ongoing debates on what music, therapy, and community could be. The interrelations between action and reflection are made quite explicit in Part VII where Cochavit Elefant reflects on a project that was developed as Participatory Action Research, but they are central to all the projects that we describe.

When selecting the eight case studies, we have sought out projects that represent at least part of the diversity of contemporary Community Music Therapy. Contexts include Western Europe, the Middle East, South Africa, and Scandinavia. In the portfolio of cases presented in this book there are Community Music Therapy projects that are quite new and emerging, such as the two South African projects and one of the Israeli projects, there are projects that have a few years history, such as the English projects, and there are projects that have a history of 15–20 years, such as the two Norwegian projects. Seven of the eight projects reported in the book were ongoing at the time they were tracked, which mostly happened in the period between autumn 2004 and spring 2007. We have also included one retrospective case study of a project that was developed about a decade earlier (see Part III).[10] The eight projects have been chosen in order to represent other forms of diversity as well. There is a range of age-groups, from school children and adolescents to adults and elderly people, and the problems that they live and work with cover a spectrum from the physical to the cognitive, emotional, and social spheres. Finally, in reading the case stories and studies you will discover that the music therapists sometimes are working in places where you traditionally would expect to find music therapists, such as special schools or neurological rehabilitation units, but other times they work in "unexpected" places such as churches and festivals.

The process of writing this book has been intensively collaborative, yet there are some clear differences between the various parts concerning writing style as well as use of concepts and theory. For instance, while Gary Ansdell in Part II explores concepts of *communication community* and *community of practice* as alternatives to the more established concept of *local community*, Cochavit Elefant in Part III focuses upon relationships between groups in the context of a local community. This exemplifies that the four authors have different academic and cultural backgrounds, but more interestingly (we think) it exemplifies that Community Music Therapy is *not* a unified theory and practice, but a broad perspective exploring relationships

---

[10]   This could exemplify how the relatively recent emergence of a discourse on Community Music Therapy has also been used as a tool for retrospective reflection by many music therapists. We consider this important, since community-based and community-oriented projects in our appraisal have been underreported in the music therapy literature so far.

between the individual, community, and society in relation to music and health. The final part of the book offers a contextualization of some of the descriptions and concepts developed in the previous chapters, in an appraisal of how these case studies could contribute to theory development on how music helps.

By use of a little anecdote we will try to clarify the intentions we have in writing this book. In a seminar on music and identity organized in Bergen in 2007, the first author of this book presented a Community Music Therapy project with focus upon the contextualized effects of music (Stige, 2007) and our colleague Randi Rolvsjord presented a contextual perspective on music therapy in mental health care (Rolvsjord, 2007). A discussion evolved, and one of the seminar participants, the British social theorist Paul Gilroy[11] expressed: "But all music is music therapy! All music has that potential dimension to it." We think he got it as right as you can get it in two sentences. All music may be used for health-related purposes and music therapists cannot restrict themselves to special music for special people in special places. This does not suggest that music therapists should be everywhere or are not required anywhere. It illuminates that music therapists could participate in a range of social contexts where various lay and professional agents interact, supplement, and sometimes challenge each other in relation to people's appropriations of music.

In this perspective, the role of the music therapist may often be that of making music possible; when people have been excluded from music, when they do not allow themselves to music, or when they in other ways struggle for access to the resources required for musical participation. This is a limited description, it could be argued. Music therapy is more than music-making. The professional music therapist has a research-based training and has developed a range of personal and therapeutic skills. We think that this is an important point, but only when music is possible are health-related appropriations of music possible. Therefore, what we explore in this book are projects and contexts where professional skills in tandem with lay initiatives make health-promoting musical collaboration possible.

---

[11]   Gilroy is a sociologically informed scholar of cultural studies, author of books such as *There Ain't no Black in the Union Jack* (1987/2002), *The Black Atlantic* (1993), and *After Empire* (2004).

Chapter 2
Situating Authors and Projects

Brynjulf Stige, Gary Ansdell, Cochavit Elefant and Mercédès Pavlicevic

In the following we will briefly describe the context of the four authors and the eight music projects that we have tracked. The presentation is organized according to the four national contexts involved, in the sequence that we have used to organize the case studies to follow; England, Israel, South Africa, and Norway.

England

Researcher: Gary Ansdell

I am currently Director of Education of a large music therapy organization – Nordoff-Robbins Music Therapy UK – and Research Fellow in Community Music Therapy at the University of Sheffield. I trained 20 years ago as a music therapist at the Nordoff-Robbins Centre, and have since worked in the UK and Germany as a music therapist in a variety of clinical areas (currently in a community setting for adults with enduring mental health problems). I have also been involved in training music therapists and developing contemporary educational programs for music therapy. As a writer and researcher I have concentrated on documenting and exploring innovative music therapy practice based on the Nordoff-Robbins tradition, also in examining the relationships between music therapy and its disciplinary and professional developments and collaborations with other disciplines and professions. This combination of practical work, research and training has led me increasingly to re-think the nature and role of music therapy as a practice, discipline and profession in the light of contemporary social, cultural and intellectual shifts, and, most importantly, the changing needs of clients and health and social settings for "music's help." In many ways this has involved re-examining and arguing for a contemporary return to Nordoff and Robbins's original broad-based pragmatic approach to music therapy (which 50 years ago resisted individualism, medicalism and psychologism). My collaborative involvement in the re-imagining of music therapy within the Community Music Therapy movement with my international colleagues has been one of continual practical, intellectual and aesthetic delight.

Projects in the English Context

Contemporary Britain finds itself under increasing pressure from its pioneering but aging health and social care system. Globalization and cosmopolitanism have also impacted on this situation – with refugees and migrants, and excessive patterns of human drift within society. Consequent disparities of wealth, opportunity, and social equality impact inevitably on patterns of physical, mental and social health and wellbeing. This context is increasingly the backcloth of the work that music therapists are called on to work in and with in the UK. One of the Community Music Therapy projects I tracked for this book – *Musical Minds* – relates directly to this situation.

Musical Minds is the name chosen by a group of adults with chronic mental health problems for the weekly singing group they have developed over the last ten years. The group is "hosted" within a non-governmental organization for people with long-term mental illness called *Together Tower Hamlets*. This is located in the socio-economically deprived and highly multi-cultural area of East London. The borough this resides in – Tower Hamlets – has some of the worst rates of physical and mental health for the whole of the country. The members of *Musical Minds* could be seen as living with deprivation in several senses: in terms of the quality of their local social and cultural environment, and in the poor standard of provisions for supporting them with their illness.

There are usually 8–12 people attending the group each week (ages ranging from 27–67) who have a range of mental health problems, musical interests and abilities. The group members are predominantly of white British origin, representing a sub-culture of East End Londoners now living in a local area largely populated by Asian and African families. A music therapist, Sarah Wilson, has been working with this group for six years. Her role is interesting in that she was not employed specifically as a "music therapist," but to be a "musical facilitator" for a pre-existing group who, equally, do *not* define it as "music therapy." As I will describe in Part II, the group members still seem to be happy about Sarah being a music therapist and about me studying their work for this book.

The weekly group revolves around singing: either with participants having individual "solo turns" with Sarah accompanying/advising (and with them bringing and developing their own repertoire and musical tastes) or the group learning and preparing songs together. Increasingly (under Sarah's guidance) there has been more of a move towards a balance between solo and group musical activity. She also facilitates the group's preparation and production of several performance events every year (either within their own premises or in local venues).

A particular angle of interest within my study of this project has been Sarah's thinking about how she uses her "music therapy skills" in facilitating this group and their ongoing difficulties in their self-elected task of meeting to learn and perform music. From Sarah's point of view she describes her aims with this group as "to facilitate the group within the ethos of *Together Tower Hamlets* – which aims to promote user-involvement and encourage group members to contribute and make decisions collectively. The broad aim of the group is to offer the opportunity for music-making and socializing in a musical environment." A main focus of my study of this group has been what such a "musical environment" affords this group in relation to the challenges of the surrounding physical and social environment the members live in.

The second project I have tracked for this book needs to be understood within the context of the large-scale transformation of health and social care within Britain during the lifetime of professional music therapy in this country (1970 to the present). The large asylums and hospitals have been closed, leading to the more geographically dispersed sites of so-called "community care," where continuity of care is often neglected as people move beyond acute provision, or need long-term care. Music therapists have had to adapt not only to these practical shifts, but also to the accompanying shifts of public discourse away from the exclusively psychological and medical models that formerly legitimated their work. The UK is also witnessing the development of a Music and Health movement (a sub-set of a broader Arts and Health sector, legitimated by new government-level promotion of a new theoretical alliance between thinking on health, culture and social equity). Given this situation, it is no surprise that the music therapy profession is feeling threatened, and has met the emerging Community Music Therapy movement with some distrust.

It is against this second national context that the second project I tracked is significant. Stuart Wood's work took place in a relatively affluent local area – a semi-country area bordering London, where both medical and cultural facilities are well above the national average. His work also began within a conventional medical setting – *Rayner's Hedge*, a Community Physical Rehabilitation Unit for adults with neurological impairment (mostly through brain injury) in Aylesbury, Buckinghamshire. The work Stuart did at first could be easily identified with that of his training tradition (Nordoff-Robbins music therapy), with the format, style and content of sessions varied according to the rehabilitation needs of participants, and the culture of the host institution. The project then gradually moved out from the medical context into a community setting, with sessions taking place in local venues such as an arts center, a parish church, a general hospital and in people's homes. Geographically the project was spread across about 30 miles, given that participants come from the isolated towns and villages in the county. From this varied work a specific and extremely unusual project evolved called *Scrap Metal*, culminating in a performance event in a local church. Participants were primarily people living with neurological disability, particularly people with stroke, brain injury, MS and other neurological conditions. But carers, family members and professionals were also involved as participants and supporters of the project. Because of the various host venues, and the range of professionals with whom people came into contact, the project operated within a very broad culture. For the participants it had echoes of local arts workshops, adult learning, medical rehabilitation, or "self development" and spiritual work. The demographic of participants was also mixed, leaning towards the white middle class as its dominant ethnicity.

I understood this project as an example of pioneering practice in British music therapy – explicitly attempting to link individual music therapy work to the use of musicing and performing in wider socio-cultural contexts: to move *from* therapy *to* community (as the title of the project Stuart devised suggests) as people's medical and psycho-social needs changed. It involved uncommon practices in music therapy (instrumental teaching, use of community musicians, performance occasions) and an experiment with the use of local musicians as part of the process. It revolved around performance practices and an unusual performance event in an unusual place. The therapist describes his aims as "to provide a music therapy program consisting of a broad range of musical formats, each with its own therapeutic impact, offering to participants a pathway of musical experience which accompanies them on their recovery." He explicitly linked his thinking about his practice and this project in particular with the developing Community Music Therapy movement.

Both of the projects I tracked highlight the complex relationships between the relatively established music therapy tradition in the UK and a variety of newly-evolving situations, contexts and currents now impacting upon it – including the evolving practice and discourse of Community Music Therapy.

Israel

Researcher: Cochavit Elefant

I am currently working as an Associate Professor of Music Therapy at the Grieg Academy, University of Bergen, Norway. I have worked with children with developmental disabilities for 25 years. I have researched communication in individuals with Rett syndrome and published several articles on music therapy with children, I am a co-founder and a team member of the Israeli National Rett Syndrome evaluation team, and I serve as an associate editor for the *Nordic Journal of Music Therapy.* As a group facilitator I am especially interested in the concept of the group as a medium for help and intergroup relation and how these can promote social change. As a member of the NISE Research Group I have been working with two research projects in Israel in the field of Community Music Therapy, which has given me possibilities for renewed reflection on previous work as well as for collaborative action-oriented research.

Projects in the Israeli Context

The two Israeli Community Music Therapy projects included in this book took place in two middle sized towns in the belly of Israel; Raanana and Natanya. The projects occurred at the end of the twentieth century and the beginning of the twenty-first century a few years after my return from the United States where I had been studying, working with, and teaching music therapy for 17 years. As a music therapist working within the American educational system, I had witnessed the changes and the new laws of the late 1970s and 80s towards mainstreaming and integrating the marginalized population into the community. I initiated and participated in several projects integrating the special needs children into the community utilizing music therapy as a way toward this social change.

Israel is a country situated at the western bank of the Mediterranean. It is a small country with a population of about seven million people. Israel is considered a westernized country which sets her eyes towards progress and high standards common to other western countries, yet at the same time Israel is a desert country without many natural resources. In addition to that basic condition, Israel is an immigrant country that deals with the constant flow of people from all around the world speaking different languages, coming with different customs and cultures. This ever flowing river of "strangers" forms disperse minority groups which necessitates economic means to support the melting pot of diverse populations into one community. The political regional issues concerning the neighboring Arab countries are also economically demanding. The combination of those two issues continuously occupies the Israeli public and leaders resulting in other issues such as education and social issues to only mild treatment.

Upon my return to Israel I was set to continue the work I had done in the United States. The music therapy integration project between children with and without special needs began in Raanana in 1995. To my knowledge, prior to my initiation of this project, there had not been any type of integration programs for children with severe special needs in Israel. The Israeli society was not fully ready to integrate its special population and initially there was no one who took interest in it. The project became collaboration between an elementary school and a center for children in special education. The staff, parents, the children and the municipality were all affected as a result of it. I served as the music therapist facilitating this multifaceted project which grew and developed for eight years. The description of this process will focus on intergroup relations within two diverse groups of children and how the group was utilized as a medium for help for social change. In the last few years, several music therapists have begun to integrate children with special needs in Israel, although the children with severe special needs are still segregated in many parts of this country.

The second project was ended recently after three years of collaboration between *Renanim* (a choir for individuals with severe physical disabilities), Rina Stadler (their choir leader for many years and a music therapist), and me. The *Renanim* group was seeking for individual and social change within their community and within the larger society. They wanted their voices to be heard and their means of doing so was through community musical performances. The group and the therapist decided to participate in a Participatory Action Research project in order to see whether a change could be made. The research inquiries were determined mutually by the choir and the therapist. The process of this research project led to empowerment within the group and the therapist and in some unique ways it gave an opportunity to individuals with severe physical disabilities to be heard and become accountable for a change to occur in their life.

South Africa

Researcher: Mercédès Pavlicevic

I am currently Director of Research at the Nordoff-Robbins Centre for Music Therapy in London. Until 2006, I lived in, and engaged with, the social context of South Africa for 15 years and developed an extensive feel for the country's urban spaces and musical culture. In 1998, together with Kobie Temmingh, I set up the country's first music therapy training program at the University of Pretoria and was Head of this training program for many years. Direct experiences of traditional African music healing ceremonies, as well as working with people from urban and rural areas of the country constantly nudged at my clinician's mind, uncomfortably in the main. The opportunities offered by this research project, to participate in, and observe, our graduate students immersed in innovative, courageous, and vibrant Community Music Therapy work, is helping to reframe the practice for that nation, at this time. This reframing is constantly inspired by the electrifying magic of musicing in Africa.

Projects in the South African Context

Like most other countries in Africa, South Africa is still coming to terms with a 600-year-old legacy of colonialism, together with its more recent history of apartheid. Since 1994, the country's leadership has pledged itself to socio-economic transformation and development, especially of the country's (so-called) disadvantaged places and spaces. At the same time, the ongoing narrative "framing" of places and people as "disadvantaged," or as "previously disadvantaged," ensures a continued legacy of disempowerment and need. This in turn legitimates a morally driven industry – both formal and informal – of "carers,"[1] not all visible. Part of this industry is within state structures of health and education, generally made up of professionals paid for their work and registered with the Health Professions Council of South Africa (HPCSA), or equivalent bodies. Another part of this caring industry is made up of professionally trained carers who work mostly in NGOs, relying on fund-raising, both local and international. Finally, there are many others who are neither trained (in the formal sense) nor funded (by state or other structures), and who become highly skilled through daily practice.

---

[1]   "Carers" in South Africa signifies persons with a broad range of expertise who "look after" those "in need" – whether HIV/AIDS orphans, victims of violence, drug abusers and so on.

This group (unsurprisingly made up of women) generally provide "care in the community" for those whose illness and need is socially taboo. In other words, neither the illness, nor the caring, need be talked about or formally acknowledged. This over-simplistic caricature of "caring" in South Africa is the backdrop for the two projects documented here.

The two South African Community Music Therapy endeavors tracked for this research project are located in Heideveld in the Western Cape and in Eersterust, East of Pretoria.

Heideveld is in the Cape Flats – a sprawling area outside the formerly "white and wealthy" city of Cape Town (a well-known tourist destination) to which "colored" (mixed race) people were forcibly moved, during the apartheid period of forced removals to make space for white housing (Steinberg, 2005). Heideveld has gang wars, drug syndicates, and a high incidence of alcoholism and single parent families. Its people (I was told) deny the severity of the violence. Heideveld is described by the music therapists as a community in despair, with little sense of purpose or hope in either the present or future. Two music therapists (Sunelle Fouché and Kerryn Torrance) have set up an NPO (Not for Profit Organization) called Music Therapy Community Clinic (website www.music-therapy.co.za), with the aim of working within communities rather than being a music therapy "place" that others come to. The Music Therapy Community Clinic (MTCC) has various projects, including individual and group improvisational music therapy practice (Nordoff-Robbins, 1977; Bruscia, 1987) with the children of Heideveld. This work, located in Woodlands primary school, in one of the "safer" areas of the Cape Flats, and the MTCC service covers seven schools in Heideveld and Gugulethu. Another project is called *Music for Life* and includes a choir, a marimba band with the local police, a drumming group, a rap group, and an annual weekend music camp, in preparation for the Heideveld Community Concert, set up by the music therapists. The music therapists fundraise for all of their work, much aided by Cerri Newdigate, also a music therapist, who is now the director of the MTCC.

Eersterust, 15km east of Pretoria, has a similar history and demography, with the added social complexity of "outsiders" (who have come to Eersterust more recently from Upington and Cape Town) who are perceived by the locals to have taken over their jobs as well as the social character of Eersterust. There is a sense that those who "make it" are able to move out of Eersterust to more affluent areas: those who "cannot afford to," remain – and they are seen as the ones who "haven't made it." Eersterust has the highest crime incidence in Gauteng (usually attributed to Soweto, outside Johannesburg) invisible because it is "white collar" crime. There are no overt signs of guns or drugs, with drug-dealing and crime networks operating well out of public sightings. Young folk leave school and enter a life of unemployment, with poor prospects and little hope for the future. Unemployment is between 35–45 per cent. Music therapist Carol Lotter works in a Non Government Organization *Youth Development Outreach* (YDO), which caters for young people who are considered socially and criminally "at risk." YDO runs the Adolescent Development Program (ADP) and music therapy is part of its

Indigenous Arts Program. Carol is there two days a week, one of which is as an (unpaid) volunteer. She is also developing a guitar school to provide guitar skills for youngsters to be able to play music and write their own songs after they have left the YDO program.

Norway

Researcher: Brynjulf Stige

I am working as Professor of Music Therapy at the University of Bergen and as Head of Research at GAMUT, the Grieg Academy Music Therapy Research Centre (www.gamut.no). My interest in Community Music Therapy grew out of engagement in a project on community integration in and through music which was funded by the Norwegian Arts Council from 1983 to 1986 and localized to the rural county of Sogn og Fjordane. In working with this project I realized that my music therapy training only to a limited degree had prepared me for the challenges of working with inclusion in community contexts. This was exemplified by a question posed by Knut, a man with Downs Syndrome who participated in a music therapy group and asked if he and the other group members could play in the local marching band. I realized that his question challenged my conception of what music therapy could be and that I had a too limited conception of possible relationships between music therapy and the music of everyday life. Together with the members of Knut's group and my music therapy colleague I explored possible practical answers to his question and we experienced an exciting journey towards increased community participation. Since then I have published several books and articles where I discuss music therapy in relation to culture and community, and my doctoral dissertation on the notion of Community Music Therapy could be read as my theoretical answer to Knut's question. As co-editor (together with Carolyn Kenny) of *Voices: A World Forum for Music Therapy* (www.voices.no) I currently enjoy the experience of reading and evaluating many submitted papers on Community Music Therapy from around the world.

Projects in the Norwegian Context

The two Norwegian Community Music Therapy projects included in this book are both from the county of Sogn og Fjordane, which is a rural and mountainous county in Western Norway. Since the 1980s, various music and community projects in this county have been influential for the development of Community Music Therapy in Norway, not least through the establishment of the music therapy training course in Sandane in 1988 (an academic milieu which in 2006 was moved to the University of Bergen).

A couple of generations ago many Norwegians lived with relatively meager conditions, while today – partly due to the rich oil reserves discovered in the 1960s and 70s – Norway is an affluent and technologically advanced country. Some have described Norwegian culture(s) as homogeneous, others as quite heterogeneous. Both descriptions make sense, in different ways. Norway is a homogeneous country in the sense that a large percentage of the population belong to the same ethnic group. Immigrants have been relatively rare except for the last few decades. But it is also a heterogeneous country in some ways, since there is considerable local variation in relation to language, communication style, and other cultural patterns. The latter fact is often attributed to history and topography. The Norwegian coast line is elongated and there are not many inhabitants per square kilometer, compared to most other European countries. Many regions are mountainous and "fjordous," which at times may make communication between various local communities and regions somewhat of a challenge. The cultural diversity of local variation is demonstrated by the fact that this little country with just above four million people has two official languages (New Norwegian and Dano-Norwegian) in addition to the language of the Sami people living in the northern part of the country.

Sogn og Fjordane exemplifies this mixture of homogeneous and heterogeneous culture quite well. It is a rural county, so it is not the first region of choice for many immigrants. It is also a county where traditional values are strong and local variation still cultivated quite actively (it may make a lot of difference whether you are from the northern or southern shore of a fjord). Being a rural and somewhat remote county, the average income is lower in Sogn og Fjordane than in other parts of the country, but life expectancy is the highest in Norway (Falnes-Dalheim and Slaastad, 2008). Some researchers argue that the traditional value of equity is stronger in Sogn og Fjordane than in the rest of the country and that this could be one of the factors accounting for the higher life expectancy. With equity there is more inclusiveness and less distance between people. This leads to less stress and more psychosocial trust, these researchers argue (see Elstad, 2005). Whether or not this is the explanation for the high life expectancy, equity and trust are strong values characterizing this county and of relevance for the development of Community Music Therapy practice.

The two Norwegian projects that will be presented in this book are the *Cultural Festival* tailored for the needs of adults with intellectual disabilities in the county of Sogn og Fjordane, and the *Senior Choir* located in the rural town Sandane.

The *Cultural Festival* is arranged as a happening one weekend every year, bringing together about 100 adults with intellectual disabilities and their helpers, coming from all over the county of Sogn og Fjordane. During this weekend the participants and their helpers live and work together and after three intense days of music, dance, and drama the processes are completed by performative events. The festival was established in 1988, as a joint effort between the music therapy training course in Sandane and NFU, a Norwegian organization for individuals with intellectual difficulties and their families. Norwegian national policies in relation to integration as well as problems of implementation are some of the reasons why the festival was established and why it still exists. In the late 1960s and early 1970s, many important political decisions were made at the national level that should ensure handicapped people full access to education, work, and cultural activities in the Norwegian society. In reality, many local barriers hindering participation persisted, which is one of the reasons why in the 1980s various projects on cultural community integration were funded by the Norwegian Arts Council in collaboration with some counties and municipalities. In a project localized to Sandane and Sogn og Fjordane from 1983 to 1986 the competency of three music therapists were employed. The project was evaluated positively and led to the establishment of the music therapy training course in Sandane in 1988. It was very clear, however, that a three year project could not resolve the problems hindering full community participation for all citizens. The festival was then established as an attempt to develop a tool for continued work on this problem.

The *Senior Choir* in Sandane was established in 1992, with music therapist Grete Skarpeid as the first conductor. As many other villages and towns in this part of the country, Sandane has a strong tradition of amateur musicing (especially choirs, folk music ensembles, and marching bands). There is a growing elderly population in Norway (as in most European countries), and as described above, people in this area of the country could on average expect to live for quite a long time. One of the questions that the *Senior Choir* addresses is to what degree they also could expect to live with wellbeing and participation in meaningful activities. This project thus exemplifies Norwegian music therapy's growing engagement with health promotion and public health issues.

The two projects from the Norwegian context both have a history of 15–20 years. It is a common assumption in the national literature of music therapy that community-based and community-oriented approaches are integral to this country's music therapy tradition (see e.g. Ruud, 2004c). In reality there have also been considerable criticisms and neglect of these approaches from representatives of more conventional professional practices. It is probably still correct to claim that the professionalization of music therapy in Norway has been more oriented toward sociocultural work than has been the case in many other Western countries. This is partly due to the influence of national policies stressing the democratization of cultural rights and the promotion of public health, and it is partly due to the influence of values and scholarly perspectives from cultural psychology, sociology, and anthropology in Norwegian music therapy theory.

Initial Dialogue

Gary: For me (like many of us – and many people now around the world), Community Music Therapy was action before it was reflection. There was of course community music therapy before there was "Community Music Therapy"! When people ask me what they should do in practice I sometimes say "follow where people and music lead." Looking back on my 20 years of work as a music therapist (and long before that in the path leading to training) this is basically what I think I always did

– followed where people and music led me. And where they led me was to various situations – some intimate and personal, some public and communal – but all to where music was doing something fairly unique in terms of communication, social participation, collaboration and plain enjoyment or "transcendence."

Cochavit: When hearing Gary speaking on Community Music Therapy in the 10th World Congress of Music Therapy in Oxford in 2002, and later talking with him, I finally felt a heavy load was lifted off my shoulders. You see, I had in fact been practicing Community Music Therapy for years in the USA, working with disabled children integrating them in their community or in community music schools, but after returning to Israel, integrating different groups of children in the community had become my "private secret" from the Israeli music therapy arena (during that time this type of practice was not considered music therapy). This all changed after the Oxford conference. And now as part of the NISE project as a researcher, I am closing this part of my professional life as a music therapist and am starting on a new road overlooking the Community Music Therapy of other therapists ... – Closure? Well, not actually, because at the same time it's a new beginning for me. It's the understanding of the theory behind Community Music Therapy (it is "behind" also because the theory often comes after the practice). It was as if someone had shed a light and set up signals at crossroads that I had passed before, so engulfed in my practical work.

Gary: When I began working as a music therapist (and then thinking and writing about this work) I concentrated on one dimension of the work (the intimate client-therapist dyad, dialogic communication etc) and forgot about the rest for a while! Actually most of "the rest" was already within the work of Nordoff and Robbins – but some of this breadth had been forgotten in music therapy in the 1980s–90s. My early writing (e.g. *Music for Life*) shows this. The motto I developed there – "music therapy works in the way music itself work" – I still think is true, but the formulation (like the practice) was too narrow. New contexts of practice helped at this point – working in psychiatric hospitals, a general hospital, with music therapy students ... where I found myself once again following where people and music led. And they led towards the social and communal and cultural dimensions of musicing. Or, more accurately, to how the personal and the communal, the cultural and the institutional *meet* and transform themselves in and through musicing. Music therapy still works in the ways music works, but the focus is broader – on a social phenomenology rather than an over-individualized one.

Brynjulf: This resonates with much of my own practical experience as a music therapist, whether I have been working in a special education setting, a community music school, a psychiatric hospital, a nursing home – or somewhere in between any of these places. I have gradually learnt to expect unexpected things, because music therapy is different each time; from participant to participant, group to group, place to place. The participants' needs and interests vary and the activities and agendas advance in ways I never know how to predict. Consequently, our roles as professionals fluctuate considerably also. Possibly these are trite statements to make, but they express something more and different than just the fact that music therapy is a broad practice and discipline. And they do not amount to the conclusion that music therapy processes are arbitrary either. It has something to do with the therapeutic possibilities of collaboration I think, and the unexpected connections that may grow out of that. But if music therapy is potentially different every time it happens then it is relevant to ask questions such as: How much do we know and understand about the range of possibilities of music therapy in various contexts? And: How is it possible to combine the need for flexibility, communicativeness, and context sensitivity with a request for research and theoretically informed reflexivity? I do not consider Community Music Therapy to be the answer to any of these questions, but maybe a new way of asking them, by taking sociocultural thinking and research more actively into consideration than what has been common in music therapy. To explore the range of possibilities in Community Music Therapy should probably not be done mainly in comparison with or in contrast to existing traditions of music therapy, then. This has been a necessary first step for us, but it is now more helpful, I think, to focus upon describing and comparing various Community Music Therapy projects and to relate them to other developments in academia and in the societies they are part of.

Mercédès: Yes, and in asking such questions as a researcher I have felt a need to reflect upon the increasingly personal and idiosyncratic research stance that this experience generated. Several on-site visits and direct engagements with the Community Music Therapy projects quickly unraveled any previous experiences of research as having to do with "observation" and "data collection" in a strict "research" sense. The data were live events – powerful, charged, uncomfortable at times and almost always unforgettable. The choice and the challenge were to remain focused, engaged, and to reconsider what research might possibly mean in a context such as this. Gradually over two years, I relinquished my positivist inclinations with all the connotations of being "the outsider" and became increasingly reflective about the multiple and evolving relationships and social roles generated by this project. My personal-professional relationships with the music therapists in each of the projects became multi-dimensional, generating rich dialogues that seemed to transgress research interviews and expand into conversations and collaborative explorations between fellow-professionals. Also, the music therapists in both sites said that this research study has helped them to talk about their work, to feel listened to, to "keep track" of what they have done; and also to revise it as they hear one another speak. In other words, their experience of talking about their work helped to generate new and complex meaning for themselves as practitioners, working in these contexts.

Cochavit: So reflection is action too?

Brynjulf: Yes ... like action involves reflection.

Gary: As musicians have always known ...

Mercédès: ... and as therapists we know only too well ...

PART II

Chapter 3

Action

Musicing on the Edge:
Musical Minds in East London, England

Gary Ansdell

The East End

There is a phrase that Londoners use when talking about their city: "West is Best." To some this also implies that "East is Worst"! East London has always been a socially and economically deprived area. But as I come up from Mile End tube station onto the Mile End Road I can look back along the road towards the center of London and see the gleaming office blocks of the City of London. Just a mile separates perhaps the richest area in the world from one of the poorest in the country (and we sometimes think this is a developing-world phenomenon!).

East was always the industrial quarter of London, and consequently the magnet for immigrants and refugees, minority groups and the poor across many generations. It was also the worse-bombed area of London during WWII, so is now mostly an ugly mess of badly re-built housing and tower blocks. The borough this area falls into – Tower Hamlets – is now one of the most ethnically diverse areas of the country, and gives asylum to people from many of the war and disaster-ravaged areas of the world. But it is also the area where poverty, racism and crime are endemic, and where social exclusion, isolation, physical and mental health is the worst in the country.

But there is another side to the East End. So-called "East Enders" talk of the "East End spirit" – shown during the bombing in the 1940s and in the resilience of its community throughout all its hardships. The compensatory picture to the deprivation has been a tradition of tight-knit ethnic and class-based communities, with strong cultural traditions that have often involved music (for example community singing in the pubs). Sadly, much of this is now breaking down ...

I walk along the road past St Martins, a crumbling Victorian psychiatric hospital that is probably the worst in the city. Every year they announce that it will soon close, but it lumbers on, with its poor facilities and demoralized staff. My colleague Simon Procter works there as a music therapist, but he's seconded by the Nordoff-Robbins Charity – the borough of Tower Hamlets does not pay for a single music therapist in the mental health sector. Next door to the hospital is a non-conformist church, and within its buildings is also housed a non-governmental agency called *Together Tower Hamlets*. It describes itself as: "a community project providing a range of self-help, user involvement training and social opportunities for adults experiencing mental health problems." *Together Tower Hamlets* works mostly in an informal relationship with St Martins Hospital – most of its members are people with enduring mental health illnesses, who revolve between the hospital and community support projects such as *Together Tower Hamlets*. The organization's literature emphasizes a social model, with user involvement, support and empowerment – and organizes self-help groups, activities and advocacy services.

Meeting *Musical Minds*

I find my way into the church hall *Together Tower Hamlets* uses for group activities. About eight adults are setting-up chairs, a few microphone stands, and a piano. They are mostly middle-aged and above, and white "traditional East Enders." Apart from this the members of the group all seem very individual. The group is a stable one, with a waiting list. All the members have some level of mental health problem, all live locally. Sarah greets me – she's a colleague who's trained as a music therapist, but who doesn't call or define herself as a "music therapist" for this group. Partly this is because she was not employed as one. *Together Tower Hamlets* advertised for "a musician" to facilitate an ongoing music group who called themselves *Musical Minds*. Sarah took the job of helping them to sing together and to put on occasional performances. Sarah has worked with the group for six years now, and they've put on one large show and performed for various local events. They meet every Thursday afternoon for two hours, 45 weeks of the year. *Musical Minds* themselves compiled their *Ground Rules and Aims*, which describe the group as follows: "The group meets to make and share music together with opportunities for solo and group activity" and "The group aims to prepare for and organize regular performances as well as musical fellowship on a weekly basis."

There's a sense of familiarity between the people in the room, so I stand out as someone new. People welcome me, and directly ask why I'm there. They then remember Sarah saying something about "being researched." People say things to me straight away: one man says that he's a virtual recluse and it's the only thing he comes out of his house for in the week. Another person tells me singing helps him with his problems; a third asks me how much they will get paid for being researched! Actually, it seems that they are very happy for me to "research them" – they say that it's good that I come along and see what they do, how it helps. I learn something from this project about the potential of research in giving people attention, witnessing their work, being an advocate for them and what they do.

The set-up for this group is different than you'd see for a music therapy group, where the chairs tend to be put in a circle with people facing each other. Here they are putting chairs out in an arc, facing towards a couple of microphones, with a piano to the side at one end. This set-up is more like an informal performance space. And indeed as soon as the afternoon gets going it becomes clear how what happens is both very different and somewhat similar to a traditional music therapy group. The members follow their usual routine of taking turns to go up and sing (usually at the microphone), with Sarah accompanying on the piano. Emily sings a Piaf song she's found – it's very suitable to her voice, and the rapport between her and Sarah is good. People complement her afterwards. Vick says "I'll sing 'My Way'" which he does, karaoke style (that is, he scarcely registers Sarah playing). This is the song he always sings. Neil looks incredibly insecure as he gets up to sing, and the first few phrases of "It's a Wonderful World" are disorganized, but then he and Sarah get it together and it's a moving rendition. People are finding it increasingly difficult to focus on each other, some of the members going in and out for toilet and cigarette breaks. Sarah suggests that before the tea-break could we sing something together, and we do "Daydream Believer" in preparation for the upcoming show. If I'm honest it's hardly (musically) *together* at the moment … The sense I'm rapidly getting of *Musical Minds* is an incredibly diverse group of spirited but vulnerable people, for whom it's a real challenge to achieve something together. They have their own styles, standards, talents, which they just about manage to reconcile in this group. These are people in many ways living on the edge of society, but here they manage to create their own creative and supportive community.

In the tea-break, we chat and I ask them whether they'd mind having a go at doing some of the "sentence completion tasks" the NISE Research Group has developed.[1] They're happy to do this, so I start by putting to them: "*Music is…?*" … They answer: "*Fantastic, a tonic, mental therapy, refreshing, relaxing, a release, cheerful, a godsend, helps everyone, cheers you up, being in a band … a bonus!*" One man asks me "What does it mean to *you?*" and before I can answer someone else shouts "A job!" and they all laugh. I go onto the next question: "*Without Music I'd be …?*" Which gets the answers: "*Depressed, lost, bored, fed up, lonely, low, empty, going mad … Finding the nearest pub!*" The answers are telling! Lastly I ask the group: "*Musical Minds is …?*" and I get responses such as "*Great … kind … fabulous …*" Then Emily says in a thoughtful way: "We're all individuals, and that's what makes the group strong … but it's also to do with

---

[1] Before the tracking of the eight projects started, the NISE Research Group developed a "music sentence completion task" with questions similar to the ones presented here. This sentence completion task has been employed in most of the projects tracked and is discussed in several of the narratives and essays in this volume. As the reader will discover, it has been used in various ways in various contexts. In some of the projects tracked it has been relevant to use this as a written task, while for instance Pavlicevic has developed it into a series of questions for a focus group type of situation (see Part VIII). Our purpose has not been to employ the same instrument for comparative purposes, but to develop a tool that could generate interesting empirical material in various contexts.

singing together." Vick adds: "We're all trying to justify our existence, but the main fact is that we all like music ..."

These thoughts accurately reflected all of the main themes that were to come out of my experiences of *Musical Minds* in the coming few years. It's interesting that the members make very explicit connections between music and their mental health (not just saying, for example, that it's a nice social activity).

Preparing for the Show

During the next few months (in the run-up to their April concert) I attend some more rehearsals, but also talk to Sarah about the group. I'm interested in how she sees her role and her work with *Musical Minds*. She says that in many ways it *is* very close to traditional ideas of music therapy. There's a week-by-week process which is at once both a musical and a social one. When Sarah first came to the group people would simply want do their own thing ("be a soloist"), could hardly listen to each other, and then would argue about not respecting each other, or being unable to practically coordinate the concerts they wanted to do together. The group often split up temporarily, unable to negotiate their differences. But there had been a gradual shift in the group. Sarah had used her skills as a mental health advocate to negotiate with the group, and to get them to negotiate their needs with each other. Gradually there has been more collaboration – both musically and socially. So for her the change in the musicing within the group is mirrored in their social experience together. The forthcoming concert has more duets, trios and group songs than ever before. *Musical Minds* increasingly want to music together. Sarah puts it this way:

> *What a lot of the members of the group seem anxious about is maintaining their own identity ... and of course that's exactly what it's most difficult to do with a mental health difficulty – you're labeled, and you're living in this traumatic community. So it's an irony really that as I'm pushing them together musically they're becoming better at feeling individuals! (Sarah Wilson, music therapist)*

As I watch Sarah more with the group I'm increasingly fascinated by her shifting role and responsibility throughout the different occasions (it's certainly not static). Sometimes in the group she's more like a conventional therapist: helping the group understand their conflicts, mediating, helping them negotiate, and supporting them. Then, as the preparation of the show gets underway she's treated more like a coach, helping the members get their solo and group numbers as good as possible. Then, as we'll see, something else happens in performance – she's an accompanist (be it one with unusual demands!). Sarah puts it likes this:

> *The priority for me is to make it sound musically good – as organized and prepared as possible. Then when it comes to the performance I just turn into the*

piano-player! They treat me differently – they go onto the stage and I'm on the floor at the side looking like the piano-player. Come the performance I'm happy to be there in the background. They're on the stage then, they do everything. They go: "Come on Sarah, let's start!" It's funny; I'm trying to find out what they are doing then, what's happening! (Sarah Wilson, music therapist)

This aspect is of course quite different from most work (and most role expectations) of a conventional music therapist. What is also different is the explicit shift from process (in the form of the ongoing weekly meetings), which gradually become a more focused rehearsals, and then the night itself – a performance as a product.

A few weeks later I go to a short gig given by *Musical Minds* for the Annual General Meeting of their host organization, *Together Tower Hamlets*. It's clear even from this short performance (which acts as a live rehearsal for the forthcoming concert) that performance is a completion of what the group does week by week. It's where the group raise their act, where they manage a togetherness that's more than usually possible. The group is performing for their organization, and to people from their local community. I think how good an example this is of how – as Christopher Small (1998) puts it – the group is performing not just the music, or themselves, but their whole ecology of relationships: to each other, to their context, to their culture and its many complexities and conflicts. They are *creating community* through their musical performance. Equally, the audience (including one Elvis look-alike) doesn't just sit there and listen: they join in. During and afterwards there are congratulations, but also an enhanced sense of connection and belonging for all involved.

The Show: *Band for Life*

It is April – three months after the start of the current preparation period for this year's show: *Band for Life*. I go along to this with Simon (the music therapist at St Martins, who knows and has worked with many of the people in *Musical Minds*). The concert is held in the same church hall the group rehearses in, but this time they've made a big effort to make the place special: the hall has lots of tables set out in cabaret-fashion, each with a colored table-cloth, flower and candle. There are drinks and small snacks, and already there's something of an informal party atmosphere. The members of *Musical Minds* have dressed up smartly, but are looking decidedly anxious now. The focus is the large stage, along which there's a banner with *Musical Minds* on it. Simon recognizes a few people from the local informal network of mental health users and workers.

Soon *Band for Life* is underway: Sarah is (as she described) at floor level at the piano, with Stuart a recent member of the group who's a decent drummer beside her. Emily hosts the show, announcing each item (though not always the right item!). They begin with a group medley from *West Side Story* – which begins ragged, but with help from Sarah soon finds its groove. The concert proceeds with each member singing an individual number, along with some duets. There is the wide spectrum of musical styles I'm now used to with this group: rock, pop, show songs, bossa-nova, pre-war… and also (if I'm honest) the usual spectrum of performance standard – from the very assured and polished to the tentative and mediocre. But, as ever with the group, this diversity is simply accepted and assimilated. Vick sings "My Way" on the night (as usual – but having prepared a new song in rehearsal!), and asks later whether I thought it better than other renditions I'd heard him do.

In the interval the performers are eager to share with me the highs and lows so far. I also talk to people in the room, finding out who they are and why they are there. One table consists of the sister and family of the church cleaner. "Oh, I know lots of these people – Vick sings in the pub I go to round the corner." This comment makes me think of how the network this concert plugs into is both a social and cultural one. It consists both of the loose community of users of mental health services, but also the immediate local community (still close in some ways in this area) where there's still a pub culture of community singing and karaoke. If you look carefully at the performers and what songs they choose to perform then there's a sense in which they are also performing and sharing their culture, their history and aesthetic.

The second half of the concert has more solos – one of which particularly moves me. Eric appears an isolated man, who seems to find it difficult to connect to others even in the music. He selects "You'll Never Walk Alone," and sings this beautifully. In the second verse the rest of the group join with him, the music swells … and the audience around me wave arms in the way football crowds do when they sing this "anthem." My spine tingles, not just at the symbolism of this, but at how this musicing actually *enacts* this fact: he's *not* alone now! The concert ends with a spirited version of "Daydream Believer", with audience rocking and singing along. It ends on a real high.

Thinking about the Performance

A week later Sarah and I discuss the concert. She tells me that (as often with *Musical Minds*) the group were so nervous half an hour before that it nearly didn't happen. "I don't know why they put themselves through it" she says. But she also acknowledges how the whole course of building up to this performance (including the fear before) is somehow integral to the ongoing life and creativity of this group and its members. I think of Victor Turner's definition of performance being the "finale of an experience" (1982, p. 13). We talk again about Sarah's role; how she clearly had to again support the group until the moment they themselves took over the momentum and delivered the show. I remembered something I'd discussed with Simon after the concert: how *within* each performance Sarah is more than accompanying in the traditional sense. Instead she has to be incredibly flexible in the second-by-second process of the performance – as people chop notes and even sections out. She has to deal with extreme variations in tempo and timing (as people give their unique versions of songs) as well as give the kind of moral support that these people need in the moment. Put negatively, Sarah's work is to make sure that performer's don't' fail. "Yes, that's when I'm working the hardest" says Sarah, "… to make that seamless move from one bar to another, from one section to another, and so on. It's trying to really keep with each person, keep them organized, not be ruffled when things go slightly awry!"

I ask Sarah what she thinks is most valuable about *Musical Minds* doing performances like this. For her it's the sense of being able to reconcile people feeling good about themselves as individuals, as well as feeling good about being together in music. In short the feeling of *musical community* that everyone experienced in the show. Why does being together matter? I ask. "Because then they really *belong* somewhere. They're part of something; they have an experience of being part of something that feels good. These are not people who necessarily have that many experiences of 'getting on well' with people." Again I think how much this success necessarily relies on Sarah's role in the group – which is to help them get near the place where *musical community* can be created: to help balance the people and the sounds such that they can remain there (as long as the music lasts, at least). This needs both musical and "therapeutic" work from Sarah: containing, believing, organizing and intervening into a long and sometimes difficult and frustrating process. This is why Sarah is fundamentally working as a music therapist here – and why this process and product achievement is a classic example of Community Music Therapy in action.

Sarah's "Chipped Mug Philosophy"

Sarah sends me an email a few days later, summing up her attitude towards *Musical Minds* in something she calls the "Chipped Mug Philosophy." Recently Sarah had bought new mugs for the group, since the old ones were chipped and nasty. "Why shouldn't we have a bit of class?" was the comment from one of the members. This could stand for much of what we've been talking about in relation to *Musical Minds* says Sarah – of it mattering to make things better than they usually are. Everyone bothered to make a special effort to clear up and dress up the hall for the concert. It was more of an occasion with this effort. Equally, it's worth all the work on the music that Sarah and the members make, to see that the show is as good as possible, given each person's (and the group's) ability. Sarah, as a music therapist, is attuned to the potential and the possibilities for change in both people and situations. Going one stage further in the analogy: all of this is happening in a "chipped" and damaged community – where people are trying their best, and often deserve better facilities and opportunities to improve the quality of their lives. "I guess the overall theme" says Sarah "is that it must be right to try to make 'it' (the music, and therefore everything else that goes with it) special – otherwise the situation is hopeless …" Ellen Dissanayake's (1992/1995) simple definition of art comes into my mind as Sarah says this – art as, quite simply, *making special*.

Chapter 4

Reflection
Belonging through Musicing:
Explorations of Musical Community

Gary Ansdell

Following Bourdieu, we can say that community is a set of practices that constitute belonging. Belonging today is participation in communication …

Gerard Delanty

This community is no union of the like-minded, but a genuine living together of people of similar or complementary natures but of different minds. Community is the overcoming of otherness in living unity.

Martin Buber

We're all individuals, and that's what makes the group strong … but it's also to do with singing together.

Member of *Musical Minds*

"The Dream of Community"?

In his novel *Saturday* Ian McEwan charts the growing disquiet of his character Henry over the course of a day in London in 2004. Although a rich and successful neurosurgeon, Henry begins to feel socially and culturally threatened by surrounding events – an anti-war march, unknown people around his house, a sense of personal dislocation. He begins to feel no longer quite at home in his city, or with himself. Later in this day Henry visits a jazz club where his son is performing, and as he listens he reflects on how there are sometimes "rare moments when musicians together touch something sweeter than they've ever found before in rehearsals, beyond the merely collaborative or technically proficient, when their expression becomes as easy and graceful as friendship or love." This thought brings Henry to a wider meditation on music and human relationships:

> [these moments] give us a glimpse of what we might be, of our best selves, and of an impossible world in which you give everything you have to others, but lose nothing of yourself … Only in the music, and only on rare occasions, does the

curtain actually lift on the dream of community, and it's tantalizingly conjured,
before fading away with the last notes. (McEwan, 2005, p. 171)

Henry's dream in this passage evokes what we could call the "apple-pie" view of
community – which conjures up a warm, nostalgic coziness, contrasting with what
the sociologist Zygmunt Bauman (2001) calls the uncertain chill of the "liquid
modern world." Henry believes his musical vision captures only an "impossible
world," that will fade when the music ends. It is no surprise that this particular
discourse of community seems so annoying (and possibly dangerous) to its critics.
Derrida, for example, says "I don't much like the word community, I am not even
sure I like the thing" (in Caputo, 1997, p. 107). Steven Poole (2006) goes one
stage further, citing "community" as the first term in his book on contemporary
propaganda, *Unspeak*. For him, the concept "community" is usually a loaded
political weapon, a "glib, facile word" that smuggles in false promise and
sentiment, ready to disarm us in any rational argument about people and society.
For him it is a word to be resisted, lest it lead us into "unspeak."

During the two years I tracked the group *Musical Minds* in the East End of
London I came to a way of thinking about "community" different to either of
the views I've characterized so far. Certainly, there were echoes of the fictional
character Henry's concerns in the worlds of the members of *Musical Minds*:
in their daily battles against the real or perceived hostilities of their immediate
environment; in their struggles with their illness; in their relative social and cultural
disorientation within the increasingly fragmented modern East End of London. An
echo too in how they found a "musical solution" to these problems through their
weekly singing group and its events and concerts, which came to provide them
with a sense of belonging through musicing. But, in a key difference to Henry's
formulation, their "musical community" certainly did *not* fade upon the last notes.
As I witnessed and participated in their social and musical world, "community"
felt neither a romantic nor a politically expedient notion, but an accurate descriptor
of a moving and vital human process.

This essay attempts to justify the continued descriptive and explanatory value
of the concept of "community" (as used by a variety of theoretical perspectives)
for thinking about aspects of Community Music Therapy. I explore, in particular,
how the case of *Musical Minds* highlights some of the complex relationships
between individuality and community; identity and belonging; communication,
collaboration and negotiation – especially when crossing social, cultural and
health barriers. And, of course, how music and musicing can often mediate and
illuminate such circumstances.

In the first section I begin by outlining recent thinking on the concept and
reality of "contemporary community" – in relation to my experiences of the case
of *Musical Minds*, and their development during the two years I tracked them. I
ask what kind of community *Musical Minds* is, and outline a variety of ways of
understanding it, drawing on current thinking about music, communication and
community. The best model for the group is, I suggest, a so-called "community of

musical practice." Subsequent sections of this essay explore particular aspects of this: of its value for people as a focus for belonging and learning, and for negotiating the delicate balance between identity and difference. Perhaps a prime function of a Community Music Therapy endeavor (as exemplified by Sarah Wilson's work with *Musical Minds*) is to cultivate, nurture and sustain such "communities of musical practice" in challenging circumstances where they are otherwise difficult, or yet unimagined.

Kinds of Community

> *As I arrive at the rehearsal for the first time, a few members of* Musical Minds *are setting up the chairs and instruments in the scruffy church hall. I'm noticed, some acknowledge me, but I feel an outsider. Twenty minutes later we are still waiting for people to come. One man describes himself as a virtual recluse, this group often the only thing he goes out of his house for each week. He's waiting for someone from Social Services to bring him along. Another couple arrive and anxiously tell us that on the bus they've just been on someone had kicked in the window and smashed it. "It's a terrible area!" says another member to me.*

How are the members of *Musical Minds* connected to their local, geographical community? How embedded or marginal are they within this social and cultural community? How do they connect to each other, both inside and outside of the group? I gradually discovered the complexities in these questions during the next two years. From conversations with Sarah I had learned that the group was a long-standing one, proud of its collective identity as *Musical Minds* and that most members belonged to a loose association of ex-patients in the area surrounding the next-door psychiatric hospital. They had quite close contact with each other between weekly meetings of the music group – phoning each other, meeting for a meal after their singing. Within the ethnically diverse area they lived in, the members were unusually homogeneous and historically rooted – all being white "East Enders" from a similar working-class background. Because of this they shared something in common from the traditional socio-cultural frame and history of the local East End culture – for example, its social-musical tradition of pub sing-songs, which was often reflected in the routine and style of their singing. Yet, to a varying extent all of the members were also living on the margins of society as a result of their long-term mental health problems. So there were varying senses of how they were both embedded *and* marginal to the so-called "local community."

These initial impressions perhaps convey the difficulties and complexities of thinking about "contemporary community" – about people's individual lives in relation to their surrounding physical, social and cultural context. In a modern (or post-modern) urban context like London the complications of any such description increase. When British Prime Minister Tony Blair said in a speech in 2004 "Go to any community in this country …"[1] what (or, rather, *where*) exactly did he mean? For many people now, the use of the word "community" to denote a place is, as we saw earlier, merely part of nostalgic (and often politically suspect) rhetoric. There are now, however, a range of possible uses of the word and concept "community." Whilst it can refer to a traditional geographical place, it can also indicate a spatially distributed group who identity themselves commonly (according to ethnicity, sexuality or political affiliation), or to a temporary collection of people whose "circumstantial community" may be a hospital, prison or refugee camp.[2]

The members of *Musical Minds* are certainly affected by their relatively hostile local environment, but few would call this (non-euphemistically) a "community." Many have also experienced "circumstantial communities" when in hospital, but are currently leading free, if relatively restricted, lives within a narrow local area. They would doubtless view self-styled communities of identity as a middle-class luxury. Does this mean that they are without community, or that this concept has no meaning for their lives?

The obvious form of community they *have* managed to cultivate (with Sarah's help) is a community of interest and enterprise – a working musical community. Quite simply, they belong together because they want to music together. But given their individual difficulties (and continuing challenges to their belonging-together in such a way) there is a need to think in more detailed ways about just how their "musical community" has been cultivated and is successfully sustained. The following three sections draw on a variety of interdisciplinary theory to suggest various possible ways of understanding a group such as *Musical Minds*, with its characteristic features and processes, challenges and achievements.

Musical Minds as a "Communication Community"

> *As people gather for the rehearsal, my initial perception of distinct and somewhat isolated individuals changes – as members of the group collaborate and communicate in various ways to set up for the afternoon. Tim prepares cups, milk and tea for the tea-break whilst Charlie opens up the metal cupboard on the stage, gets out some small percussion instruments and microphone stands, making a small performance area, with the piano to the side. People chat a bit to each other, tell Sarah about yesterday's day-trip to Margate that several of them went on; someone else complains about a medical problem. They clearly know each other very well – there's a short-hand way of chatting and interacting that leaves me, as an "outsider," slightly puzzled, as they obviously know more about each other, and the surrounding events, than I do. Overall there's a sense of familiarity, routine, mutual knowledge … yet it's not immediately apparent exactly how these people belong together …*

---

[1]   Quoted in Poole (2006, p. 26).

[2]   For more on types of community see Ansdell (2004).

Gerald Delanty (2003), in his book *Community*, writes that "If anything unites [the] very diverse conceptions of community it is the idea that community concerns belonging" (p. 4) and that, rather than just happening, contemporary community must be *performed,* it is something that we create, rather than somewhere we just *are,* or are "inside." This perspective emphasizes how contemporary community happens through its specific modes of communication, and relies less on traditional factors such as locality, fixed social structures, or ritual events. As Delanty writes:

> Belonging today is participation in communication more than anything else, and the multiple forms of communication are mirrored in the plurality of discourses of belonging, which we call communication communities. (Delanty, 2003, p. 187)

Such "communication communities" are dynamic, sometimes conflictual, and are created in and through their particular communicative processes. In this view, creating community today often involves actively cultivating such "communicative competences" as dialogue, collaboration and negotiation – both verbal and nonverbal. Communication communities involve the *active* search for belonging, understanding and communication in often unpromising circumstances. They suggest the search for, and creation of, forms of *communicative belonging.* Consequently, participation in such communities can often seem both communal *and* "discrepant" at the same time, as people work to reconcile their equal, but sometimes conflicting, needs for autonomy and togetherness.

> *The "performance space" is now set up, and members of* Musical Minds *suggest songs and sing them individually at first – each of them absolutely singular in style, delivery, taste. Concentration on each other's performance seems fragile to begin with. People move around, talk to someone else, go out for a cigarette. But concentration grows as the session settles, with people joining-in the chorus of the more well-known (and easy to sing) solo songs. There's a ragged togetherness at these moments. In the interval one man comes up to me and says: "They don't sing in the same way as I do – then I get my breathing wrong!" Then he adds, "But I know it's good to sing together – I've got to keep trying."*

Sarah identifies her main task as the facilitator of the group simply being to help the members to keep making music together. When she arrived six years ago the group culture was for people to just sing their own individual song (with the facilitator as just an accompanist) – "doing their own thing," as Sarah remarked. Gently and gradually Sarah has helped the group towards a more socially and musically collaborative culture, both on practical matters (such as organizing their yearly show-case concert) and within the actual musical material. The members sing more songs together now, joining in more with each others' music:

Sarah: This whole emphasis I've been trying to promote ... doing your own thing and listening to others doing *their* thing ... seemed to mean that people actually enjoyed the process more ...

Gary: Why does this matter?

Sarah: Because then they *belong* – they're part of it: they have the experience I think of being part of something that feels good, that they are contributing towards, that's different if they're not there ... and something that's fun as well. They get on well together at these times ... and they're not people that necessarily "get on well" other places ...

This tension between "doing your own thing" and "being a group" (between identity and belonging) ran through almost every facet of *Musical Minds.* Yet I also witnessed distinct progress during the two years I was around, in terms of people being increasingly able to reconcile this tension – a process quite literally achieved in and through musicing – both during the weekly rehearsals, but most powerfully in the public concert situations.

The singers are on stage for the concert, under a large banner with Musical Minds *on it. They begin the concert with a medley from* West Side Story *– with individual solos and group singing. They have some difficulties at first in getting the ensemble together – not helped by considerable nerves – but by the end of the medley they are more confident and coordinated, helped by Sarah's continual encouragement and musical direction from the piano, which is below the stage on the floor.*

I talk with Sarah about the concert:

Sarah: Some of the things we did this time were more cohesive as a group: this *West Side Story* medley we did once before ... sometimes it just goes chaotic, people speed up ... But then we talked a lot in the rehearsals about listening to each other to make it work ... and after the show this time the person who'd usually trip it all up came up to me and said that it'd gone well and thank you, you teach us to listen ... and I thought: Wow! It doesn't actually matter whether it has the desired professional musical effect, but the fact that he's thinking about listening to others, that he can actually collaborate with others without it going off the rails ... And that's a huge thing for them to be able to listen to each other ... because their ongoing constant complaint in life is that they're not listened to ... but the truth is that most people in the group do find it very difficult to tolerate others: their behavior, their stuff, their music ... they haven't wanted to hear it in the past. So this is another paradox: their whole thing is "nobody listens to me" but then they don't listen to anybody else either!

Gary: It felt to me as if this kind of [concert] event was a stepping-stone for the group to get somewhere else, using the concert as a vehicle …

Sarah: Yes … this was the first time afterwards that they said they felt good about singing together as a group. They came off and said *"Amazing Grace* is our anthem!" Actually I'd always thought that, but I'm not sure *they'd* see this before … Often they get taken off into wanting to do their own thing … perhaps it's a fear of being absorbed into a group … But this time they were saying, "Yes, it was great that we did that … as well as our own stuff …"so maybe they felt they could do *both*, without losing themselves … something shifted a little …

To characterize *Musical Minds* as a "communication community" is therefore to show how particular modes of communication (musical and non-musical) serve to actively construct, sustain and develop particular modes of community, and its accompanying experience of belonging.

Such a formulation can perhaps sound rather abstract: as if the achieved qualities of communication and belonging somehow exist for their own sake. Another view would be that the members of *Musical Minds* communicate because they need to work together to put on the concert – and this is prepared for each week by meeting, collaborating and rehearsing. Another way of talking about their type of community could be as a "community of practice."

Musical Minds as a "Community of Musical Practice"

Following some serious disagreements amongst the members, which had threatened the survival of the group, Sarah helps them formulate a set of "Ground Rules and Aims." They define their Aim as: "The group meets to make and share music together with opportunities for solo and group activity. The group aims to prepare for and organize regular performances as well as musical fellowship on a weekly basis." A typical Ground Rule is: "The group runs from 4–6 PM. From 4–5 members help set up the room and equipment and then workshop songs and music. People arriving during this time should not distract the group but join quietly and with respect for the music and musician."

In an interview Sarah comments on these "Aims and Rules," how they came out of the need to focus on why everyone was there:

> At the end of the day they make music, and appreciate each other's music, and listen to each other. I usually try to move into doing music as quickly as possible … otherwise they'll argue and row, then they'll argue about how long they've argued for and not done any music! So the bottom line is that everyone comes back to sing and play, to do music and talk about music … music is the common thing … (Sarah Wilson, music therapist)

When I talked to the members in their tea-break about the group one person says: "We're all trying to justify our existence, but the main fact is that we all like music …"

One possible model for *Musical Minds* is a "community of practice," a concept developed by the social learning theorist Etienne Wenger (Wenger, 1998; Wenger et al., 2002). It emerged from studies of the participatory learning of work groups, where the social, educational and productional aspects were closely connected. Wenger suggests that the concept "community of practice" characterizes the everyday experience of people engaged in doing and learning something together – where this is more than a transitory encounter, but less than a formal social structure. Wenger's concept has increasingly been used to describe all kinds of small-scale groups which exemplify how learning is social. It brings our attention to how such "communities of practice" catalyze fundamental social processes of participation, meaning-making, identity, and belonging. Wenger describes a "community of practice" simply, as:

> … a group of people who share a concern, a set of problems, or a passion about a topic, and who deepen their knowledge and expertise in this area by interacting on an ongoing basis. (Wenger, 2002, p. 4)

Wenger suggests the following indicators of a "community of practice" having formed:

- Sustained mutual relationships – harmonious or conflictual.
- Shared ways of engaging in doing things together for a purpose.
- Absence of pre-amble when people meet, as if conversations and interactions were a continuation of an ongoing process.
- Overlap in members' descriptions of who belongs or does not.
- Mutually defining identities in relation to a mutually identified endeavor.
- Ability to assess appropriateness of each other's actions and products.
- Use of specific tools, representations and other artifacts.
- Shared stories, jokes, references, jargon and short-cuts within communications.
- A sense of continuity and longevity of the identified group (adapted from Wenger, 1998, p. 125).

These criteria fit well with my experience of *Musical Minds*, and of the members' and Sarah's comments about their *raison d'etre* being to meet and make music. This, quite simply, is their practice. Wenger suggests three fundamental elements of a community of practice: (i) a *domain* – of interest, passion, knowledge, which defines what the focus or task is, (ii) a *group* of people who care about this task and have the opportunity to pursue …, (iii) a *shared practice*, in order to be effective in their domain.

Three typical dimensions characterize such a community: (i) *mutual engagement*, (ii) *joint enterprise*, (iii) *shared repertoire*. For *Musical Minds* the mutual engagement consists of their ongoing weekly meetings, facilitated by Sarah within and without the music making; their "joint enterprise" is defined by the planning and practicing for the regular performance events, and the "shared repertoire" is the gradual negotiation of the kind of songs and routines that make up the musical programmes for individual and group performance. Wenger suggests significant social benefits to flow from the activity of a community of practice, in how:

- It mediates the experience and negotiation of shared *meaning* within an immediate context.
- Its ongoing and disciplined shared *practice* sustains mutual engagement in action.
- Its *community* is created through participation experienced as competence in practice.
- *Identity* of members is defined and reinforced – they experience being someone, somewhere, in practice.
- Relationships of *belonging* emerge from all of the above.
  (adapted from Wenger, 1998)

Ground Rule No. 4: "Members listen to each other and offer constructive comments, suggestions and encouragement – which they can then expect to receive from others." Today, the group is preparing for their public concert in two weeks time. Tim runs through his song – "The End of the World" – but rushes breathlessly through it, with Sarah trying to encourage him to slow down through how she plays the piano accompaniment. After he's finished Sid says "You want to take that one slower, you do!" I've noticed recently that Sid has learned to put such critical comments in a more encouraging way. Tim takes the comment as it was intended. In an interview Sarah tells me how she approaches helping the group with the musical preparation for their performance events: "This concert was something that we aimed for and worked for and achieved – it gives a momentum, something to aim for, a reason for coming that gives us a musical experience today too – not just about rehearsing to do it over and over again in order to get it perfect, but working on it now, to get something out of the musical experience right now! We do a lot of preparation – I sometimes wonder whether that's me wanting that ... but actually the group do really want to do that ... and by the time we get to the concert all I do is play the piano ..."

Although Wenger meant something very broad by "practice" (the engaged social action of our lives[3]), musicians of course use this word in the very everyday sense of working on music: mostly in private to begin with, then within the more social *rehearsal* process. Normally such practice aims towards some kind of

---

[3] "Practice is, first and foremost, a process by which we can experience the world and our engagement with it as meaningful" (Wenger, 1998, p. 51).

performance situation. The two senses of "practice" are clearly related, and the music educationalist Margaret Barrett (2005) has used and extended Wenger's concept, suggesting specifically "communities of musical practice," which had specific features and affordances for the children she studied working together in school playgrounds:

> Children exercise considerable autonomy and agency in these communities, and draw on a range of communicative practices in producing and negotiating meaning. Children build and hold considerable cultural capital in these communities and demonstrate a "cultural literacy," "a feel" for negotiating the rules and conventions in a range of musics ... which assist children to take part in the large and small "conversations" of our musical worlds. (Barrett, 2005, p. 207)

Whilst Barrett's interest in appropriating Wenger's concept is to broaden our view of how musical learning takes place in informal social contexts amongst children, this characterization also fits contexts such as the *Musical Minds* group and their personal, social and cultural needs.

Modeling *Musical Minds* as a "community of musical practice" is useful in describing and summarizing its key features, as:

- *A community* ... being a sustained mutual engagement between an identified group of people, who (whether harmonious or conflictual) define their belonging in relation to the identified group *Musical Minds*, and who maintain a sense of boundary between membership and non-membership, and a sense of continuity, development and longevity of their association.
- *Of musical* ... being the commonly-held aim, purpose, focus, joint enterprise that the members articulate as being *why* they belong, keep coming and find meaning in. Their passion and their reward is music, and the group is both music-centered and music-led – in its exploration of musical repertoire, formats of musicing and routines of musical performance.
- *Practice* ... is what sustains their engagement and what defines their competence in relation to the overall joint enterprise. Practice might be rehearsing, talking about the music, negotiating practical arrangements for the concert – in short, *musicking* as defined by Christopher Small (1998) – music as ecology of interrelated social action animated by performance.

Whilst a "community of practice" is not just an educational concept, it does locate a learning focus as sometimes key to a dynamic personal and social process – aligning it with the aims of a "social therapy" perspective (Stige, 2004a; Newman and Holzman, 1997; Smail, 2005), where health is seen within an ecological and political frame. Another related alignment is to a sociological "social capital" theory, which the music therapist Simon Procter (2004, 2006) has developed recently in relation to work in mental health settings similar to *Musical Minds*.

Procter glosses the social capital concept as "… how (to put it at its very simplest) doing things together impacts on people's well-being, and can indeed benefit not only them but the community of which they are part" (2006, p. 147). Through an examination of his work with the community-based mental health group *Way Ahead* (2004) and within a closed ward of a psychiatric hospital (2006) Procter demonstrates how "social capital is accrued through musical participation" (2004, p. 228). He extends this idea to talk of a specifically "musical capital" – where the very specific forms of social-musical action promoted through music therapy situations help people and the communities they live in to develop resources that can be generalized:

> [musical capital] can be both public and private, communal and personal. It is about self-identity but also about being heard by others. It is above all about living performance, about grasping opportunities that promote well-being, as an individual, but also as a member of communities. The role of the music therapist, then, must include offering people opportunities to steer a healthy musical course, to renew and develop their health-promoting relationships with music within communities. (Procter, 2004, p. 228)

In his second (2006) publication on this subject Procter tackles the challenge that social capital theory is often seen as "broad-brush," with little specification of social processes at a micro-level. His example of the micro-musical generation of "musical capital" between four people on a psychiatric ward shows, on the contrary, how the key indicators of the generation of social capital (mutual trust and reciprocity) can indeed be shown within micro-musical communication. It is indeed a "laboratory" for observing this.

Musical Communitas as *"Belonging*-together"

I discussed one of *Musical Minds'* concerts with a colleague who had also been in the audience. We struggled to define the precise nature of the communal atmosphere of the concert. "It wasn't that there was suddenly community because these people had just gathered together there – it wasn't 'easy community'" my colleague said. For the sake of the following argument let's call this *Type A community*, or "falling into community" through bringing people artificially together. We agreed, however, that something else than this was happening at the concert. The members of the group appeared both very individual (and sometimes somewhat isolated), but whilst also achieving a togetherness, be this often a messy one. This togetherness clearly needed *work* in order to happen – both preceding and during the performance: work from themselves (to listen to, to accommodate each other), and work from Sarah to maintain and sustain the musical togetherness in the time of the musicing. Community in *this* sense, which I'll call *Type B community*, or "creating community," is not a natural product of simply "coming together," but has to be forged and maintained in the time and space of the musicing. This in turn needs skill and technique from the therapist/facilitator, as well as faith and goodwill from everyone else. It is the opposite of "easy community" (which is not to say that this does not happen too, or is valuable).

Something of the distinctions I've suggested here are similar to those made by Heidegger (1969) in his book *Identity and Difference*,[4] where he discusses two different types of unity: belonging-*together* and *belonging*-together – a subtle but meaningful distinction. In the former, the sense of belonging is determined by the togetherness, unification coming as a result of some externally-imposed order. In the latter, however, the togetherness is determined by the belonging. The togetherness happens from the inside outwards, not a forcing together.

In terms of *Musical Minds* what I called "Type A" community above would be belonging-*together*, whilst "Type B" is *belonging*-together, where belonging has been forged not by any outside conformity, but *in-and-through* musicing – the inter-subjective process of this "communication community." It is sustained and maintained through their ongoing "community of musical practice." This formulation has several implications for thinking about Community Music Therapy situations such as the *Musical Minds* group, suggesting how:

- Both kinds of "community" happen, but "Type A" is a simpler concept of community – where it happens by virtue of people finding themselves together in a place (around music or not).
- Type B better explains the skills and aims of the music therapist: to cultivate, by working on communicative competences such as listening and working-together in music, such that "musical belonging" can be built, developed, maintained and repaired; such that a particular quality of togetherness can be experienced as a result of the "musical community of practice."

This idea of a "communication community" could thus be seen as a natural extension of the music therapist's traditional concentration on the fostering of interpersonal and intersubjective communication as a prime therapeutic aim (Nordoff and Robbins, 1977; Ansdell and Pavlicevic, 2005). Whilst this has typically been modeled within dyadic work, recent work by music therapists is suggesting more collective versions of this (Pavlicevic and Ansdell, 2008).[5]

---

[4]   Heidegger's distinction is also usefully discussed by Henri Bortoft (1996).

[5]   Music therapists are of course not the only ones to be cultivating an increasingly broader understanding of intersubjectivity – taking traditional dyadic models into more collective examples – see for example Stern (2004) or Bradley (2005) or – for a more popular take on the re-thinking of "social intelligence" – Goleman (2006). Much of this is in turn pre-visaged in the sociological and music sociology tradition, see for example Schutz's pioneering essay "Making Music Together" (1964/1951) and its theory of the "tuning-in relationship" between people, explored further by Pete Martin (2006).

Several music therapists (Ruud, 1998; Aigen, 2002; Stige, 2002; Ansdell, 2004) have suggested the anthropologist Victor Turner's concept of "communitas" to be a useful one in characterizing the highly mutual state of togetherness sometimes forged during musicing (hence "musical communitas"). Turner in turn modeled this concept in relation to the social philosopher Martin Buber's dialogical "I-Thou" philosophy of human relationships.[6] Buber's own expansion of his two-person model of relationship to the sphere of community is relevant here to our ongoing exploration of the relationship between communication and belonging.

Buber suggests that you cannot abstractly plan for community – it is a concrete event that happens when people manage to really listen to one another. In a famous passage in *Between Man and Man* (1947) Buber makes the differentiation between the collective and the communal (that is, between belonging-*together* and *belonging*-together):

> Collectivity is not a binding but a bundling together: individuals packed together … But community, growing community … is the being no longer side by side but *with* one another of a multitude of persons. And this multitude, though it also moves towards one goal, yet experiences everywhere a turning to, a dynamic facing of, the other, a flowing from *I* to *Thou*. Community is where community happens. (Buber, 1947, p. 31)

Buber's social philosophy is an elaboration of the logic of his dialogical philosophy: that we typically fall into *I-It* relations to others – a collective of individuals in a place and time. Genuine community, one the other hand, arises from *I-Thou* relationships, where independent people experience a mutual and direct relationship to one another. As in *I-Thou* encounters, the "essential *we*" of community must be continually renewed through the interplay of genuine dialogues.

How is this achieved? Through the *between* – "a relational space ever and again reconstituted in our meeting with others,"[7] generating community. When greater than the dyad, community comes *not* primarily from people's personal, subjective *feelings* towards each other, but because they "stand in a living, reciprocal relationship to a single living centre," and therefore through which they also stand in living reciprocal relationship to one another. A community is built upon a living, reciprocal relationship, but the builder is the living, active center. This "generative center" of community Buber describes as *Verbundenheit* – "bonding" or "binding together" (recalling Heidegger's *belonging*-together) (Figure 4.1). As such, Buber writes:

---

[6]   Buber's dialogical principle has been applied increasingly to both music therapy theory (Ansdell, 1995; Garred, 2006) and to other evolving therapeutic models, see e.g. Evans and Gilbert's (2005) discussion of integrative psychotherapy.

[7]   Direct quotations in this section from Buber.

This community is no union of the like-minded, but a genuine living together of people of similar or complementary natures but of different minds. Community is the overcoming of *otherness* in living unity. (Buber, in Kramer, 2003, p. 95)

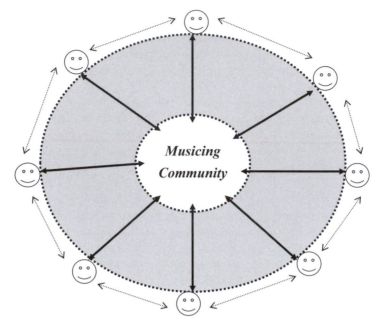

Figure 4.1   Community generated through musicing together

In this sense *Musical Minds* could be thought of as, initially, a "community of otherness," which is helped both by Sarah, but also by "music itself" to find a living and shared dialogical center. We have seen how much the central reference point of value and commitment for the members of *Musical Minds* is music and musicing. This is what creates the "between" for the group – and what continuously creates what I have previously called the *musical between* (Ansdell, 1995) that lifts them out of being just a "social group." And although they certainly have feelings for each other (and much shared history within the local community) this is clearly not enough for the group to work optimally. As such, Sarah's work (within a Community Music Therapy understanding) would be to help both imagine and mobilize *Musical Minds*' potential for *musical communitas*.

Beyond Togetherness? (Participation and Discrepancy)

My intention in outlining the various theoretical perspectives in the last three sections has been to provide tools to focus on how making music together can afford important psycho-social benefits for the members of *Musical Minds*. Hopefully these reflections have largely avoided the normal platitudes of "apple-pie community-talk." It could, however, be argued that the ideas outlined thus far still represent the phenomenon of community in too ideal and romantic a way. There is, it could be argued, still too much unity, too little discrepancy and difference in this portrayal – it is not yet true enough to the total phenomenon I experienced. In short, the "community" described is still too "cozy."

> *I notice at the first rehearsal I go to that there's a tradition of members picking their "own" songs – in a variety of styles (from 1940s show tunes to rock and pop), and then the group often joining in the chorus. In the tea-break Malcolm tells me: "They don't sing the song the same way as I do – then I get my breathing wrong." I'd noticed this earlier – Malcolm sings his preferred jazz and bossa-nova songs "swung," whilst his chorus sing them straight. "But ...," adds Malcolm, "... I know it's good to sing together – so I've got to keep trying!"*

Sarah tells me in an interview:

> *Yes, I do think that we have a sense of community ... but it's, as in any community, a variety of individuals who feel differently about different things on different days, and have different needs, talents, likes and dislikes ... but they did work well as a group this time. When they stand up to do their solos they're saying "Here's my music, here's my history ..." but it's at the same time shared with other people ... that's very nice. (Sarah Wilson, music therapist)*

Brynjulf Stige (2003) has suggested a useful model of group musical relationships that aims to accommodate the communal as both a "centered" *and* de-centered activity at the same time, and which can contain aspects of musical difference within shared musical participation. In any non-traditional community context, most people begin with an already established relationship to music, cultivated through their inborn musicality and its legacy of encounters with music throughout their life history. Stige characterizes this situation as a tri-partite pattern of reciprocal relationships between protomusicality, musics, and musicing. Music affords particular experiences to people in line with these uniquely personal sets of relationships. From this, "new meanings may then be established as new relationships between people and artifacts are built through the act of musicking in the specific social and cultural contexts of the therapy process" (Stige, 2003, p. 173). In *Musical Minds* each person's toleration of, and participation in, each other's song preferences did just this – helped along by Sarah's cultivation of more collaborative musicing and interpersonal toleration.

Within a group situation Stige's tripartite model takes an interesting form, as illustrated in Figure 4.2.

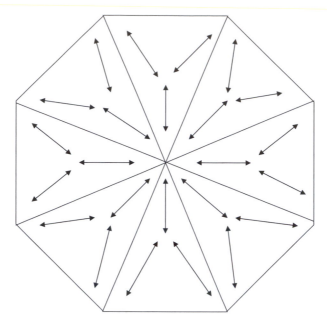

Figure 4.2   Stige's model of "communal musicking." Source: (Stige, 2003, p. 174)

Here, each triangular segment represents each person. Stige annotates this model as follows:

> Communal musicking as Centred and De-Centred Activity – Communal musicking creates shared focus of expression and experience, but each member participates in his or her specific way, based upon protomusical capacities that have been cultivated through different life histories and different encounters with musics. The meaning of the situation, as perceived affordances, will differ from participant to participant. The 8 participants in the imagined group depicted here are therefore represented as a conglomerate of protomusicality-musics-musicking constellations ... (Stige, 2003, p. 174)

In the text he further explains:

> The communal musicking is the center and shared focus, and each participant contributes with the cultivated capacities and the perceived affordances relative to his or her life history. [It demonstrates] ... *how communal musicking is at once public and private, social and personal, centred and de-centred* ... In this way, communal musicking may have a strong potential for realization of what is often considered a community ideal; *unity beyond uniformity*. (Stige, 2003, p. 173)

It is instructive to contrast Stige's model with Martin Buber's outlined above. Whilst Buber's "genuine community" is unanimously generated from a central "between," shared by all participants, Stige's model shows a simultaneously centered and *de*-centered reality, with a more diffused circulation of forces, influences and attractions. This model perhaps gives a better perspective on some of the seemingly paradoxical features of *Musical Minds* and its qualities of unity without uniformity; of a musical community which manages to live with musical differences.

During Musical Minds' *second concert in May 2005 Eric's choice of the song "You'll Never Walk Alone" feels symbolic, given he often seems an outsider, socially isolated within the group, where his musicing is often discrepant to the others. He often plays a percussion instrument in a different rhythm, or seems unengaged with other people's music. But tonight he appears confident as he takes his turn for a solo number, standing by the central mike on stage, slightly hiding behind his copy of the words, and flanked by the other members of the group who are sitting down along the stage. The main events within his performance are as follows:*

(1)   Sarah plays the piano introduction to the song, but Eric picks the cue up late, leading to discrepant timing between them (though his pitch is accurate). Sarah renegotiates the timing with Eric.

(2)   Eric had rehearsed the first verse with a parlando delivery, but tonight he spontaneously delivers it in a pitched version, with a nice tone of voice as he finds his confidence during the first few phrases.

(3)   Eric slightly rushes in Phrase 3, requiring temporal renegotiation from Sarah.

(4)   During "Walk on, Walk on …" there's a spontaneous entry of the drummer (below stage), adding in a subtle cymbal tap with brushes (the timing between the three soon becomes slightly discrepant, but gathers togetherness towards the end of the phrase).

(5)   During the final phrase, "Never walk alone …," Eric pulls the tempo up (and has slight difficulty with the high Es), leading to temporal renegotiation again between the three players, but reaching the cadence of the verse together.

(6)   In the piano transition to the chorus reprise Sarah cues Eric's re-entry through emphasis of its phrasing, plus an exaggerated upbeat. During this the "chorus" of the other members on stage gradually get up from their seats (in a ragged and individual way) and sing verse 2 together. Eric is now in the middle of the group, leading the singing…

(7)   The singing-together is often temporally discrepant, as is the textural/ timbral "blend" of their different voices (in terms of register, style of singing, timbre). In particular there is a constant micro-negotiation of

different forms of singing around the beat (before or after). This negotiation also happens between Sarah on piano, the drummer and the singers.

(8) *The camera cuts from the group to the audience, most of whom are singing along too now, swaying arms above their heads (as the UK football fans do in their traditional appropriation of this song). There's a strong sense of "all-together" now ...*

(9) *The final phrase expands in volume (more drums and piano) into a broad, generous sound. The final cadence is temporally discrepant, with individuals ending their own way – an "ending-together" which is technically not-quite-together!*

(10) *Eric waves his arms triumphantly, acknowledging the audience applause ... but also perhaps his successful arrival at this moment of belonging.*

These detailed comments on the song reveal something key to the overall focus of this essay so far: how togetherness in the musicing is negotiated through communicative processes of timing and "spacing." Then, at a level of micro-musical detail, how "discrepant timing" is reconciled with "*belonging*-together." My constant use of the term "discrepant timing" during the comments on the excerpt above suggests that Charles Keil's concept of "participatory discrepancies" may be useful here.

Against the old text-book idea[8] that successful musical togetherness is dependent upon precisely unified timing, tuning and texture Keil (1994) states, "music, to be personally and socially valuable, must be 'out of tune' and 'out of time'..." (1994, p. 4). This, of course, is relative: to the actual performance context, to the conventions of the musical style, but most of all to the form of communicative action between the musicians at that time. Keil suggests that the characteristic *groove* of many musics (especially popular and jazz styles) is created by how the participating musicians negotiate a balance between sameness and difference, their musical gestures being both collaborative and discrepant at the same time (in timing, tuning, and timbre). Negotiating and navigating this "vital drive" or groove is therefore a *social* activity, with the subtle variations of performance building a characteristic groove through what he terms *participatory discrepancies*. The musicians aren't finding some ideal time outside of their interaction, but as part of it, *between* themselves and the song or style. As Keil explains:

"Groove" ... is not some essence of all music that we can simply take for granted, but must be figured out each time between players ... [It] has to be constructed between players ... There is no essential groove, no abstract time. No "metronome sense" in the strict sense of metronome, no feeling qua feeling,

---

[8] More accurately this tendency is part of the recent cultural practice of classical music – influenced by the "conservatoire mentality" of perfectionism of technique along with the recording industry's fetishization of the "perfect musical product" to be preserved outside of the course of performance (see Small, 1998; Cook, 1998).

just constant relativity, constant relating, constant negotiation of a groove between players in a particular time and place with a complex variety of variables intersecting millisecond by millisecond. Abstract time is a nice Platonic idea, a perfect essence, but real time, natural time, human time is always variable. (Keil in Aigen, 2002, p. 35)

Ken Aigen comments on this in relation to music therapy situations:

The creation of vital, alive, quality music does not derive from the ability of musicians to link with each other around perfect tunings and precise co-temporal musical events, merging their identities into some perfect unity. Instead, music is created by an ability to connect with others in unique ways that preserve our separateness ... Hence groove is a necessarily social activity. It requires an awareness of and responsiveness to the present moment in time and to the musical contributions of other people in that moment. Thus, the establishment of groove requires moving past barriers that frequently bring clients to music therapy, particularly those which reinforce social isolation. (Aigen, 2002, p. 35)

This perspective seems directly relevant to the micro-level of what I observed happening in the excerpt I examined above from the *Musical Minds* concert. It also relates to the broader theme that has dominated this essay – the common tension between individuality and belonging. Keil's concept of *participatory discrepancies* suggests that for most live musicing a level of discrepancy is natural, in that it contributes to both the social process of the musical negotiation and the unique flavor of *these* particular performances of these songs, by *these* people in *this* place. As Keil (1994) comments: "... this loose-tuning, loose-timing way ... the very lifeblood of music, in all cultures, has to do with discrepancies."

The discrepant sounding of parts of the songs in the *Musical Minds* concert is part of their musical-social process of negotiating the groove, which is, in turn, the negotiation of individual participations in relation to levels of togetherness. In the second-by-second events in their communal singing we see (as Keil predicts) how precision and variance co-exist in the musicing. Within the negotiation process (between singer and song, singer(s) and accompanist/drummer, singers-amongst-themselves) the singers and instrumentalists are navigating and negotiating a musical "intersubjective matrix" (Stern, 2004) between themselves. They are not trying to coordinate with some externally-imposed unifying temporal or tonal standard. Instead they are negotiating the *relative* temporal/tonal/textural norm

– relative to *that* time, *that* place, *those* people.[9] Their collaborative musicing[10] actually consists of discrepant timing, tuning and texture – and its on-the-spot "repair" and transformation.

On a broader level, it is significant how this micro-level of participatory discrepancies links to the larger theme of negotiating *belonging*-together in this musical way. As Ken Aigen remarks, Keil's is a philosophy of music(ing) which acknowledges how it is possible to connect with others in ways which also preserves our separateness – exactly the issue that Sarah had identified as a basic anxiety for the members of *Musical Minds* – and one we would not be surprised to see somehow represented within their musicing. As Aigen suggests in relation to his learning disabled adolescent client Lloyd's discrepant participation in music:

> The constituents of social life lie immanently in music ... To participate in the culturally and stylistically embedded music is to participate in culture – it is to participate in the attitudes, values, feelings and experience which define the culture. For Lloyd, to create groove with his therapists is to find the comfort of a cultural home. (Aigen, 2002, p. 36)

This situation is, I would suggest, very similar for the members of *Musical Minds*. Degrees of discrepant participation ensure that a comfortable balance can be kept between togetherness and autonomy. The result for them (from what I understand from them) is, at best, a *belonging*-together forged through *musical communitas*.

> *It's the finale of the concert, with all of the members standing along the stage. The song they've chosen is an up-tempo energetic favorite with a strong groove – "Daydream Believer." Visually there's still the impression, however, of a series of individuals in a row (there's little visual sense of them being a cohesive group). The strong and relatively homogenous sound of the opening phrase gives a contradictory message to their visual appearance. The group does sound together ... but there are markedly different physical responses to the music (slight swaying/dancing, Eric still sitting whilst others stand ...). The camera switches to the audience, who are happily participating: singing and swaying sideways with rhythmic side-claps. The timing of the major phrases of the song is often discrepant (individuals arriving just before/after the beat).*

---

[9] This could be compared to Steven Feld's (1994) notion of Lift-up-over-sounding as applied to the musical aesthetic of the Kaluli – an effect termed "anarchistic synchrony" which, as Aigen (2002) comments is expressive of the Kaluli's overall egalitarian interactional style – "a cooperative and collaborative autonomy ... [which] maximizes social participation and autonomy of self" (p. 61).

[10] Mercedes Pavlicevic and I have developed this concept elsewhere (Pavlicevic and Ansdell, 2008) to characterize the functional relationship between musical and social activity, based on the psycho-biological capacity of "communicative musicality" and the culturally inducted levels of skill and style as musicianship, see also Part IV in this book.

The camera shows Sarah attempting to navigate and negotiate a "consensual beat" within all the different possibilities (or, rather, preventing the discrepancy getting too much!). The repetitive nature of the basic phrase identity of the song affords more togetherness than other songs in the concert (helped by a strong piano/drum groove/drive). There's a rather sudden final cadence (seemingly in the middle of a phrase!) leading to a rather discrepant ending (which works quite well nevertheless).

Conclusion: Towards Musical Hospitality

This essay began with the fictional character Henry's thoughts on "musical community" in the jazz club, where he hears within the music "an impossible world in which you give everything you have to others, but lose nothing of yourself." For him music evokes only a "dream of community" – which stands against the threats of the contemporary social world: how globalization and cosmopolitanism are resulting in millions of people experiencing transition, migration and displacement, finding themselves adrift from traditional forms of community and belonging. Theorists talk of "liminal communities" to characterize the transit areas, temporary or "in-between" places people end up (from refugee camps to the many "circumstantial communities"[11] where medical and social care takes place – hospitals, care centers, prisons).

My study of *Musical Minds* showed me how one aspect of Henry's diagnosis of the problem is indeed accurate: how the struggle is so often between people's wish to "give everything you have to others, but lose nothing of yourself" – that is, the struggle between belonging and identity. However, people *do* manage to, if not reconcile this tension, then to live creatively with it, and to create their own modes of community and belonging. *Musical Minds* could be seen as a heroic example of this.

Perhaps the over-use of the word "community" hinders our understanding. Recent theorists such as Derrida have, for example, suggested *hospitality* as an alternative notion – the welcoming of the other, the stranger, the giving without losing (in Caputo, 1997). Could we, he asks, create "an *open* quasi-community" which remains communicative and hospitable to difference, to the other, to different kinds of belonging, where "we do not have to choose between unity and multiplicity"? (p. 13). Wenger too concludes his study of communities of practice with an appeal for hospitality through mutuality:

> In the life-giving power of mutuality lies the miracle of parenthood, the essence of apprenticeship, the secret to the generational encounter, the key to the creation of connections across boundaries of practice: a frail bridge across the abyss, a

---

[11]   See Ansdell (2002) for a discussion of this concept in relation to Community Music Therapy.

> slight breach of the law, a small gift of undeserved trust – it is almost a theorem
> of love that we can open our practices and communities to others (newcomers,
> outsiders), invite them into our own identities of participation, let them be what
> they are not, and thus start what cannot be started. (Wenger, 1998, p. 277)

With Sarah's help, *Musical Minds* has managed to create, over the last five years,
something like this: a hospitable community of musical practice for themselves
– and with it a modest and realistic mode of belonging, which nevertheless
sustains them well in a relatively deprived and hostile environment. This, for me,
is community unencumbered with nostalgia or sentimentality, which comes with a
specification of just *how* it can be achieved, through its principal communicative
and collaborative medium – music.

The difference between this and Henry's vision (and all of those whom this
fictional character stands for) is that this is not a romantic trope of lost community,
revived only in an "impossible world" or in a dream which fades along with the
music. On the contrary, the kind of realistic musical community modeled in this
essay by *Musical Minds* is demonstrably possible (if challenging), and its effects
seems not to completely fade with the final notes – which sound out triumphantly
different in their togetherness.

PART III

Chapter 5

Action

Must We Really End? Community Integration of Children in Raanana, Israel

Cochavit Elefant

In Search for a Partner in the Community

I would like to take the reader through a journey in which two diverse groups of children ages 7–8 became united into one group during music sessions. The story is told in detail in order to illuminate the intricate but necessary intergroup relation dialogue. The two groups (one in elementary school and the other in a center for special education) attended schools in two separate parts of the town Raanana in Israel. Music was what connected these two groups. This story helps to show how children can solve social problems and how parents and schools can foster positive social relationships among children of different backgrounds. First, let us meet the children who attend the center for special education:

> *Eight young children with severe special needs are sitting in a circle during a music therapy session with me as their music therapist. We have been meeting for two years in their classroom located in a center for children with special needs, in a building away from all other buildings in a middle class town in Israel. None of the children have expressive language but all have ample nonverbal communication. We enjoy communicating with each other week after week through musical activities such as songs, vocal and instrumental improvisation and movement.*
>
> *During these meetings the staff members take a "break" from their long hours of attentive, caring and meticulous work with these children. They are tired. Some staff members stay in the room, listen to our music making as a smile of pride appears at the corner of their mouths – just like a mother watching her child perform. The children glance back at them as if saying "did you hear me play? Aren't you proud of me?" The staff who know these children very well nod with contentment.*

It took a year or so to reach the setting I have just described. Until then the staff members had actively participated in the music therapy group. I had suggested that the children didn't need much assistance during the music therapy group sessions as I wished for them to become more independent. The staff reluctantly agreed. After all, this was one of the first times they "let go" of the children. Could it be that they thought of the children's needs and disabilities rather than their abilities and resources? However, after a while the staff began to feel confident that the children could manage independently during music therapy group. The children were puzzled at first by the absence of the staff members in the circle during music, but adjusted to their autonomy with satisfaction. They began building their own identity as an independent group, which resulted in our readiness to take the children and the staff for yet another journey.

On the other side of that same town there were several elementary schools. Many children there had heard about the center for the children with special needs, but most had never met such a child. The two groups were neighbors but lived in such dissimilation. My proposal was to start a project between groups of children with and without special needs. I wished to facilitate an intergroup relationship and thought that music could become the connecting "bridge" for the purpose of uniting the groups. This was a pioneering project in Israel that was conceived and motivated out of the social exclusion and the attitude towards children with special needs.

As expected, finding an elementary school to participate in this project was not an easy task. The one exception was a school that practiced religious education and saw the opportunity to conduct "good deeds" for the children with special needs. As my intention was to find a school willing to meet the children with special needs, their personal agenda for accepting these children did not affect the plan but I took it into consideration. As a result of the school's agreement, preparation and planning for the meetings between the two institutions began. It was a long and rough four months, involving parents, staff, administrators, and of course the children who needed to be prepared for the project. In addition, funding for transportation for the children with special needs to and from the elementary school on a weekly basis needed to be found.

The parents and staff of both schools had countless concerns on behalf of their children, but they were also excited, eager and had many hopes. The parents and staff of the children with special needs were happy that this implausible dream could come true, even if it was for only one hour a week. On the other hand, many fears and concerns such as the following examples were raised: "How will my child feel if he was laughed at by the other children at the school?" Or "It is obvious that my child can benefit from meeting the children in the elementary school, but what can my kid contribute to them?"

The staff and parents of the children in the elementary school were anxious as well, raising concerns such as: "What if the children will have nightmares after meeting the children with special needs?" "What if they learn and adapt 'bad behaviors'?" Or, "I remember how terrified I was as a child when I saw these types of children. How will my kid handle it?" The parents and staff's concerns were genuine and valuable; they were in need of support and of a space for venting these concerns. As a result, I met with the parents and staff a few times and together we sorted out the different issues. Our dialogues in the meetings helped, resulting in less apprehension and in increase of motivation to let their children participate in the project.

The two groups of children were now ready to meet. My role as the music therapist expanded, and I was about to become the group's facilitator. How different could this be? Could I still function as a music therapist outside my familiar circle of children?

Forming the New Group

The children with special needs arrived for the first time at the elementary school. At the same time the other group of children was in recess playing their games and minding their own business. However, as we walked into the schoolyard, the children formed two long lines, giving us no choice but to walk in between them. This had been the first encounter for the school crowd to meet children with special needs. The uniqueness of the children with special needs was utterly exposed. Some were wheeled and others walked with an unusual gate. (The staff commented later that these had been some of their longest moments ever.) Eight children with special needs entered a classroom, in which we expected to meet eight children from the elementary school. Only four children and a teacher showed up. The staff and I were very disappointed. What a flop! Or was it? Maybe it was not such a bad idea to start a group only with children who were truly interested. We decided to begin our first meeting in spite of the few children who had showed up, but I left the classroom door open while we held the musical meeting.

This is how the situation appeared: The elementary school children sat on the chairs on one side of the circle, while the children with special needs on the other side. Tension in the air was felt …

I began singing an interactive welcome song with guitar accompaniment. The room was now filled with music that was familiar to the children with special needs, and the other children listened attentively, slowly beginning to catch up with the game involved in the song. Rhythmical instruments were handed out and, while I was distributing them, I noticed that a couple of children were standing at the doorway, peaking with their heads into the room. I invited them to join us and soon thereafter additional children waited eagerly for a pause in order to ask whether they could join us as well. Twenty minutes into the session we had twelve children from the elementary school sitting in the same circle as eight children from the center for special needs.

At that point, I decided to close the door and declared to the children that our new group has been formed and our joint journey had begun.

This filled me with excitement, while at the same time I was flooded with questions. What made all the eight children at the door join us? Was it curiosity to meet children with special needs? Was it the music? When I first decided to form a group of children with and without special needs, I kept pondering if the children with special needs could be able to represent themselves and how would they do so? What will their "identification card" look like? Maybe their love for music and their need for contact and socialization could stand out. Other internal resources would probably be discovered with time. The children with special needs had been together as a group for a few years and knew each other well. They had their own unique way of communicating with one another and they had developed an identity as a group. What about the elementary school children? They knew each other well. They also had an identity as a group since they came from the same class.

The two groups of children were very different from one another. It was understandable that each group initially stayed apart from each other, preferring to stay very close to their "home base," the one they could identify with, cautiously observing one another and trying to make sense out of the "new group." The music was the common ground, a connecting string. While the music united the two separated groups it was the children with special needs who initiated the first physical contact. This came about as early as the second meeting. One of the most vivid examples involves a boy named Eli.

> *Eli reached over to one of the elementary school girls named Abigail and removed the castanet out of her hand. Abigail, a shy and gentle child was astonished, stood up and took her instrument back from Eli. He stood up, and with a huge smile grabbed her castanet again, only this time one of the staff members pulled him away unsuccessfully. Eli and Abigail seemed to get the meaning of these moments and both burst into laughter. The staff member on the other hand, took the castanet out of Eli's hand and returned it to Abigail. From then on two staff members held Eli's hands to prevent him from attempting his "mischievous" behavior again.*
>
> *This initial attempt of interaction with Abigail was brought to a halt. The tension that was created as a result of the attempted interaction had gradually risen while Eli was kept away from Abigail. It seemed like the group needed some clarification. I asked Abigail how she had felt when Eli had taken her instrument away. She looked at me and then at Eli with a smile and said: "I think this was his way to get to know me and so it was OK." I asked her if she wouldn't mind saying it directly to Eli. She did and Eli smiled. Did he understand what Abigail was saying? We don't know, but nevertheless, he seemed pleased when she approached him directly.*

The staff had thought Abigail was in distress when Eli had taken her instrument away, and acted accordingly, but from the short conversation in the group they never again prevented Eli or any other children from making contact with one another. The "interactive game" between Abigail and Eli and the conversation thereafter gave a shift in the formation of our new group.

The Developing Group – "They are Just Like Us"

During the first few weeks the group sang songs and played musical instruments, ball, parachute games, and danced with scarves. All these activities gave the children the option to remain individuals while at the same time being connected through the music, which was heard by all, sang by all, and played by all. A balance was kept between individuality and togetherness. During this period the children had told their parents quite enthusiastically about their experiences with their new friends. The parents detected in their children eagerness and impatience while waiting for the group's music meetings. Some children used language while others used communication boards to express themselves, consequently involving and engaging their parents, resulting in the parents visiting the group. I had felt that the parents' positive response after their visit contributed to the group's cohesiveness towards a healthy group development.

Meanwhile, towards the end of every music meeting, the group held discussions about their impressions of the meetings. During the initial stage of the group, the elementary school children happily announced that: "The special children are just like us ... they laugh, and cry, they sing and play, they look normal ..." The children with special needs couldn't speak but explored the other children through other communicative means and from a close physical distance. In spite of these statements and their attempts to communicate, the children remained sitting in two separate groups in the circle. This seemed to me like an appropriate behavior for a "young" group, although the staff could not understand why this was the situation. They had felt that the initial barriers had been dropped and the elementary school children seemed to have accepted the children with special needs. As we discussed these issues, the staff acknowledged that the tempo of the group formation was slower than they had first anticipated.

About two months into the group meetings, the elementary school children began inquiring about the children with special needs. Questions such as: "Why aren't they speaking? Why are some of the children doing weird movements with their hands? Why are some drooling? Why does it look like some have diapers?"

I had anticipated that sooner or later these questions had to come and had contemplated at length beforehand how to handle these types of inquiries when they arrived. I had hoped for open discussions about these topics, but there was a challenge of how to facilitate it. I believed that their questions were part of getting to know each other. The staff members felt embarrassed by the questions and worried that the children with special needs would get hurt. They felt a danger to the group's existence and we began in our team meetings to explore themes such as caring and protecting the children versus promoting autonomy.

Group Acceptance – "Maybe They are Different after All"

As time went by, the atmosphere in the group became more relaxed. The elementary school children began feeling free to ask their questions. Their questions and inquiries perhaps came from the need to get closer to the children, from their concern for the children with special needs and as a natural flow towards intimacy. It seemed as though there was an acceptance between the sub-groups. As the facilitator, I encouraged the children to ask questions, I returned or re-phrased some of them, so that maybe the children with special needs could understand them. If they did not understand the language, maybe they did understand its quality. Here are some examples:

> While we were passing around a soft ball accompanied by a song, I noticed that some of the elementary school children held the edge of the ball. I stopped in the middle of the game and said to the children that I couldn't help but noticing that some of them were holding the ball with a pincher grip and asked if there was a reason? One of the girls said: "Yes, the ball is wet from the children's saliva. And it is disgusting!" I asked if that was what the others felt. They all replied, "Yes!"

The children came up with a solution. They suggested that the children who drooled should come with their own hand towel so that their hands could be wiped dry. What a great idea, I thought. The following meeting the elementary school children wiped the other children's hands and mouths. Was this happening because they were empowered by the responsibility they felt as a result of their solution?

> I asked the group why they thought Avi and Nadav were drooling. The children's answers and associations were amazingly colorful. They began discussing among themselves what could be the cause for their drooling. One child said that maybe Avi's and Nadav's muscles were too weak and therefore they had difficulty swallowing, another said that something was wrong with their tongues, while yet a third child, Chaim told about his twin brother who went to a special school and did exactly the same thing as Avi and Nadav. The children had not known about Chaim's twin brother. This was a new insight. Out of this topic developed yet another conversation. Nadav, at that point got up from his seat, went over to Chaim and patted his cheek.

Did Nadav understand? We will never know, but he may have felt something in Chaim's quality of voice and facial expression.

Only after many difficult topics raised by the children, they began to realize that the children with the special needs were after all different from them, and it appeared that they felt more comfortable being around them once they realized it. Some of the group members even began voicing that in the beginning they were afraid of the children, but now they understood them and themselves better.

It seemed that children with special needs felt the warmth and the caring that came from the elementary school children. For me, this was a very moving time, seeing how from being two separate groups not long ago, the group seemed to have become one whole unit with many different parts. The group had passed a period with many difficult questions; developing through a complex process and then moving on. The group atmosphere seemed freer and it looked as if one by one the children with special needs began to be more visible, and to be seen by others as individuals in the group.

The interactive musical games seemed to contribute to the phase the group was in. These included games with imitations, leader and follower games, call and response, improvisations that gave voice and a stage to the individuals. These created musical intimacy. Another favorite game during this period was the parachute game. In this game one child would be seated in the middle of the parachute while a couple of others joined him or her. In these musical games each child had a place to be heard and to be seen. There were musical and physical closeness and the sessions were full of laughter and excitement. At times the music was played quite loudly, resulting in the children shouting in order to be heard. There were many arguments and disagreements between the children as they were responsible for some of the activities, resulting in a lot of chaos. The disagreements were between all children with no difference between them. They had their own agenda; they ignored me and disregarded the rules. It was a difficult but a necessary period.

For some children the lack of authority and the lack of borders were unbearable, whilst for others it was helpful in reorganizing the group. We discussed this with the group and heard their thoughts and feelings on this topic. They began making sense out of the chaos, making up their own rules that eventually helped them to relax. Slowly each participant found a place and a role in the group and by now all 20 children were blended during circle. The group had formed its own unique personality.

Best Friends for Some, too Scary for Others

Almost six months had passed since we had begun this group and there was "love in the air." The children had become very close to each other. If a child didn't show up to the meeting, the other children looked at the empty chair and asked about him. The children with special needs inquired about the missing child by pointing at his picture or went to the empty chair, tapped the chair, made a sound, or sat on it. There seemed to be respect and caring for one another. The children shared their own music with the group in addition to the musical activities I had suggested. These included improvisation and writing songs with themes about their group. During this period the children held hands while dancing and singing. There were hugs and kisses when they met and when they departed. There appeared to be a feeling of euphoria in the group.

During the discussions, several children in the elementary school declared that the special children were their best friends. They said that they had taught them about love and friendships. Even though they didn't have language the children could understand them and they felt that they had learnt from each other. The children with special needs seemed also to have changed. Many had stopped their non-social or stereotypical behaviors such as spitting, hitting or pinching and found normative ways to communicate with one another.

After this period a few of the elementary school children began to show uneasiness in the meetings and there were times when some decided not to come. One child requested to leave the group. It seemed as if this period had been too intimate and intense for some of the children. They may have felt that they were viewed differently by others than they viewed themselves. While this was happening, other children continued to participate happily making the friendships even stronger and deeper. Most children passed this phase and moved on. The group appeared to reconstruct itself and some of the turmoil and instability began to vanish. During this period the children invited each other to their homes, to birthday parties, or to the playground.

As the school year was coming to its end, so was this group. We talked and made music around this theme. The children summarized the year by retrieving music from the group's past, they improvised about endings and they appeared fulfilled but also sad. The elementary school children were curious to know what their friends from the other side of town would be doing during the summer. They inquired of what would become of them the following school year. The children with special needs sat silently during these conversations. What were they thinking? What were they feeling? Their bodies and faces conveyed their unspoken tension.

One month before the end of our meetings (eight months into the group's life), a couple of the elementary school children came up with a proposal. They suggested that since their special friends will be staying in their special school during most part of the summer, maybe they could initiate a summer camp they could join. This came as a surprise to the staff and me. There was a lot of excitement with new opportunities. The children with special needs seemed excited as well.

The staff from both schools and the children decided to promote this remarkable idea. The parents began calling and pulling the right strings in the municipality, the staff in both schools began preparing for the summer camp, the administration of the special school committed the space and the occupational, speech, physical, music and art therapists worked as a team to develop plans to adapt "conventional therapies" into group experiential activities to better suit all the children.

Afterword

The summer camp was a success for the children, the staff and the parents. The camp was initiated by the children and was facilitated by the special education teacher and me (the music therapist). It brought the children together for an intensive one month (five hours six days a week). At the end of the camp it was decided by the group that they would like to meet the following academic year in the elementary school twice a week for music group sessions.

This group met for the total of four years. Many other such music groups developed during this period in other elementary schools. It became easier to build the groups with the years. The community became more tolerant towards the special needs population, and more funding was generated as a result of the integration law that had been subsequently incorporated in Israel seven years after the first project.

This project had made a social change in the community involving the schools, the parents of both groups, and the municipality. This was a unique transition into inclusion in a community that until then had not given many opportunities for their special residents.

Chapter 6

Reflection

Musical Inclusion, Intergroup Relations, and Community Development

Cochavit Elefant

Introduction

> *When I was about my daughter's age I became anxious each time I encountered*
> *a young man with Cerebral Palsy who lived in my neighborhood. I was certain*
> *that one day he could harm me. If my child will attend a music group with such*
> *children, she may experience the same fears (Parent).*

These words belonged to one of the parents just before her child attended a music group including children with special needs. Similar voices were made by other parents and staff in the beginning of the music inclusion program in Raanana, a middle class town in Israel. The project (as described in the narrative in Chapter 5) included two diverse groups of young children with and without special needs, joined into one new group for the purpose of the inclusion of children with special needs into the local community which until then had segregated its population with special needs.

The music therapy project involved 20 young children with and without special needs and began in 1995. To my knowledge, this was one of the first inclusion programs for children with severe special needs in Israel. I had just returned from the USA where I had integrated children with special needs through music in their local communities, and I saw an opportunity to do the same within the Israeli context. The aim of the project was to reduce prejudice towards a marginalized group and to foster awareness and appreciation for diversity among elementary school children.

My experience had sharpened in terms of the understanding of the inherent value and strength in group for the purpose of making social change. This means that for a successful inclusion process to happen with the intention to make social development and change, the focus should become on building a strong group. I have therefore chosen in this retrospective study to look at the intergroup process through social psychological perspectives on the group as a "medium for help" (Whitaker, 1985; Rosenwasser and Nathan, 1997) and on intergroup relations (Rosenwasser, 1997; Kacen, 2002; Kacen and Lev-Wiesel, 2002) and to link these to Community Music Therapy thinking. Although these theories do not adhere directly to Community Music Therapy, I see them as important when exploring the possibilities of music for successful community development.

In this project two groups of children merged into one music group. I had set to involve not only the children but their closest network systems such as parents, staff, organization leaders, and the local municipality. The real social development and change, however, occurred by and through the children. Ripples of multi-level changes were evolving in the local community; initiating from the committed children, vibrating through staff and parents, and reaching the administrational and municipal levels. The children made their way out of their own small group's boundaries towards the larger community towards a successful social change. They can therefore be viewed as a community group where the trust and cooperation created a context for dialogues and reflections for the purpose of social change. Ledwith (2005) discusses groups in community development and says that: "The group is the basis for a cultural belonging where a collective identity is formed, and from which a commitment to the process of change is much more likely to be sustained …" (p. 94). The inclusion group's collective identity and belonging developed through musicing and dialogues from which they challenged their own inner attitudes and this resulted in their commitment. In order to work with these levels of community development, the group facilitator needs to have an understanding of group dynamic and its process as well as group leadership (Ledwith, 2005).

Before I look more closely into concepts and theories that can shed light on the development of the music inclusion project, I would like to outline the integration situation in Israel at that time, in order to understand this project in its political context: The Special Education Law in Israel in 1988 specified that the placement committee in the educational system should give priority to the integration of children with special needs within the general educational framework. Unfortunately, the interpretation of the law was unfavorable to the aim of mainstreaming children with special needs. According to the ministry's interpretation, only children enrolled in separate special education schools were eligible to receive services such as therapies that were promised under the Special Education Law (Ronen, 1997). Therefore, a child with special needs who may have wanted to enroll within the general educational system was eligible for only limited services offered by the managing director of the ministry. The consequence was that most parents preferred to leave their children in special education settings in order to receive the maximal therapeutic assistance. In the year 2002 the integration law was declared in Israel and children with special needs had the right to learn together with children their own age, in a least restrictive environment in their own communities, however still today children with severe special needs are segregated in most parts of this country.

From the above description, it isn't difficult to see that in 1995 when the music inclusion project began, the Israeli society was not fully ready to include its special population. Although this project began several years ago and music inclusion projects have since been developed, there are still to my knowledge rare opportunities for children with severe special needs to participate in inclusion programs. The Israeli traditional music therapist finds it difficult to work in the community since the Israeli society is still struggling with commitment towards successful inclusion. But Israel is not alone in it as we will see in the next section.

Challenges in Inclusion of Individuals with Special Needs in the Community

There are many political, social, and economic difficulties when including a marginalized population in a local community. This is a broad subject and I will therefore only discuss it briefly in terms of its relevance to our project. The terms integration and inclusion may cause some confusion and in some areas of the world are used interchangeably. The terms are used to describe opportunities of interactions for the person with special needs with typical functioning peers in schools or in a larger community. The two terms differ in that integration denotes the placement of a person in a given setting, a mainstream classroom for example, with some adaptations and resources. Integration could be viewed as a step towards inclusion, a pre-condition of inclusion. The fundamental principles of inclusion are deeper and denote acceptance of the person with disability as a member of the overall society (Sydoriak, 1996; ICEVI, 2002). Inclusion is an ultimate social goal, multi-faceted and not easily achieved. In order to have a successful experience of inclusion it cannot be left for a mere chance but should be actively and thoroughly pursued by everyone involved.

In order to pursue a meaningful music inclusion in the community (especially one that had previously never experienced integration), the role of the music therapist is a fundamental one. It was necessary for me to examine my role as a traditional music therapist who worked with individual and group music therapy within the special education system. Taking into consideration the breadth and multi-faced considerations is what characterizes today's music therapist when working within the frame of Community Music Therapy. In this project, I had to set new boundaries and step outside the traditional setting into the community. Coordinating the project meant facilitating between two diverse groups of children, and between parents and staff, educational administrators, and the municipality. To facilitate the process also involved taking the role of social advocate for the group of children with special needs; it was necessary but not enough to work with the two groups of children, social networking in the broader community was also part of the process (Kleive and Stige, 1988; Stige, 1995). A successful inclusion process contributes to social change within the local community, but it could only work if everyone involved strive together towards the same goal and it is therefore important to understand the ecological character of the process. Ledwith (2005) believes that for any commitment to a radical social change to occur it is necessary to take into account the individual person, the small face-to-face group, the institution, and the wider society (p. 93).

In this music project, inclusion was a radical social change which took into account the individuals, the group, and the larger structure. When this happens, a strong group can be formed, which is needed if the aim is to make social change. I will therefore explore the group from a theoretical stance focusing upon the group as a "medium for help" and I will look at the intricate group development process that took place. The group's strength is in my appraisal what the music therapist can strive for, using the collective musical experiences for the purpose of contributing to change also outside the small group and into the broader community.

Group Music Therapy and Music Therapy Integration

Music is a form of non-verbal communication which can give a strong experience of being together in a group whether the child has disability or not. The group can develop through improvisation and other musical interactions for the purpose of making contact between different participants. There is vast documented literature on traditional music therapy groups in special education settings (Nordoff and Robbins, 1965/1971; Hibben, 1991; Davies and Richard, 2002; Grogan and Knak, 2002; Tyler, 2002; Walsh-Stewart, 2002; Pavlicevic, 2003).

The literature emphasizes mostly group work which encourages children's musical expression within the form of musical interaction and which fosters communication between the therapist and the client. It is less common to find literature on group process with children or how they inter-relate, collaborate or affect each other in the group. Schalkwijk (1987) found through reviewing the practice of music therapists working with people with special needs in the Netherlands that most of them use remedial music highly structured and directive resulting in a lack of focus on group processes. There may be those who would argue that it is quite impossible to work towards group process with children that are severely disabled, but my personal interest has been to not only emphasis the individual expression in the group, but also to strive towards inter relations in order to contribute to group process. My experience has been that the children with severe disability can use the music therapy group to negotiate and express different intra- and inter-relation issues and emotion through non-verbal communicative means. It does however mean that I deliberately promote this kind of work within the group. Thinking about group process is especially important when the purpose is to work on intergroup relations in order to support processes of inclusion.

There is some music therapy literature to support this broader perspective.[1] Hibben (1991) recounts a process towards group cohesion in a group music therapy

---

[1]   In addition to those discussed in this paragraph, there are other examples in the literature, such as (Kleive and Stige, 1988; Jellison and Gainer, 1995; Stige, 1995; Wilson, 1996; Jones and Cardinal, 1998; Darrow, 1999; Elefant and Agami, 2002).

with a classroom of young hyperactive children with learning disabilities. In her writings she describes the valuable accounts of using group development theories as a context for evaluating individual and group progress in social, emotional, and cognitive areas. Kern (2005) used music with individual children within the autistic spectrum in an early childhood center in the USA. She used music with the child with special needs within the frame of the day care, while the other children joined some of the activities. The purpose was to use music in order to give the children meaningful interactions. Aftret (2005) described three inclusion projects of children with special needs in Norway, at about the same period as I was working with inclusion in Israel. Together with a physiotherapist she found a neutral meeting place (outside the school vicinity) where children with and without special needs could meet in order to develop social interaction through musical and movement activities. Her interesting projects were successful in that she didn't integrate the children in isolation but worked through use of a system oriented perspective which took into consideration the child's educational and social network. Although her work had an effect on the community, she does not discuss the group's process and development and how it may have contributed to community change. In addition, the focus of her work and others are towards the functioning of the children with special needs but with less consideration to the other children or to the processes that merge two different groups.

Group as a Medium for Help

I would like to discuss the group as a "medium for help" in relation to inclusion projects and Community Music Therapy. As mentioned earlier, the concept of the group as a medium for help is borrowed from social psychology, which considers the potential of a group in making social changes in the community. The group as a medium for help is made of individuals with a mutual purpose, quest or conflict that connects them into a group (Whitaker, 1985). The individuals are gathered in search for solutions for a mutual purpose and are engaged in personal responsibility, involvement and accountability for the group. There are several beneficial characteristics that have been identified in the group as a medium for help and I would like to outline them briefly and relate them to the music inclusion project in Raanana.

The first characteristic that can contribute to the group as a medium for help is that the participants in the group identify their abilities and skills in their group. In other words, the participants operate under the assumptions that they hold the knowledge for dealing with their own concerns. They learn to help each other when group conditions allow for openness in discussions and involvement among the participants (Rosenwasser, 1997). The participants in the group become more able to scrutinize and accept decisions regarding their own lives. This notion is in congruence with the "resource oriented music therapy approach" studied by Rolvsjord (2006; 2007) where the clients are encouraged to find their own resources, develop and strengthen them. In the group as a medium for help the participants function out of the basis of their own and their group's resources. Help in this context is *mutual* help, as the group members receive and give help to each other, rather than only solve specific problems.

In the inclusion project the music had an important place in the group as it was both an individual and a common resource. The children with the special needs were able to use music to express themselves and to convey strength through the use of it. The elementary school children were exposed to the children with special needs through their musical strengths rather than their functional weaknesses. It made the children realize that people are equal when it comes to basic human emotions and expressions. This collective music making helped the group in forming cohesion towards building its strength.

Another characteristic to the group as a medium for help is the opportunity that it provides its participants for trying out diverse and meaningful roles. This can develop individual empowerment for the reason that it can offer the participants the opportunity to take meaningful responsibilities (Rappaport, 1987). When participants find out that they can also provide help and not only receive help, they begin their journey towards empowerment.

The tendency in an intergroup process such as the one in Raanana is that the elementary school children could take a paternalistic stance, believing that the other children need their protection and help. This kind of responsibility could hinder equality and mutuality and can cause the group to maintain a split. As the music therapy facilitator, I provided many opportunities for the children to try out diverse roles in the group. Individuals with a natural tendency towards a leadership role were encouraged to take a more passive or follower role for their own benefit and growth, while others were encouraged to take a more active role. Stige (Part V of this book) discusses different types of participation in a music group. He believes that all types of participation have a valid place in the group and that its members can try out different roles at different times. The role change can give the participants a glimpse into unusual positions, resulting in new responsibilities.

A third characteristic in the group as a medium for help deals with cohesion and bonding around mutual purposes. When a supportive environment is established, as in our music group, group members become free to express their thoughts and emotions with others who share a similar reality and experiences. This results in group cooperation; it enhances the members to use critical thinking, and gives them possibility to share knowledge and skills in regards to their mutual purpose. The member of the cohesive group can learn, develop and change by observing other group members in different situations (Rosenwasser, 1997). The group's cohesion can give the group strength to sustain and to be used outside the music group context. When it becomes strong enough, the group has the potential to make meaningful changes in the community hence contributing to their empowerment (Ledwith, 2005).

Empowerment is what we strive for during the group's life. One of the main expressions for empowerment in this context is that both individuals and the group develop a more critical awareness. This could be developed through the process of increasing awareness. The group's inherent structure allows the awareness to be enhanced by creating conditions for constructive verbal and musical dialogues and by processes of action and reflection. All of this assists individuals to evaluate the nature of their experience, the status of the group within the society, and their ability to take part in social reform (Rosenwasser, 1997). In Community Music Therapy dialogue, negotiation, mutuality, and empowerment are considered key elements. Musicing can strengthen the group by its collectiveness and bonding and can open up channels for intergroup communication. The group as medium for help can assist individuals in making changes in their state of affairs. Through the psychological process of empowerment, change in the perception of the self can occur within the group, including the development of group identity (Ledwith, 2005). The group is thus an important medium in developing new attitudes and in investigating the potential in community change and development.

The characteristics of the group as a medium for help are key elements in the personal development in a group process but additional considerations need to be made in relation to the music inclusion project I have described. The inclusion process included two diverse groups that merged, with the result that unique and complex intergroup relations emerged. It is therefore my intention in the next section to discuss intergroup processes.

Intergroup Relations

In order to build a strong foundation with the children towards a successful inclusion, careful facilitation of intergroup process must be considered. The condition when two diverse groups are intended to actively and efficiently combine into a unified whole group is defined as a group within a group or as intergroup (Kacen and Lev-Wiesel, 2002; Dovidio, Gaertner, and Kawakami, 2003). Intergroup relations are intended for two groups of dissimilar origin, who come together in order to hear each other and try to make a change in perception and attitudes towards each other.

This process, as difficult as it could be, is necessary when making social changes. What made our project especially intricate was that one group had intellectual disability with hardly any spoken language. Whitaker (1985) questions the ability to include this population in a group process and says that: "One cannot assume that a group experience of some kind will be good for everyone under all circumstances ... [including] the most severely mentally handicapped" (p. 10). I can see how it could be easy to agree with Whitaker's viewpoint as it could be inconceivable to perceive how children with severe disabilities could join a group with normally developed children. However, Whitaker's argument focuses upon the participants' linguistic abilities and I would like to suggest that the success of group dynamics between individuals with severe intellectual disabilities and normally developed children could be based on other communicative means such as music.

Bridging two different groups is not self evident and consists of risk taking by both sides during the entire process. In intergroup relation processes there are conflicting stance, prejudices, hostilities and fears, where high levels of difference are present (Katz and Kahanov, 1990; Bargal and Bar, 1992; Bar and Bargal, 1995; Kacen and Lev-Wiesel, 2002). This description comes from literature on intergroup work with adults. It does not necessarily reflect intergroup processes with children. The fear in meeting new people exists always, but the prejudice and hostility I believe are echoes and perceptions of adults connected to the children. With this in mind, I do think that intergroup relations with children could be less complex and more natural than with adults, but the facilitation of the group process is vital.

Whether the intergroup is with adults or children there is discrepancy between the groups that can yield strength or weakness to it. The discrepancy is enlarged by the actual act of putting the groups in one room which forces each group to look at the other. The differences between the two groups should not be blurred but viewed as natural since eventually it could be strength to the intergroup process. This strength occurs if the group frame is supportive and protective, which then enables a bridging of the gap between the two groups. In this project the music seemed to be the common ground in which the two groups found a shared supportive frame.

Another interesting point in relation to intergroup work is that there is no need to focus upon immediate individual change. The focus is in the meeting of two diverse groups, whereas for example in traditional music therapy groups the music therapist tends to look at the individual change of the child within the group. In intergroup relations there is an attempt to accept differences and the changes occur within the group. The differences and points of similarities could create an arena for discussion and music making, which may open up new routes for bonding.

Sometimes, however, dissimilarities between the groups could cause a process of collectiveness in each sub-group, leading to fortifying familiarity and preventing assimilation. This was quite apparent during the first few weeks of this new group's life as we witnessed how the children stayed in their "home" group. Although this dissimilation was also experienced in the musical activities it seemed to be an important stage that the group had to experience. If an immature process is rushed, which could especially happen when working with children (Kacen and Lev-Wiesel, 2002), then acceptance and sense of commonality is not constructed, and separation between the subgroups could occur. The progress of the group will therefore rely on the assimilation of its different parts, resulting in a feeling of togetherness. A group that is combined of two sub-groups will contain (at least during the first stages) low levels of acceptance and adherence. Consequently, the preparation stage in such situations is crucial and is expected to be long (Kacen and Lev-Wiesel, 2002).

The intergroup relations do not remain at the group level. It is "a community building process that is distinguished by changes in the group's ability to develop common membership, share priorities and meet common needs" (The Association for the Study and Development of Community, 2002, p. 3). According to this definition it might be presumed that the outcome of a successful intergroup process is a sense of fellowship, but I will discuss how this could be marked by the change it produces at the community level.

Intergroup Process: The Music Group Project Revisited

Much of our attention in Community Music Therapy deals with group work within community settings, but yet the group and its potential towards community change has not been discussed a great deal in the literature. In the narrative from Raanana I described in detail how the two groups developed through musical experiences towards inclusion. In the present section I will revisit this process through use of the intergroup theory that I have just discussed.

Twenty children (eight children with special needs and 12 elementary school children) ages 7–8 participated in the project. The group size was initially set for 16 children (eight from each educational facility), but the group size grew at the request of the children at the elementary school. A total of seven staff members took part; six belonged to the special education center (four caretakers, a special education teacher, and a music therapist) and one to the elementary school (an elementary school teacher). Most of the music group meetings were held in a classroom at the elementary school during the school year, while during the summer vacation a summer camp was held at the special education center's facility. The school didn't own musical instruments so these were brought from the special education facility.

As this is a retrospective study, the analysis is based upon video material of the sessions and a television broadcast with conversations with the children, staff and parents. I have also studied the logbook I wrote throughout the project.

Preparing the Children, Staff and Parents

Preparing the groups was vital in order to minimize the anxiety of the first meeting between the groups. The children with special needs first met alone on a weekly basis in order to become familiarized with musical activities. This gave them a head start in order to become familiar with some of the musical repertoire. They were shown pictures of the elementary school children as well as some simple explanation about the upcoming project. It was difficult to know what the children had understood, yet it seemed important. At the same time, four separate meetings with the elementary school children were held at their school. Most of the children had never seen a disabled person before. Through musical and non-musical games the children experienced and verbalized how it could feel to be a disabled child.

It is recommended that a preparation phase in intergroup projects should be held before the groups meet (Rosenwasser, 1997; Kacen and Lev-Wiesel, 2002).

The separate meetings during the preparation period help to strengthen individual group identity (Pelach-Galil, Kaushinsky, and Bargal, 2002). Once each group's identity becomes stronger within their home base, the two groups can meet (Curtis and Mercado, 2004).

The staff can be critical in supporting the group or in sabotaging it if they feel threatened or ignored; hence the staff involvement in the group's development is imperative and valuable to the group's life and in their contribution to social change (Northen and Kurland, 2001, p. 117). The staff of both educational settings was prepared as well; first separately and then together. Although I described in the narrative the many hurdles the special education staff went through during the group's process, I would like to illuminate those difficulties by bringing forth some of the statements voiced by the staff from the elementary school during the preparation period:

> *We are willing to cooperate since we see this as an opportunity to do a good deed to the weak.*
>   *It is important that our children contribute to society in this way although the only ones benefiting from this project will be the children with special needs. (Staff members)*

To hear the statements within the frame of the school's cultural context makes it more understandable from my end: The elementary school practiced religious education and was interested in helping the under-privileged people in the community. The special education staff's main concern was that "their" children would be mocked and laughed at and they felt a need to protect the children from the others. This resulted in many meetings and dialogues with the staff throughout the project. The staff can foster change in the larger community only after they would experience a change within the micro system, in this case the group of children working with the music therapist.

The attitudes of parents can support or hold back the achievements of their children. The process the parents go through is therefore another crucial ingredient for the success of a project such as this. Preparing the parents was an important step to establish their support and alliance before initiating the group process with the children (Grogan and Knak, 2002). Similarly to the staff members the parents had reservations regarding the planned project. One parent commented about her own fears from disabled children (see citation at the opening of this chapter) and was afraid her daughter would experience similar difficulties. On the other hand the parents of the children with special needs were more enthusiastic about the project, yet they were worried that their children would be laughed at by the non-disabled children or that they would be regarded as worthless, unable to contribute to the process or to the non-disabled children. After the meetings were held the support of the parents gradually became stronger as the children made the changes within their intergroup. In later stages the parents showed interest and were invited to come and observe the meetings. Such meetings had a calming effect and further enhanced the support of the parents.

In the Beginning

The beginning of an intergroup process is characterized with cautiousness and anxiety. The first meetings between the two groups magnified the discrepancies and for an external observer such discrepancies could seem too large, even hopeless. In our case however there was music which helped to establish a common ground for both groups and it wasn't long before the children found nonverbal ways of communicating with one another. The mutual musical experiences were joyous, expressive and made the children get closer to one another without actually establishing physical contact. This in turn gave the non-disabled children the courage to touch upon these discrepancies as they freely began asking questions regarding the special education kids' disabilities.

My intention was to make the group find "good enough" answers to the questions within the accepted atmosphere in which there was space for questions and discussions around the differences between the groups. The safe environment made it possible for courageous questions to be asked, thereby opening up routes and adding strength to the intergroup process. This helped the children to get closer towards acceptance of diversity within the group.

The beginning can set the tone for the intergroup relations to succeed. Initially we observed that each sub-group maintained close to their "home-base"; they sat separately and played on their own instruments. I never attempted to rush an immature group process. When the time was right, acceptance and sense of commonality did occur. This level of acceptance within the micro system of the group could determine the level of safety each participant felt to share his inner world with the others (Yalom, 1995).

The progress of the group could rely on the assimilation of its different parts, resulting in a gradual formation of a feeling of togetherness. To help in constructing commonality and assimilation certain musical activities helped.

One day I brought the big colorful parachute to use for some musical activities. I thought the parachute could represent a frame and help the group develop more safety. The song began with the children lifting the parachute up and down in order to create a feeling of wind for the "wind song." At the end of each verse I pulled the parachute out of the children's hands and with a loud wind sound I covered four children with it. They were out of sight. The children laughed and were in anticipation for their turn. After this song was over, I laid the parachute on the floor for the "ocean song" and asked if anyone wished to sit on it. Gadi jumped into the parachute. I was afraid no one from the elementary school would join him. I was pleasantly surprised when three other children jumped into the parachute and sat next to Gadi with a big smile on their face.

This was a progress into the group's development. In the first musical activity, the parachute covered individual children while they were sitting in their own sub-groups. The children had a joint emotional experience of anticipation and togetherness in the music but it occurred from a physical distance. This activity had helped them to look at each other as they disappeared under the parachute. Little moments of seeing and not seeing each other helped them to get ready for the second activity which was an attempt to narrow the physical distance. It was the children who had taken this step and the musical activity gave them the opportunity to cooperate and to choose and enjoy their togetherness for a physical proximity.

The beginning of the group's life was hesitant and careful. I was facilitating the group with caution, but with suitable structured musical activities. These activities made the children feel safe and free to express emotions within the music and within verbal conversations. This atmosphere enabled the group to gradually move into another stage.

Recognizing Abilities and Skills as Cohesion and Bonding Occurs around Mutual Purpose

As the group members formed closer relationships they began to recognize individual abilities and strengths:

> *Nina asked Amy to choose one instrument out of the two she placed in front of her. Amy leaned towards the tambourine and touched it with her face. Nina announced happily to the group: "Wow! Even though Amy can't speak she sure knows what she wants!" Then to Amy she said: "This is more than I can say about my self." Amy smiled but didn't take the tambourine (she is physically unable to hold an instrument). Nina said: "Don't worry; I'll be right back to play with you the tambourine. This suits me fine."*

We can see from this example how Nina realized Amy's strength in knowing what she wanted in comparison to her own indecisiveness. In a way their roles changed and Nina who was providing help to Amy found out that she can also receive help by not having to make her own decision. The story of Amy choosing the tambourine is an example of a child with special needs being recognized by the others for her decisiveness. Barriers fell between the children in the group, and the adults became more engaged as they viewed the positive engagements in the children. This initiated cooperation with the administration of both educational facilities which supported and later expanded the project. This process could correspond with the multi-level construct of *empowerment,* within individual, organizational, and community levels of analyze and practice (Rolvsjord, 2004) which is leading to community engagement.

Community Engagement

> *Sharon, Nina, Amy, Abigail and Mira were sitting on the bench in the schoolyard when the cameraman and a reporter from the Israeli Public Television approached them.*
>
> *"We are here to ask you a few questions about your inclusion project. We heard that this group is planning a summer camp. How is it possible that out of all the summer camps in this town you chose the one in the special education center?"*
>
> *Sharon answered: "Most friends go together to summer camps, and now that we have Amy and Mira as our friends it is only natural that we would spend the summer together."*
>
> *Nina looked at Amy (while holding Amy's hand) and said: "Do you have any idea how much I have learned from this girl?"*
>
> *"How is this possible, she doesn't even talk," replied the reporter.*
>
> *"We can't even begin to explain this; you won't understand," answered Sharon.*

The children had been through a long process of experiences in community engagement and were now contributing to that community. They knew that their interview could look good on the TV screen but they also knew it was not a shared experience, hence not understood by the reporter.

The changes that took place within the children can be viewed within the scope of community engagement (Bogdan and Taylor, 2001). The community engagement movement focuses on the importance of social context, on belonging to a community, on sharing the lives and experiences with other community members, and on contributing to that community (Bogdan and Taylor, 2001). One of the goals of community engagement today is to build and maintain friendships and positive relations between individuals with developmental disabilities and others within the community (O'Brien, 1999; Bogdan and Taylor, 2001). Such relations could be difficult to achieve due to inherent external and internal barriers for individuals with developmental disabilities (O'Brien and O'Brien, 1993), yet with appropriate mediation and intergroup process, change could be achieved at both personal and socio-cultural levels.

By highlighting the changes that occurred for the children, reduction of internal and external barriers were attained to a set where bonds of friendship were intertwined and a sense of community belonging were developed. The interview with the television at the end of the year made me "step down" from the role of a social agent for the children with special needs. I had felt that it was the children through their networking and friendships that had contributed to social change and difference within their community.

The citation I used at the beginning of this essay clearly illuminates a parent's fears of letting her child participate in the project. With such levels of anxiety and rejection, this project had to overcome not only the intricate intergroup process of the two diverse groups of children but it also had to involve the adults in order to help them to overcome some social prejudice towards the making of social change. I had hoped that the parents could become supporters of the project through the mutual work; and couldn't agree more with Kenny and Stige's (2002) assertion that "community is not only a context to work in; it is also a context to work with" (p. 10). The staff and parents were an important dimension of the project. At the end of the project the parents of the children at the elementary school were voicing completely different tunes:

> *At first it seemed that only the children with special needs would benefit from this project, but after seeing the children together there is no doubt that the elementary school children are benefiting even more from the experience. (Parent)*

I had asked the parents to explain what had made this change. Their answer was that in the beginning they believed their children's role was to give and support the "weak." They had liked that idea for their children but they never would have imagined how mature, open, and understanding their children had become. Their children had been empowered by the experience and had become the "best" social advocates for their peers with special needs. This group's strength had risen out of the growing relations among the children.

Yet some critical awareness was not easy for all. The parents of the children with special needs became critically aware of their children's limitations:

> *It was not easy to watch our children with the same age group peers. The discrepancies between them are too apparent. We thought we had accepted our children's limitations, but seeing them with regular children makes us realize how difficult this is for us as parents of disabled children. (Parent)*

On the one hand there was a sense of tension for some of the parents viewing their children together with the elementary school children which had brought back all the hopes and expectations they once had for their own children. On the other hand they felt empowered by the social change that occurred in the group and by the acceptance expressed by the elementary school children as well as by the positive excitement and anticipation for the mutual meetings expressed by their own children.

Final Thoughts

The focus of this case study was to investigate the group as a source of strength when making community change. The practice of intergroup relations for the purpose of inclusion within the theoretical frame that was put forth could be transferable to other groups beyond this study. When investigating groups it is important to consider the differences between them, however a comprehensive evaluation of groups shows that there are common traits which unite them. Kurt Lewin (1948) who contributed much to the investigation of groups believed that although groups differ in size, structure or activity, they are all established on principles of mutual dependence between its participants. Mutual dependency between participants is in many ways what defines a group.

Our group of children worked out of a mutual purpose; the process of interacting and forming relationships illuminated how they were co-dependent as they developed into one group. Through mutual music making and conversations individual changes accrued putting weight on the individual perspective within the group's development, helping each participant to know his resources and limitations. This type of cross-group contact led to a better intergroup attitude. The meetings initially enlarged the discrepancy between the sub-groups but as the group developed these diminished. There is little insight in regard to the difficulty the children with special needs underwent in understanding the other group, but if we deduce from the difficulty clearly expressed by the "normally developed" children sitting in the same circle as the children with special needs, we might infer that all members underwent some personal difficulties, gradually leading through resolutions to individual growth.

The children, staff, parents and other involved partners made a breakthrough from a position of helplessness into a standpoint of activity and participation in the community by closely observing the group process experienced by the children. It could be viewed as a ripple effect (Pavlicevic and Ansdell, 2004), where developments at the individual level had implications at group and organization levels, and vice versa. If we use the ecological terminology proposed by Bronfenbrenner (1979), we could say that individual change at the group level (micro system change) prepared the children for intergroup relations (developments in an expanded micro system), supported by the parents and staff (meso system change). The enthusiasm of both children and parents for developing similar projects achieved the support of the administrative levels at both educational facilities, reaching up to the municipality (exo system change). As indicated in the introduction to this chapter, processes at the macro system level (the authorities' interpretation of The Special Education Law in Israel) made this process more difficult but therefore also more important, in my view.[2]

---

[2]   The model used here for description of the ecological character of human development was pioneered by Urie Bronfenbrenner in the 1970s. Later theorists have developed other terms, specifying ecological levels in between the micro system and the macro system differently, for instance by describing the levels of organizations and locations. Types of organizations include schools, work places, religious congregations, and community coalitions, which are larger than microsystems and also have a formal structure. Localities have a geographical delimitation, and are usually organized with local economies and governments and with local systems for health, education, culture, etc. (see e.g. Dalton, Elias, and Wandersman, 2007).

The influence the music group had on the community could be described through use of the concept of the group as a medium for help. The group assisted the individuals to make changes in their state of affairs, through psychological processes of empowerment and change in the perception of the self, including the development of group identity. It could be said that this project re-established the group as an important medium in developing new attitudes and in investigating potentials for community change and development.

In this project dialogues were established in order to prevent the blur of otherness. The children learnt to know themselves as a foundation for identity in order to be able to make confrontation with otherness. It required moving towards the other in an empathetic way, moving into the "other person's shoe." People quite rarely move into the "other side" to something that is foreign. What is discovered from this experience (which takes a lot of daring and generosity), is not only the otherness of the other but of one self. This "other world," the foreign far-away-world makes myself different and brings into consciousness my own difference. This self-divergence, which is reflexive and self-conscious, sheds a light on the "otherness part" and not the identity part of oneself. This can be threatening and anxiety provoking and give an experience of weakness in identity, but it also makes place for opening wider circles; it can give strength and new knowledge and the freedom of acceptance (Gorevitz, 2001, p. 41).

The opening of wider circles is what Community Music Therapy would like to be identified with, expanding conventional music therapy practices and entering into new and sometimes unknown arenas. The professional definition and boundaries of the music therapist is expanded from working with individuals and groups towards socially oriented roles. The therapist's theoretical thinking needs to be ecological and socially oriented. My focus has been to explore the understanding of group dynamics and intergroup relation theories with the motivation of making social changes. This type of standpoint can contribute to the thinking of Community Music Therapy when working within the frame of the group involvement in the community. Although some may think that group process considerations are valuable only within the frame of micro systems change, it could be considered within the larger community frame as well. My personal and professional experiences have shown that group strength has potential in making a community change.

PART IV

Chapter 7

Action

Because It's Cool. Community Music Therapy in Heideveld, South Africa

Mercédès Pavlicevic

Music for Life

Whenever I arrive in Heideveld (about 15km outside Cape Town) my thoughts and familiar habits no longer fit, and today is no different. We've left Cape Town, one of the world's beautiful places, and are speeding along the motorway, towards Heideveld. Music therapists Sunelle Fouché and Kerryn Torrance are in front, planning their day's work, and I look at the muddy road alongside the motorway; the tin shacks, the skinny stray dog drinking out of a puddle of water, and the low grey clouds that only just enable me to see Table Mountain, now far away. I wonder about music therapy in a place like this. We've left the 3-lane motorway for Khayelitsha, where Kerryn dropped off some music therapy reports at the orphanage, and we're now weaving our way through narrow roads, small houses – this place here seems slightly better off than the shacks near the motorway. I start noticing children in school uniform walking in the same direction, with their dark green sweaters and grey skirts or pants, and eventually arrive at a 6-foot-high fenced-off property that has barbed wire at the top. This shocks me: Woodlands school, here in Heideveld, needs to protect its children. From whom, I wonder.

Sunelle reminded me in the car that they provide the only music the children ever get each week: there is no music-provision by the state, and she and Kerryn often talk about providing music and providing therapy. Their *Music for Life* programme is part of the voluntary or NGO-funded "caring industry,"[1] and always at risk of having to be stopped because of shortage of funds. I can't help wondering about how this worry must add significantly to their responsibilities, and this puts me in something of a dilemma, in terms of adding to their time constraints by needing research time with them in Heideveld.

We're carrying instruments and video equipment towards the classroom, the wind is cold with bits of rain, and we greet everyone along the way. This is a place of greeting – you cannot walk past anyone without a thorough good morning how are you fine thank you. We're walking under a tin-roof, cemented corridor that

---

[1] NGO is an abbreviation of "Non Government Organization."

attaches one of the long concrete buildings to another, and this is the overriding image of Woodlands school: low grey cloud, chilly wind, green tin roofs, and grey concrete buildings. Not much garden. The playgrounds are concrete too. There is nothing comfortable or cozy about this place. I should have brought a warmer jacket. The music room is pretty chilly, and we're going to first make some tea, and watch a video of last year's Heideveld Community Concert, since we have one hour before the choir rehearsal.

We're huddled round a small TV monitor, clutching our mugs of tea while Kerryn and Sunelle tell me about the concert. They planned it as part of the *Music for Life* project: so that the community could be a part of the children's musical lives. On the video you see that the hall is full – some 400 people of all sizes and ages – and the energy and excitement are palpable. The whole of Heideveld seems to be here. "It was amazing, we expected maybe 100 people – I don't think we'd even sold 100 tickets – and then on the evening – everyone just arrived. We were shocked! And excited! And thinking – what do we think we're doing ..."

Kerryn says that the concert offered the neighborhood a chance to come together in a new way. Sunelle speaks about Heideveld's pride in hearing the children and the choir sing for the first time – "for many parents, it was the first time they had any idea that their children could do anything like this!" The music therapists tell of how this event galvanized everyone: it brought together gangsters who not only helped to set up the chairs in the afternoon of the concert, but also asked whether they could take part. On the video we see a bizarrely attired group of young folk up on stage: young men mostly, some dressed as old Malay women – these are one of the local gangs, I'm told, performing their local traditional musical genre (Kaapse Klopse).[2] We also watch an adolescent group sing a song from their group music therapy. On the video, the audience listens intently to the song, which is about needing the community to believe in them and to believe in love and not remain silent about crime and abuse ... . Sunelle says:

> *Through the whole evening if children sang or danced, the community would stand up and clap, and if they knew the song they would sing with them ... and also the response we got from the adults and the parents and ... people from all over who came, ... they said we didn't know that our children could do this, we didn't know that they had this potential and also, you know, just saying how wonderful it is to hear these stories from the children, to see that these children can blossom on a stage ... (Sunelle Fouché, music therapist)*

The children's performance is vibrant, alive; it is overwhelming to watch ... Kerryn continues:

---

[2]   Kaapse Klopse refers to a minstrel-like dance troupe tradition in the Cape Flats Colored communities in the Western Cape. Traditionally, these perform in the city of Cape Town on 2 January which is known as "die tweede nuwe jaar" – the second new year.

A concert is such an energetic, vibrant thing and we experienced this through the rehearsals ... and when we had our dress rehearsal and all the teachers were there and seeing the children perform for the first time and you get this kind of exhilarating, this hopeful feeling ... Also that evening, there was this feeling of hope and energy in the community and in the audience. And also, the music that the children were performing was their music, it was Kaapse Klopse music and Xhosa songs and things that they could relate to, and they joined in, so I think definitely it also had an effect on them. And also bringing these Colored and Xhosa communities together – they were sitting together and clapping and singing to the same songs. (Kerryn Torrance, music therapist)

Kerryn and Sunelle tell me that the Heideveld community has claimed the concert as theirs, and that their own role has shifted from initiating and organizing the concert to now simply providing musical support.

Alternative Rehearsal

It is almost time for the choir rehearsal, and we quickly put away the TV monitor, our tea cups, and clear the rest of the room. As I check the white balance and label the video tapes, I think of what Kerryn said when I asked her earlier why she and Sunelle established the choir (and haven't they got enough to do without it). She said,

We felt that there was such an enormous need in the community, especially with the children, and we decided that all the children don't necessarily need music therapy, they don't necessarily need to come for therapy, but they're in this community, they're quite disempowered about the violence – all the violence going on around them. They get involved in the gangs and they get involved in drugs, so we wanted to find some other way to draw them in ... and music is such a powerful way of getting people together ... it wasn't really about the music, you know, the skills they were learning, it was more about the fact that they were there and singing and being part of a group through music ... [the choir] is giving them a group that they belong to, and also a positive group experience which is very difficult for them to find, in their neighborhood, in Heideveld. The groups that function in Heideveld are gangs or drugs ... So we wanted to provide an alternative. (Kerryn Torrance, music therapist)

As I think about this conversation, I remind myself of my "secret" agenda: to document their work as best I can, so as to give this work a voice; to make it known, and filming is part of this. Kerryn and Sunelle are practicing a song at the piano, and my eye is drawn to a poster on the notice board, with Choir Rules. I zoom in the camera lens to have a look (Figure 7.1).

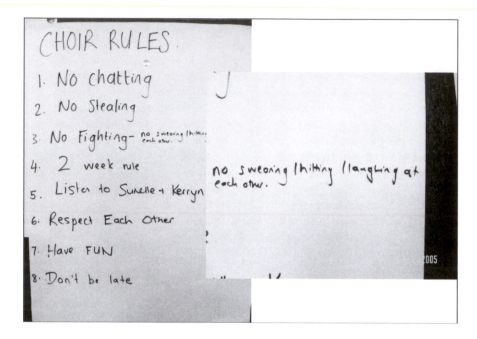

Figure 7.1   Choir rules

Kerryn sees me and laughs: "Ja! We're strict! If you want to be in the choir, you need to behave and the kids know this. We worked out these rules together, it took an entire choir rehearsal to do this, and now the kids themselves enforce the choir rules if someone slips up – they do our job for us!" At that instant there is a commotion outside the door, a knock and then a pouring in of some 35 children, aged between 6 and 14. The noise is unbelievable – I haven't been in a school classroom for many years … They're all in different school uniforms – I remember now that they come from seven different schools ("We also arrange all the transport – part of our music therapy work").

The children make a beeline for me, cluster around the video camera pulling faces. We all hear Sunelle's stern voice: "Remember what we talked about last week? This is Mercédès, she's come to watch us practice and also to video us – so let's get going quickly and then perhaps there will be time for Mercédès to show us some of the film." The children leap into rows, and within moments, are doing vocal warm-ups. Out of tune. How on earth does this cackle become a choir, I wonder … I film from the back of the classroom, and as the choir warms up, I find the children's energy thrilling. And loud! Energy just seems to pour out of them … I decide to move to the front, which means I'll be a lot more noticeable, but in any case, so many keep turning around to look at me I don't think this will make much difference. From the front, I notice two girls who are not participating. They look sullen and unhappy, I wonder what's happened to them. I must remember to ask the music therapists afterwards. (It turns out that they are newcomers, and

Sunelle and Kerryn are giving them time to find their own voice within the choir, so not pressurizing them to "do" – despite the concert deadline.) I also notice that when the choir practices the words of the songs, there are clear linguistic fault lines. All children say the English words; the "colored" children say the Afrikaans words while the Xhosa children the Xhosa words. A fractured social landscape in a microcosm: ethnicity, language, and geography.[3]

Soon the choir rehearsal is in full swing, and the children less and less interested in me. I too am less and less interested in the filming, and spontaneously feel the music inside my body as they sing. I have to stop myself from humming along, because of the microphone on the camera. At one point in the rehearsal, the choir has been rehearsing a song called "Kan'n man dan nie," and at the end of the song, there is general chatter and noise in the room, as Sunelle and Kerryn confer at the piano. Out of the corner of my eye I notice the back-row – seven of the oldest children in the choir – clustered around a table. I zoom the camera in towards them and film the children spontaneously continuing to create music and dancing without the need for the therapists … This becomes one of the many "magic moments" in Heideveld … . Soon after this, the rehearsal ends, and Sunelle reminds me that I wanted to ask the children some questions about the choir and choir rehearsal.

I'd Like to Know Why You are in the Choir

I feel rather self conscious standing in front of the children without a camera to hide behind. I speak hesitantly, "I want to say thank you for allowing me to be here and listen to you all and film your work. I enjoyed it a lot" (spontaneous clapping and "you're very welcome" from the children, who look at Sunelle and Kerryn when they answer me).

I say to them, "I'd like to know why you are in the choir." There is a barrage of comments –

"Because it's cool"
"It's fun"
"You learn more about music"
"You learn things you never knew before"

---

[3]   I use the term "colored" here as it is used locally. This usage is related to an incredibly complex demographic-identity landscape and language. Folk use different categories to identify themselves and others – some to do with language (English, Afrikaans, Zulu, Xhosa, Pedi, Venda, Shangaan etc), some with skin color (white, black, coloreds), and some with ethnicity (Zulus, Xhosas, Pedi, Shangaan, Venda, North Sotho, South Sotho, and more). None of these align very neatly. The "colored" folk are also a demographic group, and their language is proudly Afrikaans (they are the largest Afrikaans speaking group in the country), so the "colored" bit is (ironically) more complex than skin color.

"We've made new friends in the choir"
"Our friends are jealous because we will be performing in the concert"
"We like to dance ... dancing helps you sing ... singing helps you dance ...
singing without dance is boring"
"We sing the songs afterwards when we walk home."

I ask the children what they think about Kerryn and Sunelle. There is much laughter in the room, and Sunelle and Kerryn say: "you can tell Mercédès whatever you want to tell her ..." More laughter. The children say –

"They are very much *all right!"*
"They are our mother and our father... our aunties, our uncles" (much laughter)
"They are kind ... Not strict. Noooo – oh ... They are strict! Sometimes ... always ..."
"They love us" (lots of laughter).

It is time to end, the children are getting restless, there is a knock at the door – it is the driver from one of the schools, come to fetch the children. Suddenly the room becomes noisy and disheveled once again, as the children pour out into the afternoon.

On the flight back to Johannesburg that evening I write notes on the day's events, surrounded by businessmen and corporate executives. I can smell Woodlands school on my jeans and sweater. I feel lucky to be a music therapist and a researcher in South Africa.

Chapter 8

Reflection
Let the Music Work:
Optimal Moments of Collaborative Musicing

Mercédès Pavlicevic

Introduction

This chapter is grounded in enthusiasm about music's power to "make things happen": within and between people, however well or unwell, in intimate settings, in closed small group settings or in wide spaces. The setting is Community Music Therapy work in South Africa in Heideveld in the Western Cape. Numerous on-site research visits enabled direct musical participation, filming, photographing, interviews (individual and group, semi-structured and open ended), direct observation and "corridor chats," all of which together grew a substantial data corpus.

Throughout the three years of data collection, it was undoubtedly the musicing events themselves that conveyed music's powerful work more directly and clearly than any number of in-depth interviews, conversations, or field notes. At the same time, "music's power" was not a "given," so to speak, but needed to be evoked, invoked, crafted, shared, and worked with in a very particular way. And it was this that became increasingly fascinating: how did music work in these music therapy group events? How did music therapists make "it" happen? How did all the participants seem to know, with apparently minimal musical formal knowledge or experience, that singing-dancing-moving together is "magic"?

To address these questions I selected "magic moments" from videos of group music therapy work, showing a group doing music together. At these moments, each group was in optimal flow: in other words, they were "peak" moments when the groups seemed propelled within highly fluid musical groove; moments that – frankly – electrified me. The nearest analogy being moments in a live jazz concert when the improvisation "takes off," with corresponding whooping, cheering, whistling, and clapping by the audience. At such moments in group music therapy, the (socially assigned) identities and roles of therapist and clients seemed to meld: all became people doing "magic" music. Crucially, opposite moments were equally easy to identify. These were moments where the groups remained a collection of individuals, or splinter groups, with low level collaboration and musical incoherence. These non-magic moments have remained a useful backdrop for considering how and when music works – and how and when it doesn't. Although it might seem curious to "reduce" three years of data work to "moments," I drew encouragement from the writings of Tia DeNora (2003) and Eric Clarke (2005), both of whom are inspired by Gibson's attentiveness to the "right level" of analysis being informed by the phenomenon's ecological scale.

At this point, a brief detour is needed to clarify the second half of this essay title. Before this research project, Gary Ansdell and I began to work on the notion of *collaborative musicing* (Ansdell and Pavlicevic, 2005; Pavlicevic and Ansdell, 2007) to explain group events in music therapy. This was, in part, to redress a dearth in group music therapy literature (in contrast with literature portraying one-on-one or individual work), and also to consider the complexities of group music therapy in the light of a broader intellectual stream; this, in contrast to the theoretical emphases on group dynamics and group psychoanalysis that characterizes much group music therapy literature. Lastly, we were inspired to do justice to the richness and complexity of group work both in our own clinical practice as well as that of our colleagues. Since this work overlapped with, and consequently informed, the data work presented here, a short description seems appropriate.

Briefly, collaborative musicing identifies and describes the acts and intentions of all participants in group music therapy, as they collaboratively enact optimal group musicing. In optimal collaborative musicing, the distinction between being a therapist and a client is replaced by a collaboration between participants that is emphatically musical, calling on all participants to sustain a unified musicing organism. To make sense of this collaborative work, we framed group music therapy as a complex social-musical event, expanding its traditional frame as a "relational" and "therapeutic" event. These descriptions seemed insufficient, especially in the context of current theories and research (e.g., Bradley, 2005; Small, 1998; Davidson and Good, 2002; Sawyer, 2003, 2005; Stern, 2004). At the same time, though, we were clear that collaborative musicing has a "musical-therapeutic" agenda. In other words, group music therapy generally happens with "vulnerable" people, and its task is to ensure that all participate in, and co-generate as optimally as possible, collective musicing. In keeping with a music-centered practice (Nordoff and Robbins, 1977; Aigen, 2005), where the nature of participants' vulnerabilities may restrict optimal collaborative musicing (e.g. through neurological damage, or physical/mental incapacities, and so on), the music therapist's skills are called upon to address and repair these restrictions through musicing (Pavlicevic, 2003).

Thus, the musicing events in this essay are framed by this understanding of the musical-and-social nature of group music therapy. The second part of this essay title also signifies the enactment of interactive social networks and of social life through collective musical action in group music therapy. The "magic moments" selected for micro-analysis provided empirical substance to collaborative musicing as "micro social action." They also enabled a moment-by-moment analysis that revealed a rich musical-temporal-kinesthetic-social event. In this chapter, only one excerpt is presented; not a distilling of a vast ranging practice, but rather, a purposive exemplar chosen as a result of (collaborative) thinking with the music therapists on site.

The essay is underpinned by a (fairly) straightforward question, which is this: What happens when a group of people make music together in music therapy? Irresistibly, other questions begin to appear in rapid succession: How does music "work," here? What is the nature of the group in music? How are the music therapists part of this event? And what implications might we draw from such events, in terms of "everyday life"? I now consider this "magic moment" in some detail and will then give an "intuitive commentary" followed by the research questions and analytic themes that emerged from the micro-analysis of this work. (Note: it will become evident that some themes "bulge" while others appear empirically slender – the result of a commentary based on micro-analysis of several excerpts, not presented here.)

A Magic Moment in Heideveld

This moment, alluded to earlier, happened while filming the Heideveld Children's Choir rehearsal in a classroom in Heideveld with about 35 children aged 6 to 14. This was in preparation for the Heideveld Community Concert, due to take place in a local church hall some months away. The choir had been rehearsing a (Cape Malay) song called *Kan'n man dan nie*, at the end of which there was general chatter and disarray in the room as Kerryn and Sunelle, the two music therapists, conferred at the piano. In the midst of this disarray, as I was about to switch off the camera, my eye was drawn to the back-row of the choir – 7 of the oldest children (11–14 yr olds) – clustered around a small table at the back of the room, doing spontaneous and informal singing and dancing. Sensing something interesting, I zoomed in. What follows is a summary description of this "in-between" part of the choir rehearsal.

1. Seven children are clustered around the table, facing one another with heads lowered as they spontaneously sing the last line of "Kan'n man dan nie" and move their hips. Half the group taps the song's rhythm on the table, which tapping anchors and drives the continuing *crescendo* and tightening of the singing, towards a sudden *sforzando* of vocal and physical energy with exclamations of Ya-Ya-Ya!. Simultaneously, all jump backwards, away from the table, laughing, and almost immediately forming various looser pairs.

2. A girl, "X," then begins tapping a new but related rhythm on the table while everyone still laughs. She nods, claps, chats and moves at the same time, and the various dyads re-position themselves around her clapping and nodding, singing DU-DU-DU, and doing rap/hip-hop body movements, moving closer together around the table.

3. Sunelle's voice emerges forcefully from the general chatter, querying something, and the Back Row looks instantly towards her as one, imperceptibly interrupting their singing, clapping, and dancing, which continues.
4. Kerryn, seated at the piano, begins to play in a way both relating to, and mismatching, the back row's singing-dancing. Kerryn continues to play in this "partial" matching mode (the meter and pitch are partially matched, while her playing is recognizably related to the children's musicing).
5. The back-row begins to re-organize its singing and dancing towards the piano's ongoing rhythmic ground, until piano and the group are in the same groove.
6. Sunelle's voice is heard (off camera) organizing the rest of the choir into one large circle. The back-row continues to dance, sing, clap with the piano, while loosening and opening their cluster to form a line, eventually becoming one side of this large circle.
7. The back row and the choir are increasingly one musical event as the rest of the choir begin to sway and clap (the camera zoom widens). There is a long period of musical and bodily adjustments by all, and a sense of gathering momentum, as the piano moves, with the choir, towards the next song in the rehearsal, which is "Catch a Falling Star and Put it in Your Pocket." The rehearsal continues.

Intuitive Commentary and Some Research Questions

What emerged during micro-analytic study of this (and other excerpts) is the effortless synchronic musicing within and between each of the young folk. To think in terms of a number of youngsters singing and dancing "together as one" falls qualitatively short of explaining their supra-individual choreographed elegance. It is as though, during optimal moments, there is no phenomenological distinction between the group's musical sounds, movements, and use of space. Thus, the *crescendo* of sounds and body movements also correspond with a tightening of the group's clustering towards one another, while a *diminuendo* corresponds to its loosening cluster, away from one another. The musical and spatial phenomena seem to become one, so much so, that to speak of intersections of space-and-time feels limiting. Equally limiting is to think of the sharing of musical minds and space," with the implications that it is separate minds (or experiences) that come together. More apt, perhaps, is the notion of unified and unifying time and space, which moments became recognizable in the data analysis. Perhaps, at times such as these when the group is in peak flow, the axes of time and space need melding; as do those of separateness and collectiveness, musicing and mind. In reflecting on the virtuosic group choreography and synchronicity, I saw a social-musical improvisation in which musical space is generated, molded, occupied and dismissed with split-second precision and collective dexterity. This social-musical improvisation seemed to be known within and between all minds and bodies as one, complex, phenomenon. This optimal experience of collaborative musicing can be thought of as one of the therapeutic aims of such work.

Three questions emerged from the data work, from the intuitive insights and discussions with research colleagues in our group and with the music therapists. These are,

- What is the configuration of collective and complex group musicing events in Community Music Therapy?
- How is collaborative musicing regulated by the participants?
- What strategies do music therapists use to generate optimal collaborative musicing?

I will now explore these questions directly, drawing from the data analysis. The process of micro-analysis involved identifying the segments, doing thick descriptions of each, coding this and doing cross-segment comparisons for emerging themes. These are now presented as addressing each question, although to think of these as addressing mutually exclusive aspects of group musicing would be to limit the complexities of the event.

The Configuration of Collective and Complex Musicing Events

Here I focus on the role of the song, and the group's choreography.

Whose Songs? How Shall We Sing It?

The excerpt shows the ensemble using a song that already exists in the social domain that is the choir rehearsal. The back-row "claims" or "borrows" for itself this song (*Kan'n man dan nie*) and makes it its own. In this sense, the song represents the larger social domain (the choir), to which all participants belong. In that distinctive time and space, i.e., the "formal" part of the rehearsal, the song has a particular role and function. In this "magic moment," equally, the song's everyday idiomatic form and content "frames" how the back-row "moves'n grooves" together. Here, however, the song's everyday conventions are interwoven with idiosyncratic musicing that seem to belong in *this* time and space.

With improvisatory flair, the children propel and enact the song, tipping from one social-musical genre to another, (e.g. melding hip-hop type movements with Kaapse Klopse idioms for *Kan'n man dan nie*). The back-row flows in and around these conventional/cultural idiomatic frames with seamless fluidity, and also discards any aspect of the musical conventions with ease, once no longer needed. Thus, in the excerpt, the children don't limit themselves to the song's everyday conventions; they don't need to complete its conventional phrasing or reproduce it "exactly"; quite the contrary, at times. It seems that a highly mutual, reflexive loop is enacted, with musicing "creating" the back-row, who in turn *(re-)create* the song.

The enacting of the song seems to be about more than accurate enactment – about more than musical virtuosity for its own sake. How might we understand the song's function? Or rather, its multiple functions since, for the choir especially, the same song seems to have multiple uses and purposes. Whereas, for the whole choir, the song was being rehearsed for a performance, the back-row's idiosyncratic use can be understood as a signal (to itself and to the rest of the choir) of its distinctive identity and skills – possibly a kind of social "preening." Its enactment signals the back-row as a separate entity from, as well as part of, the larger corpus: the song that previously "belonged" to the entire choir is "borrowed," and this distinctive enactment generates the back-row's social and musical identity. It is worth considering that instead of enacting the song, the back-row could stand around, giggle and chat, which would distinguish it as a cohort separate from the rest. However, this would generate an identity that is less unusual, less distinctive, less different from everyday life (after all, in Heideveld as in many places, clusters of teenagers often stand around giggling, wriggling and chattering, often with animated body movements). Instead, the back-row displays its virtuosity as a tightly choreographed unit, drawing admiration (at the very least) from the music therapists and researchers who watched this film. Indeed, they could have been performing to the video camera filming them (though this is fairly unlikely, given the chaotic melée in the room, and given that they remained unaware of my covert activities).

These events are not dissimilar to professional musicians in rehearsal (Davidson and Good, 2002), or to Keith Sawyer's (2003) descriptions of a jazz ensemble, although both describe experienced amateur and professional musicians familiar with their repertoire and its conventions. Sawyer describes jazz musicians' effortless jamming, continuously experimenting re what works and what doesn't regarding the musical conventions. But what of the young people depicted here? They have little experience of playing musical instruments – or, indeed, of unimposed social co-operation. Their virtuosity, I propose, is in their tightly negotiated, collaboratively idiosyncratic use of the song's cultural imperatives. The song, in turn, provides a collectively acknowledged scaffold for the group's collaborative musicing: its structures of phrasing, melodic contours, of rhythmic patterning, places particular demands on the body, enabling bodies and minds to entrain, and to collaborate synchronically.

The next theme describes the forming of the group: How do we describe this, what is its nature, its configurations?

The Choreography and Its Topography

In South Africa, (perhaps more than in "The North") musicing is a physically active social event, and is overtly conveyed through the body – this includes choral concerts and hymn singing in church, where to sing while standing (still) would be considered rather unsociable. In the film are young persons singing, tapping, and dancing with their entire bodies, moving effortlessly between talking, laughing, gesturing, and musicing (1, 2).

This choreography has various topographies. The participants group, ungroup, and regroup into various configurations. They form tight clusters (1), and reconfigure into loosened clusters (2). We see them in scattered formations (1) that nevertheless remain a group, we see them opening outwards (6, 7), and we see parallel clusters musicing concurrently – including the back-row and the piano, the various pairs, and the back-row and the larger choir (2, 3, 4). Some configurations can be described in terms of musical performance conventions: we see what resembles a soloist and group (2); an entire ensemble (1, 5, 6, 7); and parallel ensembles (2).

It seems that a single temporal stream holds and propels each micro-event, each person and each collection of persons in this Magic moment, propelling the children seamlessly from one configuration to another. The same temporal stream seems to happen within each child, between the children, and to the group as a whole. Moreover, this single temporal stream appears in multiple modalities: it is "musical" (in the idiomatic, conventional cultural sense as the children sing and dance), prosodic (in the children's laughter and chattering), and kinesthetic (in their movements and gestures). The same temporal stream is enacted as their singing becomes chattering and wriggling (1), becomes dancing, wriggling, re-grouping, and more.

A foundation for this temporal stream is aptly identified by Malloch and Trevarthen's (2000; 2009) notion of *communicative musicality:* a neurologically facility, anchored by our Intrinsic Motive Pulse (Trevarthen, 2000), and activated in a particular way through musicing with others. Here, we have an ongoing stream enabled by communicative musicality that flows through, generates and "holds" the children's magic moment. Communicative musicality is underpinned by the unifying functions of *vitality affects* (Stern, 1985, 2004), whose dynamic temporal qualities are to do with the expressive qualities of any animate or inanimate act or action.

In the magic moment, it seems that a unified vitality affect happens within each person as well as between them, held by the group musicing. Thus, as the music intensifies, not only does each person's body movements intensify, but correspondingly, the ensemble moves closer together spatially. At another event, at the very point of musical climax/exclamation, the back-row jumps back as one, the children loosen away from one another spatially, and each individual body's tension releases.

These moments of optimal collaborative musicing can be described as intra-personal as well as inter-personal animation through one common temporal musicing stream. We can think in terms of group musicing as gathering and animating one supra-subjective Vitality Affect, enabling the ensemble to function as one musicing organism. The function of musicing, here, seems to be about generating inter-subjectivity as part of collective or supra-subjectivity; creating a unified and unifying experience of time, place, and person.

All of this prompts a consideration of the group's optimal collaborative musicing as a distinctive qualitative phenomenon, with a distinctive "topography." This experience echoes Sawyer's (2003, 2005) notion of the collaborative emergent as "ephemeral"; an ongoing, easy-to-miss happening that continuously unfolds.

Close analysis of this magic moment revealed finely honed skills by the participants. They are able to regulate constantly, enacting multiple ways of dancing, of using space and of musicing, closely tied to the ongoing ebb and flow of their own musicing as well as that of the ensemble. So far, we've seen the ensemble operating at times as one organism, at times as a collection of persons, as having various spatial and musical configurations, as flowing easily and virtuosically in, with, around, and through musicing. The next two questions explore the participants' acts: what are they doing and how? How do they engage in musicing? How do they music collaboratively? (if such questions can really be formulated).

How is Collaborative Musicing Regulated by the Participants?

Two aspects are addressed here: who's in charge of what, when; and the multiplicity of events in collaborative musicing. For the sake of analytic distinction, I distinguish between "the participants'" and "the music therapist's" strategies (addressed in the next question). This is because of the distinctive social nature of music therapy group work. Thus in addressing the second question, the spotlight is trained more sharply on the young participants.

Taking Charge and Taking Care: Switched Roles, Tasks and Skills

In all the excerpts studied, young folk assume and discard a number of roles in the interest of sustaining the musicing stream. The roles are in the interest of a particular task, and seem to be elicited in the musicing moment and in response to it.

The roles are enacted through a range of body-musicing and include those of initiating (girl X taps a "new but related" rhythm on the table in (1)), leading (various children at different moments lead the step and dance inwards or outwards and draw the rest of the group), following, flowing with, interrupting (in this exemplar, it is the music therapist who interrupts (3); in other examples studied, it is the children who do so, in the interests of shifting or altering the musicing event), prompting (through exaggerated enactment to ensure unified temporal enactment), supporting (re-orienting oneself in order to become "part of"), and so on. Each of these is enacted with skilful agility and dexterity, and the switch in roles and enactment is swift and nuanced, and at first glance, not especially noticeable. Thus, "leadership" is relinquished when the collaborative singing-dancing intensifies, with the "leader" then becoming part of the entire organism in music. The ensemble seems to accord musical and aesthetic authority to that person, at that moment.

Any of these roles seem to have one common purpose, which is to sustain a collaborative, temporal musicing stream. This task also has a social dimension; that of ensuring that the collection of persons becomes entrained, neurologically, musically, spatially, socially, so that the ensemble can shift towards (and also release from) being as one. In the interest of this task, each role is taken on and discarded by any participant at any time, and, critically, this highly fluid social "hierarchy" is accepted by the group. (In other examples studied, the same roles are taken on and passed around between participants at different times during the same musicing event.)

The collective event, then, is at times the responsibility and property of the entire ensemble, and at times the responsibility of any topographical combinations: one person, of duos, trios, or of all. Also, it seems that taking charge and taking care pertains to more than what's happening within the ensemble. The next theme highlights the group's attentiveness to what's happening around it.

Attending to Multiple Spaces

Whilst absorbed in musicing, the back-row is alert to Sunelle's interjection (3), to Kerryn's piano mismatching (4), and to the larger choir beginning to re group (6). This suggests a concurrent alertness: engagement and participation in the back-row's musicing, and moment-by-moment attentiveness to all events. The back-row straddles, and remains committed to, two "memberships": their own, distinctive one, and that of the larger whole, able to respond equally to internal and external events, absorbing these as part of its ensemble musicing. At the end of the excerpt, the back-row de-clusters as a spatial and musical group, and is re-absorbed by the larger circle. At the same time, though, the back-row retains its distinctive identity: the children remain together, forming one side of the larger choir circle (7).

The back-row musicing is not exclusive (or excluding), and the children hear, listen, and respond to, events around them, whilst also remaining committed to their continuing enactment. The music therapists emerge increasingly in the second half of the film, as they increasingly draw the multiple events in the room towards one, larger participatory event. This is the "formal" part of the rehearsal. Their increasing prominence offers a good moment in this narrative to now consider the music therapists' stance, with the final question.

How Do Music Therapists Generate Optimal Collaborative Musicing?

As intimated earlier, in the various "magic moments" studied, the music therapist is part of the musicing ensemble. They are on camera present throughout and part of the group musicing – so much so that to distinguish between questions 2 and

3 seems somewhat artificial. However, the music therapist regulates herself as having two roles: as the music therapist, as well as her role as a member of the ensemble. It is this dual stance that is of interest here. In attempting to make sense of the "therapeutic" aspect of collaborative musicing, as represented by events such as these, the data analytic work closely trained the spotlight onto the therapists' acts, as participants with roles and tasks distinct from the rest of the members. The segment reveals a rich range of strategies, despite the visual absence of Sunelle and Kerryn.

The question concerning music therapists' musicing strategies needs some broader reflection and contextualizing at this point, and for this I draw from various semi-structured interviews (some of this is elaborated in Part VIII). One aspect has to do with the social–professional identity assigned to the music therapist by the work contexts; i.e., by the teachers and children at Heideveld. This "music therapist identity" (similar to that of a "teacher," a "pupil," or a "choir member"), can be thought of as a social "given," no matter how implicit, covert, or contrary the therapists' actions in the film. This identity is, however, more than given, it is also "taken" – in other words, the therapists assume their responsibilities and roles as therapists, albeit in less-than conventional therapeutic ways. In our interviews, Sunelle and Kerryn talk of being white, outsiders, not from Heideveld – and over the years, gradually becoming accepted by the people of Heideveld – as "white" (a good thing) rather than "whiteys." When watching the excerpts together, the therapists described their stance, their thinking and their doing in each of the excerpts as "part of" music therapy work, framed by music therapy professional knowledge and skill.

Music therapy work demands considerable preparation before the group event. The music therapists ensure that various scaffolds are in place, and remain so during group musicing. These are physical, musical, temporal, and social scaffolds, and in music therapy professional practice, these are usually described as part of therapeutic boundaries (Darnley-Smith and Patey, 2003). Rather like any music rehearsals, the physical space (the room) needs to be dedicated to the event, and clearly delineated as such to others – in other words, this space needs to be (more or less) free from interruptions. The physical space needs to be amenable to group musicing, so that the beginning and end of sessions are generally spent reconfiguring it by rearranging school desks, chairs, and so on. Similarly, the timing and duration of the event is delineated: sessions begin and end at a certain time, with a commitment by all, to be there for that duration of time – although everyday events inevitably intrude on these delineations. In the various examples studied, the music therapists provide instruments, musical material (where necessary), clear the physical space or prepare it in other ways (including chiding cleaners and chasing up drivers and handymen). As we'll see in Part VIII, part of ensuring optimal social scaffolding can mean that they relinquish their role and professional identity.

During group music therapy work, the music therapists' strategies can be summed up as enabling and ensuring that optimal possibilities for collaborative musicing are created, sustained, and acted upon. These strategies are enacted in multiple ways, ways that are fluid and flexible, that are at times imperceptible, covert, and at other times strident and startling in their suddenness and interruptions. In other words, the quality of enacting their strategies is tightly coupled with the entire group's enactment at that moment. In this sense, it is as unpredictable and improvisatory as demanded by the (social-musical) totality of the moment.

I now consider the music therapists' strategies within group musicing by focusing on their complex attentiveness to the moment, and collaborative enabling.

A Complex Attentiveness to the Moment – and "Doing as Little as Possible"

The complexity of the therapists' stance is such that it cannot be (conveniently) described in any one way. A series of micro events illustrated some characteristics of this stance.

In one of the magic moments studied, the music therapist remains silent throughout, alert and ready to do whatever is needed at any moment (which may or may not be "strictly musical" – it may be moving a chair to one side as the group begins to dance and move around). Often the music therapists did not play, and if and when they joined in with the playing, it was quiet, as though "feeling their way" into the group musicing. I also experienced music therapists assigning authority and leadership to someone in the group at times, and acting as "sous-chef" – responding as need be, to ensure that the leader's leading, and the group's responsiveness are as effective as possible.

In the back-row magic moment, the music therapists' absence is punctuated by sudden, dramatic appearances. Music therapist Sunelle interrupts the back-row's musicing volubly and decisively (3), while, some moments later, Kerryn also does a musical interruption, and, moreover, does not adjust her piano mis-matching (4). Both acts seem counter-intuitive and rather unconventional, socially (interrupting or interfering) and musically (not adjusting or accommodating). However, throughout the excerpt the two therapists (off-camera) seem to tolerate what looks and sounds like chaos and disorder (the rest of the choir can be heard noisily chattering and giggling), and seem to suspend their responsibility. It is as though they have their own business to attend to, while the children chatter. At the same time, though, there is a sense of their multiple attentiveness: they attend to their business, they are aware of "what's going on" in the room, and aware of the back-row. Kerryn's partial piano matching is nevertheless a matching of sorts – and attests to a listening – or at least to hearing – the back-row's singing, albeit peripherally.

Thus the therapists' attentiveness can seem ambiguous, at times almost indecisive; generally not at the forefront of either event, but appearing as and when needed. Overall, in the magic moments, I had a sense of their feeling the flow, sensing the musicing's energy with optimal and unobtrusive alertness, and intervening only as needed.

Enabling Collaborative Enactment and Shifting of Roles, Skills, and Tasks

By apparently "doing as little as possible," the therapists enable a truly *collaborative* enactment. We've seen already that roles are apportioned to, and shared by all. In none of the excerpt do we see any one person being the "expert," the "leader," "musical conductor" or "soloist" for the entire event. Similarly with other roles: those of following, supporting, observing, attending, being "part of" are taken on and discarded by any member of the ensemble, at any time – although the timing, as we saw earlier, seems to have everything to do with the musicing's form and content, and with the group's energy. While part of the collective event, and even when engaged in different tasks, the music therapists also retain their distinctive identity, not attempting to be the "same as" the group, even when flowing as part of the ensemble musicing.

In all magic moments, the music therapists multi-task and sustain multi-attentiveness. They flow in and out of overtly "therapy role," able to switch between being therapist, director, co-musician, facilitator, collaborator, at the same time, with nuanced shifts between and among these tasks. At times they can be seen to enact multiple tasks (listening while clearing the floor of instruments; talking with co-therapist while also listening to the back-row and to the rest of the choir); while at others they seem to be "doing nothing" – just listening and paying attention.

This unobtrusive strategy of what I call "enabling" seems to subvert the notion of the therapist having authority or even responsibility for what goes on. In this sense the events are collaborative and democratic. However, none of this means that the therapists are not "at work," or not needed. It seems that their work is a complex mixture of being, doing, and, at times, not doing.

Music Rules

Having addressed the three questions with themes that emerged directly from the data work, I conclude this essay by returning to the "straightforward" questions at the start of the essay, such as: How does music "work" in group music therapy? What happens when people are together in music? What is the nature of the group in music? What implications for everyday life?

Music, as such, does not work. What is described here is collaborative enactment driven by the imperatives of musicing. The song's imperatives of phrasing, rhythm, melodic contours, and meter are refracted and collaboratively enacted through each of the participants' proto-musical capacities (Pavlicevic, 1997; Trevarthen, 2000; Stige, 2002; Cross, 2003; Ansdell and Pavlicevic, 2005). At the same time, these enactments are activated and shaped by the conventions of social engagements, e.g. doing to, receiving from, and doing with (or without), one another, and so on. Each – the musical and the social (conventions and enactments) – needs the other, and neither exists without the other. Thus, the song needs bodies, and bodies need other bodies and minds for singing-and-dancing-together.

We see in this magic moment, socio-musicing enactments within the delineated social space of group music therapy work. Collaborative musicing, here, affords relationships and interactions to be enacted with all the improvisatory complexities of everyday life. The cultural musicing convention is that of improvisation, which has a long tradition in music therapy practice, and in this (and other) magic moments – the cultural artifact is a song. The song, in this example, is "borrowed" and becomes a common ground for the group's work together. The song's cultural-idiomatic conventions provide a sonar and temporal scaffold for the ensemble's energy and momentum to constantly merge, emerge, diverge, and converge. The ensembles' use of this song is flexible, spontaneous, elaborate, multi-idiomatic, and is process specific. This "improvisatory" stance goes beyond "musical" improvisation, and absorbs events, speech, and interruptions and intrusions from its periphery. Optimal collaborative musicing conveys through joint musical action, the fluidity and permeability of minds and bodies in unified time and space, propelled by, and propelling, a unified musicing stream. We might say that musicing is the property of the group as much as the group is a property of musicing.

Collaborative musicing, then, is characterized by synchronic space-time choreography – akin to Condon and Ogston's (1966) descriptions of interactional synchrony between conversing adult dyads, but far more complex. Optimal collaborative musicing suggests more than a sharing of musicing patterns that exist in separate, individual minds and bodies. This choreography is also about more than individual acts that are temporally co-ordinated or entrained. Rather, the emergent needs constantly negotiated and re-crafted choreography, working around and towards one kinesthetic shaping of the present, which can be described as "group mind experiencing group time" in music (Bradley, 2005; Sawyer, 2003; Stern, 2004). Such optimal moments of collaborative musicing seem to be the socio-musicing pivot around which the group constantly gathers and releases, temporally and spatially, almost too powerfully bonding to be sustained for too long.

In all the excerpts studied, the music therapists' stance is paradoxical. She "holds in mind" the social-musical complexity of collaborative musicing as she listens, attends, "does nothing," does something – delicately at times, stridently at others. It is the therapist's multiple attentiveness that enables the social democracy of collaborative musicing; with multiple identities, roles and tasks evoked and enacted within and by each member of the group, at different times, in response to the group-musicing needs and demands.

Finally, then, in these social contexts, what are the implications of this work for everyday life? We've established the social-musical work that is collaborative musicing. It's worth recalling that in this site (as in the other South African site discussed in Part VIII), the youngsters playing music are well versed in crime, gang violence, fighting their corner, cheating, stealing, lying (see the choir rules in the narrative in Chapter 7). There is little tolerance for "difference" in everyday life. We might describe the social co-operation that happens in the streets and playgrounds as coerced; with insidiously (and at times brutally) enforced alliances and allegiances.

Collaborative musicing, as portrayed here, offers ways of being different in a different way. Not difference that is ethnic, geographical or territorial, but a difference generated by musicing's needs and demands. We see roles and responsibilities collaboratively assumed and discarded in response to social-musical imperatives. Difference of skills, acts, roles and tasks is enacted and accepted and absorbed as necessary for optimal crafting of the present musical moment. Thus, the children's social skills, which may be distorted or coerced in everyday life, are refracted and recrafted here, through collaborative musicing. Music therapy's task here, to both refract everyday life, and also to recast this refraction through collaborative work, offering a range of possibilities for enacting social collaborations in everyday life.

To conclude, the Community Music Therapy work that I have documented and tracked in the two South African sites was with vulnerable young people. Young persons whose everyday life offers few possibilities for social collaboration – unless imposed, at times, ruthlessly. In these two projects, rules are negotiated by all, and nobody rules anyone else. Clearly, music rules.

PART V

Chapter 9

Action

A Society for All? The *Cultural Festival* in Sogn og Fjordane, Norway

Brynjulf Stige

A Society for All

As I drive through Våtedalen, a narrow gorge beneath the glacier that runs through the central part of the county of Sogn og Fjordane in Western Norway, I notice that there is not much snow left in the fields. It's April and I'm on my way to *The Cultural Festival.* Spring must be coming up soon.

I start thinking about the name of the event. "The Cultural Festival." It is kind of hard to tell if its humility or hubris that has given it such an unspecified name, suggesting that it's nothing, or – *the* thing. The festival has established itself as a happening one weekend every year, bringing around 100 adults with intellectual disabilities and their helpers together, coming from the small towns and remote valleys of this rural county. During the festival all participants, helpers, instructors, and organizers live, work, and play together. The days are packed with workshops and performances and lots of social events. After three intense days of music, dance, drama, and art, the processes and products merge in a final performance.

Four cars full of music therapists and students left the university college in Sandane this morning, headed for the festival. How many times have I been driving like this? I'm not quite sure. As Head of Studies in the music therapy training course in Sandane I was part of the group that established the festival back in 1988, in collaboration with the local division of NFU, a Norwegian organization for individuals with intellectual disabilities and their families. I remember that we had two ambitions at that time; to create a cultural event that could be inspiring and meaningful for the participants and to create an arena for cultural politics, so that the process of developing inclusive cultural activities in local communities could be supported. An important backdrop for our efforts at that time was the fact that the Norwegian government was just about to de-institutionalize the care for people with intellectual disabilities, delegating the responsibility to all municipalities to establish community-based care for this group. We had reasons to believe that the municipalities' capacities for this challenge would vary considerably. Very few municipalities had developed decent cultural activities for this group of citizens and the government reform of the late 1980s did not regulate public responsibilities in relation to such activities in the same way as it did secure the rights to housing and schooling.

For many years I came back every spring for this festival, being one of the instructors and organizers. Then I had a break for a few years, due to responsibilities in other contexts. After that I had again found myself as music therapist and instructor in the festival, and had enjoyed it. This time will be different, however, since I am coming in the role as researcher. I have taken interest in studying what this festival affords for the participants.

When we approach the hotel where the festival is arranged, it starts snowing. All of a sudden the glacier has got company of millions of snowflakes dancing before our eyes. We jump out of the car, manage to get the musical instruments safely in place, install ourselves in our rooms, and then head for the opening ceremony.

Among the guests at the ceremony is the director of culture in the county of Sogn og Fjordane. She gives an opening note and expresses that this is one of the more established festivals in this rural region and that it is also one of the more important. Of course she is flattering the audience, but she has some arguments to support her claim too: She talks about the importance of bringing people together for company and cultural experiences. "Participation in cultural activities gives us shared experiences," she says, "It gives us something to talk about." "The festival is a place where we can receive, but also give," she continues. "It's a place where you can build surplus energy, have inspiration, and experience joy." And she claims that joy maybe is underestimated as the basis for cultural activities. Then her talk moves into wider circles and she links the festival to public health, a topic of current interest since a recent Norwegian white paper on health promotion had stimulated new awareness about relationships between health and society. The director finishes her opening note by stating that the county wants to continue to support this festival in the years to come and she gives tribute to NFU, the music therapists, and the other festival workers for the work they are doing for the festival.

After a musical performance and some enthusiastic community singing, the assistant mayor of the municipality where the festival is located has a few words to say. She is also a member of NFU and one of the founders of the festival. First she describes the festival as a place where people could meet and have new friends and new experiences. Then she talks about cultural politics and the need to support events like this, before she reads a poem about friendship. I think to myself: "This is what NFU is all about; politics and friendship." The assistant mayor finishes her talk abruptly, exclaiming: "Let's hope it stops snowing!" There is lots of laughter in the audience. Then we sing NFU's song of morale: "A Society for All." That's NFU's dream; an inclusive and open society with no discrimination.

Later that afternoon I interview three of the volunteers from NFU. Despite the responsibilities and burdens of having a handicapped member in their close family, they've had the devotion to come together and work for a better society. They explain to me that NFU defines itself as a watchdog for the rights of people with intellectual disabilities and also aims at offering their members support and solidarity, for instance through courses and workshops. The three women talk about some disturbing tendencies in the development of the Norwegian welfare state; juridical complexities, tendencies to re-segregation in schools, lack of financial and practical support to parents, and lack of inclusive cultural activities. This is where *The Cultural Festival* comes in, they claim, not only as an arena for cultural activities *per se*, but as an arena for cultivation of *respect*. One of the three organizers in particular claims that *respect* is the main term that characterizes the goals of NFU. "The festival is about *participation*," she says; "it is about creating a space where nobody is excluded." "And this is why we want to collaborate with music therapists," she adds, "because they know how to make that happen."

The values of these women resonate with my own, and they resound when I start observing the activities, trying to understand more of the festival as an *inclusive social space*. There are four music groups to observe, with different foci, depending on the participants' strengths and interest. Group A is called "Together in Music"[1] and includes many participants with severe physical and cognitive challenges. Group B is "Singing and Playing," with a focus upon community singing, improvisation, and ensemble playing with various easy-to-play instruments. Group C is "The Rock Group," while Group D is "The Music and Theater Group." Usually two music therapists and two students work with each group.

The Theater is Right Here!

I decide to go to group D first. As I come in, one of the music therapists welcomes the participants and explains that this group is called *Music and Theater.*

"Theater?" one of the participants asks, "where is the theater?"

"It's right here!" the music therapist responds and points at the circular space created by the chairs that the participants sit on.

"Right here?" the participant chuckles.

It is an intriguing opening to a session. I feel that a scene is being set and observe how the music therapists proceed by introducing each participant in a greeting song. Over the years I have observed and used numerous greeting songs like the one I now observe. The need for such songs should not be taken for granted, but I have experienced again and again how they may transform and intensify a situation. So I watch and listen closely to see how it works this time. One of the music therapists holds a drum and sings one verse of a song to each participant, inviting them to beat the rhythm of their own name on the drum. Some of the participants join in and seem to enjoy. Others don't get the point or miss the beat. The helpers sitting in the circle in between the participants sometimes

---

[1]   This, and the three other group names, are free translations of the Norwegian terms used in the festival.

smile at each other. Sometimes they laugh mutely. There is some insecurity and uncertainty in the air. My feeling is that this specific greeting ritual doesn't really work for this group. There doesn't seem to be space enough for various ways of taking part.

The music therapists continue their work by introducing some movement activities. One of the participants is rather reluctant. We are all asked to lift our two hands, but he refuses to do so. His neighbor, who is there as a helper, persuades him to lift at least one hand. "He's probably shy," I am thinking. But is he? It looks like there is a lot of strength and humor in that guy too. I don't have to wait for long before these parts of him become more visible. While the two music therapists are introducing a movement activity, all of a sudden he stands right up, enters the circular space, and starts moving with them. Gradually he transforms the movement activity into a dance. He snaps his fingers and starts moving his hips in a spectacular way before he grabs the first music therapist with his left hand and the other with his right, while he is smiling in a peculiarly charming way to the group. All of a sudden the situation is transformed. He's taking the lead and creating a dance, using the activity the music therapists had introduced but changing it into something quite different. He's now the "director" of the musical interplay, so to say.

As I observe this I start thinking back to the many years that I've worked as a music therapist with adults with intellectual disabilities. I've often experienced similar situations. Suddenly somebody puts up a show so that everything I've planned falls apart, while something new and often more interesting emerges instead. In observing this group, the performative character of almost any music therapy session becomes clearer to me. And a drama is certainly unfolding in front of my eyes: Some of the participants are mostly doing what the music therapists seem to expect, while others are twisting and bending words and sounds and rules and movements, elaborating on what's going on, smiling and looking at each other and waiting for response. In a way, the music therapists are part of this. They seem to expect unexpected things to happen.

Bringing Music to the People

After the music and drama session I walk through the lobby. Everything is silent. I can smell the cooking in the kitchen. Preparations are being made for the big dinner tonight. I walk by the white grand piano and the instruments that the dance band is going to use. I can see a cook flirting with one of the receptionists. Maybe this belongs to this story too?

I stop outside the door to the room where group A, "Together in Music," is having a workshop. I can hear folk music. It's music for dancing. Then I hear the voice of the music therapist and I hear several group members laughing. Are they dancing in their wheelchairs? I enter the room. What meets me is a circle of people playing together, using a huge parachute as the center of action. The warmth and intensity of the atmosphere is striking. I sit down to watch and listen.

The next activity is a musical improvisation. One student sings while another plays the violin. The music therapist is walking around with the ocean drum, producing sounds; sometimes soft and sometimes quite rough. She challenges the participants by holding the drum above their heads. When the drum gets louder one of the helpers says to her neighbor participant: "This sounds like a storm at Verlandet" (an outer island of the rough North Atlantic coast). I don't know if the participant understands the words, but the two of them smile at each other.

I feel that the activity I'm observing is somewhat symbolic. The group consists of people with very serious handicaps. Most of them not only have grave cognitive problems, they have severe problems with body functions too. It is not easy for these people to come to music, either physically or socially, but the music therapist brings it to them. Sometimes the music even gets alarmingly close. Still, the participants are not just silent recipients. As I observe more of the details of the interactions in the group it becomes very clear that the participants contribute actively in many different ways. In a greeting song, for instance, one of the participants lifts his arm quite a bit higher than required and then drops it with some force and an extra humorous twist. The situation is changed, if only slightly; a fermata is created in the song and the music therapist and many of the participants giggle.

After the workshop there is a break. Later there is a big dinner with music and songs. And then time for dancing. But I don't feel like dancing. The dance band musicians know their chords and melodies and it's technically OK, but I find it a little lifeless and boring. The floor is full of life, however; it's full of participants who want to dance, and they expect students and music therapists to join in. That's also part of the ethos of the festival. I feel obliged to take a dance or two, and I enjoy it too, but then I feel that it's enough. It's been a long day and I'm getting tired.

I walk through the lobby. It's packed with people now. One of the members of "The Music and Theater Group" grabs me when I pass him. He wants to tell me something, but has no words. He points at his shirt, which is dark with various white patterns, and makes quick movements with his hand. It's pretty obvious that he wants me to acknowledge his new shirt, which I tell him that I like. He waves his hand, let the fingers run through his hair and I really don't know what's going on. I don't know his language. "There is so much he wants to tell you, but he's not able to get the words out," a female participant sitting right next to him says. "You may tell him," she says to the man – or rather, on behalf of him – "that you've been dancing with me!" She becomes his mediator, but his own media are not without messages either; listening to the grain of his voice and looking at the flow of his hands I can experience and share some of his excitement and enthusiasm.

Humor in Time

The next morning I go for a swim in the swimming pool. It is warm and pleasant and a nice contrast to the snow-covered fields outside. After breakfast I go for the workshop of Group B, "Singing and Playing." As usual, the first song is a greeting song. One of the music therapists takes the lead and presents each participant to the group. When it comes to a female participant in her fifties, the music therapist sings her name and asks if she's here, as the lyrics of the song suggest. The woman answers loudly: "No, she ain't around today" and then laughs vigorously, as the music therapist and the rest of the group do too.

Another participant, sitting in his wheelchair, looks like he's falling asleep. But when the song comes to him he's awake indeed. He sings, softly but lively, a whole verse of the song, beautifully performed. He sings to a young woman next to him, whom he knows well. The music therapist adjusts the volume and the tempo of the song to attune to his way of singing.

Then there is "Fun for four drums," the classic Nordoff composition, or rather, an abbreviated and simplified version of it which now seems to be part of an oral tradition of music therapy songs that many Norwegian music therapists use. One elderly man is eager to play, but he is never on the beat. He is always too early. He looks pleased, though. He laughs and seems to be proud of his achievement. Didn't he notice the rhythmical discrepancies? Later in the session I observe that probably he does. When playing piano together with the music therapist he has a strong sense of rhythm and phrasing, so maybe the rhythmical discrepancies in his playing in "Fun for four drums" were part of the fun? I talk with the music therapist about this afterwards. She laughs and says: "These participants have been living in institutions most of their life and they have been trained to be so conformist. It's quite important – and fun too – to give space for these kinds of humorous actions 'going across' the musical expectations."

Humor seems to be one of the main points on this group's agenda. It is also present in the music therapist's way of leading the group; she seems to be playing with discrepancies in time, space, and sound. The songs are simple indeed, with quite uncomplicated structures. But the use of them is sophisticated; there are changes in tempi and volumes and a lot of creative use of rubato and fermatas. And the participants join in; sometimes they play many beats instead of one, or they are loud when they should be silent, or fast when the music is slow. It is quite enjoyable.

With a Little Help from Your Friends

I left the hotel for the neighboring community center where Group C, "The Rock Group" of the festival, is practicing. I had heard rumors from the day before: Some wild subversive musicing is going on in this group.

Yesterday, one of the music therapists had arranged a song which the participants had found a little difficult to play. The music therapist had been helping and advising the various band members about how to play the drums, the synthesizer, the base, and the guitars. There was a little "choir" involved too. It should have been interesting, but it didn't really work. The synthesizer player was just silent; he didn't join in at all. And one of the guitarists had problems with his part, he didn't quite get it. The music therapist kneeled down to help him. In the resulting silence the synthesizer player woke up, seized the moment and pressed the button for some pre-programmed synthesizer music. Some strong rhythms came out of the loud-speakers, and loudly too. Immediately, everybody were on their feet, singing and dancing. The "mutiny" didn't last for ever. After a while the dancing died out and things turned back to normal. Again the group tried to play the song arranged by the music therapist. And again the synthesizer player was silent and the guitarist found his part too difficult. Once more the music therapist knelt down to help him, and once more a moment of silence occurred. This time the synthesizer player pushed no buttons for automatic music; he started to play the national anthem on the keyboard. Everybody joined him instantly, singing loudly and marching around!

This was the story I'd heard from the day before. When I came in there were no subversive activities going on. It was an unplugged experience this time. The group was singing "Evening song for you and me," with the striking opening line "The pig stands and howls in the silent night's chill (even though there's no sign that anybody's gonna kill)."[2] The song – a mixture of Norwegian folk music and American country music – was very popular in Norway at this point. Afterwards the group starts practicing a new song for the band: "All I have to do is dream" (the Everly Brothers song). It's a simple and nice little tune, very well-known for the participants from a humorous ice cream commercial on one of the Norwegian television channels. "Good choice of song," I think, while observing the efforts of getting it together.

It is not easy. Some of the participants lose track of what their role in the song is. The synthesizer player and the guitarist become passive, looking out the window or not looking anywhere special. Are they listening? One of the drummers seems to be able to keep track of what he's supposed to do, synchronizing with the others and joining in as well as he can. His co-drummer, however, is struggling with the beat. Some of the singers in the little "choir" are having a more enjoyable experience; they move around, show off, and stand out in more than one way. There's a rich variety of initiatives and responses involved, so rich that it almost gets cacophonic. People seem to be moving in many directions, but strangely enough the song keeps going and never falls apart completely.

---

[2] My translation of "Grisen står og hyler i den stille kveld. (Han skal ikkje slaktast, men hyler likevel)." Lyrics by Ragnar Hovland. Music by Odd Nordstoga.

Performing the Community

I have shared glimpses from my first round of observations in the four music groups of this cultural festival. I make a second round too. I see how "The Music and Theater Group" work with a fairytale and I'm struck by the talents in gesticulation that some of the participants demonstrate. I go back to "Together in Music" and see how they continue to explore musical companionship through sounds and movements. "Singing and Playing" is still deep in musical humor when I come back, but something has changed too. The music therapists allow for more silence and there seems to be more *listening* involved in the activities.

In "The Rock Group," where silences could lead to "mutinies," things really have changed when I come back. Every member of the group is now able to take part, in some way or another. The participant on the synthesizer is improvising, following the basic beat. Both drum players are more on track, one of them also starting to improvise. The guitar player is also part of it now, in the B section of a song where he's supposed to strum the strings to a simple but salient syncopated pattern. He smiles; waits for the occasion, strums, waits, smiles, strums. He is proudly taking part in a way I haven't often seen him. "The Rock Group" has really been able to pull it together. It almost looks like a miracle, but there has been some hard work involved, I know.

The third day is the final day of the festival. In the meeting of instructors the second day, the organizers had underlined that they wanted the final "concert" not to be a conventional one, but a performance that could represent closure and completion.

It's time to say goodbye. The MC of the closing ceremony is one of the volunteers from NFU that I had interviewed. She expresses appreciation of the efforts made by all participants, helpers and instructors and she claims that the festival has been characterized by *joy, communication*, and *collaboration.* "Thank you, and please come back next year!" she says and is met by applause and enthusiastic shouts. Then we sing one of NFU's songs: "Come let's create a new world."[3] The sight and sound of this volunteer singing this song fascinates me. She is a mild, middle-aged, middleclass woman. She doesn't look like a romantic revolutionary. But you could see in her eyes that she's seen things. She's seen ignorance and injustice, and she wants to fight it.

After the introduction and our enthusiastic community singing, the various groups present themselves for the audience. First, "The Rock Group" walks on stage. The members find their places behind the instruments and microphones.

---

[3] My translation of "Kom la oss skape ei ny verd." After the ceremony I ask the NFU representative about the origin of this song. She tells me that she thinks it is a union song from the 1930s, about equity and solidarity: "It's a song that we found appropriate for our needs, so we translated it [from Dano-Norwegian to New Norwegian] and started to use it." I'm struck by the pragmatic attitude and ask myself if it is an expression of the view that oppressed groups share interests.

The music therapist is there, helping out and checking that everything is working. When everybody is in place he carefully makes sure that the amplifiers and micro- phones are working and that the sound is OK. This is a practical necessity, but it seems to be something more too. As he inspects these practical matters he is at the same time checking if everybody in the group is OK, helping the group members to calm down and to make themselves ready.

When the group starts playing it sounds quite good; it starts with the cowbell, then the djembes. After a while the drums join in and finally the bass, the guitar, and the synthesizer. It looks good too, since the musicians clearly enjoy the situation. In an improvised section three of the participants create solos on a djembe. It's a sequence full of energy, humor and unexpected micro-events and it receives lots of applause. In the B section of the song I watch the guitar player carefully. How is this setting working for him? Not as well as in the workshop, I realize. He loses some of his concentration and plays vaguely and quite softly, not at all with the power and precision I'd seen in the workshop. This may be the exception here; the others in the group seem to be doing fine. When the music is over, the group is given a big hand from the audience. One of the drum players leaves his chair, enters central stage and makes an elegant leap for the audience. Then one of the singers takes over and sends her greetings to the audience: "Thanks. Thanks a lot! Thank you everybody!"

"Together in Music" enters with all their wheel chairs. They need quite some time to get ready and the instructors and helpers and participants use the time they need. This builds a positive atmosphere. As a member of the audience I get time to see who's in the group and what instrument each one is going to play. The quiet and slow process in a way prepares me for the music to come. I get the time I need to become curious and to build expectations.

The music starts with one of the music therapy students playing a steady pattern on the djembe. Through use of body language the participants are invited to join in with their own sound, one after the other. After a while the student starts singing, without words, and by this introduces a new idea. The music therapist brings in a microphone and some of the members of the group are given the possibility to add their voice. She walks around and supports and encourages the participants to play or sing. Then the pattern is reversed. Through use of signs and body language the music therapist communicates to one of the participants that it is time to stop. Then she approaches the next participant. One by one the participants are given signs of silence. The group sound diminishes until there are no sounds left. There is a pause and then there is applause. I'm quite moved and also left wondering what performing means for this group of participants.

"Singing and Playing" come in and start with a rain jingle. "At least it's not snowing anymore" somebody says and many laugh. The jingle is part of the performance but it also prepares the group for the more demanding parts of it. The group starts singing a spring song. The "No-she-ain't-around-today-lady" stands up. Obviously, she has been given the responsibility to introduce the piece. "I'm nervous" I can hear her tell the music therapist, who smiles mildly and encourages her to keep going. The lady presents the piece for the audience, receives her applause and sits down smiling. The music starts softly. The pianist begins to improvise, with the participant of the "too-early-on-the-beat-humor" playing beautifully together with her, with perfect timing. Improvisations on flutes and percussion come in. It sounds like a spring in the forest and we all join in and sing a verse of the song. After that there is a solo on the chimes. It's soft and it's beautiful. Thinking it over it's not only the sound that I find beautiful; maybe it's just as much the participants' faces and the concentration and the pleasure that I read on them?

Finally, "The Music and Theater Group" comes, in a procession. The group members enter the stage to Billy Joel's "Uptown Girl," which some of the younger participants in the audience obviously know well. Again, I feel that the opening activity has been very cleverly selected: It introduces the group and it's a simple but activating experience that eases the group's challenge of getting the performance started. After the procession one of the music therapists explains for the audience how the group has been working. I understand that the performance is really a completion in this case, in a very concrete sense.

The participants present the different characters that they have been playing, in their costumes. Some of the characters just walk forward when presented, give a bow, and receive applause. Others give a bow and a show. After this the group plays one of the songs they have been using in the workshops. I sit and watch the djembe group. One of the participants is quite old. I've known him for more than 20 years and I know that he cannot see very much anymore, so how is he actually able to understand what's going on and when it's his turn to play? He probably sees nothing of the quite clear and lively conducting that the music therapist performs. I watch him and notice that he always starts a beat or two late. Obviously he listens carefully and joins in as soon as he's able to. I can see how he sits waiting, concentrated and eager to participate. I'm moved by this music, not only because of what I hear but because of moments of sound and gesture linked to a shared history.

We've heard beautiful songs of spring and hope. The snow is gone and the *Cultural Festival* is over. It may have been a society for all who were there, but soon there will be no signs of this festival in this little town. The participants will be heading back for the municipalities where they live. What could they bring with them back to their own local communities? Before they leave, some of the participants approach the organizers and start inquiring about next year's festival. It tells me something about the value of it, but maybe also about its limitations. We need to ask: What are these people's possibilities for musical participation in the contexts of their everyday life?

Chapter 10

Reflection

Musical Participation, Social Space, and Everyday Ritual

Brynjulf Stige

Art is not a mirror held up to reality, but a hammer with which to shape it.

Bertolt Brecht

The "commonality" which is found in community need not be a uniformity. It does not clone behaviour or ideas. It is a commonality of forms (ways of behaving) whose content (meanings) may vary considerably among its members. The triumph of community is to so contain this variety that its inherent discordance does not subvert the apparent coherence which is expressed by its boundaries.

Anthony Cohen

Politics of Participation

Music therapists often work with groups that have been marginalized in society and they therefore encounter people and situations where problems of participation are serious and far-reaching. Obviously, this is so in contexts with problems of poverty and other forms of explicit social exclusion, but if you take a closer look this is so also in relatively well-functioning welfare states, such as the Norwegian society where I live and work. I live in a country with politics that are supposed to support the value of equal possibilities, but there are cracks in the polished surface, including discrimination of groups that do not belong to the established "we." These cracks are all but uninteresting and unimportant. They are critical for those who experience them and reflect deficiencies in the system as well as in the humanity of dominating groups.

One such crack that has attracted my attention is the segregation of people with various disabilities from the ordinary musical activities of many Norwegian communities. I have had the privilege to be involved in several practical projects focusing upon the rights of people that have experienced such exclusion (Kleive and Stige, 1988; Stige, 1993; 2002). Rephrasing a saying from the feminist movement, this work has made me aware of how *the situational is political*. How people interact and make music in a given context may have political origins and outcomes. A case that has stimulated me to revisit and rethink this theme is the *Cultural Festival* for adults with intellectual disabilities that I described in the narrative preceding this chapter.

I studied this festival in 2005 and 2006, through participant observation, interviews, and video recordings of workshops and performances. In spring 2005 I interviewed three representatives of NFU, a Norwegian organization for individuals with intellectual disabilities and their families. I then learnt that these representatives asserted *respect* to be the central value informing their own engagement for the festival and that they considered this value a central guide to the formation of the political goals of NFU. If there is respect, society and the local communities will be more inclusive, they argued. In conclusion they claimed that "the *Cultural Festival* is all about *participation*; it is about creating a space where nobody is excluded." The NFU representatives made it clear that their appraisal was that the profession of music therapy seemed to share these values and perspectives and that this was a major reason why NFU wanted to collaborate with music therapists in developing this festival. My goal as researcher in relation to the festival could hardly be to verify or falsify these claims. Rather, I decided I wanted to develop a better understanding of processes of participation as they would unfold in this festival.

I have previously discussed the notion of participation, with the objective of stimulating more systematic reflection on its relevance in music therapy theory (Stige, 2006b). In reading the music therapy literature, I discovered that most music therapy researchers employing the notion have taken it for granted, not giving it any specific conceptual consideration, and they have for a large part concentrated on participation as "joining in," that is; taking part in a pre-defined activity. Joining in, or behaving in ways adjusted to a context, is of course valuable in many ways. It can lead to learning, to the experience of being accepted by others, etc. But this is a very limited notion of participation. What about the cases when joining in is unachievable or unacceptable for the individual, due to differences in skills, interests, or values? There must be alternatives in between joining in and not taking part. If we think of participation as mutual and collaborative activity, there is more space for diversity in production of *communal experience* and there is also potentially space for *political action* (citizen participation) (Stige, 2006b).

A notion of participation could be linked quite closely to the notion of music. When Christopher Small (1998, p. 9) treats the word "music" as a verb he proposes that when we music we *take part* in a musical performance. The notion of performance that Small then employs is a broad one; he talks about the "performance of relationships" (his work is explicitly informed by Bateson's ecology of mind). In Small's perspective, musical meaning is not immanent and originating from the structures of musical works, it emerges through collaborative action in context. When music is considered participation in performance, discussions on the notion of performance are inevitable, and this theme will be discussed in detail in Part VI of this book. In this essay I will focus upon another aspect, namely how the possibilities for musical participation are negotiated in context. A brief detour to an experience I had when writing the essay may give us a starting point:

> *I find myself in the Grieg Hall, listening to the Bergen Philharmonic Orchestra performing Mozart's* Requiem. *I think of the work being performed as a great one and the orchestra plays well, so I enjoy the performance. My eyes wander back and forth, from instrument to instrument, musician to musician, group to group. My ears turn to various parts and take pleasure in how the sounds mingle together and establish larger wholes. Of course I'm not listening with my ears only. Memories, ideas, and emotional responses accompany the sounds that I hear. And my body is central to it all. As the music at points grow strong and rhythmically driving, I start tapping my foot, without even knowing. "Highly inappropriate behavior in a concert hall, and especially in relation to a requiem," my neighbor perhaps thinks. She whispers, but not softly: "Stop that tapping!" I so do, and I'm back to the silent participation that is expected of a member of the audience in this context.*

This experience from a classical concert exemplifies an episode of silenced participation. I was going beyond the space that was given me by the conventions of this context. This would not be easy for me to change or challenge. I did not even bother to try. I knew that if I wanted to be more active than what the membership of a classical audience allows for, I am lucky enough to have access to the resources required to search out other events and contexts – such as for instance a jazz concert – where more active and involved styles of audience participation are accepted and even encouraged. But not every person has access to the resources that enable them to search out contexts that fit their participatory needs and tendencies, and various problems of participation may be linked to discrepancies between personal qualifications and the expectations of a given community. This illuminates how such problems usually are linked to values and sociocultural processes of exclusion, repression, and silencing.

In studying processes of participation in the *Cultural Festival*, I therefore will not focus entirely upon the acts and possible intentions of individuals, but also upon negotiations among participants and between participants and music therapists. In addition I will reflect upon the relationships between the music workshops and broader community contexts. Much of the analysis will be based upon "readings" of one selected video-recording of a greeting song used by the group "Singing and Playing." This will be supplemented by material from field notes based upon participant observation and developed through use of relevant literature. The approach to the analysis of the empirical material is thus interpretive and – as mentioned in the Introduction – the case study is informed by Charles Taylor's (1985) discussion of research as *aspect seeing* and Kirsten Hastrup's (1999) discussion of *knowledge as produced in communities*. Instead of picturing the festival "as it is," the notions I will develop hopefully could articulate *specific aspects* of the workshops studied, aspects that – to my knowledge – have not previously found an expression.

In the following I will produce three various interpretations; participation as style of self-presentation, participation as co-creation of social space, and participation as ritual negotiation. According to the account given above, these interpretations capture aspects that gradually came into my awareness when studying video recordings of the festival. The various interpretations are partly re-descriptions of the same situations, as continued reflection, theoretical studies, and discussion with colleagues reformed my understanding.

First Interpretation: Participation as Style of Self-presentation

As participant observer in the various music workshops of the festival I was fascinated about how the music therapists and participants were collaborating in establishing the scene of the play and work that constituted the workshops of music therapy. I was immediately reminded about Goffman's (1959/1990) dramaturgical theory of social interaction. Human encounters may be understood as participation in "dramas" with certain "scripts" where our actions relate to available roles and constitute a presentation of self in the given situation.

In the narrative preceding this essay (Chapter 9) I described the first seconds of the first workshop I observed in the 2005 festival, where a participant and a music therapist negotiated about what "Music and Theater" could mean. I described this opening interaction as intriguing. Still, it turned out that the greeting song ritual that followed did not work particularly well. Why was this situation not working for these participants? And which criteria do I actually use when evaluating this? As I participated in the festival, questions like these were articulated only as vague thoughts and feelings, but they became clarified during my observations and influenced the analysis and interpretation of the empirical material.

One way of describing the problem of this greeting ritual would be that it was not spacious enough; it did not accommodate unexpected events very well. And unpredicted acts seemed to be central to this festival. Some "breaking of rules" and "diversified action" happened in all the workshops that I observed. In the movement activity following the greeting song in "The Music and Theater Group," for instance, I had observed a "shy guy" who did not really take part in the movements proposed by the music therapists. His participation was silent, until all of a sudden he stood right up, entered the center of action, took the leadership, and transformed the movements into a dance. Similar, if less dramatic, diversifications were added in the greeting song in "Together in Music," where one of the participants lifted his arm a little more than the others, let it go with an extra twist and humorous force, and broke the beat so that the movement of the song had to halt for a moment. Likewise, the play and work of "Singing and Playing" was abundant with humorous diversifications like this. And in the "The Rock Group" there had even been tendencies toward "subversive action." At times, some of the participants would break out and lead in completely different directions than those originally suggested by the music therapists.

Any description of the participation in this festival would need to account for these *participatory diversifications*, events when the participation of individuals (or sub-groups) was not conventional, but introduced something new and different to the situation. We would not be able to understand these diversifications, however, if we did not have some concept of *conventional participation*. As I suggested in the comments to the vignette from my experience of Mozart's *Requiem* in the Grieg Hall, conventional participation is relative to context. What is expected of you in one situation may be off beam in the next. When we take part in an activity, we do assess what the available roles and the rules of the game are. In the workshops of the festival that I studied, these roles and rules were often defined by the songs and activities.

The term "conventional" is not used negatively here. I am not referring to connotations such as "conformist" or "conservative," rather to connotations such as "usual" and "traditional." As suggested above, the *Cultural Festival* is a context where participation is diversified. Unusual and unpredictable contributions are quite common. But conventional participation is not rare in this context either, as when participants try to play the basic beat on a drum or decide to take up the microphone to sing a song. And the fact that participation may be conventional

Figure 10.1   Conventional participation as high achievement. Photo: Ragnar Albertsen

does not mean that it is flat or without engagement or enthusiasm. Participants may well internalize the values and rules of the situation and be expressive through use of the involved conventions.

One aspect of the idea that participants may be expressive through personal elaboration within musical and social conventions has been explored by the ethnomusicologist Charles Keil (1994), in an essay on the complexities of the "how-we-play-what-we-play." Keil's focus is on the ongoing musical process when a group of musicians play together and he claims that when we play and listen to music it is often the *participatory discrepancies* that interest us. Participatory discrepancies may be described as the "out-of time-and-out-of-tune" aspects of the music-making. In line with this, Keil suggests that much live music-making is not mainly about the development of advanced musical motifs and structures, it is about "getting into the groove" through advanced play with participatory discrepancies. In the *Cultural Festival* I observed many instances of what I would describe as participatory discrepancies, although it was sometimes necessary to discriminate between situations where participants were searching for the tune or the beat and when they actively played with discrepancies and variations after having found it. For many of the participants in this festival, conventional participation is a high achievement (Figure 10.1).

The description so far suggests that the participants of the *Cultural Festival* explored different styles of self-presentation, ranging from conventional participation to various participatory diversifications. Based on observations of the various workshops of the festival, an analysis of the video material, and consultation with relevant literature, I will offer a description of five different styles of self-presentation:

- Non-participation (not being there).
- Silent participation (being there but not joining in).
- Conventional participation (joining in but not standing out).
- Adventurous participation (standing out but not going across).
- Eccentric participation (going across).

I can briefly explicate each category.

Non-participation involves "not being there," which could at least take on two different forms; literally not being in the setting (leaving or never arriving), or physically being there but with no sign of being psychologically and socially present. The first alternative was very rare in this *Cultural Festival*, possibly because there was already a selection involved; the participants had chosen to come to the festival and to be part of one of the music groups there. While this festival, then, did not provide me with much information on this type of non-participation, the category may be quite important in other contexts of music therapy. (How much of a free and active choice is participation in music therapy for people with intellectual disabilities? What options exist for making real choices available and when and how should non-participation be acknowledged?)[1] The second form of non-participation was observed occasionally in the festival, when some of the participants would withdraw, look out the window, take a walk in the room, etc. This of course at times would influence the other participants, so that one could imagine complex patterns of "being there by not being there."

Silent participation involves being there but not joining in or taking part in any conventional way. In contrast to the passive form of non-participation described above, silent participation involves giving some impression of being mentally and socially present. In the case of watching or not watching, this is usually pretty obvious. It is more difficult to know whether or not a silent participant is listening, even though we usually have a feeling whether or not this is taking place. This feeling is probably based on observations of posture, body language, and mimics.

Conventional participation involves joining in and performing what is expected in the situation, in one of the roles available (say singing, playing, dancing, or conducting). Conventional participation involves imitation of and/ or synchronization with what others are or have been doing. Some degree of amplification or personal embellishment may be involved, however, such as in the participatory discrepancies described above.

Adventurous participation is different from conventional participation in that the individual's contribution is standing out. It is not just an embellishment of what would be expected, it is a deviation that contributes with something essentially new in the situation. It could be described as a divergence that requires considerable active adjustment by the other people present in the social-musical situation. Several examples have already been given, such as the contribution by the "shy guy" in "The Music and Theater Group," whose participation in the movement activity prescribed by the music therapists was silent, until he unexpectedly entered the center of action and transformed the activity into a dance.

Eccentric participation is more dramatic than adventurous participation. It goes across what is happening in the group. An example was given in the narrative, where one participant all of a sudden introduced a completely different song than what the music therapists had introduced. Eccentric musical participation of this type goes beyond transforming what is already happening and it can rarely be ignored. It will usually either establish a new center of mutual attention and action or it will break up the existing structures. In the first case, leadership is challenged. In the second case the coherence of the group is challenged.

---

[1]   See e.g. Warner's (2005) discussion of such questions in relation to music therapy with adults with serious learning problems and behavioral problems.

Commentary

The five forms of participation in music that I propose do not represent discrete categories. Non-participation, for instance, may gradually be transformed into silent
participation which again may turn into conventional participation. Elaborated
conventional participation at some point becomes adventurous, and if escalated
further may turn into eccentric participation. The process is not necessarily
linear, however. As we have seen, silent participation may at times turn into say
adventurous participation. And eccentric participation, at the extreme, may turn
into non-participation. Together the forms of participation represent a repertoire
of possibilities, as illustrated in Figure 10.2.

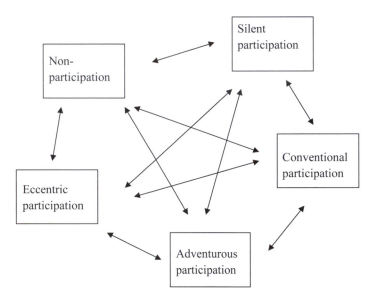

Figure 10.2   Forms of participation as a repertoire of possibilities

To think of participation as *mutual process* (Stige, 2006b) has implications
for the understanding of the five forms of participation that I have described. For
instance; in relation to silent participation the question is not just whether or not
the participant is watching or listening, but whether or not his or her presence
is witnessed by other people in the situation. Similarly, we could describe non-
participation and conventional, adventurous, and eccentric participation as mutual
process leading to co-created events. This will become clearer in the next section.

Second Interpretation: Participation as Co-creation of Social Space

At this point, it could be suggested that the ability to deal with a diversity of forms of participation, ranging from that of persons who are silent to that of persons who introduce completely new directions of action and thus challenge the music therapist's leadership and/or the coherence of the group itself, is very relevant in relation to the values described by the organizers of the festival; *respect* and *inclusiveness* in relation to *participation*.

The observations made suggest that the music therapists worked quite flexibly in order to achieve this. Through selection of adequate musical material, sensitive affect attunement when approaching each participant, flexible shifts in the role taken, and responsive and respectful use of humor, they were able to contribute to the formation of situations that would enable each participant to participate in a way meaningful for him or her.

This list of therapeutic actions already suggests that the perspective implied in the five categories developed above needs to be expanded: The categories "punctuate" the flow of acts and events by paying attention to the self-presentation of each participant but they do not clarify the interactional sequences that precede and surround this manifestation. In other words; we need a conceptual framework that enables us to understand and talk about how these moments are *co-created*.

One central observation made is that most music therapists in most sessions of the festival were willing to let scripts go, activities go, and even their roles as leaders of the group go, as long as there was mutual focus of attention and emotional entrainment in the group. Examples even include moments of "musical mutiny," where the music therapists accepted that one participant abruptly introduced a new song in the middle of another activity, as long as this new song was taken up by the others in the group. In situations where eccentric contributions were not taken up by the group, the music therapists would take a more active role in re-establishing a focus of attention and action.[2]

This way of describing the workshops reveals that what may look very different at first glance, such as e.g. silent participation and adventurous participation, may contribute in comparable ways in a given situation, if our focus is not just various self-presentations, but the co-creation of social space. If the self-presentation of therapists and other "helpers" is just as crucial to examine as that of the participants, we need to understand more of the collaborative dimension of participation. I have chosen to use ritual theory in the exploration of this, since rituals may be understood as co-created processes where individuals take various roles that supplement each other.

The idea that ritual theory may inform music therapy is not new, as exemplified by the work of Carolyn Kenny and Even Ruud who both build upon the anthropological literature of ritual studies, in the tradition pioneered by van Gennep (1909/1999)

---

[2]   It is, by the way, interesting to note that eccentric participation at times seemed to energize the groups, possibly because of the antinomian element that had been added.

and later developed by Victor Turner (1967a, 1967b, 1969) and numerous other researchers. Kenny has been especially interested in relationships between myths and rituals (1982) and has supplemented this with discussions of play, creativity, and aesthetics (1989, 1994/2006, 2002a, 2002b). Ruud (1991, 1995) has taken interest in the liminal phase of *rites de passage*, exploring the possibilities for communitas and change that they may embody. Both Kenny and Ruud, then, describe rituals as *supportive contexts* that may enable communal, creative, and critical processes. I will follow in Kenny's and Ruud's spirit, but not in their letter, since I have chosen to take a slightly different path when exploring rituals in music therapy. I will be concentrating on the sociological tradition of ritual studies, as pioneered by Durkheim (1912/1995) and Goffman (1967) and later developed by Collins (2004). This is a tradition that has insisted on secular interpretations of rituals, with less focus upon ritual as special occasion and ceremony and more upon ritual as an everyday activity essential for the construction of social life.

I find Collins's (2004) elaboration of Goffman's concept of *interaction rituals* to be especially relevant for the understanding of the workshops of the *Cultural Festival*. According to Collins, interaction rituals are characterized by *mutual foci of attention* and *increased emotional energy among participants* and they build *community* and *group membership*. In order to explore the relevance of these notions for appreciation of the practice that I have studied, I will revisit some situations from the workshops of the festival. Let us start with a closer look at one of the greeting rituals that started almost all sessions for the groups participating in the festival.

The greeting ritual that we will examine is a song used by the group "Singing and Playing," in a session in the second day of the festival. This is the group where in one session one of the participants answered "No, she ain't around today" when the music therapist sang a verse of the greeting song and asked if she was there. This response produced lots of laughter in the group. My interpretation is that this humor was an acknowledgement of the line delivered by this woman rather than a critique of the simple and somewhat naïve lyrics of the song. Asking somebody if she is there may be seen as a redundant and rather stupid action, but only if practical information is your focus of attention. The function of this song seemed to be of a different kind.

While one music therapist accompanies on guitar or piano, the other walks around in the open space created by the semicircle of participants. She looks at each person with anticipation. As she starts to sing her eyes wander around, sometimes focusing upon one participant, sometimes upon another seated somewhere else in the room. As an observer I cannot help but being pulled into the situation: Who is going to have the next verse? It's Maria. The music therapist approaches her and addresses her with words, sounds, and movements. The therapist slows down her singing, to adjust to the singing of Maria, who knows the words and the tune well but joins in with a somewhat different pace. Both persons stretch out their hands and they touch each other delicately. In this position, with the music therapist kneeling and Maria sitting with her hands planted in the open hands of the therapist, they sing a slow and sensitive version of the verse that the conventions of this greeting ritual have assigned for this moment. As they sing, the surrounding participants turn their heads and bodies toward Maria and the music therapist. They watch closely, they seem to listen carefully, and they smile (Figure 10.3).

Figure 10.3   Greeting ritual establishing bodily co-presence, mutual focus, and shared mood. Photo: Ragnar Albertsen

The above is an example of a partially scripted ritual; the song was well-known to the participants and provided a frame that allowed them to predict the forthcoming actions to some degree and to contribute in active ways. Following the logic of interaction ritual theory, this pre-established structure is not the central element of the ritual, however. It is a supportive arrangement, a scaffolding so to speak. The central ingredients of the ritual are bodily co-presence, "barrier" to outsiders, mutual focus of attention, and shared mood (Collins, 2004, pp. 47–101). Let us take a look at how these ingredients are established in this specific case.

Bodily co-presence is established at two levels. First, the group is assembled in a room and seated in a semicircle, and are thus visibly present for each other in a very clear and orderly way.[3] Second, the structure of the song is arranged so that each verse gives attention to one participant at the time. The music therapist then

---

[3]   This arrangement also created the required barriers to others, in a flexible way. The doors of the workshops of the Cultural Festival were to some degree open. People could walk into the room, but they would generally not be considered participants in a workshop before they took a seat in the semicircle.

intensifies the bodily co-presence by approaching the person in question, kneeling down in front of her. A rationale for kneeling down could be that this establishes eye-contact at the same horizontal level and thus could promote interaction at an equal level. But, as Figure 10.3 demonstrated, the therapist at times puts herself in a lower position than that of the other person. This could be arbitrary, but it could also be interpreted as an act communicating deference. This would suggest that part of the process involves what we could call "sanctification" of the other participant's face. As mentioned earlier, Goffman (1955/1967) argued that one's face is a sacred thing in ordinary face-to-face interaction. By exaggerating everyday procedures in greeting the other, the music therapist could be interpreted as attempting to approve the other's face. And it seems to work, I hardly observed that the act was interpreted as over-the-top and thus "sacrilegious."

How is the mutual focus of attention established in the greeting ritual of this song? Before answering this, we may halt a second to reflect upon what the mutual focus of attention in fact is. Is it the person introduced by the lyrics of the song or is it the shared activity? It seems to be both; the process is *social-musical*. To address one person at a time ensures that he or she gets involved and engaged in the activity and the group's attention is drawn to the person in question. But it is not just the person; the person's participation in the musical activity is essential, both for the music therapist and for the other participants in the group.

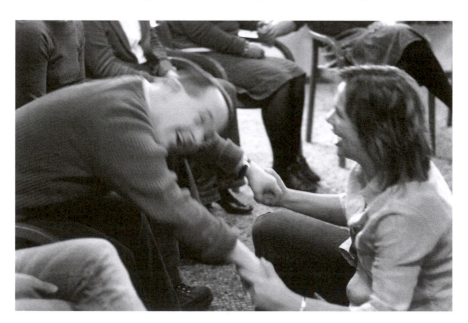

Figure 10.4   Greeting ritual developing into adventurous participation. Photo: Ragnar Albertsen

This observation relates to the next point in Collins's list of interaction ritual ingredients; the establishment of shared mood. He describes interaction rituals as "emotion transformers" (Collins, 2004, p. 92) which could, for instance, turn negative emotions into positive ones. In the case of this group, emotions were transformed in the sequences that each participant's verse represented. With Maria, a certain delicacy was introduced. The music therapist slowed down the tempo of the song and also sang more softly, in order to adjust to Maria's contributions. With John, it was a completely different story.

John sat patiently, but with visible eagerness, waiting for his turn. When the music therapist came to his verse, the song and the situation was immediately transformed. John grabbed the hands of the music therapist and initiated a rocking movement and an acceleration of the speed of the song. The music therapist attuned her contribution by increasing the volume of her singing and the situation was energized considerably (Figure 10.4).

With use of the categories developed in the previous section we could call John's contribution *adventurous,* but we must also pay attention to how others in the situation attune to the adventure. In this case the music therapist allowed the adventure, perhaps to some degree anticipated it, and accommodated it quite actively. Both were adjusting their participation in relation to each other. And it did not stop with increased speed and volume of the song and rocking movements from where John was sitting on the chair. All of a sudden he stood up and hugged the music therapist warmly and enthusiastically, and for a long time (Figure 10.5).

Figure 10.5   The pleasure of adventurous participation. Photo: Ragnar Albertsen

The little sequence that I have described here exemplifies that even though a ritual may be scripted, in this case through use of a well-known song, the participants in a group can only to some degree predict forthcoming actions and events. There is always room for improvisation and more or less unexpected episodes. There is, of course, immense variation among rituals concerning the space allowed for spontaneous events. A classical concert with performance of works such as Mozart's *Requiem* and a music therapy activity such as the greeting song described here are probably at different poles of a scale. In the concert hall only the conductor and the soloists are usually allowed space for anything close to adventurous participation. As a member of the audience the space is limited. To tap your foot to the music would in most cases be considered to be too active and spontaneous. The greeting song of "Singing and Playing" is certainly different. The performance of it seems to be designed to give space for each participant, and the attitude of the "conductor" (the music therapist) is to warmly welcome personal and spontaneous contributions from anyone.

The broad range of possible styles of self-presentations in music described earlier therefore does not necessarily imply fragmented situations with a series of individual foci so that things fall apart. If integrated in interaction rituals, these various styles of self-presentation may become part of the co-creation of a more inclusive social space. *Participatory spaciousness* implies that there is room for unity beyond uniformity. While Anthony Cohen (1985/1993, p. 20) clarified that community may involve commonality of ways of behaving combined with meanings that vary among members, the interaction rituals of the music therapy workshops described here illuminate a specific form of participatory spaciousness, involving variance in behavior constituting relationships that to varying degrees imply shared meanings.

Third Interpretation: Participation as Ritual Negotiation

Sometimes, rituals are spontaneous, created in the spur of the moment. In the group "Together in Music," for instance, similar rituals as those described above – with mutual adjustment of tempo, tonality, timbre and volume – were developed through improvisation, on the basis of unprompted sounds or movements from some of the participants. Scripts (and stereotyped actions) are not what constitute rituals. Mutual focus of attention and emotional entrainment is much more central. As mentioned above, scripts may function as scaffolding, as a container for actions and emotions.

In this case study five styles of self-presentation in music have been described as a repertoire of participatory possibilities and the shared task of all participants (including helpers and music therapists) has been described as that of creating an inclusive social space. This seems to have the potential of making interaction rituals work in ways that combine each individual's need for spaciousness with the group's need for mutual focus and attention. This does not mean that all possibilities are equal at any point of time or that every participant could move freely between every form of participation. Therefore, the description requests that we approach the question of describing what a successful ritual would be in this context. In other words; we need to reflect upon *ritual outcomes*. As a step in this direction, I will examine incidents of *ritual intensification* and the issue of *situational stratification* in the music therapy activities.

Collins links ritual intensification to the establishment of a mutual focus of attention and the development of shared emotion:

> Once the bodies are together, there may take place a process of intensification of shared experience, which Durkheim called collective effervescence, and the formation of collective conscience or collective consciousness. We might refer to it as a condition of heightened intersubjectivity. (Collins, 2004, p. 35)

Durkheim (1912/1995, p. 217) used the metaphor of "electricity" to describe the extraordinary degree of exaltation that a ritual can create. Shared emotions intensify as they are expressed through rhythmic entrainment. As Clayton, Sager and Will (2003, p. 22) suggest, there is a tradition for sophisticated work with rhythmic entrainment in music therapy, e.g. through the improvisational approach pioneered by Nordoff and Robbins. This approach involves musicing where the therapist's music imitates and incorporates the sounds and rhythms of the client. If performed with respect and sensitivity, this could lead to an affective change that makes the client more willing to enter into musical collaboration and eventually a therapeutic relationship.[4] The music therapists working in this particular *Cultural Festival* all worked in a tradition informed by this approach. In the group situation, imitation of and synchronization with each individual's contributions were supplemented by even more intensifying strategies. Individual and dyadic improvisations were typically interspersed with sequences of community singing, often with rhythmic movements, which obviously intensified the situation. Also, the music therapist would sometimes enthusiastically exaggerate his or her response to the participant's contribution, through "amplified" mimics and/or sounds, see Figure 10.6.

These forms of ritual intensification seemed to be used in order to help participants to move from one form of participation to another, say from silent participation to conventional participation. Or it was used to intensify the participation within one form (in direction of more elaborate and expressive conventional participation, for instance). Quite often these strategies of ritual

---

[4]   This is a way of working that lately has been put in a theoretical context by Trevarthen and Malloch in their discussion of *communicative musicality*, with focus upon the mutuality of "mirroring" capacities and activities in human communication. See (Trevarthen and Malloch, 2000; Malloch and Trevarthen, 2009). See also Pavlicevic's discussion in Part IV of this book.

intensification worked. Clients were encouraged to take part and to take part with more emotional energy. There is, however, a therapeutic dilemma to be discussed in relation to this: If the music therapists are very active in intensifying a ritual, they also run the risk of putting themselves in the center of action and attention, which according to interaction ritual theory could have negative effects for other participants with more limited expressive resources. Collins (2004, pp. 102–40) discusses the problem of stratification of emotional energy in rituals. "Energy stars" may use a ritual to "charge their batteries" of emotional energy, while participants who find themselves in subordinate roles may experience the same ritual as an energy drainer.

This puts the music therapists' willingness to accept and acknowledge adventurous and eccentric participation in perspective. These forms of participation challenge the established order, where the music therapists usually are "sociometric stars." While in this style of working, the music therapists are almost always where the action is, adventurous and eccentric participation may put other participants in the center. This, then, adds to our understanding of the importance of "musical mutinies."

Figure 10.6   Ritual intensification. Photo: Ragnar Albertsen

Adventurous and eccentric participation may contribute to democratization of the ritual, but it is worth noting that such participation usually requires trans-situational resources of some sort – such as personal skills in dancing or in playing an instrument – in order to be effective in transforming the situation and influencing the whole group. Possibilities for adventurous and eccentric participation are therefore never equally distributed in a group.

In the second interpretation of this essay the focus was upon everyday rituals in music as possible scaffolds for the co-creation of an inclusive social space. The third interpretation that I have presented here suggests a focus upon the need to negotiate on the formation of the rituals themselves. This requires reflexivity on behalf of helpers and therapists, who need to develop consciousness about themselves as participants in interaction rituals, for instance in relation to self-evaluative questions such as: How and when do I contribute in the process of creating shared foci of attention? How and when do I allow for diversity in participatory inputs? How and when do I empower participants who may struggle to find resources that enable them to shape rituals through say adventurous participation?

Discussion: Participatory Spaciousness and Ritual Outcomes

I have studied the *Cultural Festival* run by NFU, a vital Norwegian organization for individuals with intellectual disabilities and their families. The basic values of this organization are equality, respect, and justice, expressed in slogans such as: "Society for all" and "Together for inclusive communities." The organization defines their role as that of being: a supportive network for its members, a watchdog in the society, and an active agent for positive change. The festival is part of the latter ambition, and the local leaders of NFU have decided to collaborate with music therapists in order to take steps in the direction of achieving this. One of the arguments for this choice given by the NFU representatives was that music therapists take great interest in and know how to show respect for each person's way of participating.

The first interpretation I made was that five different forms of participation as self-representation could be identified, namely non-participation, silent participation, conventional participation, adventurous participation, and eccentric participation. Whether this description could be generalized to other contexts is a question that could be explored both empirically and theoretically. In light of the interaction ritual theory that I have employed, it could be argued that these five categories represent contingent constellations of two more general dimensions; level of energy and degree of mutual focus. Some forms of participation are very energetic, others are more lethargic. In relation to the established focus of attention, some forms of participation are centripetal, others are more centrifugal. Figure 10.7 demonstrates these possibilities in a matrix:

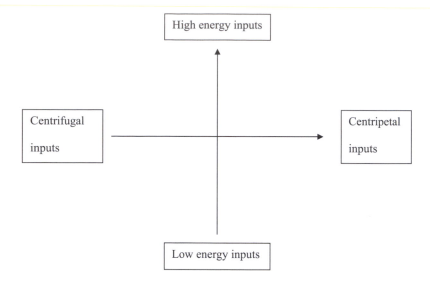

Figure 10.7   Levels of energy and degrees of mutual focus in musical
             interaction

An inclusive social space for musical participation allows for low energy as well
as high energy inputs, and for both centrifugal and centripetal contributions (actions
that challenge or support the established focus, respectively). The workshops of
the *Cultural Festival* demonstrate how such a social space could be co-created,
while the vignette from the classical concert hall that I presented in the beginning
of the essay illuminates a more exclusive context with a much smaller range of
possible inputs. It would probably be a mistake, however, to take for granted that
the five forms of participation identified in the *Cultural Festival* necessarily could
be identified in any other inclusive settings. This should be explored empirically,
but I would speculate that conventional participation in any given context could
be identified at various levels of the two dimensions of Figure 10.7. For instance;
a choir would usually require moderate energy inputs while a heavy metal band
would require high energy inputs. Most choirs clearly require centripetal inputs.
This is probably the case for many heavy metal bands also, while some of them
would cultivate a larger range of contributions concerning degree of mutual focus.
These simple examples illuminate how definitions of conventional participation
vary substantially from context to context, which suggests that terms such as
non-participation, silent participation, adventurous participation, and eccentric
participation would make more sense in some contexts than in others, and that
they make sense in different ways.

     The second and third interpretations in this essay were informed by interaction
ritual theory, and these interpretations require that we address the question of
what the *ritual outcomes* could be. Based on the pioneering work of Durkheim
(1912/1995) and later research in this tradition, Collins (2004) has developed

a general discussion of this question. He suggests that if the ritual ingredients (bodily co-presence, barrier to outsiders, mutual focus of attention, and shared mood) successfully combine and build up to high levels of emotionally shared attention, participants have the experience of:

1. group solidarity, a feeling of membership;
2. emotional energy [EE] in the individual: a feeling of confidence, elation, strength, enthusiasm, and initiative in taking action;
3. symbols that represent the group: emblems or other representations (visual icons, words, gestures) that members feel are associated with themselves collectively; these are Durkheim's "sacred objects." Persons pumped up with feelings of group solidarity treat symbols with great respect and defend them against the disrespect of outsiders, and even more, of renegade insiders;
4. feelings of morality: the sense of rightness in adhering to the group, respecting its symbols, and defending both against transgressors. Along with this goes the sense of moral evil or impropriety in violating the group's solidarity and its symbolic representations. (Collins, 2004, p. 49)

The empirical material that I have gathered runs somewhat short of suggesting what the specific outcomes of the rituals of the *Cultural Festival* were. I had no possibility of interviewing participants about their appraisal of this or of observing them over a longer period of time. This is then a question which should be investigated in future studies. The most obvious outcome that I could observe was production of emotional energy in each workshop. It was sometimes very striking to observe how a group of somewhat silent participants could be energized and transformed to a group of vigorous actors during successful ritual sequences, as demonstrated by Figure 10.8.

The question is, of course, if and how emotional energy carries over to other contexts. One way of addressing this question is to examine relationships *between* the ritual outcomes. A simplified summary of two central contentions in interaction ritual theory would be: *Group solidarity is a precondition for the production of emotional energy, while symbols are a condition for the preservation of it* (Collins, 2004).

The first contention has already been discussed. We remember from the discussion of emotional stratification that if a feeling of membership is replaced by the feeling of being subordinate, rituals could be energy drainers instead of energy chargers. This does not mean that every person needs to have an equal role in order for the ritual to be effective. Spectators in a soccer match may well experience collective effervescence, if they identify with one of the playing teams and intensify the experience of watching through community singing, shouting, and/or moving. I would speculate that what matters is the feeling of *participating*, which, according to the perspective employed in this chapter, involves the experience of contributing and collaborating. If we review the workshops with this lens established, it becomes quite clear how the music therapists worked quite actively to establish conditions for group collaboration and for each participant's contribution. Obvious examples in all groups were sequences of community singing with possibilities for personal inputs in shape of solos, and these situations could give space for quite diverse contributions.

Figure 10.8   Ritual outcomes: Energy, symbols, and solidarity. Photo: Ragnar Albertsen

As I also have described, the rituals of the festival indeed seemed to be successful in relation to the production of emotional energy in each workshop. What, then, are the implications of the claim that symbols are a condition for the preservation of emotional energy?[5] Durkheim wrote about the importance of symbols in relation to emotional energy (which he called social feelings) in the following way:

> Without symbols, social feelings could have only an unstable existence. Those feelings are very strong as long as men are assembled, mutually influencing one another, but when the gathering is over, they survive only in the form of

[5]   It is important to distinguish this claim from the much debated claim in psychoanalytically informed therapy that therapeutic experiences must be verbally processed in order to have a lasting effect. Interaction ritual theory builds upon a different metatheory on human consciousness and there is no claim made in relation to verbal insights on previously unconscious material.

memories that gradually dim and fade away if left to themselves. Since the group is no longer present and active, the individual temperaments quickly take over again. … But if the movements by which these feelings have been expressed eventually become inscribed on things that are durable, then they too become durable. These things keep bringing the feelings to individual minds and keep them perpetually aroused, just as would happen if the cause that first called them forth was still acting. (Durkheim, 1912/1995, pp. 232–3)

Durkheim describes this process as *emblematizing* and suggests that it is required for the group to become conscious of itself and also for the perpetuation of that consciousness. Emblems could be words and narratives, but as the citation reveals, it could be all sorts of things, as long as it is durable and "inscribed" in some way or another. It is important to note that this is a dynamic and reciprocal process; symbols are durable only to the degree that they are (re)charged. In other words; rituals must be repeated in due time in order for this process to work (Collins, 2004, p. 37).

Popular music groups emblematizes their concerts and public performances by having a distinct name, by feeding the media with narratives about themselves, by producing all types of effects such as T-shirts and pins, etc. In comparison, what were the processes of emblematizing in the music groups of the *Cultural Festival*? I observed no attempt of giving the groups especially intriguing names or of producing fascinating narratives for the media … What I did observe was that many of the participants were quite active in documenting their participation. They would bring with them digital cameras and video cameras (this goes mainly for "The Rock Group" and "The Music and Theater Group"). These cameras were, by the way, rarely in use in the workshops themselves, where the active musicing seemed to take all the energy and concentration. But in breaks between workshops cameras would pop up and there was also a great deal of interest for sharing the footage. A related phenomenon was that some of the participants showed great interest for the video recordings that I was making.

What other symbols were produced in the groups? "The Music and Theater Group" used costumes actively, which probably not only contributed to the music theater production but also symbolized group membership, as long as the workshops lasted, that is. Work with more lasting symbols was a bit more difficult to identify. I suggest, however, that the songs that most groups worked with could have emblematizing functions, to the degree that these songs are remembered by the participants after the festival. There is some evidence that this is actually happening. In the workshops many participants immediately recognized songs that had been used in previous years and joined in with visible pleasure and satisfaction. Also, many of the participants had favorite songs and activities from previous festivals that they proposed should be used this year too. Other examples could probably be added, and the work with symbols of group membership and ritual participation for participants with intellectual disabilities is in my judgment an area that deserves further investigation.

What are the relationships between ritual outcomes and therapeutic outcomes, then? My preliminary answer is simple. In the case of the *Cultural Festival, the ritual outcomes are the therapeutic outcomes.* While empirical research on this is still wanting, I suggest that there are theoretical reasons for suggesting that ritual outcomes of solidarity, emotional energy, use of symbols, and possibly also development of morality, are therapeutic outcomes. One theoretical link could be made to Even Ruud's (1997a) work on the relationship between music and quality of life. Ruud suggests that music could contribute to the quality of life by (1) increasing our feelings of vitality and our awareness of feelings, (2) providing opportunities for increased sense of agency, (3) providing a sense of belonging and communality, and (4) creating a sense of meaning and coherence in life. There are some interesting and quite strong parallels between Ruud's list and the list of ritual outcomes, but the details of these parallels will need to be examined in later studies.

Conclusion

In this essay I have examined the issue of participation by putting it in the context of ritual collaboration. I have argued that interaction ritual theory, as pioneered by Durkheim (1912/1995) and Goffman (1967) and more lately developed by Collins (2004), provides us with a lens that may help us discover important aspects of this kind of work. The observations of the festival, and the interpretations and reflections I made in relation to them, suggest that:

- The music therapy workshops studied include use of four central interaction ritual ingredients; bodily co-presence, barrier to outsiders, mutual focus of attention, and shared mood.
- Five different forms of participation as styles of self-presentation could be identified; non-participation (not being there), silent participation (being there), conventional participation (joining in), adventurous participation (standing out), and eccentric participation (going across).
- If integrated in interaction rituals, a broad range of styles of self-presentations in music does not necessarily imply fragmented situations with a series of individual foci but could create an inclusive social space. This implies that there is room for unity beyond uniformity.
- Participation may involve negotiations on the formation of the interaction ritual itself, which may involve negotiations on problems of stratification.
- The above puts the music therapists' willingness to accept and acknowledge adventurous and eccentric participation in perspective, since this could put other participants in the center of action and to some degree democratize the ritual.
- Ritual outcomes that seemed to be present in the festival include production of group solidarity, accumulation of emotional energy, and the use of

symbols, and it is suggested that these ritual outcomes may be understood as the therapeutic outcomes.

It is worth noting that the latter proposal could have implications for our notion of music therapy practice. It would support the idea that Community Music Therapy is not only or mainly oriented toward producing individual change but also toward *ritual change*, which implies that we not only take interest in how the ritual affects the individual but also in how the individual affects the ritual. For groups such as those participating in the *Cultural Festival*, Community Music Therapy is not something that necessarily could or should be restricted to a limited period of time, then. Like all other rituals, rituals of Community Music Therapy may need to be repeated regularly. As Collins (2004) would argue; rituals pump the participants up with emotional energy that contributes to their feeling of agency and belonging in the society. Even though various symbols could make such ritual experiences last longer, rituals still need to be repeated in order to work. It could then be argued that the participants of the *Cultural Festival* need and deserve much more regular gatherings than the existing pattern of one "corroboree" every year. If we in this way start exploring to what degree a society or local community gives space to spacious rituals, we start realizing that ritual change may be closely linked to social change.

PART VI

Chapter 11

Action
Can Everything Become Music?
Scrap Metal in Southern England

Gary Ansdell

Tonight's Music is Unique

The program for *Scrap Metal*'s concert tells you straight away that the evening is
not going to be a conventional event. It "warns" us: "Tonight's music is unique.
You have not heard it anywhere before, and you will never hear it again." The
facilitator of the Scrap Music Ensemble, Stuart Wood, wrote these words, and
they are an accurate description – I've never heard or seen anything quite like this
before! Look again at the program, with its diagram of the instruments used: a car
bonnet, typewriter, "strung sink," bicycle wheel, three buckets ... (Figure 11.1).[1]

   Some of the audience probably felt they'd arrived at the wrong event as they
sat down in a church used to more conventional cultural events in this small town
in Buckinghamshire.[2] Perhaps they thought they'd mistakenly arrived at some
neo-1970s "musical happening." In a sense it *was* a musical happening, probably
a unique one in most people's cultural experience. It proved a unique musical and
social event. I will describe here some of the background and careful preparation,
what happened on the night, and some of the challenging consequences of *Scrap
Metal*.

From Therapy to Community

The *Scrap Metal* concert was the logical and practical outcome of a broader
Community Music Therapy project Stuart had been working on for the last few

---

[1]   The last of the acknowledgments in the program is to "The Tip." In England "the tip" is
the equivalent to a "scrap yard" – where we take discarded household things, like washing
machines, old bicycles etc.

[2]   Buckinghamshire is a relatively affluent semi-rural area about 30 miles from outer
London. Its many small towns mean that health services are widely distributed, and isolation
is sometimes a problem for people. Cultural life is organized around the towns, though like
many semi-rural communities is weaker than it was in previous times.

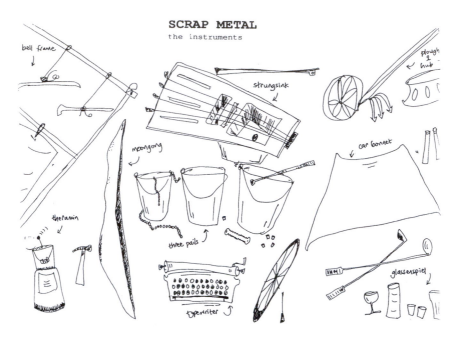

Tonight's music is unique. You have not heard it anywhere before, and you will never hear it again.

There are several precomposed pieces in among our improvisation. You will hear parts of **Suite for Toy Piano** by John Cage. We also play **Can Everything Become Music?** by Jane Lawrence, a **Gregorian Chant**, and the folk round **I Have Nothing to Declare**, by Richard and Caroline Harman. Along the way, we have been listening to works by John Cage, Takemitsu, Steve Reich and Keith Jarret. We have also been influenced by jazz music and Gregorian chant. This may flavour what we do when we play tonight.

Often the music that emerges from our improvising sounds unusual at first, even to us! That's part of the fun. Maybe, by the end of the concert, you will fancy having a go on something yourself?

Special thanks to: St. Mary's Church, VOA-PCT, Nordoff-Robbins Music Therapy, AVAC, The Rhys Davis Trust, The Speedwell Trust, and The Tip

The SCRAP METAL Ensemble

Organ	fraser, caryl, barbara
Toy piano	mikako
Three pails	jane
Moon gong	mark
Strungsink	mark & others
Mixed percussion	lynne & others
Drum & Cymbal	les
Typewriter	wendy
Voices	olivia, christine, roger, richard, caroline, jeannor
Theramin	mark & others
Theramin design	paddy & larry
Construction	roger
Piano	stuart

Figure 11.1   The program for *Scrap Metal*'s concert

years. The title of a published account of this work describes it succinctly: "From Therapy to Community: Making Music in Neurological Rehabilitation" (Wood, Verney, and Atkinson, 2004).[3] The chapter describes a pioneering project to follow his patients' social and musical needs – wherever these led. It was based on two values: First, that people's commitment to their musical activity is the basis for their therapeutic progress; second, a belief in music's role in creating community.

The initial setting for this project was a medical one: a neurological rehabilitation unit for adults with acquired brain injury (typically through strokes or head injury). Starting off with relatively conventional individual work with patients, Stuart found himself challenged to deal with the changing needs of these people as they developed beyond the acute stages of their illness. Now the need was rather how to re-integrate people back again into their family and community life (and how they could live resourcefully with a chronic illness). In his account Stuart makes a simple but rather profound observation: "[O]ften the outcome of therapy is as much in musical and social skills as it is in personal process" (p. 49). But therapy for these patients had typically stopped when they left such medically-based services. Stuart's question was simply "What next?" – how could these people's newly-found engagement with music and musicing through music therapy help them in the necessary next stage of their journey: re-finding a place in life as someone "differently abled"?

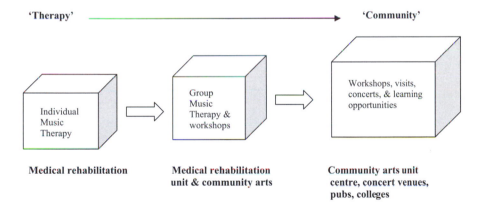

Figure 11.2   Stuart Wood's three stage program of Community Music Therapy work. Source: Wood, Verney, and Atkinson (2004), *From Therapy to Community: Making Music in Neurological Rehabilitation.* London: Jessica Kingsley Publishers, p. 52. Reproduced with permission from Jessica Kingsley Publishers

---

[3]   I shall report the project here using Stuart's voice, although the chapter being quoted is written jointly by Stuart Wood, Rachel Verney, and Jessica Atkinson.

Stuart's practical answer was his "three stage program" of work (Figure 11.2):

People mostly started in individual music therapy during the acute stage of their illness, where music therapy was seen (in a Nordoff-Robbins fashion) as the "skill of drawing out personal responses and developing them into personal growth and change" (p. 51). However, it became clear to Stuart that this was not where music therapy stopped: he found his individual patients leading him into the next stages of their musical pathways – as music helped them make the physical and psycho-social re-connections they needed. One man wanted to make music with his wife – to help them find a new and more equal way of communicating and collaborating. Another woman wanted to learn the piano – to work on the physical and cognitive aspects of her rehabilitation, but also simply just to learn the piano! Then soon she wanted to compose for herself. Many of these people led to Stage 2 of the model: group music therapy and musical workshop experiences, which both brought local musicians *into* the medical setting and took patients *out* of them.

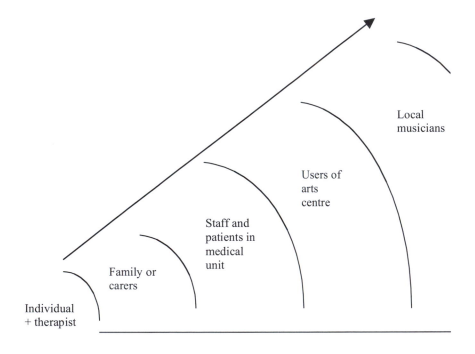

Figure 11.3   The "ripple effect" in action. Source: Wood, Verney, and Atkinson (2004), *From Therapy to Community: Making Music in Neurological Rehabilitation*. London: Jessica Kingsley Publishers, p. 61. Reproduced with permission from Jessica Kingsley Publishers.

At the same time, musicing within the unit was achieving the other aim of the project: to develop musical community within the medical setting – for patients, staff, visitors alike. "Music," writes Stuart, "was a way into social interaction, and it was the interaction itself." An open group on Friday afternoons, music for special occasions ... all of these activities proved complementary to the developing individual musical pathways of the patients. As Stuart comments: "There is no contradiction between the growing social network and the individual rigor of each participants' work" (p. 55). By nurturing these connections that musicing created (in all of the formats tried – both with a social and a learning focus), something interesting was happening: a natural outward movement for people. As hoped, music was an ideal bridge-building activity, which helped people re-integrate back into the outside community once they were ready for this step. Stage 3 of the programme was a carefully-managed series of workshops and small musical events away from the medical unit – where "participants" naturally integrated with people from the wider community. The programme graphically showed the "ripple effect" in action (Figure 11.3).

At this stage the program also had the important aspect of people being able to *offer* something, as well as receiving. Stuart comments: "What seemed at first to be contradictions between 'therapy' and 'community' are in fact points of tension which are overcome by the continual commitment of participants to their changing musical work" (p. 59). In this brave and original project many of the traditional conventional patterns of music therapy were supervened by a process of simply following where people and music needed to go, in the best interests of those people and the community they lived in. Another original aspect is the way that this project is prepared to harness *any* type of music or musicing which can be of benefit to these people. It shows just how little some music therapy has used the broad affordances of music, and how few links are typically made to broader musical culture.

Stuart ends his chapter describing the project at the point where he was about to embark on its logical consequence (the process and event I'm about to describe here). Stuart comments at the end of his account:

> At last the participants had reached a stage where they could be contributing members within a community of musicians and concert-goers, in their own town and out into the wider geographical area. (Wood, Verney, and Atkinson, 2004, p. 62)

The Idea and the Preparation

I started tracking Stuart's *Scrap Metal* project during its three months of preparation for the concert. He talked to me about how the idea had emerged and of the ongoing process of developing the project. The "seed" for the project was startlingly simple and profound: at once both powerful symbol and practical solution. Stuart was working with a woman in individual music therapy whose neurological tremor had meant that many things in her life had ended: job, relationship, hobbies … She said it was like being on the scrap-heap – she felt useless, scrap. Except that music therapy was gradually making her feel differently about herself – increasingly as creative, able to make something beautiful. She and Stuart linked this to a television program, when people go to a scrap-yard and have to make something out of what they find. "So we thought *we* could do this too! Make instruments out of scrap!" said Stuart. The idea fired the imagination of this woman, and she told Stuart how she'd find old things in her house and try to see what kind of music she could get out of them. Stuart continues:

> *She'd bring these "instruments" in and we'd play them: a bucket played with a bike chain or with thimbles on her fingers; a type-writer (she'd been a typist!). And gradually for me this all took on an extra resonance … Here I was working as a music therapist in neuro-rehab, where often someone's coming to me in an awful state in their life – they feel like they're on the scrap-heap, as this woman said. But then something else happens, a transformation occurs. And it's often in music you hear it first … it's instantaneous, you experience this transformation … (Stuart Wood, music therapist)*

Stuart and the woman introduced the scrap metal idea to other people in the rehabilitation community (the people involved in the three-stage Community Music Therapy program outlined above). It instantly had a great resonance for others: many said that they too had felt like scrap, but also felt music to be something transformational for them. It was the right idea for the right people – and at the right time, given the preparations of the "From Therapy to Community Project":

> *So I thought, there's a way of enacting this "scrap" symbol in a musical project. After three years of the project people are used to developing things, through workshops and performances. We can pull in other help – a metalworker, other musicians. So we did it! We literally enacted the idea by me and this lady going to a scrap yard one misty Monday morning. She got very excited, she found a chimney flue, leant it against a skip and played it. We chose stuff to take back for the metalworker to make into something playable: we're making a gong out of a car bonnet, a bass out of a kitchen sink with added strings … a car hub…*
>
> *The whole project was in a sense a musical ritual: these patients went somewhere where there was just useless, discarded things; and they investigated this junk … they interrogated these things they found until they found the music in it. This was for many people the embodiment of what they'd found their music therapy to be … (Stuart Wood, music therapist)*

Three months of preparation and collaboration started: building instruments (with the aid of a local metalworker), improvising with them in a workshop format, and gradually crafting semi-prepared pieces which were then rehearsed for performance. Part of the creative process was also listening to music which used similar instruments and techniques, or had the same spirit: Cage, Takemitsu, Reich, Jarrett ...

The playing group was extremely varied: people in states of illness and recovery; physical and cognitive ability and disability; musical training and no musical training; people from a variety of local areas. There were people Stuart had worked with in the previous program, carers and family, the instrument maker and his girlfriend and two fellow music therapists (one usefully a church organist). What they all had in common, commented Stuart, was that they wanted to make music together. So the performance group and its music began to take shape. At this stage when I talked to Stuart he was both exhilarated and daunted: by both the scale and logistics of this project, but also in terms of managing the expectations of everyone involved, and not least ensuring the physical safety of the participants.

The Concert

We gather in a church in the town of Aylesbury for the concert, on a warm summer evening. There's been a summer arts festival, so already the church has an unusual feeling, with modern acetate sculptures hung above people's heads. The audience is mixed, perhaps half having come after hearing about the concert after looking at the art. The remainder of the hundred or so people are family and friends of the performers. In many ways it is just a usual concert for this community – socially and culturally. But having said this, the usual concert style in this church (organ recitals) does *not* look like this: a stage set with all of the instruments in Figure 11.1; several performers in wheelchairs. The atmosphere on both sides (performers and audience) is expectant of something different. Perhaps each has a different idea in mind of what will or will not happen in the next hour.

Stuart frames the evening with a short talk on the basic idea of *Scrap Metal* – stressing, as he tells me later, the "human condition angle" – the fact that there are times we *all* feel we're on the scrap-heap. When you looked at the stage it was actually difficult to tell who was who, and this was intentional. In terms of what we were about to hear the only clues were the "instruments" we could see, and the program notes mentioning several modern composers.

Many things were of course exactly the same as any concert: the expectation, sense of nerves, then the tipping-over into music and performance. The concert starts without any obvious sign, an airy improvisation without pulsed sounds ... then suddenly there's the click of the typewriter (and its bell!) cutting through the texture. We the audience somehow relax into the bizarre, surreal musical world the concert has conjured already – and listen to what sounds and people can do ... How one man in a wheelchair who can only make a limited movement with one arm does just this (with some vigor) upon the gong made out of a car bonnet and strung up near his right side,[4] how the former typist plays along just so, and how all help each other both to play and to listen in this unique way.

The music lasts for about 45 minutes, broken up into about seven sections, which consist of different combinations of the people playing different instruments, in semi-prepared pieces. There are some lovely surprises and jokes – my colleague Mika plays John Cage's *Suite for Toy Piano* on a toy piano resting on a bucket! The woman who started off the whole idea of *Scrap Music* plays a duet with Stuart, based on a random word game alternating with her playing an upturned bucket with thimbled fingers! The audience listen, smile, seem totally absorbed by the ingenuity and unique sound-world being created.

The first and the last pieces have the church organ too. Fraser (a music therapist as well as organist) has done some organ-based workshops with the group, out of which these pieces developed. The last builds to a thrilling climax with full organ – its sustained chords the perfect complement to the scrap percussion.

Stuart rounds off the evening by teaching us, the audience, a round – written by a member of the group who can't be here. We all end up as musical participators too.

Afterwards

"We pulled it off!" says Stuart when we meet a few weeks after the performance. We look at the video of the event and discuss some of the details of the pieces. We also talk about the audience's reactions. "Someone told me," says Stuart, "this is music as it should be!" This person talked of how the concert made him listen differently, to feel part of the musicing in a different way than in a conventional concert. There seemed to be a thirst for people to make music together – not just the participants, but everyone. There was also a noticeable paradox in how people commented on the concert afterwards. We heard nobody say something like "how marvelous for '*them*' to manage that"! Instead people commented on aesthetic features of the event – things like "that kitchen sink sounded fantastic!" At the same time many of the audience members clearly did identify with the players, in just the kind of "human condition" stance that Stuart had outlined in his opening words. Someone said: "the instruments looked really incomplete on the stage at first, but then when the people were playing them they just transformed them – it sounded amazing!"… or: "When that lady played the buckets with the bicycle chain it really lifted me – I found it inspiring!" So clearly people made sense of what was happening in many ways – aesthetically, humanly, socially.

Stuart summed up this unique event: "It was a concert, but not a concert; a performance but not a performance; an audience, but not an audience … using scrap metal that became something other than scrap metal …" I came away feeling that John Cage (something of an inspiration for this event) would have enjoyed it,

---

[4]   In the end, the gong was beaten out of sheet metal. The bonnet became a large drum.

would have approved of the paradoxical description Stuart gave. Cage's manifesto statement – in the essay *The Future of Music: A Credo* – gives a good alternative description of the *Scrap Metal* project:

> Though the doors will always remain open for the musical expression of personal feelings, what will more and more come through is the expression of the pleasures of conviviality … And beyond that a non-intentional expressivity, a being together of sound and people (where sounds are sounds and people are people). A walk, so to speak, in the woods of music, or in the world itself. (Cage, 1980)

Chapter 12

Reflection

Where Performing Helps:
Processes and Affordances of Performance
in Community Music Therapy[1]

Gary Ansdell

If Man is a sapient animal, a tool-making animal, a self-making animal, a symbol-using animal, he is no less a performing animal, *Homo Performans* ... His performances are *reflexive* – in performing he reveals himself to himself.

Victor Turner

Performing arts like music reveal the collaborative elements in the expressive practice of mutual respect.

Richard Sennett

This is music as it should be ...

Audience member of *Scrap Music* concert

Introduction: Musical-Social Performances

A reviewer on the BBC Radio 3 "CD Review" program comments on a new batch of Beethoven Symphonies. Two performances he critiques are by unusual orchestras – Daniel Barenboim's *West-Eastern Divan Orchestra,* and the *Simon Bolivar Youth Orchestra of Venezuela.* Whilst the reviewer maintains that his inclusion of these recordings in his selection is based purely on musical criteria, he cannot help but outline their social story too. The orchestra Barenboim set up (with Edward Said) has an explicit political and social agenda of creating a practical way for young people across the Middle East fault-lines to play music together. The Venezuelan orchestra is part of a country-wide social program which gives children from the slum areas instruments, musical tuition and opportunities to play within a network of orchestras. Such stories are becoming increasingly common – presenting musical and social projects together. The next day I hear

---

[1]   Some material in this chapter appeared previously in Ansdell (2005c).

about a London opera company mounting an opera with homeless people. This engagement of the arts with a contemporary social agenda seems increasingly legitimated within public discourse. Notably, most of these musical-social projects revolve around performances, with the implicit recognition that performing helps with the social, psychological, cultural and political issues these projects address.

Formerly, music therapy has cultivated the main discourse around "music's help" for people. Now, others are building alternatives. Music therapy's response to these newer and broader musical-social practices and narratives has been an ambivalent one – as has its view of the role and value of performance within music therapy itself.[2] The development of Community Music Therapy discourse is, however, opening up professional and theoretical discussion within music therapy to the potentials and problems of working with clients across the full continuum of private to public music therapy, and to the place of performance practices within this spectrum. It is also linking (or re-linking) music therapy as a practice, discipline, and profession more directly to broader current debates on cultural politics in relation to health, social care, and social action. In my own British context this relates to the shifting relationships between music therapy, community music and the developing "music and health" movement, and how these relate to strategy and resourcing within the health, education, and social care sectors. In other national contexts the players in this scenario may be different, but I suspect that the professional politics will be similar.

In this essay I explore this shifting area of how and when performance may help people, by presenting two successful Community Music Therapy projects in which performance was central: *Musical Minds* and their ongoing rehearsal and performance process in the East End of London, and the *Scrap Metal* project and its one-off performance event in a church in a rural area of South-East England. Through these case studies I explore the sometimes paradoxical aspects of performing with vulnerable people in sensitive circumstances. I also attempt to build up a picture of "how performing helps" by looking at these two case examples in relation to developing multi-disciplinary theoretical perspectives on performance – in particular on "musicing-as-performing" and its potential for personal and social transformation. I also attend to potential professional and ethical dilemmas associated with performance practices within music therapy.

The current debate within the music therapy profession could perhaps be simply summarized as: Is performance in music therapy a "good thing" – and if so, why? Many music therapists remain to be convinced. My alternative question is: Can performance in music therapy be a resource rather than a problem? To answer this we need to look at both the *process* of performing, and its outcomes – what precisely performing affords people, situations, and communities.

Firstly, however, we need to understand how both traditional music therapy and traditional musicology came to marginalize performance, and how recent

---

[2]   In print the evidence for this is more by omission than commission. Of the more explicit statements is that of Streeter (2006).

thinking has challenged this. The next section shows how these two cases are interestingly parallel.

Re-considering Performance: Within and Without Music Therapy

From the Margins of Music Therapy

The pre-history of contemporary professional music therapy presents a diversity of practices reflecting local, socio-cultural and philosophical factors (Gouk, 2000; Horden, 2000; Ansdell, 2003). In Europe, musical performances by the healthy to the ill have been relatively common in one way or another within a thousand-year history. Within its modern (twentieth-century, post-war) development as a health profession music therapy has, however, been increasingly ambivalent towards using the performance dimension of music.[3] The early music therapy pioneers clearly incorporated public and performance aspects into their work in hospitals, special schools and care homes. At the same time, probably for the first time in music therapy history, they also emphasized playing music *with* patients. Their work showed a fluid movement between private and public musical events, entertainment and therapy, psychological and social aims.[4]

Interestingly, even within this pioneering generation there are few references to musical performance in music therapy within their published texts. We know that explicit performance work was going on at this time, but when it comes to their written texts it is the individual or "private group" work that is theorized as music therapy (almost as if perhaps the public performance aspects were self-evident – or else difficult to integrate into developing theory). As music therapy became increasingly institutionalized and professionalized in the 1980s (within Europe and North America at least) its attitude to musical performance changed in a negative direction. Along with its new legitimation as a paramedical/ psychological intervention came the normative conventions of these clinical practices, and the development of what I've dubbed the "consensus model" of

---

[3]   As I don't intend this as an extensive literature study of this area I have limited this characterization to European tradition (see Priestley, 1975; Ruud, 1980a; Everitt, 1997; Tyler, 2000; Stige, 2002, 2003).

[4]   These pioneers include Juliette Alvin, Nordoff and Robbins, Mary Priestley, Florence Tyson (see Stige, 2003 for more detail). Nordoff and Robbins, for example, wrote the following in their book *Therapy in Music for Handicapped Children* (1971), as a caption for a photograph of a musical play they had worked on and performed with a group of children: "The therapeutic impact of the play lay in both rehearsals and performance, the performance being the summation of a therapeutic process that had its origin and development in the rehearsals" [Appendix 2].

music therapy.[5] This led to an increasing "privatization" of practice – individual or closed-group sessions becoming the norm, with therapists clearly experiencing (for disciplinary and professional reasons) discomfort integrating performance practically or theoretically into their work.

To caricature only slightly, the consensus model of music therapy has considered "therapy" and "performance" as antithetical concepts, and that (at worst) performing for ill, vulnerable, troubled people is counter-indicated, counterproductive, coercive, ethically dubious, professionally confusing and possibly dangerous. Such therapists will tell you that "putting on a performance" (variously described in the consensus model as "acting-out," "narcissistic," "being inauthentic," or "hiding behind a persona") is what therapy is trying to *treat*, not encourage! Therapy is about *process*, not product, and its core conditions for being an effective treatment are privacy, confidentiality, concentration on individual authenticity, and care with theoretically-conceived boundaries of time, space and person.

The Community Music Therapy movement is partly a response to these attitudes and assumptions, especially in relation to how music's social, cultural and performative dimensions *can* be necessary and helpful (Ruud, 1998; Stige, 2003; Pavlicevic and Ansdell, 2004; Turry, 2005; Jampel, 2006; O'Brien, 2006; Pavlicevic, 2006b; Wood, 2006).[6] In contrast to the attitudes of the consensus

---

[5]   I called this normative development the "consensus model" (see Ansdell, 2002; Pavlicevic and Ansdell, 2004). Clearly some of this picture is an over-simplification, both of modes of practice and theory. Many music therapists during the 1960s–90s continued to use aspects of performance in music therapy (but seldom to present this aspect or write about it). It could be argued then that performance practices in music therapy have consistently been "marginally widespread." Equally, some theorists were also the exception, articulating performative dimensions within their thinking (particularly Even Ruud and David Aldridge).

[6]   The dimension of "performance" could be seen as an indicator of these changes between the "consensus model" and an evolving Community Music Therapy view. For example, whilst few texts in the previous (1960–90) music therapy literature carry (if any) no more than one or two indexed references to "performance," a change can be seen in recent years. Even Ruud's influential book *Music Therapy: Improvisation, Communication and Culture* (1998) has 12 references to performance, whilst Pavlicevic and Ansdell's edited book of chapters by 16 music therapists, *Community Music Therapy* (2004) has 43. An added complexity here is the recent discussion as to what extent "performance" is the defining feature of Community Music Therapy. A recent web-debate ensued from Even Ruud's (2004b) short discussion paper entitled "Defining Community Music Therapy" in which he tried to do just this, using the notion of performance: "Community Music Therapy, then, may be defined as the reflexive use of performance based music therapy within a systemic perspective" (Ruud, 2004b). This suggestion was followed by a lively debate by further discussants (Stige, 2004b; Ruud, 2004b; Ansdell, 2005a; Ruud, 2005; Pavlicevic, 2005, Garred, 2005). The gist of this discussion is a resistance to *defining* Community Music Therapy by exclusive reference to performance, whilst acknowledging that the potential

model towards performance, a Community Music Therapy perspective has suggested that:

- Performance occasions *can* be an appropriate therapeutic medium – providing a site, focus, tool or occasion for music therapy to work with both individual and socio-cultural dimensions of human need.
- "Giving a performance" can have positive, healthy connotations that relate to a fundamental and natural mode of musicing, and also to a fundamental psychological and social reality – that "performing ourselves" in the world is both natural and necessary.
- Performance work in music therapy can keep a focus on *process* whilst also working for outcomes; can balance individual and communal needs.
- Performances create and sustain networks of relationships between and amongst people, institutions and communities.

So rather than the ambivalent (or hostile) pairing of music therapy and performance we have seen within the consensus model, there is growing understanding that performing in music therapy can be a legitimate practice, and one well aligned to contemporary interdisciplinary theory on personal and social health and wellbeing.

From the Margins of Music Studies

A parallel "turn to performance" has been happening within a variety of disciplines studying music, countering traditional musicology's project of analyzing (in Peter Kivy's phrase) "music alone." This ideology of so-called "musical autonomy" saw music as a set of abstracted texts – with performance and performer grudgingly admitted only as supplementary to the musical work and its internal workings. Performance became denigrated as mere reproduction of musical objects, leading at best to a concept of "music *and* performance" (Godlovitch, 1998; Cook, 2003). As Love (2003) suggests, this was part of academe's continued Cartesian split: since composition is a mental phenomenon it deserves serious study, whilst performance is a bodily one (and best ignored). In the last 20 years or so, however, a growing movement of "new musicology" (along with sister disciplines of ethnomusicology and music sociology) has de-mythologized this structuralist trope, and re-focused music studies on situated performance, worldly uses of music and the

---

value of performance is indeed one vital characteristic of most Community Music Therapy work – and that reflexive thinking on this is relatively new. Performance can be key (at some times, in some places), but is also not central. It is one possibility, richly connected to other possibilities. Ruud, however, holds to his view that what is definitional of Community Music Therapy is that it uses performance to "negotiate the space between the private and the public, the client and the institution/other staff, or the client and the community" (2004b).

bodies that produce it. In short, music *as* performance. As Nicholas Cook writes in his book *Analysing Musical Multi-media* (2001) "music is never alone" – it is always part of a cross-modal production (of sight, sound, gesture, collaboration, event) and it always takes place somewhere, with someone, doing something, for some reason.

What Cook calls a "culturally-oriented musicology"[7] increasingly studies music *as* performance, as a situated, contextualized social event, within which there is an improvised dialogue with a text or a tradition in real social time, nurtured through rehearsal and inter-performer multi-media collaboration. This has been a major shift of emphasis, as Cook explains:

> Instead of seeing musical works as texts within which social structures are encoded, we see them as *scripts*, in response to which social relationships are enacted. ... To call music a performing art, then, is not just to say that we are performing it, it is to say that through it we perform social meaning. (Cook, 2003, p. 206)

Working from a similar premise, both Benson (2003) and Godlovitch (1998) elaborate a much more personal and social account of musical performance than has previously been the case in musicological writing. Benson's is based on a Gadamer-inspired dialogical theory, where the whole musical process – composing, performing, "audiencing" – is seen as one unbroken and improvised interpersonal and intercultural dialogue which happens through musicing. Performance for Benson is elaborative, improvisatory, transformative – it brings music quite literally to life again. "All performance is resuscitation" he writes (p. 179). This in turn lends performing an interesting social and ethical dimension:

> The challenge facing the performer is that of speaking both in the name of others – the composer, performers of the past, and the whole tradition in which one lives – and in one's own name, as well as *to* those who listen. (Benson, 2003, p. 188)

Paul Atkinson (2006), in a detailed ethnographic study of the Welsh National Opera Company, calls this "dual" or "double" performance. We can both be ourselves *and* perform the voice of another. Similarly, Godlovitch's more philosophical analysis of musical performance takes him to what he calls a personalist conclusion. "Why do we attend a musical performance?" he asks. Not just to hear a text being

---

[7] This movement developed out of interdisciplinary contact between musicologists, ethnomusicologists, sociologists, and philosophers of music, pop and jazz studies. For more on the origins of the disciplinary shift in musicology (see Ansdell, 1997, 2001, 2004; Cook, 1998; Cook and Everist, 1999; Williams, 2001). For a critique of "new musicology" from a cultural sociology perspective (see DeNora, 2000, 2003; Martin, 2006).

reproduced but to hear *people* performing, to witness something being at stake for these people, and of this situation being something humanly vital:

> Personalism reminds us that performance is a way of communicating, not especially a work or a composer's notions, but a person, the performer, through music. Personalism intimates that a proper understanding of performance must … appreciate ritual, forms of communication, action and its significance, human benefit and reciprocity, and a good many other concerns belonging naturally to social conduct. (Godlovitch, 1998, p. 145)

Such ideas have always perhaps been more central to pop and jazz studies (Frith, 1996; Fischlin and Heble, 2004; Clarke, 2005; Martin, 2006), which are increasingly influencing thinking on any type of performance. Within popular music practice and studies the traditional art music problem of musical works is less apparent, and the approach to the issue more pragmatic. Jason Toynbee (2000), for example, writes the following in a chapter called "Making up and Showing off: What Musicians Do":

> So far … I have not made a distinction between authorship and performance. For in an important sense it is the elision of these moments which distinguishes popular music's mode of production … In short, performance refers to creation-in-*progress* … to carrying on production. (Toynbee, 2000, p. 53)

In pop performance there is then the whole theatrical side of showing-off (as arguably there is in *any* performative genre). What gets usefully emphasized in much analysis of pop, rock and jazz performance is just how key this aspect of communicating to the audience is. This sensitizes us also to the various modes of communication itself (musical and non-musical) within this heightened context – turning the spotlight particularly on how the body and its gestures mediate form, content, and context (as we will see later in respect of the music psychologist Jane Davidson's research).

Overall, this new consensus attitude towards musical performance is perhaps most famously conveyed by Christopher Small's (1998) concept of *musicking* (and his book of this name), which is achieving a popular reorientation of thinking about music – towards activity, relationships and context.[8] Performance is central to

---

[8]   Sociologists of music (e.g. Martin, 2006) have argued that a socio-cultural discourse (such as Small's or Cook's) was already there in earlier writing about music by non-musicologists. The pioneer sociologist Alfred Schutz, for example, wrote decades ago about the social intersubjective relationships between performers in his famous essay "Making Music Together: A Study in Social Relationship" (1964). Equally, the cultural theorist Edward Said (1991) has written about performance as an "extreme occasion" that reveals the paradox of being utterly socially situated whilst also being removed and protected from everyday life within the self-sufficiency of a "musical world" (Barenboim and Said, 2002, p. 37).

Small's ecological model of musical activity – indeed performing is unashamedly simply what music is all about:

> To music is to take part, in any capacity, in a musical performance, whether by performing, by listening, by rehearsing or practicing, by providing material for performance (what is called composing), or by dancing. (Small, 1998, p. 9)

> Musicking is about the creation and performance of relationships ... It is the relationships that it brings into existence in which the meaning of a musical performance lies. (Small, 1998, p. 193)

Moving Performance Back to the Center

To summarize, performance is shifting from the margin to the center of both music studies and music therapy. Performing has shifted from being seen as just reproducing musical works to instead creating and sustaining social relationships through musicing. This view links musical performance to the wider inter-disciplinary "performance studies paradigm,"[9] which Nicholas Cook helpfully summarizes as follows:

> The contemporary performance studies paradigm stresses the extent to which signification is constructed through the act of performance, and generally through acts of negotiation either between performers, or between them and the audience. In other words, performative meaning is understood as subsisting in process, and hence by definition is irreducible to product. (Cook, 2003, p. 205)

For these reasons, musical performance takes a key place within an emerging ecological theory of music[10] (Small, 1998; DeNora, 2000, 2003, 2005; Clarke, 2005), where music(ing) is *never* "alone," never abstract. Rather, musical performance is crucially about people: here, now, in these particular circumstances, with these particular needs, and where it helps them to do particular musical things.

It is against this background of thinking about musical performing that I want to look in more detail at the processes and affordances of performance for the people involved in the *Musical Minds* and *Scrap Metal* projects. From my analysis of these projects emerged two axes of significance, which will structure the following account. First, a synchronic vertical axis that concentrates on the importance of particular here-and-now moments of performance, "synchronized"

---

[9] See Schechner (2002) for a detailed characterization of the performance studies paradigm.
[10] An ecological theory of music sees the phenomenon of music(ing) as a distributed but interdependent variety of musical resources, forms, agents, processes, purposes and "habitats" – from which collaboratively emerge a network of micro to macro "musicworlds."

with the people co-witnessing the events in that unique context. These moments consisted of both very personal and individual performances (which I call "self performances") and more collaborative ones.[11] The second, horizontal or diachronic axis is temporal-developmental, tracing how performances emerged through time, in a before-during-after process. I've called the latter "preparing and completing performance."[12]

Self Performances

Pam[13] had been a typist, but her worsening neurological tremor has increasingly affected her life, leading to many losses: her job, relationships, and hobbies. She is the person whose comments had unexpectedly inspired the whole Scrap Music *concept and concert, with its musical enactment of the fact that, as music therapist Stuart Wood comments, "... people in neuro-rehabilitation often feel they they're on the scrap-heap ... but then something else happens, a transformation occurs. And it's often in music you hear it first – it's instantaneous, you experience this transformation ..." During her individual music therapy sessions with Stuart, Pam would bring in various "instruments" she'd found in her house – a bucket she'd play with a bike chain, or with thimbles on her fingers. She also brought in her typewriter, and they'd make music with these spontaneous instruments.*

Pam had wanted to do a solo in the concert, but was worried about having to do exactly the right thing each time in a public setting. So through the preparation she and Stuart had developed a semi-structured piece as a duet between them. They call the piece "Can Everything Become Music?" Stuart comments that "there's a lovely sense of a balance between structure and freedom in this piece – Pam needed some kind of anchoring to the freedom of the improvisation." The improvisation was inspired by an avant-garde Japanese piece they'd listened to, and the possibilities of her "found" instruments: three different sizes of metal

---

[11] This distinction is not of course to suggest that "individual" performances are not socially mediated, or that more communal performances do not consist of individual contributions. Nevertheless, in the two cases I studied there was clearly a difference in emphasis between the two categories of performance I suggest here.

[12] These two axes (synchronic/diachronic) echo (and take some inspiration from) the psychologist Benjamin Bradley's central argument in his book *Psychology and Experience* (2005) that to explain psycho-social experience adequately we need methodologically to be able to reconcile accounts of *here-and-now* ("out-of-time") intersubjective and uniquely contextualized significant experience with developmental ("through-time") and often abstracted causal accounts. Similarly I would argue that any adequate account of the affordances of performance for people necessarily involve the reconciliation of these two axes, but arguably with an emphasis on the synchronic, "intersubjective matrix."

[13] Pam's particular story and work within the project that built up to the *Scrap Metal Concert* was central to the *Scrap Metal* concept – see the narrative preceding this chapter.

bucket that made varying sounds. She plays these with metal thimbles on the fingers of the hand of her "good arm," articulating short phrases of rhythms. Then there's a pause and Stuart responds to her music, by picking up randomly and reading out words from post-cards thrown onto the floor. The words make random lines of poetry: "Freedom of Pattern in Loose Rhythm ..." Then Pam plays the buckets again with variations on her rhythmic patterns. Again a pause, and Stuart reads: "In total structure ... deal with what you've got ..." This time Pam plays the buckets with a bicycle chain ... "Infinity" comes the final word from the postcards.

As we look later at the video recording of this piece Stuart comments:

There's a lot of applause after this piece ... it's wonderful to see Pam's face ... she's so relaxed about the occasion. It wasn't just confidence, she needed a reason to perform like this. She needed to find a way of being herself properly amongst other people in public. It was a kind of performed experimentation. Probably more than most she was very aware of what being "disabled" means ... Doing this piece gave her a different way of being herself in public – it gave her a reason to just be herself, rather than to just subscribe to the conventional label "disabled." Being public was important for Pam – being witnessed by others ... (Stuart Wood, music therapist)

Being publicly witnessed is also important for Vick, a key member of the *Musical Minds* group, who struggles with his mental health and alcohol problems within a socially deprived area of East London. In the *Band for Life* concert Vick takes the microphone for one of the solo spots. "My Way" is a song he identifies with and others think of this as "Vick's song." Vick is part of the East End pub-singing culture and regularly sings this karaoke-style in the local area. He has a good strong voice and gives the song all he's got, though Sarah the music therapist, who accompanies Vick on the piano, has to work hard to get Vick's performance more communicative (rather than a monologue in karaoke singing-it-out style). But how Vick sings changes during the song and he ends on an exciting climax, leading to rich applause. Vick is somehow both totally himself in his spot whilst also being a Sinatra tribute; both giving an individual performance, but also really engaging with the social situation.

This is characteristic of many of the solo "spots" in the concert, and Sarah comments on this solo performance dimension of the concert:

The group is incredibly various: their likes, dislikes, abilities, issues, age, background, difficulties ... everything. The variety of songs is extreme! As professionals you'd never programme such variety, so you've got individuality at the same time! But when people stand up to do their solos, they're saying "Here's my music, here's my history ..." There's a strong sense of individuality as people come up to the mike and do their song. It's interesting then that what these people are often so anxious about is maintaining their own identity. Of course that's exactly what it's most difficult to do with a mental health difficulty – they're labeled, and there in this East London community which is a traumatic place to be ... so it's an irony really that as I'm pushing them together musically they're becoming better at being individual ... So the programme represents this idea of each person really being themselves through their choice of song and style, but also what's been achieved is a togetherness ... (Sarah Wilson, music therapist)

These examples, and the comments Stuart and Sarah make about them, suggest that we should think of them as much more than reproducing a musical text, or "putting on a performance." Rather, I suggest, these are "self performances," where something personal and crucial is at stake. Recent theory on performance helps suggest why this might be so.

David Aldridge (1996, 2004) has outlined a performative concept for music therapy, suggesting the motto *"argo ergo sum* – I perform therefore I am" (instead of the Cartesian "cogito ergo sum") (1996, p. 27). "Performing the self" is here not just a psychological or sociological concept, but a physiological one too (the performance, for example, of our immune system or motor coordination). This becomes clearer when such performance "fails" or is severely restricted through acute or chronic illness – at a physical, cognitive, expressive, or social level. At a more existential level we can also see how our illness-health and our identity are performative. So when patients play in music therapy with us they "perform their lives before us" (p. 27) – who they are now (their illness *and* their health) and who they *can* be. Their musicing is thus a "health performance." Aldridge also suggests how music therapy can offer a form of help or "repair," with the music therapist's job being to provide sites for performance such that the performance of the self can continue and elaborate.

There is an almost homeopathic logic here: failing performance at one level needs performance at another as its "remedy." Pam's "failing performance" of her physical self has paradoxically increased her need for such a public performance site in order to perform her emerging new identity or social self creatively to others – as "differently abled." As Stuart comments, Pam needed "to find a way of being herself properly amongst other people in public." This reminds us of the complementary aspect to Pam (or Vick's) life performance – the audience's witnessing of it, and response to it. Sarah describes the solo members of *Musical Minds* like Vick as coming up to the mike and saying "Here's *my* music, here's *my* history ..." – again in a personal and social situation where identity is challenged. The audience in both concerts consisted of family, friends and supporters of the performers (as well as some who did not have such personal connections). Their part is crucial in creating Pam or Vick's "health performance" in that they mostly knew, and were invested in, what was personally at stake for the performers in those moments on stage. This brings us back to the Godlovitch's *personalism* theory of performance I outlined above, where he reminds us that in most concerts it is the *person*-in-the-music that we are interested in, where something is at stake for them (and thus for *us*) during the time of performance. We are not just interested in the sound of Pam's bucket, or Vick's *My Way*, but in what is at stake for them *during* the performance. This is also of course the logic of Small's *musicking* concept; that the meaning of a performance lies in the quality of the social relationships it articulates and creates. In the two examples we have been looking at this local ecology has created a supported site for two self performances, where they can experiment with different forms of identity, social connection, and ability. As they music Pam and Vick are very much saying "*argo ergo sum*"!

Another dimension to these solo performances is how very specific performance skills determine what the music psychologist Jane Davidson has called "optimal performance" (Davidson, 2001, 2002, 2005; Williamon and Davidson, 2002; Faulkner and Davidson, 2004), where "the expression of the musical sounds and the social intentions of the performer in context are integrated in the bodily production" (2005, p. 232). Her detailed empirical work on how musicians perform has emphasized how embodied this process is, and how it depends on an integrated hierarchy of skills[14] – from basic psycho-physical coordination to expressive socio-cultural conventions – simultaneously communicating both the music and the person musicing.

Davidson's perspective suggests in more detail how, whilst for Vick and Pam their need to retain and enhance their performance of the self within illness is crucial, such performance is also a many-layered challenge. The significance of this work for our current investigation concerns how a music therapist using performance as a legitimate site for client needs can try to ensure optimal performance at the levels Davidson suggests. I will look more at this below – in terms of the careful professional work it entails from the music therapist – preparing performances and coping during them. For the time being, Davidson's work serves to remind us what is behind optimal performance, how fragile it can be, and how its achievement will often be a difficult challenge rather than an everyday achievement.

As I stated earlier, music therapists have for some decades been troubled by musical performance being part of music therapy, as it seems to conflict with

---

[14]   Davidson argues that earlier empirical research on performance tended to study the production of sound from a somewhat disembodied stance. She has instead developed a broader bio-psycho-socio-cultural perspective. Her various studies of individual and group performance show an evolving holistic sequence of embodied performance. Firstly, the individual free-moving body works within its biomechanical constraints to produce a complex task. In music this is, at the same time, an expressive performance produced via a bodily "center of movement" (e.g. a pianist's swaying from the hips). In addition to this performers also produce a whole repertoire of non-verbal movements which serve to coordinate their expressive musical actions with co-performers and audience (these being embedded in a socio-cultural framework). Lastly, performers convey something about themselves in the music through their bodily conduct, which is accessible to (and desired by) audiences.

psychoanalytic theory's concept of "authenticity" (or rather it's assumption that performance is inauthentic).[15] Therapy, in this view should be helping people get more insight into their "real" self. Much contemporary psycho-social theory would, however, take serious issue with such a narrowly psychological concept of personhood, instead suggesting how the self (and its constant shifts) is a socially and culturally constructed entity, whose nature is indeed performative.[16] An interesting example of such a perspective comes from the radical "social therapist" Fred Newman, who colorfully describes performance as "being who you aren't, doing what you can't ..." A main inspiration for Newman's method and theory (which is a thorough critique of traditional therapy) is the early Russian developmental psychologist Vygotsky. The latter's theory of child language development caught Newman's interest; how Vygotsky suggested that children perform "a head taller than they are" when surrounded and inducted into a cultural *zone of proximal development* (for example, a conversation, or playing music together). Adults literally talk (or play) above the child's developmental level, but whilst in that cultural performance space the child performs beyond himself. Thus, these "performance spaces" ("ZPDs") are *both* the tool for development but also the experienced result (a "tool-and-result" phenomenon in Newman's theory):

> In this way, human development is an "unnatural act"; we become who we "are" by continuously "being who we are not," as the tool-and-result of our activity. (Newman in Holzman, 1999, p. 100)

Newman wants to get away from an idea of therapy as just people finding out who they "really" are, from expressing inner content "outwards."[17] Instead he developed a performative stance on therapy itself – where for him people learn to perform themselves differently in ensemble with others. The aim is to transform the whole zone of relational experience such that people experience themselves differently together. "I'm not concerned to help people to discover self. I'm concerned to help people discover life" says Newman:

---

[15] This psychoanalytic modeling of music therapy I've called the "consensus model." For more detailed comment and critique of its attitudes and assumptions (and a comparison of these to emerging Community Music Therapy thinking (see Ansdell, 2002; Pavlicevic and Ansdell, 2004).

[16] This is not the place for a detailed account of social constructionist ideas of the self, but see – for discussions of how these ideas relate to Community Music Therapy – Stewart (2004) and Ansdell (2004). For a perspective from cultural psychology see Stige (2003). On "performativity" from a Performance Studies perspective, see Schechner (2002).

[17] Newman takes inspiration here from Vygotsky, who famously wrote: "The relationship between thinking and speaking is not the relationship of one being the expression of the other ... When you speak you are not expressing what it was that you were thinking, you're *completing it*" (Vygotsky in Holzman, 1999, p. 127).

> What we were creating in therapy … was *performance* … and that performance
> was of wonderful, developmental, therapeutic value. People were learning how
> to perform – going back to Vygotsky's language – people were learning to
> perform *beyond themselves*. They were breaking out of the habit of simply *being*
> themselves to discovering not who they were but *who they were not*. (Newman
> in Holzman, 1999, p. 129)

In these terms the *Musical Minds* and *Scrap Metal* performances were certainly a
form of "social therapy." Instinctively the members of both groups (with the help
of their music therapists and the audience) literally staged for themselves a zone
of proximal development, an environment in which to perform a head taller than
they usually can in everyday life. The fundamental paradox of "becoming who we
'are' by continuously 'being who we are not'" was readily apparent for many of
the participants of the performances – for Pam and Vick especially.

   The conventional therapy model of "expressing yourself" was hardly adequate
to what happened, not only therapeutically, but also musically. An alternative
possibility is suggested by Jason Toynbee (2000), who mounts a critique of naive
expressionism within his theory of popular music. Instead of thinking of musical
creators (along lines popularized by Romantic pictures of classical composers
expressing their souls through unique musical expressions), Toynbee suggests
that most musicians create *in* performing – that "making up" and "showing off"
are one fluid continuum. And they do this by selecting possible voices from the
already-available cultural stock, and then speak through these musical voices with
personal agency. He calls this "social authorship." Here again is the paradox of
performance: being your own musical voice through being someone else's:

> It represents another nail banged in the coffin of expressionism. For not only are
> voice-ingredients located in the social world, so too is the creative act. Never a
> pure enactment of subjective intention, it must, as a condition of its possibility,
> have an awareness of itself as a performed act in a social milieu, at a particular
> time and place … Effective social authorship produces thick texts which speak
> of the social lives of people, particularly oppressed people, but which also
> promise the possibility of change. (Toynbee, 2000, pp. 58–66)

Vick's rendition of *My Way* comes to mind here. Toynbee's view explains how
performing is seldom so simple as the traditional model of expressing yourself
or communicating the song. Vick instead took part exactly in a process of social
authorship – taking a cultural voice (a style, a song, a performer) and transforming
it in the course of performance, so that the performance event was both
characteristically Vick *and* Frank Sinatra – a "dual performance" in Atkinson's
(2006) phrase. It was both of the moment, and woven within a cultural and social
tradition. Vick was "being who you aren't; doing what you can't." Equally, the
more improvisational, avant-garde quality of the *Scrap Metal* concert had its

combination of negotiated cultural conventionalism and performed personalism (Pam's bucket piece, for example).

So here we have two examples of mainly solo performances, where the total ecology of the situation created unique moments for two individuals. For Pam and Vick musical performance affords them a resource for performing a self through a social performance, and hence the potential for individual transformation.

Collaborative Performances

Both concerts I witnessed also contained group performances in which the whole became more than the sum of its parts, and where community was being performed – just as Vick and Pam had performed their individual lives. For both therapists such collaborative work was important – creating a situation where the often socially isolated members of their groups could create something together. Sarah talked a lot about the relationship between individuality and togetherness in her work with *Musical Minds* – how the group had developed in the last few years from a rather individualistic "doing their own thing" style to, more recently, building both musical and organizational collaboration. Sarah has encouraged the group to listen more to each others' songs, and to join in and work on group numbers. Social collaboration seems to have followed musical collaboration.

> Musical Minds' Band for Life *concert begins with a* West Side Story *medley. All of the group of ten performers are on stage together, singing an ensemble number. Nerves are bad and the beginning is musically ragged. Sarah works hard (on the piano, along with gestures to the group) to motivate musical collaboration. The success of the performance is partly related to Sarah's preparation with the group, and by her in-the-moment musical accommodation to the contingencies of their singing. But there is also an obvious autonomy of the group during the performance – they find their own accommodation to each other and to the situation. The creation of a togetherness finds another dimension at the end of the concert when the whole group again get up on the stage and sing the war-time classic "We'll Meet Again" – encouraging the audience to join in (which they do).*

The group is now promoting other people's ability to participate too – creating musical community for everyone.[18] Sarah comments:

---

[18]   There are two interesting dimensions to this. First, such communal singing relates to the local East End of London tradition of pub and community singing, so what was being enacted by the group at this point was as much to do with a *musical* tradition as it was with the loose mental health community this was taking part within. Second, the audience consisted of some people who had only just come out of the neighboring hospital

This was the first time afterwards that they said they felt good about singing together as a group. Why? Because I think it's when they really feel they belong – they're part of it: they have that experience I think of being part of something that feels good, that they are contributing, that's different if they're not there ... and something that's fun as well! They got on well! And they're not people that necessarily "get on well" other places ... (Sarah Wilson, music therapist)

At one level the contrast with the *Scrap Metal* concert could not be greater.

The opening minutes of their concert presents us with a seemingly avant-garde musical idiom, with a loose airy coincidence of sounds and people in the resonant acoustic of the church. Short thuds of drums, a squeak from the organ ... the texture building, but also people characterizing themselves and their unusual instruments ... Then responses – this sound answering that one ... and soon the tentative sounds build into a huge climax of pulsed percussive sound. This is not "therapy music" as I know it! People are not just "expressing themselves" here. But neither is it conventional avant-garde professional music – here people are deeply personally invested in their performance, but variously challenged by their physical and musical abilities.

The next piece in the concert is a continuation of this play between structure and chance. This time the group use as their starting point John Cage's "Suite for Toy Piano." Appropriately the soloist for this is professional pianist and music therapist Mika – who sits on the stage on a bucket, with her toy piano resting on a wooden crate. After she plays a section of the piece a pre-arranged nod from Mika gradually cues in the other players: first the typewriter, then the bicycle wheel, gong, pan-lids, and teapot theramin ... moving from set piece to improvisation, each voice entering and re-orientating the music. As the improvisation develops the idiom changes slightly, towards perhaps the jazz drumming style of one of the workshops that have led up to this concert. There's a successful cohesion in the music, coming from the musical collaboration of the players. The theramin successfully breaks up the group beat for a while, and then the piano reorients the group within a more melodic and harmonic idiom.

Stuart comments on this overall process:

In improvisation you don't know what combinations are going to happen next! I love that moment when people start listening to the theramin, and they hear something that isn't a pulse, but is a continuous sound ... and then they all try to dissolve what they're doing to make space for this new thing. And of course what they're also doing here is making space for a person in that, as well as making

themselves (and were brought along by some other professional). This communal singing gave everyone the chance to join in, whoever they were, wherever they'd come from.

space for a sound, because the two things are wrapped up in one. I find that level of listening profound, moving...

So each gesture or accident of sound instantly takes on an importance to the whole, and creates the future of the piece. I love this sense in improvised music where a small gesture has a big effect, where the ripples from a sound go a long way. As a music therapist I see this as a true performance: where people are being formed by music, and then forming music in turn ... it's a continual musical looping ... Now for some members of the group this looping has an individual significance, it helps them do something more than they can usually do ... whilst for others it's more social: it involves their whole social life, it's the only thing that creates them as social beings again when they've had this illness or disability that so isolates them socially. So someone can be formed within themselves, but they can also be formed and form others on a social level ... (Stuart Wood, music therapist)

Stuart's words here tantalizingly suggest some of the recent theorizing on how group improvisational processes (for example in music or drama) can be models for "social emergence" – how social group phenomena emerge from individual communicative action. Equally, this theory could provide us with tools for thinking about how and why musical and social emergence seems isomorphic in situations such as these two music therapy group performances. The communications theorist Keith Sawyer (2003, 2005) has developed a sociocultural theory of group creativity based on his close study of improvising jazz musicians and actors. He suggests how creativity is as much a socio-cultural process as a psychological one; that it happens as much *between* people, as "within" them, and its main characteristics are improvisation, emergence and interaction. Group creativity is achieved through coordination, communication and collaboration in the improvised moment. Especially in performance situations (and within performance groups) something new *emerges* through the constant micro-communications that mediate the cultural materials the performers are working with and through (i.e. the musical or dramatic formats or set-pieces). Overall, writes Sawyer:

... in emergent groups, the whole is greater than the sum of the parts; the performance is greater than the individual performers. A performing group is a complex dynamical system. (Sawyer, 2003, p. 163)[19]

Independently of Sawyer, Mercédès Pavlicevic and I (Ansdell and Pavlicevic, 2005; Pavlicevic and Ansdell, 2009), have suggested that the psychobiological foundation of communicative musicality (Malloch and Trevarthen, 2009) is naturally followed by a second "function" of *collaborative musicing* – which

---

[19]   In his most recent work Sawyer (2005) has developed the implications of this statement into a theory of social emergence, which gives detailed attention to how a "third wave systems theory" can help model the emergence of social phenomena.

naturally couples social and musical emergence through performance and quasi-performance practices. People want to music together, to perform together, for adaptive human reasons.[20]

These two theoretical perspectives on group musical processes are interesting in relation to the "collaborative performances" described above. The more improvisational of the two was the *Scrap Metal* concert, where the communication and collaboration process that was carefully built up during the workshops enabled an emergent level of creativity, performance, and social collaboration to happen on the night. Here it was very apparent that the performed whole of the concert was greater than the sum of its parts. Physically and musically, the "group flow" within the performance situation afforded a unique experience for many of the participants. Although *Musical Minds* rely less on improvisational procedures there is nonetheless an important sense in which their performance events, and their increasing social collaboration, are co-emergent too.

We have seen how, in one sense, what happens in these "collaborative performances" is similar to the "self performances" of Pam and Vick: people are working simultaneously at a bodily, psychological, and socio-cultural level; they are somehow performing a head taller than they usually are; they are somehow both themselves and "someone other" within the course of performance. But there is a difference too: the matter of what the collaborative musicing of the performance ensemble affords – which is these people's creation (or re-creation, as Stuart puts it) as social beings against the losses of their illness.

Preparing and Completing Performances

The previous two sections have presented the synchronic axis of performance: the in-the-moment constellations of experience that are so powerful for performers and audience alike. But this is not the whole story. You would be forgiven for assuming that the etymology of "performance" indicates "through the form." The anthropologist Victor Turner (who made an extensive study of performance cross-culturally) gives, however, another interesting possibility:

> *Performance* ... is derived from the Middle English *parfournen*, later *parfourmen*, which is itself from the Old French, *parfournir* – par ("thoroughly"), + fournir ("to furnish") – hence performance does not necessarily have the structuralist implications of manifesting form, but rather the processual sense of "bringing to completion," or "accomplishing." To perform is thus to complete a more of less involved process rather than to do a single deed or act. (Turner, 1982, p. 91)

This sense of performance as *completion* assumes then that something *needs* completing, both in the cultural form which is the performance vehicle, but perhaps

---

[20]   For more on "collaborative musicing," see Part IV in this volume.

also in the personal and social life of those who participate in the performance event. It suggests how in the creative "carrying out" of performance something is transformed, personally and socially. In this sense performance events are close to ritual events in being both experiential (going with the liminal flow of musical *communitas*), but also potentially reflexive – showing people back something about themselves and their society. Turner became especially interested in the rehearsal or preparation process for performance. He commented on how an actor moves from taking up a role (= "not me") to assimilating this in performance as "not not me." The aim, says Turner, is "*poiesis*, rather than *mimesis*: making, not faking." He sums up his concept of performance: "A performance, then, is the proper finale of an experience" (Turner, 1982, p. 13). In this sense I follow now the two performance events I studied from the diachronic (over-time) axis: the before-during-after process – from preparation to completion.

Before

Musical Minds have been preparing for four months for the upcoming concert during their weekly rehearsal time (from 4–6pm every Thursday). They start after Christmas for the April concert, with the urgency increasing in the final six weeks. There's an important relationship between the ongoing week-by-week musical and social process of the group and this "concert highlight." When I join them for a rehearsal three weeks before the concert there's anxious talk of whether there will be enough people in the audience; whether the staff will manage to do the food and drink; how to clear the stage area of junk. Gradually the group moves on to the more musical aspects. They try out songs they will perform: some solo items, a few duets and trios, and several chorus numbers. Tim rehearses his song, but he can't help rushing ahead with the music. Sarah tries to pull him back through her piano accompaniment, and after he's finished Sid gives him quite tactful feedback about singing it a bit slower. The next try he's a little better. Some of the communal songs are ragged at first, but there's discussion about listening to each other, trying to get it together. They try again, listen a bit more to each other, and the music begins to cohere. The group is keen to put on the best show they can, both musically and in the presentation aspects. Sarah, as the professional facilitator of the group, works hard with a skilled and subtle behind-the-scenes support, which seems crucial to the performance event being a success. She keeps members collaborating during rehearsals, her support seeming at the same time musical, organizational, and "moral." Sarah comments:

> This concert is a big event for us ... it's something that we aimed for and worked for and achieved – it gives a momentum, something to aim for, a reason for coming that will give you a musical experience today ... It's not about rehearsing to do it over and over again in order to get it perfect, but working on it now, to get something out of the musical experience right now ... In terms of the music I'm finding a way [during rehearsal] for a song or chorus to actually work ...

given that many of the members don't *actually sing what's written! So working out how to make suggestions about tempo, pitch, but also how much to let it go. I don't spend much time note-bashing ... but there is a limit: you heard a few people chop notes, bars, leave sections out! [laughs] (Sarah Wilson, music therapist)*

So Sarah sees her role in this preparatory stage as helping the members to get their performance as right as they can, or want it to be. It's not a case of musical perfection for perfection's sake, but of being sensitive to what the members themselves want to do with their music. Sarah manages this (as do the group) without comparing people too much – given there are marked difference of ability, talent, and awareness in the group.

Again, there are similarities and differences with the *Scrap Metal* project. This is more explicitly a one-off, time-limited project – though at the same time it (and many of its participants) are part of the ongoing process of Stuart's Community Music Therapy work in the neurological rehabilitation unit. In common with *Musical Minds* is the careful preparation that goes into both the musical, personal and social aspects of the *Scrap Metal* concert. From the forging of the scrap metal idea in Pam's music therapy, to the collecting of the instruments, to the emergence of the musical pieces is something of a musical ritual process (a description used by several of the participants I talk to). The preparatory stages involved regular improvising groups along with musical workshops (on jazz drumming, Gregorian chant, and playing with an organ). Music therapy doesn't usually, of course, happen in a church (but then this isn't typical music therapy). The group's musicing, however, develops very much in response to the acoustic space and atmosphere of this church, with its availability of the organ. The musical workshops build on musics the participants have become interested in. These are not necessarily those either the participants are used to, or those usual to music therapy work: Gregorian chant, jazz drumming, opera, organ music. The group also increasingly listen to recordings of the kind of improvisatory idiom that reflects the scrap metal sounds and ways of musicing – John Cage, Takemitsu, Japanese contemporary avant-garde music. Their aesthetic responds both to this music, but also to the sounds of the scrap instruments, the space of the church, the confluence of their tastes, gestures, and physical abilities.

The place of the preparatory work and the performance also has some cultural and political resonances: these people have left a medical setting and are trying to take their place again in their natural community and its cultural life. The concert is scheduled as part of a summer festival in the town, so the concert also takes its place alongside other arts events. As the concert comes nearer the meetings take on more of the character of rehearsals – doing things again and again, working at something for a purpose. But the notion of "rehearsal" isn't quite right for this ever-changing musical creation. As Stuart comments:

The other thing that's interesting is the notion of rehearsal ... *the Friday before the event everyone was talking about the final rehearsal, and I was saying, "You do know that we won't be doing the same thing then as we're doing now!" ... On the night is a performance, but tonight, now, is also a performance ... (Stuart Wood, music therapist)*

Stuart and Sarah's words about the "before process," and the events I witnessed, show something interesting about the development of both of these groups in terms of how process (as rehearsal or preparation) and outcome (as performance) relate. Put simply, their ongoing musicing is the most important thing – whether this is part of preparing or part of completing in performance. This phenomenon echoes some interesting writing of the sociologist and amateur musician Richard Sennett in his book *Respect* (2003). He explores how it is possible in our world today to keep our self-respect, and to respect others. When inequality (of health, money, opportunity) is unavoidable, how can people retain their self-respect? When well-meaning social and health workers give aid, therapy and advice, is mutual respect ever possible, Sennett asks. In seeking an answer he suggests a surprising analogy: that practicing and performing music may be a paradigm for thinking about mutual respect in these situations. Respect, Sennett suggests, cannot just be intended, it must be *performed*: "Respect is an expressive performance. That is, treating others with respect doesn't just happen, even with the best will in the world" (p. 207). What people want, suggests Sennett, is usually something more collaborative and less personal. Musicing is exemplary here of collaborative "respect-in-action," of "taking the other seriously" (p. 52).

His examples of the fruits of musical participation seem directly applicable to *Musical Minds*. Firstly, as Sennett suggests, the skill and craft element of learning something like music, of rehearsing and performing it, illuminates how self-respect develops. The members of *Musical Minds* engage with their music primarily for its own sake: to get it as right as possible, to make their shared performance a quality event. This palpably cultivates what Sennett calls "secure self-respect." Their investment of participation, rehearsal and mastery reaps dividends in dignity and self-respect. Secondly, *mutual respect* flows from such musical collaboration. Sennett uses the example of chamber music to illustrate this:

> ... ensemble work requires collaboration. Unless the musicians are playing in unison, they have to sort out differences and inequalities, loud against soft parts, or soloists and accompanists working together ... This is mutual respect as musicians perform it, a matter of recognizing someone else who is doing something different. (Sennett, 2004, p. 6)

This performative enactment of mutual respect describes well the narrative of the rehearsal and performance aspects of *Musical Minds* and *Scrap Metal*: the balancing of autonomy within community; of how Sarah and Stuart's role naturally shifts as the situation changes; of how self-respect and mutual respect is generated through musicing and performing. Stuart is explicit that *Scrap Metal* is not a group for people with disabilities but a group for those people to make the music they want. Both performances were fine demonstrations of how, in Sennett's words, "performing arts like music reveal the collaborative elements in the expressive practice of mutual respect" (2003, p. 263).

During

"Suddenly the Group is on the stage and they do everything then – you heard them shout to me: 'Come on Sarah, let's start' – It's funny! I'm trying to find where *they* are, what's happening!" This is Sarah describing what happens when the weeks of preparation end and the concert begins, at which point, as she says:

> *When it comes to the performance all I do is play the piano – I don't go on stage at all. Someone hosts, I just stay below the stage at the piano – as far as the audience is concerned I'm the piano-player! (Sarah Wilson, music therapist)*

There's a subtle shift of role for Sarah here – the therapist who also seems "just" the piano player – one which matches her overall strategy of balancing her musical and therapeutic support for the group with a respect for their autonomy. I find a similar subtlety of role-shift with Stuart, who also guides the group through the preparation process, but is far from center-stage when the performance happens. I ask him whether he still feels a music therapist at this stage:

> *I did feel like a music therapist all the time. After all I was responsible, and it was part of the music therapy program. But I know what I feel like when I'm a music therapist ... and that I can rely on this without being too conscious of it. It's my sense of accountability ... if there was a problem for anyone or a safety issue, then it would be my fault ... But I could also forget this role to some extent when I'm paying attention to the bigger picture ... (Stuart Wood, music therapist)*

I became increasingly interested in how both therapists negotiated these subtle variations within their basic role, but also how they managed the detailed craft aspects of ensuring an "optimal performance" for both individuals and the event as a whole (performers and audience). It will be clear by now that I don't mean by this the setting of some objective aesthetic standard which is independent of the participants, but of helping them to achieve what they want to according to their own standards and hopes. This brings to mind Turner's definition of performance as the "carrying-through" or "carrying-out" of something crucial. How then do Sarah and Stuart manage this in the second-by-second musicing?

I made a performance analysis of Vick's performance of *My Way*, and Sarah's skilled accompanying of this. The analysis uses criteria for identifying "musical performatives" based on Jane Davidson's work on embodied performance process (see above). The micro-analysis showed how Sarah's piano accompaniment helps Vick to regulate the timing, co-timing, and expressive organization of his performance. In short, to optimize this (against the de-optimizing effects of his illness) through Sarah's help. Describing her strategy for supporting and intervening musically into the performances (both in rehearsal and during the performance) Sarah comments:

> *Some people always make the same mistake of course, but others it just comes out differently every time ... I might say things like "slow down"... and then in the group stuff I'll sometimes be very directive, and wave a hand around, but then they'll get up on the stage and it'll all go haywire! So it's getting balance between letting things happen and saying something. I think it's not right to say "Everything's great!" when it's not ... because many of the members are musically sensitive, and they can tell the difference ... (Sarah Wilson, music therapist)*

The flexibility of professional and social roles is more marked within the *Scrap Metal* performance. Certainly an audience member who simply turned up to the concert (not knowing any of the participants) would not necessarily know "who's who" – by which I mean who of the 12 people on stage is a professional musician, music therapist, carer, patient ... or the man who designed and made the scrap instruments. Within the concert the music further leveled the social roles (an unusual situation in both music therapy and music professional circles). There was also another leveling – the performers and the audience were in a different relationship to each other than in a conventional concert. Stuart talks of "setting up a performance practice into which the audience are invited." Given the social aims of this project – to give people a way of re-negotiating their social identity as "differently abled" people – this was important, akin to how Victor Turner describes performance situations as examples of *communitas,* where structural roles are leveled whilst the music lasts.[21]

After

"A Performance," writes Turner, "is the proper finale of an experience" (1982, p. 13). Both concerts ended with the traditional finale of a lived-through process – a climax, followed by applause, relaxation, appreciation and an "after-glow." Concerts have been referred to as ritual events (Small, 1998), and ritual metaphors were common in people I spoke to about these two events. The organist of the *Scrap Metal* project, Fraser Simpson, said this:

---

[21] For more on Turner's concept of "communitas" in relation to Community Music Therapy (see Stige, 2003; Pavlicevic and Ansdell, 2004).

> *There was something really ritualistic about the performance as a whole ... It left me thinking how much performance itself is a form of ritual ... and how in traditional music therapy you don't get this – you don't have performance and so you don't have ritual.[22] Another thing that struck me was the energy of the music. There's something very special about the experience of working towards a performance, and then giving a performance ... the adrenalin, the excitement. Will it work or won't it? This is something that's such a vital basic part of music making ... which again gets completely left out of the traditional music therapy set-up (Fraser Simpson, music therapist)*

The performance event, at best, is something that is lived-through together, leading to a sense of completion and fulfillment. The ritual quality was both in its outer form but also in its function as a transformative event in relation to participants' identity, illness, health, and social being. The performers (individually, collectively) did not merely communicate the "form" of the songs; they somehow *completed* both the songs and themselves in the course of performance. Stuart talked of how the event was simultaneously forming people's experience and being formed by it. It often felt (for both audience and performers) as exactly the "proper finale of an experience," a carrying-out of something personal, communal, and cultural at the same time.

The week after the concert the *Musical Minds* group gets together, has a party and talks about the concert. A video was made, and all of the group want a copy of this – it's very important for them to show others, to have a record that they really did do it! Sarah comments:

> *The concert went better than I'd hoped: and it was a great atmosphere! The Group really enjoyed it I think ... and also I think they saw that there was something so good to be had about getting involved (in the long-term and immediate preparation for the event) ... and something so good to be had from good music, from listening to each other, being listened to by others... (Sarah Wilson, music therapist)*

There was also in both concerts (and their consequences) the sense of the *reflexivity* mentioned by Turner: the performances being a comment to society about what these people *could* do (marginalized as they are). On a more personal level, the choice of songs and pieces, and the ways participants chose to perform them gave subtle messages on, as Turner writes, "the nature, texture, style and given meanings of their own lives as members of a sociocultural community" (1987, p. 22). Somewhere here a magic mirror was at work.

A member of the *Scrap Metal* concert audience said afterwards: "This is music as it should be ..."

---

[22]   Various music therapists and theorists would no doubt enjoy challenging Fraser on this point!

Conclusion: The Affordances and Risks of Performing

I hope that the above discussion conveys how for the members of *Musical Minds* and *Scrap Metal* performing was certainly helpful within the situations they found themselves in. I hope also that the varying theoretical perspectives I have outlined in relation to the process and events I witnessed demonstrate how such performative aspects of Community Music Therapy practice can be in alignment both with contemporary psycho-sociocultural theory, and with a broadened therapeutic agenda of providing transformative experiences for people at individual, social, and political levels.

What, however, of the *risks* of performing, for potentially vulnerable people, in sometimes sensitive situations? The examples and the theories also highlight some of the paradoxes and potential difficulties of performance. It is perhaps no surprise that music therapy has been traditionally wary of entering into the performance zone – and rightly so. It is necessary to keep looking both at the benefits and the problems of performance for music therapy. The cultural theorist Edward Said has called performance "an extreme occasion … the central and most socially stressed musical experience in modern Western society" (Said, 1991, p. 12). It may be helpful to think of performance having two faces:

- *Performance as pressure:* the discourse of socio-economic performance (with its performance "targets" and "indicators") has burdened the modern notion of performance with negative/stress-laden connotations. This is also part of the reality of much musical life now – of competitions and performance situations loaded with expectation, pressure, and judgment. All of this could become unwittingly part of music therapy situations if we are not mindful.
- *Performance as epiphany:* this is the other face – performance as peak experience, "natural high," as "completion," not competition; as site for identity work, *musical communitas* and social hope.

My witnessing of the before, during, and after process of the two performances described in this essay have showed me overall how it was the consummate skill of the two music therapists, Sarah and Stuart, that ensured the safety of these events, and minimized (as far as humanly possible) "counter-therapeutic" aspects. This involved preparing performers (who all had a previous trusting relationship with the therapist); "thinking around" and intervening into emerging or potential problems; managing the audience's expectations; coping in the heat of the moment (musically and socially) with the minute-by-minute contingencies of the performances. This suggests the absolute necessity of a professional stance for this work, one informed by training and experience, and able to balance the risks of the event against the potential benefits. Recent discussions on the processes and ethics of Community Music Therapy (Aigen, 2004; Ruud, 2004b, 2005; Turry, 2005) have coined this attitude as one of "reflexive performance." One of the intentions of constructing a new discourse of Community Music Therapy is precisely to open up professional discussion of the potentials and pitfalls of accompanying clients across the full continuum of private to public music therapy, so that we can share experiences and concerns, and can encourage rich but safe practice.

My case for performance within music therapy stands currently against an ongoing belief within much of the current music therapy profession that performance is an unsuitable musical activity. In contrast, as I hope much of this book demonstrates, Community Music Therapy is developing a more nuanced understanding of the affordances and varying suitability of the private and public aspects of musicing within broadly-defined therapeutic contexts. A major part of this re-thinking involves a re-assessment of performance, and how it can be thought of as a possible resource rather than a problem. Current thinking, after all, argues that music should be defined as a performance art through and through – "music *as* performance." And if we follow where music and people lead, then both often lead up the steps, onto the stage, and towards the lights and the microphone! Mostly this is a good thing.

PART VII

Chapter 13

Action

Whose Voice is Heard? Performances and Voices of the *Renanim* Choir in Israel

Cochavit Elefant

Introduction

I first heard or rather saw *Renanim* choir three years ago while they were performing together with another choir in a mutual concert in Natanya, a town in mid Israel. They drew my attention during the concert and made me feel somewhat uncomfortable. I was not sure then if it was because of their severe physical handicaps or because of their strong effort in singing while not being heard. The other group performing in this concert, *Idud* (with singers with intellectual disabilities) did not provoke this type of feeling in me when they sang together with *Renanim*.

A few weeks before the performance, Rina Stadler, the music therapist, told me about the two choirs and about her interest in talking to someone about her work. At the same time, I was looking for a Community Music Therapy project in Israel and her work was intriguing and made me curious. I had known Rina, her motivation and energy of working and developing the choirs. Her insights and reflections over her work excited me. This time she had felt uncertain of her decision to merge the two choirs and wanted an outside participant observer to enter her work arena in order to take part in thinking about the development of the choirs. Her key statement was that she wanted to mix the groups in order to "give voice" to the *Renanim* choir.

My original thought was that it would be interesting to understand the two choirs' interest and perception towards music and performance in the community and to observe intergroup relations between the two choirs. It turned out that the choir members had questions, concerns, and goals that they wanted to pursue too. This resulted in the development of our collaboration inspired by the tradition of Participatory Action Research (PAR). I followed and documented the choirs for two years. The research took a sharp turn after the next concert, resulting in the continuation of a collaborative research project only with *Renanim*, as they voiced a concern that we could work with. The theme of "Whose voice is being heard?" gradually emerged as the main research focus. The story here is told in chronological sequence as the project developed.

Introducing the Two Choirs *Renanim* and *Idud*

The *Renanim* group consists of about 20 members between the ages 30–50. All members have quadriplegia.[1] Despite their severe physical handicaps they function at a normal cognitive level. All choir members live in a segregated village for individuals with physical disabilities called Maon Nechim,[2] situated at the outskirts of Natanya. During the daytime some study and others work in sheltered vocation in the village. In the afternoons they have several recreational activities, including the choir, which have rehearsed once a week for the past eight years with Rina, the village's music therapist.

The *Idud* group is made of about 45 adults with intellectual and developmental disabilities (at a mild to moderate level) around the same age range as the other group. They also live in a segregated village located outside of Natanya, but at quite a distance from *Renanim*'s village. They work at sheltered vocation in their village and have several recreational activities during the afternoon, including the choir with Rina. This choir has also been singing for the past eight years.

The group members have only rare opportunities to leave their segregated villages. However, yearly concerts take place in a location in town or in one of the two villages and they create an opportunity for them to be in contact with a broader community. Rina says:

> *I have been directing the choirs for the past eight years and feel that the end of the year concert is an expansion of the groups' therapeutic experiences; some of the members have individual music therapy in addition to singing in the choir. The two groups are confined to their own little circle of community; however, the concerts give them an opportunity to sing together and meet an audience that can give them feedback for the end results of what they have been rehearsing all year. (Rina Stadler, music therapist)*

Rina is one of the few music therapists in Israel who works flexibly with open boundaries within music therapy and doesn't only confine her practice to individual or group sessions within traditional therapeutic thinking. The performances with the two groups are her way of expanding the choirs' therapeutic experiences. The year I joined the project was when Rina had decided to try and merge the groups during the annual concert. The rationale behind it was to give voice to *Renanim*, who in her opinion was not heard loud enough when singing alone.

---

[1]   Quadriplegia is also known as tetraplegia and is a symptom in which a human experiences paralysis affecting all four limbs, although there is not necessarily a total paralysis or loss of function.

[2]   Maon Nechim means in Hebrew "Hostel for the Handicapped."

The First Joint Performance – and After

The first joint performance took place in a hot summer evening July 2004, in a large dining hall which was converted into a concert hall for the evening, in *Idud*'s village. The *Renanim* choir was transported with special vehicles to the arena. The concert was a tribute to a very famous Israeli song writer, Ehud Manor, who attended the concert and expressed his gratitude and warmth towards hearing his songs performed by the two choirs. Many attended the concert; family and friends and also some music therapists. The larger sized choir (*Idud*) wore colorful robes and stood on the stage, while the smaller sized choir (*Renanim*) wore white shirts with black pants and sat in their wheelchairs apart from the other choir. Both choirs were relatively motionless, adhering to conventional "concert rules." It seemed impressive but the atmosphere felt somewhat tense, perhaps caused by the discrepancy in choir size, clothes and sitting arrangements. In front of the choirs stood the music therapist, ready to lead the singers, and on the side of the stage the pianist was seated, ready to accompany.

Then the singing began and I became mesmerized. The sounds coming from the stage were loud and impressive. I was surprised, and so was the audience. During the first song my attention went to *Idud.* There was something powerful in the way they were standing and singing; they were vivacious and secure. They sang and moved with strength and passion, communicating musically with the audience. But then I zoomed towards *Renanim* and saw something totally different. The proud stance of *Idud* was contrasted by the severely handicapped group of people sitting in their wheelchairs. The colorful dresses of *Idud* won over the simple black and white outfit of the *Renanim* group. But the most striking difference was the sound; the powerful voices of *Idud* overshadowed *Renanim*'s silent voices. The group was "voiceless"; only their uncontrollable strong body movements and gestures were "heard." This unfortunate situation was made even more problematic by the fact that the pianist did little to attune his tempi to the singing gestures of *Renanim*. These images were quite strong and my experience was that this performance simply put the spotlight on *Renanim*'s weaknesses and pathologies.

At the end of the performance the hall roared with excitement, the audience was very moved by the concert and there wasn't a dry eye in the house. The song writer Ehud Manor congratulated both groups and said that the evening had been one of the highlights of his life. He added that their singing connected him strongly to the naivety and love that drives him when writing his songs. At this point it seemed as if everything in the concert was flawless and successful. The audience and the singers mingled after the concert, exchanging views and experiences, yet when I came to congratulate *Renanim*, they thanked me with a polite head nod. It was quite clear that they were not in congruence with the rest of the crowd.

Shortly after the performance I met with Rina who also seemed unhappy about *Renanim*'s experience in the performance and said:

> Renanim's *voices vanished behind* Idud's *voices. This was not my intention and I*
> *had not anticipated this to happen. (Rina Stadler, music therapist)*

She revealed that *Renanim* was extremely disappointed because their voices were
shadowed and overtaken by the other choir. These are some of her reflections:

> *When I decided to merge the groups I think I was caring more for the end result.*
> *I didn't want* Renanim *to sing alone because of their weak voices, but I didn't*
> *think of what this performance might do to them. Maybe a joint performance*
> *must not be achieved at all costs? (Rina Stadler, music therapist)*

I met the two choirs separately to discuss the performance and to hold an open
conversation around the "music sentence completion task." Some of the phrases
were: "Music is …," "For me Music is …," "Without Music …," "Performing is
… ." The groups were very different in views and feelings towards the performance
and towards music. The *Idud* choir was very positive about the performance. These
were some of their statements about the performance:

> *"I had a great time."*
> *"It was fantastic."*
> *"I love to perform."*
> *"I love to perform and sing with different groups."*
> *"Ehud Manor loved us."*

These statements revealed genuine aspects of these singers' experience, but there
were also quite clear limitations to their verbal expression and several participants
seemed to echo each other. In my experience the discrepancy between their
capacity for musical communication on the stage and their verbal conversation
in our meeting was immense. They had their own unique expressive voices when
singing on the stage. They were communicating and collaborating as long as
they were musicing and had said all they needed during the performance. Words
were not their strongest avenue and had limited meaning at that point. I asked
Idud if there was anything they wished to change either in rehearsals or in the
performances and their wish was to continue just as things were. At that point they
asked me with no hesitation to stop talking so that they could get back to their
rehearsal. I was interfering with their precious musical time with my meaningless
questions.

After my conversation with *Idud*, Rina and I concluded that the group seemed
content and did not wish for a change to take place. It seemed less relevant and
urgent to continue involving them in a Participatory Action Research project.
The meeting with *Renanim* choir was different. The group had many things they
wished to share and to discuss with Rina, me, and amongst themselves. They were
uninhibited and expressed their emotions and thoughts openly about their singing
and performing. These were some of their comments about the performance:

"The performance was too scary for me."
"We were swallowed by the other group."
"We were hardly heard."
"I hate to perform."
"People need to get to know us in a better way."
"The performance took away the fun."

Listening to them made me hear how loud their "silent" voices spoke. Their voices were an out loud expression of their internal being and their need for dignity and self-esteem. Rina and I valued their comments and found them both relevant and important and I had then wished to develop a relationship that would be mutual and reciprocal. They were lively thinkers, eager to discuss, develop, change and work around issues regarding their rehearsals and performances. One of the members said:

I hope the tradition of performing will continue but differently!

Although the experience of merging the two groups during the performance left them unhappy and disappointed, they didn't want to give up the experience of performing. At that point, I explained what Participatory Action Research in music therapy was and that it meant that we were all acting and collaborating together. It was agreed by the group, Rina (the music therapist) and I that I will participate in some of their rehearsals and all concerts for the next two years. Our meetings would be audio-taped and the concerts videotaped, and we would observe the videos together and discuss and reflect throughout the project.

When I left the group I was deeply moved and inspired. My uneasy feelings towards this group during the concert were overtaken by warmth, respect, and strength towards the group and I was looking forward to continue working with them and Rina. I met *Renanim* again a few weeks later after they had watched the video tape of their performance with Rina. We discussed the performance one more time and their action was that they decided to perform the next concert without the *Idud* choir. They discussed the fact that their voices did not sound well during previous concerts but that it was important for them to work on their voices so that they could be heard. They continued to discuss this theme with Rina during the upcoming rehearsals.

Death of Ehud Manor, and an Enlightening Turn

The sudden death of Ehud Manor, which shocked the whole country, happened a few months after the concert. *Renanim* responded to his death very emotionally. Their meeting with Ehud Manor during the performance had been very meaningful for the choir. In addition to Ehud Manor's death another sad death occurred to one of the choir members. The choir and Rina were devastated. The two traumatic

occurrences had affected everyone. Several members left the group, some due to
health problems and others due to fear of performing.

The year was a difficult one for the choir and Rina. She was unsure whether
she could prepare the group for a concert. The group was now quite small (about
15 people) but nevertheless wanted to continue singing and preparing for the next
concert. Two months before the second concert I received an e-mail from Rina
which presented the various aspects of the choir and her problem:

> Hi,
>
> It's really a very complicated situation. I want to be convinced that all I'm doing
> is for their [the *Renanim* choir]'s sake. On the one hand the process is important,
> that's true, and not the finished product, but the process is directed towards this
> final show. Everything that happened this year and the process that took place
> are all leading towards this concert. I can't disappoint them now. I must accept
> all these problems as part of the process.
>
> Do you think I can tell them that they'll not sing in the concert this year? I
> don't think so.
>
> I hope I'm not doing it for myself. It's crossing my mind once in a while. I
> don't know, I think I'm doing the right thing as a therapist for her patients.
>
> It has really been a hard year for me and the group but nevertheless very
> teaching and very interesting. I learn a lot …
>
> Rina

These are sincere words expressed by Rina to her several dilemmas. Is it a good
idea to let the group perform or not? Will the quality of the performance influence
the group? Do we want to separate the process from the product?

The group's mood was at its worse, the quality of singing had deteriorated and
Rina was worried that another disappointing performance would completely drain
the last bits of strength the group members had. However, Rina did not want to
disappoint the group by not performing. Rina's dilemmas were openly discussed
with the group. This was an important direction that Rina took and would become
a regular practice by her. By doing so, she had passed some of the responsibility to
them. The group held loud discussions regarding the performance and decided to
perform despite the loss of some members and vocal abilities. Another important
outcome of that meeting was that the group and Rina decided to ask two staff
members from the village to join the choir during rehearsals and the concert to
strengthen the choir's voice. The group members once again gained control over
the situation and made their own decisions as to what they wished to do.

In the meantime, as the group's identity and collective action became
strengthened, a couple of members returned to the choir. This contributed to the
group's confidence and pride and uplifted the atmosphere along with the extra

voices of the staff members. They all agreed that it was better singing with the staff members than with the *Idud* group.

I joined a rehearsal just before the concert. The atmosphere was relaxed and humorous even though there was hard work going on. Rina had suggested a new musical direction; Middle Eastern type Israeli songs. Some of the discussion during the rehearsal was:

> *Rina:* These songs are easier to sing, with simpler rhythm and the melodies are easier to learn. You all have to take responsibility when you perform. You need to try and do your best at the performance.

She was supportive and at the same time firm, while repositioning the responsibility towards the group. The conversations between Rina and the group became more fluid while ideas and thoughts were discussed. The motivation during the rehearsal was high as they rehearsed the same phrases over and over with the intention and willingness to succeed.

> *Rina:* Did you notice that most of the songs are quite sad?
> *Orit:* I love to sing sad songs.
> *Avi:* Yes, they touch you right in the heart.

I left the group thinking that they will make it in the next performance.

The Second Concert – and After

Once more, I felt that there was tension in the air, but this time it came from the excitement of being "one" of the *Renanim* group. I was really proud of them, even before they began singing. They sat in their wheelchairs on the stage with smiles of excitement and confidence. I felt their strength and dignity.

The pianist was a little more attuned to the group than he had been the previous performance. They sang several Middle-Eastern genre songs with wonderful nuances of the musical ornamentations characteristic to that style. Some members had solo pieces in which they sang with so much soul and power, and some pieces were sung by the whole choir (Figure 13.1).

Their singing went very well and they were heard! The audience's attention went to the group while they performed. The performance was powerful and in control. It wasn't difficult to detect the grimaces on the choir members' faces as people waited in line to congratulate them after the concert. They seemed proud and enjoyed every moment of their connection to the audience.

Two weeks after the concert we met in order to reflect and evaluate the concert. The group was very pleased with the performance and eager to start rehearsing to prepare for another performance. The following comments were made by some of the members:

Figure 13.1   The *Renanim* choir during performance

> *Avi:*   I feel great with the performance. There were several slip-ups, but these
>   were caused by excitement. I think we sang better this year than last
>   year.
> *Dorit:*   My voice was used up in the rehearsals but I was very excited to sing
>   alone in the performance, a positive excitement.
> *Orit:*   It was too short. I am really glad we sang alone. *Idud* has a different
>   disability.
> *Dorit:*   I was so moved when Avi had his solo.

The group was still very excited and stirred by their achievement. The meeting
was more of a platform to ventilate their feelings and we agreed to meet in two
months to watch the video of the concert and to discuss the next action.

Watching the video provoked a lively discussion. They were pleased that they
had been "heard" by Rina who had agreed to let them perform in spite of the
difficult experiences during the year. And they were pleased that the audience had
finally heard their voices. They had the space to individually and collaboratively
express themselves in public and felt a pride with their identity in spite of their
disabilities in relation to the world.

They began discussing the next action in the Participatory Action Research
cycle; raising once again the idea of singing with the *Idud* choir.

> *Chagit:*   This was a good performance. Maybe we are now ready to sing
>   together with another group.

Orit:	I have a problem singing with *Idud*. Different types of disabilities shouldn't be performing together. The singing needs are different. We are not heard when we sing with them, but now that we sang alone we were heard!
Pitzi:	*Idud* is far better than us.
Rina:	The idea behind the performing is for you to enjoy it. Your group has less than 20 members while they have more than 40, so why compare?

Their discussion took a different direction.

Dorit:	Actually, singing the medley alone this year wasn't easy. Idud can strengthen us.
Rina:	What do you think about the idea of rehearsing throughout the year with *Idud*?
Pitzi:	I think that we either merge all the way or stay alone.
Orit:	Maybe it will become interesting to do it that way.
Maxim:	I think it could be great to merge.
Avi:	I will be heard less with a big choir.
Orit:	It is not enough to sing with them only during the concert. Either we sing together all year long or we sing alone! I'm interested in merging the groups!
Cochavit:	I'm hearing more voices for merging than singing alone. What made you change your minds about singing together with the other group?
Several voices:	It is more fun to sing together in a larger group.
Dorit:	*Idud* can amplify our voices.
Orit:	We have strong enough voices to sing with other groups.

There were many different voices that were expressed and the discussions were at times heated and loud. Some members were more opinionated than others. My role was that of a group facilitator during this process. Individuals learned to listen while others dared to speak. The group learnt to negotiate and compromises were made.

Closure

"Idud can amplify our voices," said Dorit. These were the exact words Rina also had used two years earlier when she first had tried to merge the two groups during performance. So what was the difference? This time the words were said by *Renanim* after a long process of evaluating, reflecting, acting, and reflecting again. Rina's attempt then in merging the groups gave them an opportunity to build something new all by themselves. "We were heard!" they declared in the second performance.

Another cycle in our Participatory Action Research project had come to an end and I had to leave the project. Yet a new decision was made by the choir and it could mean that a new and exciting cycle could begin. *Renanim* had experienced that doing Participatory Action Research meant "taking a journey … it is about movement from the way things are to the way things could be" (Smith, Willms, and Johnson, 1997, p. 8). My journey with the group had ended, while they continued.

During the following year they had a very successful performance in which they sang partly alone and partly with *Idud*. I didn't attend that performance but watched it on video and can testify that their voices were heard while they sang alone and with *Idud* – at least I heard it. I would like to end with one of the citations of our last conversation:

> *Avi:*   What a great voice I have! Finally I'm being heard! This needs to be heard internationally (Figure 13.2).

Avi and the group had known that I had been discussing the project with my international research colleagues and they were always eager to hear the opinion of the "experts." However, I am led to believe that Avi's last statement came from pride and strength and a wish to share his voice with others. I was glad to tell Avi and the group that their voices will be heard internationally as my intention was to bring their story to international conferences and to a written testimony.

Figure 13.2   Avi's solo

Chapter 14

Reflection

Giving Voice: Participatory Action Research with a Marginalized Group

Cochavit Elefant

Giving voice to silenced voices is the beginning of emancipatory practice.

Margaret Ledwith

Introduction

In the narrative in Chapter 13, a detailed story was told about *Renanim*, a choir whose members are adults with severe physical impairment. The choir and their music therapist took part in almost three years of a Participatory Action Research (PAR) project. The group was motivated to change a shared issue of importance, namely their concern of not being "heard" during a public performance. Through their PAR journey they regained their voices and with it enhanced their experience of dignity.

This chapter will describe the process of making change with a marginalized population, and then focus on the main outcome themes weaved out of the PAR project: "Whose voice is heard?," "Musical performance," "The role of the music therapist in Community Music Therapy," and finally; "Time and Timing." The themes were developed through an etic and emic dialectics,[1] which enabled the sharing of different perspectives related to *Renanim*, Rina Stadler (the music therapist) and me (the academic researcher), informing each other for the purpose of dialogue and understanding.

Adults with Disabilities – The Israeli Context

Adults with disabilities in Israel are still segregated and isolated from the larger society. Like the two choirs, they typically live in group homes or villages for people with disabilities (Lifshitz and Merrick, 2004). These are located at the outskirts of a town or city, with limited social integration in the community. Various

---

[1]   Etic perspective is an outsider's view (researcher) of an account, and emic perspective is the local or native's (insider) view of understanding an account.

environmental constraints impede their participation in the everyday activities that individuals without disabilities experience. These environmental constraints include physical, social, institutional, economic, and cultural factors in their home and within their community (Law, 1997). As a result of the limited control over their day-to-day life, they tend to spend most of their time in passivity, cared and led by others which create limited experience in decision making in their lives, all of which fosters dependency.

Individuals in a group such as *Renanim* experience intense physical disability and chronic pain from degeneration of muscles and bones. In addition, they are occupied with the theme of *loss* in their life. There is the loss of physical abilities, loss of loved ones (due to isolation), loss of friends (who pass away), and loss of vitality. They have very little power, status, or influence in their own small community or within the larger society. Their voices are rarely heard and when it happens, they are often misunderstood or misinterpreted.

The attitude towards the disabled in Israel is a disputed subject and has caused criticism among concerned citizen groups. The large amount of immigrants settling in Israel leads to development of segregated minority groups, which necessitates use of economic means to support contact and integration. In addition, the political and military realities become a heavy economical constrain for the country, leaving behind social, educational, and cultural issues. On many levels this type of neglect and distance from the population with special needs can result in deep social and psychological effects among them.

The *Renanim* project was about a group of individuals unwilling to accept the Israeli social stance towards marginalized groups. They were concerned with overcoming and changing values and attitudes towards them. Participating in the choir was an important activity for this group and a social symbol for their strength. One member expressed the meaningfulness of performing with these words:

So that the people out there could see and hear what the disabled can do.

The group had only one or two opportunities each year to make a difference, which may explain why those performances were significant and essential to most of them. Through the research project the rehearsals and the performances became one of very few arenas for independence, dialogues and democracy. There, they could choose and negotiate repertoire; relate and communicate to each other about musical and personal issues in their lives. This process was documented as it grew and developed, inspired and informed by the Participatory Action Research process.

The Process of Making Change with a Marginalized Group

Participatory Action Research (PAR) was practiced during this research project. Stige describes Participatory Action Research as:

... a communicative approach, where collective reflections for identification of problems and solutions are essential. But the process does not stop with thinking and talking; practical actions are implemented and evaluated as a basis for new collective reflections. (Stige, 2005a, p. 405)

PAR is characterized by its cyclic approach of assessment, planning, action, evaluation, and reflection. The cycles allow the participants to develop and learn from the actual process, to rethink, return to the problem, attempt and act on a new strategy, evaluate, reflect, etc. The process is motivated by a quest to improve practice and understand ideas; by acting and changing the direction and by learning how to improve the course (McTaggart, 1997). The PAR process carries ingredients quite similar to a therapeutic experience and it could therefore be natural for the music therapist to collaborate in such a process without losing the professional identity.

In other words, those who are involved in a PAR are likely to influence the direction of the research, by communicating, changing, and developing ideas. The PAR approach carries a potential tool to help improve the lives of the marginalized groups, as Stige writes:

Participatory action research is about giving marginalized people voice and about listening to the voices of others. (Stige, 2005a, p. 408)

There are relatively few PAR examples in the music therapy literature. The first project using aspects and principles of PAR was carried out by Stige and Kleive in the mid 1980s (Kleive and Stige, 1988; Stige, 2002). In this example the music therapists and *Upbeat*, a group of adults with developmental disabilities in Norway, brought about social change in the municipality where they lived. The change occurred when the group's musical experiences became more inclusive and was heard within the local community. A more recent PAR project was completed by Warner (2005), set in a community home for people with learning difficulties. The uniqueness of Warner's study is that the PAR approach in music therapy was developed with people with very limited or no language. In this research she managed to include the residents, music therapist, and care workers as co-researchers.

PAR means partnership and collaboration with an emphasis on mutuality with shared values and visions. There are several ways of defining the roles of the people involved in the research process (see e.g. McTaggart, 1997; Stige, 2005a). I have come to define my role as an academic researcher, while the music therapist and the choir members were defined as co-researchers. My role as the academic researcher at the outset of this project was to elucidate the PAR as an approach to work towards reflective action cycles and to bring my perspectives as an outsider into the dialogue. I attempted at giving boundaries to help move the participants from one place to another, and yet at the same time maintain flexibility to enable new actions posed by the participants. My intention was also to attempt at helping to bring and create tools for the participants to build trust and cooperation in order to create a context critical for challenges and reflection; to navigate but to know when not to, as the participants become emancipated.

> The process of doing participatory action research may be conceptualized as a cycle of collaborative activities that starts with a thematic concern. (Stige, 2005a, p. 410)

In this project, PAR approach was born out of a desire to change and improve a quest namely giving voice to the *Renanim* choir. This became a joint motivation for us all; the choir members wanted to be heard and Rina wanted to improve the performance so that the group could be heard. As a researcher I was dedicated to the process and to the responsibility of documenting it.

The first cycle started with a thematic concern; *Renanim* was not heard loudly enough when singing alone. Rina, the music therapist, examined the theme from her viewpoint and values and then pursued by merging the two choirs. Thereafter, she involved *Renanim* in rethinking and reflecting on the theme, thus examining her internal motives and challenging her own inner attitudes and stance. Eventually the PAR process lead to the same quest of "giving voice," only this time it was a mutual desire. This theme had many variations and developments; from a more concrete physical level in which the choir wanted to sing well and be heard, to a more social value focal point of being heard and accepted by society. This thematic concern was a development from Rina's monologic frame of decision making towards a more dialogic mode in which all of the participants were involved and inherently could deal with differences in views and agendas which arose during discussions. However challenging, the dialogical perspective is an important aspect of PAR, as Warner writes:

> Clearly different agendas are likely to exist ... by identifying agendas and subjecting them to critically reflexive processes, new solutions might become evident. (Warner, 2005, p. 78)

The concept of "allowing" differences in views within a frame of people who aren't used to negotiations is to go beyond their boundaries. These boundaries expanded as the group's coping skills and confidence grew.

Data Collection and Analysis

My participation and observation as researcher took place during two concerts and during several rehearsals and conversations before and after the concerts (Figure 14.1). The data collection was multilayered and included:

Audio:
- Semi structured interviews and discussions with therapist before and after both performances.
- Semi structured interviews and discussions with both choirs after the first performance, including the sentence completion task about music.
- Several discussions with *Renanim* before and after the second performance.

Video:
- Both groups in performances.

Log writing:
- Including my reflections; personal correspondence with the therapist, including e-mails and phone conversations.

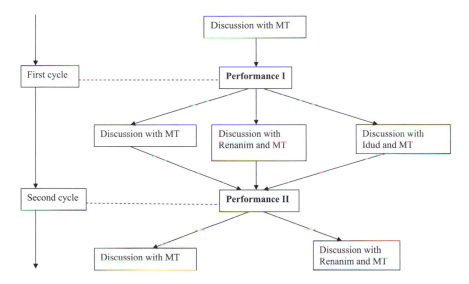

Figure 14.1   Collaboration between academic researcher and co-researchers in PAR cycles (discussions focused upon assessment, planning, evaluation, and reflection)

Throughout the project, the data was collected, transcribed, and analyzed by me. Every new text was read by Rina as well as read out loud to *Renanim*. The content was discussed and reflected upon and through cycles of comments and feedback, new reflections and themes were developed. The main theme that was discussed was "Whose voice is heard?," which occupied all of us and which I will discuss in relation to empowerment philosophy. Another theme developed by the *Renanim* group, Rina and me was "Musical performance," while "The role of the music therapist in Community Music Therapy" was a theme drawn out and communicated by Rina. The theme "Time and Timing" was chosen by me as a result of reflection on the research material. However, the themes were discussed with all the participants and resulted in multiple insights and perspectives which will be considered as I discuss them.

Whose Voice is Heard?

Representing and interpreting marginalized groups' voice can be treacherous and risky; viewing them as vulnerable and seeking for ways to act on behalf of them. The act of listening and connecting to people's accounts from their cultural and political perspective could prevent misinterpretations.

> Without some thought about the politics of interpretation and the agenda of each party, the vulnerable voice can easily become submerged, or, worse, misrepresented. (Warner, 2005, p. 17)

In the case of *Renanim*, the music therapist had voiced an agenda and utilized her personal point of reference without taking the group's position sufficiently into consideration. She merged the two choirs so that *Renanim*'s voice could be heard. Were the group misrepresented? Here are four of the members' voices after the first concert:

> *"I feel that we were swallowed by the other group."*
> *"We were hardly heard. There were more of them [*Idud choir*], while we had fewer voices."*
> *"Because our disability is different, we need to let our voices be heard."*
> *"We weren't heard at all."*

The above statements are in dissonance with the therapist's initial belief and action, which she understood retrospectively. However, I believe that her position promoted an opportunity for renewal and growth as implied in one of the above statements:

> *Because our disability is different, we need to let our voices be heard.*

This was not only a statement of not being heard musically during the concert, as many of the others also had voiced. This was a powerful political statement coming from a severe disabled person, and it was a statement I believe could have been echoed by other choir members. Other nuances could be depicted out of this statement, namely the claim that the group needs to take responsibility for being heard, to take ownership for their own unique voices, "… advocating the primacy of the voices and goals of the participants themselves" (Stige, 2005a, p. 404). The group wanted to represent themselves; shifting from being passive and dependent to becoming active and gaining control. This shift within the group could take place only when the therapist moved from a monologic to a dialogic mode concerning decisions about performance.

The PAR process allowed for a space to critique, negotiate, listen, and reflect on issues connected to the participants' limitations and possibilities. They began voicing their position, they began acting on them, and they began to be heard. The facilitation and my collaboration in the process helped them to hear each other. The discussions before the second concert were important but limited to the rehearsals. Eventually, it was their musical voice that helped them to regain their individual and collective voice. It was through the audience's response to their remarkable singing during the second concert that made them feel recognized. In their singing one could notice the determination and will which was a result of their powerful discussions.

By now the above statement was replicated by other members, from a stance of strength and determination. These were some of their voices after the second concert:

> *"People need to get to know us."*
> *"People should get to know us as human beings and not just as wheel chairs users."*
> *"If we would only sing here [in their own residential setting], no one will actually hear us or know about us."*
> *"People from the outside can see what 'handicapped people' can do."*

These were multiple declarations of wanting a social change. The group's collective identity had been formed in which "... a commitment to the process of change is much more likely to be sustained" (Ledwith, 2005, p. 94). Regaining their musical voices enabled them to advocate social change and justice, utilizing the performance as a channel towards their quest. This type of self advocacy is an important part of community engagement with its purpose to improve the group's lives in the community (Curtis and Mercado, 2004).

Empowerment

Through the cyclic process of moving forward and regaining their voices it could be said that *Renanim* gained empowerment through their actions. There are many types of definitions for empowerment which are subject to different social constructions. Servian's working definition from 1996, in which he says that empowerment occurs when a person has enough power to meet his or her needs (Servian in Warner, 2005, p. 72) is the closest to what one can expect in the Israeli context in relation to people with disabilities. Perhaps with the critical reflexivity in groups such as *Renanim*, the day will come when empowerment will become rights of the disabled people in Israel.

Law (1997) in her study of parents of disabled children found that her study group experienced personal empowerment as they achieved increasing control over various aspects of their lives in the community. This could be said about the *Renanim* choir who initially had limited control over the rehearsals and concerts but who gradually gained more control, changing and reaching closer towards their vision.

Rolvsjord (2004) discusses in detail the philosophy of empowerment and illustrates it by her client's metaphoric use of the Beatles song "Blackbird." Her client, a person in mental health care, uses the process of therapy as empowering. This type of process helped her in finding and using her resources and abilities, nurture them and building up her strengths. Rolvsjord says that: "Therapy is not only about curing illness or solving conflicts and problems; it is also about nurturing and developing strengths and potential" (Rolvsjord, 2004, p.100). Similarly to empowering through a therapeutic process, the process of PAR and its attributes may offer empowerment. Prior to the PAR process the power was distributed unequally between the therapist and the group members.

However, during the PAR process, the group members became empowered; they had an opportunity to build their self esteem and self determination and to face their own strength which resulted in mutual collaboration. The participants became accountable for themselves as stated by Ledwith (2005): "Without a sense of one's own personal autonomy, collective action is weakened" (p. 66). The group managed to build up their own identity; showing their strength and abilities for themselves and others. This supports the views of Warner (2005), who argues against the notion that people with disabilities don't have the capacity to take responsibility and to be accountable for themselves. In this case the PAR intention was to empower the marginalized group. Their frustrations transformed into initiation and action for their own wishes and thoughts, and from helplessness and vulnerability they were strengthened and empowered. The process of PAR helped the group take a stance by "declaring their voices."

My role as the academic researcher was initially to assist the therapist to identify her stance and ways; however my own process was also to change my own beliefs in valuing the group's resources and abilities. The process took its shape by bearing in mind that as the therapist saw the group's development towards independence it became transferred into the group's gaining control. The change the group had undergone made it meaningful to themselves and to the therapist and would hopefully expand further into other practices in the community in which this group lived. By making their own critical analysis of their choir situation, the *Renanim* members as participatory action researchers could understand how "resistances are rooted in conflicts among competing kinds of practices" (McTaggart, 1997, p. 37). This could help them to take other actions in other issues of their concern.

Musical Performances

Gary Ansdell has devoted a whole essay in this book to the topic of musical performance and so it is my intention to write one section in this chapter relating performance to the *Renanim* project.

> Performance occasions *can* be an appropriate therapeutic medium – providing a site, focus, tool or occasion for music therapy to work with both individual and socio-cultural dimensions of human need. (Ansdell, Part VI, this volume)

Ansdell promotes performance as an appropriate therapeutic music therapy medium. This could very well work for some while not for others. For a performance to have a meaning there needs essentially to be relationship between performer, spectator, and the space in which it all meets (McAuley, 1999). This may become quite multifaceted when dealing with performance with marginalized individuals. Such a situation, I believe, requires extra care and attention. From the spectator's view, a performance could easily be exhilarating; viewing society's "weak link" perform, presenting their healthy capabilities by expressing musically what cannot be said with words. As we have seen; from the performer's view, this may be experienced quite differently.

Ansdell refers to two axes in performances; the synchronic and the diachronic, and the narrative of the two choirs *Idud* and *Renanim* clearly illuminate how the experience of these two dimensions are related. For *Idud*, the "here-and-now" moments of the synchronic axis of performance were experienced positively, and this was synchronized with the experience and expression of the audience that co-witnessed the performance. These experiences did not lead to a strong focus upon the diachronic axis (except that the choir members were interested in performing again). In contrast, *Renanim* had a strong focus upon this axis; they also wanted to perform again, but in a different way, which led to a clear motivation for the PAR project that could facilitate such change. This focus upon the diachronic axis, with repeated cycles of assessment, planning, action, evaluation, and reflection, was deeply rooted however in the experience of the here-and-now of the first joint performance, where their voices had not been heard, where the pianist did little do attune his tempi to their singing, and where there had been considerable difference between their own emotional experience and that of the other participants and the audience.

The relationship between the performers and the audience in the *Idud* choir was maintained throughout the performance within a shared physical and emotional space. There was mutual expectation and collaboration between everyone involved; there was a "giver" and a "receiver" and they seemed to be on an equal position. The *Idud* choir performed in their best possible way and the audience responded accordingly, nourishing each other in an exchangeable fluid manner. However, this inter-relationship between performer and audience is not always the case, as for example in *Renanim*'s experience. The first performance (where the choirs sang together) did not work for *Renanim* and their conductor (therapist). The audience responded enthusiastically from their point of view, but with no reciprocity from the choir's end. The audience did not notice, since they were occupied with and nourished by *Idud*. There was a discrepancy between *Renanim* and the audience and although they shared a physical space, they did not share the same emotional space.

The outcome of that performance was positive for *Idud* and for the audience but it was a devastating experience for *Renanim*. Fortunately, this negative incident turned into a constructive journey in which the group made growth and developed into a group of strength making their resources available. In that sense it also became a therapeutic medium for them. One of the singers in *Renanim* didn't want to return to the choir after that experience. Rina suggested that he should consider individual music therapy. He returned to one of the group's last meetings and joined the conversation. This is what he said to the group:

> *Do you know why I left the choir? I know that performances pressure me. I go to the performance with a lot of worries and anxieties. But when we sing in the rehearsals it is very different. (male singer in* Renanim*)*

For him, performance, did not work but individual music therapy had helped him to work out issues, enabling him to express the reason why he had left the choir. This project illuminates how sensitive performances can be for some people and how imperative the therapist's role becomes in dealing with individual, group, and institutional needs. This example also illuminates relationships between what Ansdell (see Part VI) calls "self performances" and what he describes as "collaborative performances." For the audience, this joint performance would look very much like a collaborative performance, but for this participant it was simultaneously a self performance (unfortunately a negative one in this case). Something personal and crucial was at stake, but he was unable to voice it and the audience did not seem to be ready.

Performances provoke dilemmas between processes versus outcomes. The music therapist may fluctuate between the two, or weigh one over the other. These concerns and others need to be thoroughly considered by therapists before they go public. Rina voiced quite clearly her dilemmas:

> *On the one hand the process is important, that's true, and not the end product, but the process is directed towards this final show. Everything that happened this year and the process that took place all lead towards this concert. (Rina Stadler, music therapist)*

The therapist can maintain the focus on the process while working towards the outcome, but also the outcome/performance becomes a part of the process as was seen after the first and second concerts. Rina's hesitation to let the group perform in the second concert was based upon her established professional musical and therapeutic lenses; she didn't think they were musically ready to perform and she was apprehensive about their emotional being. The group was however, emotionally ready to perform alone, they had worked on the music during the year and wanted to perform. The following comments had managed to liberate Rina and me by realizing that *Renanim* had taken responsibility for their performance:

> *"We will give all we got during the performance."*
> *"We are here to sing, to have fun."*
> *"Why do we work and prepare during the whole year?"*
> *"So that we can perform and people can see what we have been working on."*

A performance, when it takes into consideration contextual concerns, can motivate and benefit a group of severely disabled people who want to be heard and seen in a different manner than merely as wheelchair bound individuals. The second performance had a positive musical and psychological effect on an individual as well as on a communal basis.

The Role of the Music Therapist in Community Music Therapy

When I asked the *Renanim* group to complete the following item in the sentence completion task: "For me music is …," several members spontaneously shouted – *Rina*! For this group music and Rina are synonyms; the music is the person and the person is the music. It is through the therapist that the group had gained access to music. This heroic group with severe physical challenges, and therefore limitations in singing, managed to rise beyond their disabilities and bring out their most inner and personal music through the therapist's sensitivity and skillfulness. She gave musical meaning to each member through her close musical and personal contact with them.

This is not where it ends. The music therapist has led the choir for many years but she was also working in the village as a traditional music therapist in individual and group therapy. We are witnessing more and more therapists expanding their role in their work placements, including work outside the therapy room (e.g. Aasgaard, 2004; Zharinova-Sanderson, 2004; Elefant, Part III in this book; Warner, 2005; Wood, 2006). This ecological frame of working can bring more possibilities and also difficulties for the clients and the therapists. A number of today's therapists find the therapy room limiting to some of their clients and see an advantage in taking their work publicly. The role becomes multi-layered and complex within the professional thinking and not least in reference to institutional and work placements.

Working within a wide spectrum of music therapy approaches raises questions and issues. Some may assert that this flexible position is in conflict with a more defined and clear music therapy position and that the same therapist can find it difficult to work with individual and group therapy while at the same time lead a choir with the same people. For some clients this could pose a problem that must be taken into consideration, while it could serve and benefit others.

As mentioned earlier, the therapist in this project worked within a wide spectrum in music therapy. Prior to the project Rina was preoccupied and questioned her role as a music therapist within the community frame. She regularly changed between her role as a traditional therapist who listens, accepts, reflects, and follows her clients during individual and group work to that of a choir leader who (according to common choir conventions) often follows her own sets of beliefs and values. However, the continuous dialogues and reflection with the group in the PAR process made her see that her roles as a therapist were less different in the different settings. There were many more layers and responsibilities to the work in the community, but the actual work with people, whether in individual settings or in choir rehearsals was not so different. In working with the choirs, the music therapist faces the challenges of using her therapeutic skills to help and take care of the welfare of the clients into the community in a safe and successful way.

I believe that when the music therapist is able to broaden her professional identity so that it is possible for her to move from one form of therapy setting to the other, she will be more available to help her client move from one setting to the other. The "Matrix-model" of music therapy developed by Wood (2006) elegantly illuminates the many possibilities participants can have as they progress in music therapy. This non-hierarchical model depicts the possibility of movement from individual music therapy, to group music therapy, ensemble participation, choir singing, etc. A client can participate in one "format" of therapy or more, and can also move from one to the other as needed. This type of a model could be an excellent tool for negotiation between therapist and client and can also assist the music therapist when she or he moves from one context to the other.

In the case of *Renanim*, this type of movement between formats was possible both for the group members and the therapist. Rina had slowly changed her position from one who makes the decisions for the group to a position where the decisions were made through discussions on shared experiences. The group was able to discuss and negotiate their wishes and in one example presented above one of the participants who had left the choir because the performances were too stressful returned to sing in the choir, after he had discussed his reasons for leaving with the group. The group's "new" dialoguing manner had an important influence on his return.

What we see here is not simply a movement in the direction of user-led services; it is a mutually empowering process. In the negotiations between the music therapist and the participants the decision making process is important, but for any one party this "does not necessarily mean holding the power to control all decisions, but having possibility to influence and making one's voice heard" (Rolvsjord, 2007, p. 236). A relationship of mutuality, openness, and collaboration has the potential to empower on individual and on group levels. It is with this frame of mind that the music therapist needs to enter into Community Music Therapy.

Time and Timing

A public choir performance is an event where the choir members and the audience experience and live jointly the same music at a given time. However, the times before and after the performance are equally important as during the performance. Ansdell (Part VI, this volume) has an intriguing discussion of the "diachronic axis" where a performance emerges over time (the before, during, and after). He portrays the temporal development of the performances of the *Scrap Metal* concert and the *Musical Minds* groups which vividly shows the complexity of such a development. As we have seen in this essay also, this axis must be explored in relation to the "here-and-now" event of the performance, where the participants' experience of their self performance, often as part of a collaborative performance, is central.

When discussing the concept of time in this project, I would like to consider two forms of time references made by the Ancient Greeks, *chronos* and *kairos* (see e.g. Aldridge, 1996; Stern, 2004). *Chronos* is the objective view of linear clock time where "… the present instant is a moving point in time headed only towards a future" (Stern, 2004, p. 5). *Kairos* is an alternative conceptualization of time, with focus upon "… the passing moment in which something happens as the time unfolds" (Stern, 2004, p. 7). This is a subjective consideration of time. In relation to *Renanim*, I would like to consider external and internal influences of time such as objective and subjective time and how it was negotiated and utilized by the choir members, the therapist, and the academic researcher.

Prior to the research project, the time was valued in reference to the group's achievement in preparing the repertoire in time for the performance. In other words, whether or not the group was able to prepare the repertoire within the external and objective time frame allotted prior to the performance. The therapist had put a time frame in which the group had to rehearse and prepare towards a product. This focus upon objective time became quite demanding for this group.

The concept of time during the rehearsals changed during the research project, as the music therapist moved from a monologic stance and started to consider how time could be approached in a dialogic one. In a monologic stance there was a conservation of time, which we could describe as economical. The time was utilized for work; for practicing melodies and for learning lyrics. Less time was considered for personal, social, or relationships issues. There was one person leading while the others followed; an external body judged, directed, organized, and carried out. During the development of the research project a dialogic stance took the place of the monologic stance. The dialogic conceptualization of time is "… concerned with flexibility and the convergence of multiple tasks" (Aldridge, 1996, p. 37) and it is seen as springing from the individual and interpersonal interaction rather than external forces. Time as *kairos* therefore has a different quality in which it confers more space for thinking and reflecting by all participants. This type of time has an internal flow of its own and could be perceived as time consuming from the more economical chronos perspective.

With *Renanim* fluctuation was seen as time and timing was sometimes slow, sometimes faster. It moved forwards at times and regressed at other times, as the participants acted, evaluated, and reflected on their quest. Part of the process in the group was the negotiation between the objective external and the subjective internal times. Every so often there was tension between them, which Aldridge (1996) has described as "... private and public time resulting in stress and anxiety" (p. 37). On the one hand, there was an external performance deadline, and on the other hand there was the time needed for interaction, reflection, music sharing, and processing. The solution to the dilemma was that a performance date would be agreed on, but only when the group was ready. The time frame towards the performance was flexible and spacious, rather than fixed and specific. There were important moments in which the group experienced a timeless qualitative reality and the subjective time provided the group with a psychological way of fitting their lives into the reality of the time frame of *chronos*.

One of the purposes of the performance for the *Renanim* group was community engagement and the opportunity to interact with others outside their restricted community. However before they could enter an unknown situation they needed the time to build relationships between their group members as well as strengthening group identity. The time during rehearsals and after the performance was used not only for learning the music but also for those important elements which led and contributed to community engagement. Flexibility in time could therefore be considered a major condition for community engagement to develop. PAR, with its continuous process of thinking, talking, acting, and evaluating, brings forth renewed collective reflections in a cyclic form. This type of practice will naturally require time if the quests are to be achieved in a manner that most participants are in mutual concurrence with.

Also for the academic researcher time and timing was critical. One of my roles was to attempt to identify when the time was appropriate to enter or exit the discussions. Although I was a mutual partner in the project, one of my contributions was to bring forth my group facilitation skills. Listening to the discussions and concerns, learn from the group and either reflect, reiterate, summarize, elaborate, or search with the group for new action strategies were all part of the role in which the timing was essential. The therapist also needed time to rely on the choir as they moved from being led to becoming a much more independent group, which influenced the pace and time of events too. This trust was not only built through everyone's negotiations during the meetings but was especially a result of the second concert, as the therapist felt that the group then achieved control over their situation in a new way.

This change in frame turned time from moving as a point headed towards the future to becoming an experience *kairos*. "This type of time entails a personal attempt to maintain identity in the face of imposed environmental constraints" (Aldridge, 1996, p. 37). The dialogues between the members of *Renanim*, the music therapist, and the academic researcher made us all understand that time was a central component in the process. Without taking time into serious consideration, the outcome would have been different. The group was seeking for and committed to social change and they understood that this not only takes time, but requires sensitive timing also. These considerations suggest that Community Music Therapy projects and performances can be as process-oriented as traditional music therapy.

Summing Up a Beginning

The *Renanim* project was about the heroic efforts of a group of individuals wishing to make a change in the Israeli social attitudes towards marginalized people. The PAR project was created with the aim to advocate an opportunity for a dialogic and democratic approach towards their inquiry of social change; overcoming negative values and attitudes towards them. By adapting a dialogic approach through actions and reflections (through discussions), these individuals formed a group that managed to develop and strengthen their collectiveness, resulting in empowerment and in the shaping of their future. The participants in this project learned to think democratically and critically and to continually question established meanings and conventions.

Participating in the choir was an important activity for this group and a social symbol for their strength. One member expressed the meaningfulness of performing with these words:

> So that the people out there could see and hear what the disabled can do.

The group had only one or two opportunities each year to make their voices heard in this way, and this was an opportunity they wanted to use.

We can see this in relation to the perspectives advocated by a PAR pioneer such as Paulo Freire, who advocated a dialogic and democratic approach to education and inquiry, aiming to restore oppressed people's ability to create knowledge and practice in their own interests (Stige, 2005a). In the case of *Renanim*, the group was developed and strengthened by regular and steady discussions and reflections throughout the research project, which for the choir members led to a better understanding of themselves in relation to their situation in the village and the broader community of this mid-Israeli town. This was in accordance with the PAR process as discussed in the literature: "Collective evaluations and reflections based upon negotiated role definitions are continuous elements in the process and form the basis for refined diagnosis of the situation of concern and for the development of new plans of actions" (Stige, 2005a, p. 410).

The PAR project took place in different arenas and different formats; open discussions during rehearsals; semi-structured interviews; and meetings to (re)view concert videos. In addition there were the shared experiences of performances and various forms of communication between the choir, the music therapist, and the academic researcher before and after these performances. All these types of meeting places and arenas required flexibility and tolerance but provided multi-perspective opportunities for all the participants. It provided occasions and sufficient time for growth and development, as the experience of time changed in the direction of the subjective narrative time of *kairos*. Although the time frame of the project was predetermined to take place during two years, it became clear to the choir and the therapist that despite the ending of the project the change that had occurred will enable the group to continue its process.

The idea that a marginalized group of people could become influential participants in a research project was not only powerful for the participants but also for the community in which they lived. Empowering them and other marginalized groups of people can enhance self-advocacy in which the group could choose to self-disclose and represent themselves in a dignified way (Curtis and Mercado, 2004). The *Renanim* members were committed and accountable to their change; they exercised their power to shape the process and took action in order to create more space for their voices. The performances gave the group a platform and an awareness of how they wanted to be viewed by others. On the basis of their choir experience, which they developed, their voices could carry them into a more democratic collaboration and action within their village and in the larger community. If the group is able to continue the process the way they hope, the critical analysis they made of their choir situation and the fostering of change described in this essay could be just a first step for *Renanim*. They could be able to take other actions in relation to other issues of their concern.

This example illustrates how Community Music Therapy and performances within a community frame can provide a foundation for marginalized groups in relation to self-growth and the experience of becoming citizens with some influence. The experience of collaborating in this PAR project helped the therapist in relation to her doubts on her many music therapy roles, moving back and forth within the spectrum of conventional work into Community Music Therapy. Although it may have seemed that the therapist was flexible within the boundaries of music therapy, her own doubts about not adhering to one stance in music therapy were not always easy. The PAR process weakened this doubt and confusion and made her more secure when moving from one context to the other. She valued this experience of documenting, self-critiquing, and reflecting on her work where the ethical dilemmas about representing the group's voice became one of the central issues. The PAR process made her recognize that shifting from a monologic approach to a dialogic one did not only empower the choir members but also her. This approach promoted independence which contributed to the therapist's self-growth.

The experience of being a researcher with the PAR project attempting to understand the group's world from a different angle was a novel one. In this study I entered the arena of a group with a shared culture, and I did so with the idea of learning from the group (Stige, 2002). I had to learn about that culture to understand the "local people's world," their thinking, and their actions. Entering with this type of belief and respect made it possible to form a relationship with both the choir members and the music therapist. My entrance gave the group access to external verification and the hope that through a collaborative journey they could be able to work with and reach their goal. Becoming a close collaborating partner changed my concept of the researcher too; from that of the expert who brings in knowledge to that of the (experienced) learner. When I communicated to the group that my perspective as researcher had been changed through the PAR process and that I had become very close and connected to them, the group was quick to remind me that we were mutual collaborators. They also reminded me about the lyrics of one of the songs by Ehud Manor that they had been singing:

> At the end of the day when you pick up the pieces; what is essentially left? Only a few friends ... (Ehud Manor)

> ... *and you became one of them.* (Renanim *2006*)

In the Israeli music therapy context this project was quite unique for several reasons. First, it is quite exceptional to meet a therapist such as Rina who is committed to social change and is flexible enough to work both traditionally and with the larger groups outside the therapy room. Her work is beginning to be recognized and with time similar approaches will become more prevalent among music therapists in Israel and elsewhere. Second, the Participatory Action Research process was the first of its kind within the Israeli music therapy research milieu. Perhaps in the future the relevance of collaborative and activist approaches to research will become more evident in the music therapy community in Israel and elsewhere.

PART VIII

Chapter 15

Action

Music in an Ambiguous Place: *Youth Development Outreach* in Eersterust, South Africa

Mercédès Pavlicevic

Safe?

I am driving out of the University of Pretoria with my car boot full of camera equipment, and wonder (yet again) whether I'll manage to slip past the security guards without the car being searched. Theft has gotten worse recently and the guards are doing their job. I have forgotten my signed permission form. I smile broadly and am waved through. Mildly triumphant I speed eastwards. Fifteen kilometers later, approaching Eersterust, I slow down and check my rear view mirrors and lock my doors. As I turn off the railway bridge and into the narrower, dirt road on the left, my senses are on high alert. Something to do with being a woman, perhaps? – and not entirely confident about my ability to react like James Bond should I need to. Eventually I'm in the car park at YDO – *Youth Development Outreach* – where music therapist Carol Lotter works two days a week. The cement building is long and low, with high windows, so that you can't really see what's happening inside. The lawn is patchy as the rains haven't yet begun; the thorn trees offer scant shade. I open the car boot self-consciously given the value of the equipment, and start unloading. Two young men approach: can we help? I try not to let them know that I am checking them out – and know that they know I am. After all, they are part of the "youth at risk" and here for social rehabilitation because they've been in trouble with the law. Carol has told me that most are on "good behavior" at YDO, since they need to complete the Adolescent Development Program instead of being criminally prosecuted.

Carol is already in the hall, stacking chairs. The high windows will be problematic for filming – they're all around, I'll have to work out the best angle for the camera. Carol greets the young men, who smile and seem somewhat embarrassed and awkward. They put my bags down and get out of the hall quickly – leaving the two of us to continue stacking the chairs. "Will you join in?," she asks, "it will make your presence less intrusive." OK I know about the researcher as participant-observer but my drumming skills are appalling. I agree reluctantly;

my hands always hurt with drumming. I'll join in for a bit and then return to filming. Safer than drumming. Carol says she's not sure who's here today, never knows who's coming, and this is part of her work here: to be here on Monday and Tuesday afternoons, and see what happens. While I connect the camera and do a white balance check, Carol tells me about the guitar school that she's setting up not only to teach youngsters to play but also to encourage them to write their own songs after they have left the YDO programme. This will happen at a regular time, and YDO has just received a donation of seven guitars. Practicing will be done at YDO, says Carol, because of the risk of taking guitars home – either they or significant others would possibly sell the guitars.

Suddenly

The door is flung open and its force blasts five or six young men into the room. They're dressed in baggy shorts, trainers, baggy t-shirts, one has a white hat, another a baseball cap, two are those who helped me in the car park. With barely a glance at Carol, they cluster around the instruments on the floor – there are various hand percussion instruments, a rainmaker, some Djembe drums – and continue to talk in an animated way, at times interrupting one another, at times gesticulating. Although I don't understand the language, which is in the African vernacular, I sense their personal investment in the talk. The energy is high with much gesticulating and exclamations. Carol is among them, listening intently and looking to the young man with the white hat, on her left, who seems to be the leader in the discussion. At one point, after someone else has said something, everyone exclaims "ja!, ja!" and "the leader" begins playing on the drums. This is interrupted by more animated discussion, until, without cueing, the young men begin drumming, dancing, and singing together. Carol joins in, drumming and dancing with a lower level of intensity than the young men. The singing and dancing gathers intensity, and the tempo and dynamic level, as well as the body movement become tighter and more energized. The entire group "grooves" and, just as suddenly, the singing moves into laughter and exclamations, and a rapid diminuendo. Drums are returned to the floor. It's all taken about five or six minutes …

Some moments later, something similar happens, except that this time while the young men talk and gesticulate, Carol clears the floor of other instruments. The young men "jump" into singing and playing almost immediately. Their force is extraordinary. Carol clears the floor as they dance and sing, and she joins in on the Djembe drum. Her presence seems ambiguous: she is both part of and not part of what's going on, which seems to have its own voltage (high) and momentum (fast). I hope she doesn't ask me to join in. Suddenly the stacked chairs are being dismantled and dragged to form a circle, around a flipchart. My attention has been drifting. Everyone sits with a Djembe drum in front of them. Carol is part of the circle, with the keyboard behind her: she could turn round and play, and remain part of this circle. This time round, Carol seems to be in the role of musical conductor.

The energy level is lower. She guides the group through a reading of the words on the flipchart. These have a strong anti-crime message. The words "Just don't do it" are a play on Nike's "Just do it." The words of the song are –

> Please guys, drugs and crime are no solution to any problem in life
> Instead they lead one to end up in jail or dead
> .... *Just don't do it* ....
> Today's youth have no future
> Due to dangerous substances
> It leads them to steal and commit a lot of crime
> .... *Just don't do it* ....
> Parents, teachers, the police and the community
> Must stand together to fight evil deeds
> .... *Just don't do it* ....

After reading the song together, they speak it once again, but this time it sounds like a rap song, and as they recite it, some start moving different parts of their bodies, swaying from side to side, clicking their fingers … and this quite naturally becomes a rap … Please guys … Different people at various times offer suggestions, and repeat the song using their bodies more forcefully – finger clicking, foot-tapping, body swaying movements while they sing; Carol makes a suggestion, and they ask her to do something at the piano. She starts a series of chords and together the group moves together to what suddenly becomes a performance of the song as though for an audience. At the end there is laughter, clapping and back slapping. The door opens, two teenage girls, in short skirts and sleeveless tops arrive – sorry we're late, they chorus. The young men jeer. Carol turns to me.

> *"This is Mercédès, as you can see she's videoing us today."*
> *"Can we see it?" they ask.*
> *"Of course" I say. (It will save me having to do some drumming.) The TV*
> *   monitor is at the other side of the hall.*
> *"Wait, can we first do some drumming, seeing that Lisa and Michelle are here"*
> *   (Blast, I knew this would happen.)*
> *"Mercédès come and join us"*
> *"Of course, thanks."*

Seated in the circle I feel affluent and old. White. The researcher. Carol explains how we will do it. I remove my rings and put them safely in my pocket.

That is Just Awesome

Luckily the drumming is over fairly quickly, and we then regroup around the video monitor, to watch the recording together. This is much more fun! There is a running commentary throughout

> *"Look at this, check that, hey you can sing! Look at that dancing! That's not bad!"*
> *"Carol do you think it's ready?" (Ready for what? Have I missed something?)*
> *"Well if we're going to perform it, then you need to make sure the whole band is here, else ..."*

Perform? What? Where? One week later, Carol pops into the office to tell me that she has a recording of the same songs being performed with a visiting musician who plays keyboard. We watch the video together. Solly, a YDO staff member who runs the Indigenous Arts Programme, and Jabu, one of the young men, take turns at the microphone, singing "Just don't do it" while other young men clap and dance and sing the chorus together. At the end of the song Solly cries, "Awesome! That is just awesome, you guys!" Solly opens out his arms towards Jabu in delight, saluting and celebrating the performance.

Chapter 16

Reflection

Crime, Community, and Everyday Practice: Music Therapy as Social Activism

Mercédès Pavlicevic

Please guys, drugs and crime are no solution to any problem in life
Instead they lead one to end up in jail or dead
………… *Just don't do it* ………… *(refrain x 4)*

Jabu, participant in YDO

By considering music in terms of its affordances, discussions of musical meaning … can combine with a consideration of its social uses and functions in a manner that recognises the plurality of music's social functions without being swept away by total relativism.

Eric F. Clarke

… I often found that music is linked to a greater awareness of our own possibilities of action, a feeling of mastery, or increased basic social communicative skills.

Even Ruud

The young men clustered around a sheet of paper lying on the floor barely know one another, and have a common focus: co-creating a song whose message they hope will reach other young men in Eersterust: crime doesn't pay, it's not cool. They are together thanks to the rehabilitation program run by *Youth Development Outreach* (YDO). The song, they say, needs to get out of YDO and into the community – they hope a local community radio station will perform it so that others can hear what they now know. As the young men practice, discuss turns, suggest body movements, and try any of these in different ways, an atmosphere emerges of mutual respect, fun, and friendship.

Community Music Therapy and Social Life: Considering Situated Practice

This essay considers music therapy as "everyday work": part of a complex social web, and thoroughly engaged with the social issues of its time and place. This is inspired by documenting work at Eersterust and Heideveld,[1] work whose embeddedness in everyday life distinguishes the work from music therapy practice that is distinctively to do with "health," "education," or "music." None of these quite does justice to the music therapists' multiple social responsibilities, or to a practice that appears so permeable to the different layers and niches of the social world. Exploring and documenting this work made me consider the nature of the embeddedness of Community Music Therapy in social life in South Africa – especially given the implicit social activist stance of this work. This consideration is, in part, informed by academic texts in "new" musicology, music sociology and social music psychology (Cook, 1990, 1998; Martin, 1995, 2006; DeNora, 2000, 2004; Clarke, 2003; Clayton, Herbert and Middleton, 2003), whilst also acknowledging that any of these are firmly situated in Northern discourses far away from Africa. (It is for this reason that, unless unavoidable, I avoid referencing during the text, and let the data speak directly.) In (sub-Saharan) Africa, to talk and think about something called "music" or "musicians" is somewhat risible (Blacking, 1973; Mereni, 1996, 1997; Karolyi, 1998; Janzen, 2000; Agawu, 2003; Pavlicevic, 2004, 2006a). Anthropologist John Janzen writes,

> The point is that the Western definition of music suggests performers or players before an audience, rather than music emanating from amongst the participants for whom the rhythm, bodily movement, sounds and words are a conversation that grows in intensity and fullness and movement as it progresses. (Janzen, 2000, p. 47)

Correspondingly, the music therapy practice documented here is enacted in "music and singing and dancing together" – an extension of everyday musicing. The work refracts local norms regarding time, place, and persons and may seem haphazard and un-delineated in terms of physical space, time limits, or "professional" roles in contrast to work that embraces more "formal" (global?) disciplinary norms.

The practitioners' implicit social activism makes sense in both Eersterust and Heideveld, where the dramatic nature of everyday life is refracted in an equally dramatic practice that flows with, within, and through it. As participant-observer, I experienced socially reflexive musical happenings, embedded in insistent and at times dramatic social worlds that refuse to remain "outside"; while music therapy participants equally, refuse to leave the work "inside."

Many of these deliberations have emerged directly from the data work, leading to an enquiry about the nature of the refractions between music therapy and everyday life (that includes everyday musical life). This is not to separate the two artificially (and then consider how one might impact on the other), but rather, to consider how each is part of the other. More specifically (and to use explicitly sociological constructions from "The North"), this essay considers how Community Music Therapy appropriates the social-musical affordances of its

---

[1]   The work in Heideveld is discussed in Part IV of this volume.

contexts (in this instance, of Heideveld and Eersterust) and how these contexts in turn appropriate the affordances of Community Music Therapy. Corresponding questions emerge: How do these affordances and appropriations happen? What is appropriated and afforded? And finally: What can Community Music Therapy work on these two sites tell us about music and social action?

I now move directly to the themes that arose out of data analysis, in a spirit of adventurous enquiry:

1. Listening to local knowledge.
2. Outside in: negotiating distant and close-up social spaces.
3. Networking, sharing, and "attuned expertise."
4. Health talk, lay talk, research talk, and music talk.
5. From mentors to musicians, from strangers to musical friendships.
6. The silence, the medium, and the emergent message.
7. The concert as the meeting place of secrets.
8. Everyday music therapy and making a difference.

The data collection itself needs a brief explanation: although the data examined here are mostly from the work at *Youth Development Outreach* (YDO) in Eersterust, at times in this essay I also draw from Heideveld work to explicate themes. The YDO data consist of interviews with music therapist Carol Lotter, sentence completion tasks with the young folk at YDO, my own notes after participating in drumming groups, listening to comments while we all watched the video together, studying of video recordings alone and with Carol, as well as informal chats with folk in and around the music therapy events.

Theme 1: Listening to Local Knowledge

At the beginning of our interview, Carol describes Eersterust:

> *Well what you do see when you drive around the streets of Eersterust in the afternoons for example is a lot of men who are unemployed, just either sitting around in their gardens or walking around. I think one of the other realities of the area is that those that can afford to go to schools in the Pretoria suburbs leave the area during the day and come to school in Pretoria schools, and you have the more economically disadvantaged children going to the schools in Eersterust. (Carol Lotter, music therapist)*

It is the kind of knowledge that comes from being there for some years, rather than armchair knowledge from a newspaper. As Carol drives around, it seems, she notices things about the place; men hanging around, with little to do, and she think about what this might mean in terms of the young men with whom she works. Some of her knowledge comes from knowing an Eersterust family, whose mother she knew as a student in another part of the country; some is gleaned from local papers, some from talking with YDO mentors and other staff members – and some from "hanging about."

In Heideveld, Sunelle's local knowledge is multifaceted:

> *OK, about the suburb ... people were moved there during apartheid, so the older people in both Mannenberg and Heideveld still remember being moved from the city to Heideveld. That's about 20km from the city center, in the Cape flats. There's houses, small houses ... I heard that about 14 people live in one two-room house. So very overcrowded, high, very high unemployment rates. They've got extreme drug problems, and well, alcohol and dagga abuse problems. The older people, the adults, and the children, specially. There's a new drug out in the Cape flats now – "Tik," and it's just taken over. And what makes it different from other drugs – it's manufactured in the Cape flats. It's very dangerous, very chemical, and it's a huge problem. (Sunelle Fouché, music therapist)*

Sunelle's talk reveals macro and micro knowledge; distant and close-up knowledge, political-historical as well as personal knowledge, and that 14 people live in a two-roomed home. She also has "casual" knowledge: "Tik" is a new drug out on the streets, locally manufactured and cheap. This informal, current knowledge is imparted by children in music therapy work – and Sunelle connects this kind of knowledge with music therapy work: drugs are linked to gang wars that are linked to unsafe streets, which are linked to children being unable to come to music therapy at times, and safe transport needing to be provided. The music therapists set up a transport network with the help of the teachers. Not only this, but they have the drivers' telephone numbers, are alert for children being late (which at times interrupts our interviews). Moreover, they keep themselves informed about daily events in the neighborhood. They also know the local police station staff and talk with them frequently, and they know the local gangs and which gang the children or adolescents belong to – this I glean from the music therapists' reflections about children: names often have an addendum ... she's from the "Cats," he's from the "Black Mambas," and so on.

I gain first-hand experience of the music therapists' social networks when, because of endless interruptions, we decide to continue our discussions in the (new) Heideveld mall coffee shop. A constant stream of shoppers points to the music therapists, comes to greet them, and they wave in return (that's so-and-so's mother, the one who Brenda told us about last week; or gosh how he's grown, and he seems to have a little brother now ...). This is everyday coffee shop chat, and hardly conducive to focused research discussions.

The music therapists' attentiveness to local knowledge does not imply that this replaces the disciplinary norms of global music therapy knowledge. Rather, they convey an alertness to the inadequacies of colonizing the local with the global (Smith, 1999). Instead, they listen to formal talk and to gossip; they listen to talk not meant to be heard, and on the basis of these listenings, negotiate norms for this practice, in this place, at this time.

Theme 2: Outside In: Negotiating Distant and Close-up Social Spaces

South Africa's colonial history has ensured a well-established separation of socio-economic class. The music therapists are educated professionals who travel to work in places that are geographically, economically and socially distant and different. Carol positions herself on the outside when she says,

> *I am aware at times that I'm a middle-aged white woman going into a context that's very different from my own and therefore being very careful about not wanting to impose an agenda which may come from my background, or my training or my music ... (Carol Lotter, music therapist)*

In Heideveld, Sunelle is more explicit about being on the "outside": I've asked her to comment on whether people in Heideveld have a cohesive sense of identity.

> *That's so difficult for me to answer ... I think as an outsider looking at the community, I can see – this is who they are, this is the music they listen to or, this is their religion, this is the way in which they talk and the things they talk about. (Sunelle Fouché, music therapist)*

However, the rest of her sentence suggests that her "outsideness" is close-up: so close that she hears what folk talk about:

> *But if you listen to conversations, or listen to what's happening in the community, there's not really a sense of support or of people standing together to solve problems. (Sunelle Fouché, music therapist)*

This kind of close-up listening happens in the car park while negotiating with bus drivers; walking to the stall-shack to get a coke; chatting to the teachers at tea-break. In both sites, the practitioners retain an awareness of difference, while also recounting how their work has created pathways from the outside into the local social space. Sunelle tells me that she and Kerryn are now on the Heideveld Safe Room committee (which ensures that each school has a secure physical space for children needing protection). The committee members (she says) invited them to join once they realized that the music therapists weren't simply "fly by night do gooders" from wealthy suburbs. This refers to one of the complexities of socio-economic asymmetries: "poor" communities wanting expert help to solve "problems" without being patronized (implicitly at times) by "do gooders." In South Africa, this kind of helping scenario is often funded by foreign donors, with "helpers" darting in and out of under-resourced spaces). The ultimate social acceptance comes from the Heideveld choir children who inform the therapists that they are not "whiteys" (a derogatory term for those who live "over there in Cape Town" but "white." "White," say the children, "is ok."

It is not only the music therapists who negotiate pathways into social musicing spaces. In preparing the local church hall for the Heideveld Community Concert, some young men appear and offer to help setting out the chairs. Sunelle and Kerryn accept gratefully, and ask them who they are – they've heard about the concert, they say, and want to know whether they too can perform. Which they do – and it then transpires that they are members of a local gang. Word about the concert has got around Heideveld – enabling gang members to negotiate a pathway towards the concert.

It seems that here, community music therapy opens social borders for all, acting as a social magnet that attracts folk who would normally be on other sides of the social divides, and enabling them to cross-over, make links, become part of, and generate another kind of everyday life. This social and territorial fluidity is reflected in the Music Therapy Community Clinic's ethos: disinterested in having a fixed base, the MTCC is a "traveling service," able to shift to and from whichever place and event asks for music therapy – and able to withdraw and move on, once no longer needed.

This everyday work offers possibilities for other social rules, which enable anyone to negotiate and reposition themselves within a pliable and permeable social field; one where outside and inside has the possibility of dissolving. In other words, the social field is reconfigured by these re-positionings: the music therapists can be outsiders and insiders, gang members can cross over into other gangs' territories for the concert.

Theme 3: Networking, Sharing, and "Attuned Expertise"

Rather than expertise being an abstract, absolute notion linked to everyday status, whether a gang member's expertise, that of a mentor, a young criminal or a music therapist, it seems that different folk enact expertise in a range of ways, for a different "time, place or purpose." Any of these are evoked and enacted as part of the "Community Music Therapy worlds."

Carol says that despite her own expertise in music therapy work, she is aware of her lack of expertise when it comes to local music genres and events. Rather than borrowing CDs by local artists, she decides to attend the local arts festival over a weekend, outside work hours, in order to get a direct experience of the musical events, to listen to what people in the street say about the various musical performances. She chats with folk wherever she is. Their opinions and descriptions, she hopes, will educate her. From this experience she describes gaining a sense of local music *in situ*, learning about local opinions (of which there are plenty), local attitudes and norms. It is her engagement within this social event that affords her a direct, experience-based "knowing" of what musicing goes on where and how and with whom, and for this to happen, she assigns respect to the opinions and knowledge of local folk-in-the-street. They are the experts in Eersterust's musical happenings, and she is there to learn from them.

She describes experiencing all of this with an agenda of how to adapt her practice to local resources and opportunities for performance. Her own music therapy expertise is unattuned to Eersterust, and needs refining and elaborating for her work with the young folk at YDO. It is not a transportable commodity, to be enacted in all times and places. On the contrary, it is a negotiated commodity, needing the help of those with whom she works. Carol says,

> *I have expertise that can be channeled ... and so it's more a negotiation with the group of saying where would you like to go? (Carol Lotter, music therapist)*

This suggests that music therapy know-how is not an absolute, but negotiated according to time, place and participants. Some music-skills need teaching and learning and practicing. Carol has started a guitar school, hoping that guitar skills will provide social opportunities for the young musicians. She says,

> *And I will for example prepare with the group a chord progression that we will practice over a period of a few weeks and then these jazz musicians would come in and improvise over the chord progression and it will hopefully give them a real sense of having achieved something, of having learnt a musical skill, but also the importance of playing music with other people, ...and we're hoping to almost make that into a sort of mini-concert even if its just for the staff of YDO that they come in and listen to what has been produced. (Carol Lotter, Music Therapist)*

Precisely this happens when a visiting keyboard player arrives at YDO, and an impromptu performance ensues. In the video recording, Carol and I together watch Solly dancing and joining in as Jabu and a collection of other young folk sing "Just don't do it" with a visiting musician. Jabu holds the microphone and is clearly the prominent person here – with an enthusiastic, participative small audience.

In Heideveld, when the music therapists are considering starting a choir, they first talk to the teachers. It seems that the teachers know "how Heideveld works."

> *And every decision we make, we first discuss with them ... so we said that we would like to start a choir and what would they think and they said yes it would be a good idea and we started from there. (Sunelle Fouché, music therapist)*

It is the teachers who help the music therapists access the schools and arrange choir auditions, and help the music therapists get to know the drivers (and their phone numbers). At the end of the year, the members of the local committee take over organizing the concert after the therapists tell them of their difficulties in securing a venue. "Leave it to us," says the committee, and the concert comes together in two weeks. Not only that, the therapists tell me, but the concert is claimed by the community as belonging to them – and their roles have now shifted from arranging and organizing, to providing some of the musical items for this event.

> *Just about the concert, what was interesting was that Kerryn and I were very involved in the organization and we kind of planted the seed for this whole concert and did all the organizing and so on, and at the end of the day, the teachers and the children really took the concert, and it was their concert. It wasn't about something that we've organized and they're just taking part in, it was definitely their concert, and we played a very minor role at the night, which I think was exactly what we had in mind. It was really a community initiative. (Sunelle Fouché, music therapist)*

Here is social collaboration in action. An everyday local network is activated by the concert, on the basis of who knows what for what purpose. The music therapists' access to the network is pre-established by the ongoing sharing, negotiating and mutually attuning pathways. The network secures a concert venue, sets a date, arranges printing and selling tickets, secures an MC, prints programmes. There is also the matter of printing t-shirts for the choir members, and organizing transport. Word gets around, enacting and transmitting local knowledge, skills and expertise: the expertise needed by this event, in this time and space, with these persons.

Generating networks can be thought of as a kind of socio-musical activism based on collective affordances and appropriations around specific events. The harnessing of expertise generates a new sense of collegiality and social collaboration: one in which all are a part of various dimensions of the tasks in hand, with permeability and flexibility of roles and enactments. These music-based networks are pliable, affording new social symmetries between folk of different social class, language background, and between folk from different parts of town.

It is not only expertise and networks that are negotiated and permeable. It seems that Community music therapy changes other social rules: those of language and of talking. I experienced these as constantly negotiated, rather than "owned" and "imposed" by any group.

Theme 4: Health Talk, Lay Talk, Research Talk, and Music Talk

On both sites I became aware that music therapists usually legitimate their work much like any health-care profession. The work is narrated as "needed" by those who have "problems" of one or other sort (Delanty, 2003; Furedi, 2004). The problems in the sites studied here have replaced those that characterize music therapy as a health profession, (i.e., of pathology, disability and disorder). Instead, they are everyday problems: problems of unemployment, substance abuse, crime, gang wars, and the absence of male role models. I barely heard words such as "clients," "Attention Deficit Disorder," "Depression," etc. Instead the music therapists talked of the "children," the "adolescents" and "the kids," and, as we'll see later, the music therapists are simply Carol, Sunelle, and so on.

Carol is clear that she would like to move away from "problem-based" music therapy work. Of her work at one of the schools that forms part of YDO's Outreach work, she says

> I am wanting to say to the school let's just work term by term where different groups of children per grade are exposed to music therapy whether they have so called problems or not ... the problems were a starting point for the educators and the school to justify having music therapy in the school in the first place ... (Carol Lotter, music therapist)

It seems that problem-based work has its own problems. Carol continues...

> I certainly am moving towards that simply because of the response of the children, and the other side of it is also one does not want them to feel labeled if they are referred for music therapy. One of the Group 7 children actually said to me, "so if you're a music therapist are my brains cooked?" (Carol Lotter, music therapist)

Cooked brains carry social stigma, while also, apparently, enabling you to have fun.

In Heideveld, music therapy "referrals" (to use a health talk term) are negotiated between all in a common language. Here, the teachers suggest that a child has music therapy because the child is "quieter than usual," is "not playing with others," because they've heard that the child has seen a violent crime, or because the child seems to have "something wrong but don't really know what's going on" (SSI/SQ/4:5–19). Lay talk is negotiated, and health talk seems to be discarded, perhaps a signal of the professional and social symmetries and respect between adults.

Everyday talk, it seems, is part of music therapy work – and in observing musicing work, I became aware of the music therapists' skills in navigating between talking-talk, body-talk and music-talk. In Eersterust, I watch Carol with a group of young men speaking a language inaccessible to her – she listens attentively, alert to the prosody, gestures, spatial configurations and intensity of the group talk, which moves seamlessly into "music talk," and then shifts constantly between word-talk and music-talk. Carol's listening is effortless, and her lack of semantic understanding barely features after the session, when Carol and I discuss this event, so fluid and agile the shifts between various "talks," and so consistent, apparently, their meanings.

Research talk is, equally, negotiated. As part of the data collection, our NISE research group devised a simple sentence completion task. Sentences began with "Music is ...," "For me, music ...," and "Without music ... ." When Carol does this task at YDO, there is a distinct feeling of malaise during this task and the

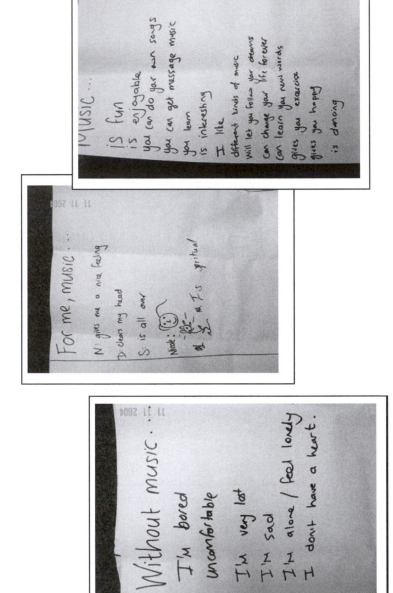

Figure 16.1 Group-talk on music

individual written products are limited. Carol intuits that writing is problematic for the youngsters who have a well developed sense of failing in "school work." She decides on a collective discussion, interspersed with drumming. In this way, energy generated by drumming, she hopes, will filter into animated group-talk (Figure 16.1). The result is enthusiastic talk, disagreement, giggling and teasing – and shared ideas.

Perhaps the ongoing negotiations of "talk" in these contexts (which at times seemed paradoxical), best portray the complexities of navigating between a local, everyday practice and its global norms. The collaborative negotiations of talk conveyed a spirit of democratic participation and empowerment – one that afforded possibilities for "making friends."

Theme 5: From Mentors to Musicians, from Strangers to Musical Friendships

These spirited collaborations seemed to reflect an ongoing fluidity regarding the flattening of social hierarchies, generating status on the basis of the needs and demands of the moment. For instance, mentors and their charges became co-musicians, while children from different parts of the Cape Flats became choir members and friends, music therapists were like the children's parents, and "white" rather than "whiteys."

Similarly at YDO, one of the mentors asks to become part of the music therapy group. Within the organization, mentors are responsible for the young folk attending the Adolescent Development Program, and their social status within YDO is one of responsibility and authority over the young folk who are at YDO for "social rehabilitation." The request to join generates a way of being together in which social ranking dissolves. Carol describes:

> We began to sing a song which he [the mentor] assisted the group in negotiating how the song would be sung. He started it, the group then continued and then suddenly the focus shifted completely away from him into the hands of the group. I, as music therapist, took an even more backseat role in that particular session where all I did was provide a musical support and basis ... in many ways it actually facilitated and released the group I think to experience something that they may not have if it was just me working with them. (Carol Lotter, music therapist)

From Carol's description, the mentor becomes part of group musicing together with his young charges. Musicing together enables all to relinquish their YDO-defined identities and social hierarchies, and instead become collaborative musicians. The same happens to Carol – she becomes the "backup musician."

In Heideveld, Sunelle explains that rather than the capacity to "sing in tune," the choir auditions are to do with selecting children who might benefit the most from being in the choir; those who seem most alone, most lonely, and in need of friendship.

Envy in their friends makes the children realize (if they didn't know this beforehand) that singing in the concert makes them "special"; this in an environment where there's not too many opportunities to be "special" and "cool" – unless as a gang member or glue sniffer. "We" is to do with being together in a different way, and also with being seen by others as having status, that seems to be assigned to them by their friends. The children say,

> *"The choir is cool."*
> *"It's fun."*
> *"You learn more about music."*
> *"You learn things you never knew before."*
> *"We've made friends in the choir."*
> *"Our friends are jealous because we will be performing in the concert."*

Musical action generates friendship based on having fun, on co-operating and on learning, where everyday life fails to provide for these kinds of friendships. The choir children speak of their (other) friends' envy, in a social context without too many offerings for being "special" or being "envied" for having something different to or more than others (unless a gang member with status).

Something else makes the choir "special": the songs that they choose to sing, and that dare to speak of secret things.

Theme 6: The Silence, the Medium and the Emergent Message

In both sites, singing songs is a substantial aspect of Community Music Therapy work, and I was intrigued as to which songs were sung, how these were selected, and whether (and how) some were adapted, composed – by whom and to what purpose. This was especially intriguing in a nation where songs continue to be powerful instruments of social activism.

In Eersterust, Carol has encouraged 18-year-old Jabu to work on a song. He has been reading the local papers and conveys to her his dismay at so much "bad news." She suggests that he draws together some of the newspaper headlines into a song text, and then bring it to music therapy so that they can work on it together. I observe Jabu, Carol and another three young men from Mamelodi working on Jabu's text. The song is entitled "Just don't do it" – a subversion of Nike's "Just do it."

The words address the entire Eersterust community: the youngsters involved in crime, as well as those who are supposed to be responsible for social order. Its message is that, whereas drugs and crime are indeed a solution where there is no other work (*drugs and crime are no solution*), their consequences are serious (*Instead they lead one to end up in jail or dead*), as Jabu has experienced first hand. The song paints a bleak picture of current social norms (*Today's youth have no future*), and issues a veiled critique towards "parents, teachers, and the police," who are clearly not fulfilling their social responsibilities and need to be doing more in order to protect the young people (*Must stand together to fight evil deeds*). The words of *Just don't do it* issue a moral imperative: crime doesn't "pay" in the social currency of Eersterust.

In observing the group working collectively on the song, I am struck by how Jabu's text accumulates co-operative meaning between all group members as they craft the song together. The song's message seems inseparable from its singing, which is constantly modified and negotiated between all. They learn not just the words – the words are part of moving their bodies in an emergent quasi-kwaito-rap genre, they are part of generating a collective rhythm, phrasing, melody and harmony of bodies, voices, instruments. It seems that the song does not really exist without its being worked and played and negotiated socially and musically between the young men. Singing the song reconstitutes the young men as civic messengers and as social activists.

A thousand miles away in Heideveld, Sunelle and Kerryn talk about songs they are preparing for the Heideveld Community Concert at the end of the school year.

> One of the things that inspired the concert was the stories that we were hearing in music therapy. Children telling the stories about the gangs and the violence and the poverty and the unemployment and the drug abuse. These were all things that we were hearing in the music therapy sessions that the adults in the community almost never really told ... they didn't even always speak to us about the gang violence ... not like we heard from the children, so we felt that we wanted to give the children a chance to give their message to the community of how they felt about what was happening in their community. (Sunelle Fouché, music therapist)

In a social environment where children are "seen and not heard," songs are chosen on the basis of a strong belief in the power of singing to convey the messengers' forceful and unambiguous message.

> One of the songs was about singing and how singing makes you feel better, makes you feel less blue or something, and when you're feeling blue you must sing a song, and the other song was "Tomorrow," then which is about tomorrow the future's going to be better. And we also chose a song which is about District 6, but also about a Colored community and the content of the song's also has lots to do with the Colored community ... it's also a hopeful song ... The music we chose was also not really about the musical value of it, but more about the words and the emotional value. (Sunelle Fouché, music therapist)

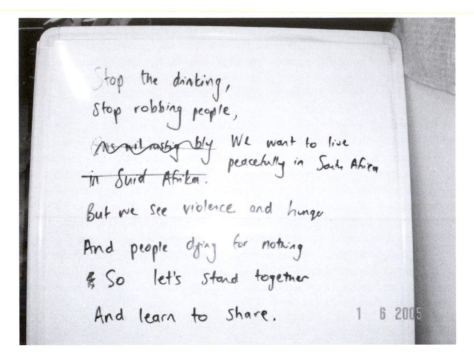

Figure 16.2   Adapting known songs by creating words that are relevant to the
               present

Here are songs already in the public domain ("Tomorrow" and "District 6");
songs that evoke a collective history. Later in the interview, Sunelle speaks of
adapting known songs by creating words that are relevant to the present (Figure
16.2).

> *And then the other music therapy group was also Kerryn's group, they were*
> *older children, between 14 and 16 – very difficult group, very adolescent, going*
> *through difficult times and, but the group kind of shifted when Kerryn asked them*
> *if they would like to write a rap about Heideveld. So they, she took a familiar*
> *song – it's the "Black Eyed Peas" song, "Where is the Love?" and they wrote*
> *their own words and used the chorus of the original song, so it's a wonderful*
> *song about – they don't want violence and they don't want fighting and they want*
> *peace in their lives and loving. So that was the words of their song, and they also*
> *performed at the concert. (Sunelle Fouché, music therapist)*

The choice of songs for the concert has everything to do with what needs to be
conveyed and to whom: songs are chosen and adapted with particular listeners in
mind, and in Heideveld a social ritual is enacted that enables attentive listening. In
each of these scenarios, the song selected, adapted or created embodies something
akin to "discursive activism": an utterance, a message, a statement conveyed

through joint musical action. To return to Janzen's quote earlier in this essay, the song emanates not only from the performers to the audience: rather, it gains collective meaning through growing amongst all participants, animating each person towards and with others, and intensifying the human bonds between all.

Theme 7: The Concert as the Meeting Place of Secrets

The concert brings together people who would otherwise have no reason to do so. As we've already seen, singing seems to dissolve difference and enable friendships. Sunelle describes:

> *The music that the children were performing (at the concert) was ... Kaapse Klopse music and Xhosa songs and things that they (the audience) could relate to, and they joined in ... bringing these Colored and Xhosa communities together – they were sitting together and clapping and singing to the same songs. (Sunelle Fouché, music therapist)*

Before the concert, however, are rehearsals and dress rehearsals, each of which affords all the identities of performers with status, skills, and "sass." There is a more nuanced affordance too: to do with the minds of the teachers who hear the children in the dress rehearsal.

> *When we had our dress rehearsal and all the teachers were there and seeing it for the first time and looking at the children and you get this kind of exhilarating, this hopeful feeling ... many people said we didn't know that our children could do this, we didn't know that they had this potential and also, you know, just saying how wonderful it is to hear these stories from the children, to see that these children can blossom on a stage, so I think that they did get the idea. (Sunelle Fouché, music therapist)*

A new social awareness emerges here, to do with teachers' respect for the school children and their skills, which suggests other ways of relating to one another – this in an environment where, at times, Sunelle and Kerryn observe difficult relationships in the classroom. At the concert, the music therapists introduce the audience to the kind of music they are about to hear, and why.

> *So, in the beginning, right in the beginning of the concert when we had to do all the introductions, Kerryn and I briefly spoke about music therapy and said, we hear all these stories in music therapy and it seems that Heideveld can be a very hard place for children to grow up in, but these children also have this enormous potential, and that's what they're going to show you tonight, and you're welcome to join in, and they were so responsive. (Sunelle Fouché, music therapist)*

The concert enables the children to address their elders in a way that would be unthinkable in daily life. Singing conveys their fears about their lives, as well as the fact that there is a social collusion in Heideveld about "keeping quiet." The concert does several things: it assigns the children the role of being the "prophets" of their communities: those who see and speak out. The children become the moral conscience, by saying (singing) what is unspeakable – what is generally hidden and silenced. The collective musical event also permits these things to be heard by the adults in their role as audience, without taking offence at the words – but on the contrary, with great pride in what "their" children are able to do on stage. The performance alters the social relationships in Heideveld for some hours – generating another kind of social network, based on collective musicing that is both fun and very serious (Figure 16.3).

Figure 16.3   Heideveld Community Concert

The community's response to hearing the children perform is similar to the teachers' reported earlier. This is that they had no idea that the children could "do" music; let alone write their own songs, adapt known songs and perform them on stage. The concert generates for the adults, a new way of seeing the children, and for the children a new way of being seen: as children with skills, with potential, children who can stand up on stage and sing.

The social ritual that is the concert (Small, 1998) creates a magic social space; one where the performers remain themselves (the children) and at the same time become the messengers of powerful social messages. This ritual enables certain things to be said. The silence is replaced by singing. The singing conveys what cannot be said. That which cannot be said is heard. Here is Community Music

Therapy work in the public domain, addressing attitudes, local taboos, and reconfiguring social networks.

The final theme from the data situates this practice firmly within everyday life, life that happens in the car park, the playground, the public domain – and also able to make a difference, with an agenda of activism that is at times explicit, at other times more nuanced.

Theme 8: Everyday Music Therapy and Making a Difference

We saw earlier that one of Carol's visions is to get music therapy out of "problem-based" work and into everyday life. For this, she drives out of YDO to local schools, where something surprising happens.

> *Well, last week when I arrived at the school the children ran out to the car to come and fetch the djembe drums and they drummed all the way down the corridor to the music room where I work. That was on the Wednesday morning. On the Thursday morning the same thing happened but this time they stayed and played and there where three children per drum and they took turns and so the first three would come and play and then another three would push their way to the front to try and play and those that weren't playing were dancing ... It was bringing them together where otherwise they would be just slouching around outside the school probably not even talking to each other and yet this activity brought them together ... it eventually became something you could hear throughout the school. (Carol Lotter, music therapist)*

Here is an unscheduled event, in an unscheduled spot, where it is the children that decide how the drumming happens – something akin to playground songs and games. In YDO, similarly, a drumming group becomes an unexpected event.

> *And at the end of the music therapy where (there was) an improvisation with the staff and we had about 40 people together ... and the doors of the complex where left wide open and we even had a few people coming in off the street and just joining, if you like, a music party, because that's what it was. People were dancing, they were drumming, there were instruments all over the show. It was, I suppose, very much a free-for-all where I was monitoring but not leading. It was their moment. (Carol Lotter, music therapist)*

My own sense in listening to Carol is that it was everyone's moment; one that was a social magnet, generating a kind of party, a celebration of doing music together, of being together in music. Musicing transforms YDO into a place where music happens, from being a place where folk are in trouble to being a place where folk do music.

Party talk seems a good time to conclude this essay, and I conclude by returning to the questions formulated at the start.

Closing Questions, Closing Answers

The data commentary in this essay has been anchored by an assumption that in these sites, Community Music Therapy is everyday practice. In each site, as in South Africa generally, musicing is part of (rather than distinct from) everyday life. How, then, do we make sense of music therapy as part of a social musical world, where therapy (it must be said) is a rather odd notion? And indeed, how might we consider the question of affordance and appropriation without risking a colonizing construction about this work (Smith, 1999). Since some of these issues are addressed in other parts of this book, I focus on the one question that, on the basis of this work, can be addressed "authentically," emanating from the data itself as well as from my own position that is both inside and outside the work described in these pages.

The question is this one: What can Community Music Therapy work on these two sites tell us about music and social action, and in turn what might social action mean in the context of this everyday practice? I start with a general statement, which I then explicate. For this general statement, I use the term "work" to signify "Community Music Therapy as everyday practice."

First of all, (to separate these for a moment), we've seen that the work in these sites has parallels with everyday life. The practitioners (i.e., all who take part in the work) are part of existing everyday networks of interactions. These everyday networks flow throughout the work and its structures (whether these be transport, concert programs, playground drumming, language, gangs), enabling the work to be animated by them (in French everyday talk, the verb "animer" is often used in musicing contexts, and I use this everyday word here to signify the reciprocal animation of the work and everyday life). Animated collaborative musicing – which, to repeat, has everything to do with everyday life – empowers all participants in the work to influence one another, irrespective of expertise or socially assigned status. This mutual influencing, I propose, is refracted in the everyday interactive networks. These networks (now infused with animated musicing), are, in turn refracted in the lives of participants. We have here an ongoing cycle of affordance and appropriation, collaboratively created and inspired by animated musicing.

This ongoing cycle is characterized by the participants' attentiveness, their respectful listening, their receptivity and their capacity and willingness to negotiate, whether this be to do with language, talk, skills, attitudes, values, knowledge, status and roles. At the same time, the whole of the work is available to its time, place, and purpose. None of these mean that the work or its actors dissolve into everyday networks and disappear – on the contrary, it seems that the everyday nature of the work enables the work and its social field to refract one another. The social field, on both sites, narrates itself as having problems, be these overcrowding, guns, or glue. Its rules are its social order, and obeying these rules means that children join gangs, children buy cheap drugs, gang leaders rule, and men drink. There is a powerful social investment in maintaining these rules – after all gang leaders also support local churches and football teams. Gangs impose silence and secrets, and in this, the children of Heideveld are well schooled. Similarly, Community Music Therapy too, has emergent "rules": global orthodoxies that are fast describing its norms and values (Stige, 2002, 2003; Ansdell, 2004; Pavlicevic and Ansdell, 2004).

It seems that the work in these two sites provides possibilities for all participants to break the social rules – or at least reframe them; and the sites themselves afford the work this possibility. The therapists' alertness to ongoing possibilities for social-musical affordance and appropriation characterizes the social activism of this practice. The data from both sites convey the practices' deliberate agenda to "make a difference," and to do things differently; to be a catalyst for altering networks and their actors in specific ways. For this to happen, this everyday work is constantly negotiated in its everyday contexts. The music therapists listen, look, ask for help and advice, and come to understand how aspects of everyday life offer possibilities for musical-social action. They don't do this alone! Part of their activism is to relinquish their expertise and authority (legitimated by the institutions and by the profession) and create networks based on shared and collaborative expertise and authority. (Let's remember that the choir rules are negotiated together with the children!) This deliberate stance becomes refracted in all actors relinquishing their expertise and authority in and around musicing. Thus, in musicing, gang leaders, mentors, and silenced children enact "other rules" of social interactions; to do with respectful listening, with being attentive and receptive to one another, and with ongoing negotiating. These values are crafted and refracted in community music therapy work, so that revised social rules can be created by all and for all, at this time and place.

Finally, the work in these sites enables another kind of everyday life to be collaboratively enacted by all, whatever their social position, status and role. This collaborative enactment affords possibilities for an ongoing cycle of revising social rules by all social participants, rather than living with everyday rules bound by orthodoxies that are authoritarian and un-pliable.

Perhaps the last word in this essay is best left to a young person from Eersterust:

Without music, I'm alone.

PART IX

Chapter 17

Action

Caring for Music:
The *Senior Choir* in Sandane, Norway

Brynjulf Stige

Music is Really Good for these People

In Sandane, a tiny town in rural Western Norway, a group of pensioners has created a choir in collaboration with one of the music therapists in town. They call it the *Senior Choir*.[1] Most of the singers are in their 70s or 80s, some even in their 90s. They live in their own houses and are relatively healthy. In fact, only one member is living in an institution and is dependent upon the health care system. But of course, being above 70, most of the choir members have some health concerns and feel that they know little about the future, even less than they used to do.

The choir has given me permission to join some of their rehearsals, as participant observer. Just before one of the first rehearsals that I was part of begins, I find myself talking to a female member of the choir. I am interested in her motivation for choir participation, but before talking about that, there are other things she wants to explain to me.

> *There is a great future for music therapy. I'm quite sure that in the next few years more and more people will discover how they can use it.*

Probably I am not among the most difficult to persuade on this issue, but she sounds very convincing. While she talks, she sometimes looks up. Now and then there is a brief break in the conversation, as she wants to say hello to the singers that come into the room. She nods towards some of the singers, turns towards me again, and says:

> *Music is really good for these people.*

I am kind of puzzled by the third person perspective used, but assume that indirectly she is also talking about her own experience. In a second I am reminded about the fact that these reflections are informed by this lady's previous professional

---

[1] "Pensjonistkoret" in Norwegian.

experience. She tells me about her past career as headmistress of a local primary school. In the 1980s, when integration of handicapped children became common in Norway, she had started to include music therapy in the services of the school and had felt that music engaged these children in a very special way, which she describes as "deeper than words," involving both the bodies and the minds of the pupils, preparing them for learning.

"And for collaborative action too?" I ask. – "Oh yes, of course," she responds.

There is no more time for talking. Solgunn Knardal, the music therapist conducting the choir, calls for attention. The singers gather together and sit down on their respective chairs. I approach the small group of three or four men that sing in this mixed choir of about 20 senior singers. One of the men leans over to me and asks:

Is it true, that the music therapy training course is going to be moved from Sandane to Bergen? And does that mean that you are leaving too?

It is true, and I realize that this choir is one of the things that I am going to miss. I have heard them sing in many various performance situations and every time I have experienced their energy and joy when singing as contagious. I have seen many new groups of music therapy students work with them in their practicum placements, and usually it has been a pleasure to see the musical and often humorous interaction across generations. I remember especially well one of the performances the students arranged together with the *Senior Choir*. The whole thing started as a conventional concert but things spiraled in more and more creative directions. Some of the seniors wanted to improvise like the students did, and when they discovered that some of the students knew how to play Norwegian folk music on violin and accordion they were on their feet immediately. They came walking to the concert on feeble legs, but their dancing was something different. They came to sing and stayed to dance …

The male singer's question stimulates a series of memories. As a researcher I am reminded that I am and have been part of the larger community that these singers belong to. It requires consideration but in many ways it is an advantage, since it gives me easier access to the "world" of the choir.

"Do you want to sing with us?" the old man asks me, in a friendly voice.

I know that the music will not be too complex and that the male singers could use an extra voice, so musically I can easily accept the invitation. The simple gesture of asking me exemplifies the hospitality that I have noted as typical for the choir's activities.

"I hope I don't blow it," I respond.

Community Connections

The music therapist-cum-conductor, Solgunn, usually starts each rehearsal with a series of physical and vocal exercises. It prepares the singers for practicing the actual songs and on several occasions I have heard many of them express that these exercises are helpful not only for the singing, but also for their efforts of maintaining as much as possible of their own physical and vocal capacity.

Today, there are a few words to say before the exercises. Solgunn talks about their previous concert and praises their performance more than just a little, before she informs the choir that they have received news about forthcoming financial support from a local bank as well as from the music council of the municipality.

Solgunn tells the singers that after the previous concert she had spoken with a member of the audience; a local book seller and well-known man in town. He had been surprised, he had told her. The choir's singing had been so vivid and energetic.

> "*I guess he was disappointed ...?" one singer laughs.*
> "*Well, at least we smashed some misled prejudgments, again," another singer responds.*

For a moment I find myself placed in a group of community activists. The humorous comments given seem to resonate with some serious issues, namely the feeling that many Norwegian seniors have of being devalued in society.

After a time of activist atmosphere, things calm down and the seniors start discussing other aspects of their recent performance. Even though the conductor and the singers obviously are quite pleased with this concert and its impact on the audience, they soon also enter a conversation on possible improvements, not least concerning how they present themselves on the stage. One of the changes Solgunn wants to introduce is to make the male singers more visible in the choir, since they have had a tendency to hide in the back-row. Several of the singers have opinions on this issue, and a vivid discussion on presentation before an audience evolves. After a while Solgunn suggests that they close this discussion. She has got some more news she wants to share.

The county administration is about to celebrate an anniversary of the cultural department and they have decided to invite the *Senior Choir* to perform on this occasion! Everybody is very pleased, but soon some practical issues emerge: How could they arrange the transportation to the neighboring town where the anniversary would be held? It turns out that Solgunn has been thinking about this too. She has been talking to the administrative leader of the cultural department of the municipality who had not been negative to the idea of giving financial support so that they could rent a bus for this event.

Working on a Wedding March

"That's enough talking for now, let's start singing," Solgunn then says.

The singers make themselves ready. First, it is the warming-up exercises, then a few songs that the singers know really well, and they sing energetically. Then there is some hard work waiting. Solgunn has arranged a new song for the choir. It is a wedding march composed by a jazz musician using the idiom of Norwegian folk songs. The lyrics are not so hard: "Tra-di-da dam-da-da-di dei a / Tra di da dideli du dei." I cannot stop myself from thinking that with these lyrics the singers at least get around their usual intense identity debates about which language should be used in the lyrics they sing; the New Norwegian typical of rural areas or the Dano-Norwegian dominating in the more urban parts of the country.

But words aside; what matters now is music, and it turns out that it is quite demanding. The melody is new for the singers, and even though the idiom is well-known, the melody is a little "different," with some challenging intervals and harmonies, so the learning is not easy. They have to try again, and again, and then again. It is hard work. I can see that the senior singers really concentrate. My impression is that Solgunn uses all the communicative skills and the capacity for encouragement that she can muster in order to keep things going. There are numerous repetitions and many questions. I can see that some of the singers struggle somewhat and a few of them start saying that they are never going to make it.

"Oh yes we are. Of course we are going to make it. In time!" one of the singers says.

Solgunn supports this statement, and as I sing together with the men's group I start thinking about the variety of roles that she takes as music therapist working with this choir. She is obviously not "just" a conductor and instructor, but also a motivator, mediator, and manager. As conductor she is quite directive, but this is combined with an attentiveness to what is going on at any moment, so that initiatives and responses from the singers are seen and heard. It seems like there is some kind of sensitive "semi-directed dialogue" involved.

I start looking around in the choir, observing some of the interpersonal processes going on. I note that some singers have more problems than others with finding the right sheets of music, knowing where they are in the score, and reading the lyrics. I also note that several of the other singers find ways of supporting their neighbors, when that is required. I am struck by the flexibility and humor used in the supportive acts. The support is given quite subtly, in ways that – in my impression – ensure that the dignity of the person needing help is not threatened.

After quite a long sequence of hard work with the wedding march, there is time for something else. The choir starts singing a humorous love song called "Viss du var ei båre" (If you were a wave). The singers know the song very well and their voices carry strongly. There is joy and power in the air and they sing as if they are really surfing on the wave that they are singing about. Given the realities of urbanization, older people are obviously the future of this rural town. But this is not in the mind of the singers of the *Senior Choir* right now, I am quite sure. They sing almost like they are a bunch of youngsters, falling in love for the first time.

I Don't Need Money for Having Ladies in the Car ...

There is a short break, and some new issues are now discussed among the members of the choir. Two ladies from the board step in front of the others and start informing them about one question that has been much discussed lately: How should they share the costs for transport to and from the rehearsals? Some think that everybody should pay a regular amount and that the board then could redistribute the money so that those that have cars and take passengers could have their costs refunded. Others suggest that each passenger could pay a price for each trip, directly to the driver. The issue seems to be difficult to resolve, and there is some tension in the air, until one of the men says:

> *I don't need money for having ladies in the car...*

One of the other male drivers takes the word too:

> *We shouldn't think about money all the time. I drive 60 km to come to this rehearsal every Thursday, and it's worth it!*

As in almost any type of participatory democracy, there seems to be considerable debate and tension in this choir. But even more striking is the humor and the generosity that many of the members communicate. After the rehearsal is over, I start talking with the man that drives 60 km every Thursday, just to sing. He is well over 80 and lives on a farm in one of the remote valleys of this municipality, just beneath the blue ice of a large glacier. I can see that his shoulder is hurting, so I ask him what happened.

> *"Oh, I've just been working too hard in the cowshed lately," he responds. – "It's kind of strange," he laughs. – "It's work that I've been doing since I was a kid, so my shoulder should have been able to take it by now ..."*

We get into a long conversation about life on the farm when he was a kid. The kids worked from early morning to late in the night, he tells me. He remembers running home from school in the lunch break in order to feed the horses. He grew up on an isolated farm in a country which at that time was relatively poor, and he makes it quite clear that life was not easy. As he tells about this, something else emerges too, namely his memories of the strong sense of community among the kids when working together.[2] This had been especially strong, he told me, when the lines between work and play became more invisible, as when the children in the bright summer nights would be sent out to collect the cows in the woods. They would then run together, find some huge rocks that the glacier had carried in earlier times, climb them and look for the cows. There would be rivers to cross and new rocks to climb. Searching for the cattle was part of the game, but not the whole thing.

As he talks, I start thinking about the *Senior Choir* as a community of practice. Much of what is going on in the rehearsal seems to be hard work; on how to sing new tunes and harmonies, on how to remember the lyrics, etc. The singers seem to enjoy the work, however. They take it seriously and are themselves taken seriously, both by the conductor and by the community where they belong and for whom they perform. The work is so hard that at times there is considerable tension involved. There is no kidding around. But then there is the joy of climbing rocks together too, as they finally succeed in singing a new song confidently or as they burst into laughter from something someone said.

Without Music, Life Would be Dry and Boring

I have heard this choir many times since they started in the mid-nineties. I have heard them in concerts and I have been at rehearsals supervising music therapy students having their practicum here. Also, I know many of the members of the choir from other situations. I have had professional relationships with some of them, as with the headmaster of the local primary school. Some have been working in shops where I've been. Others are parents of colleagues or friends. I can see their engagement and hear their enthusiasm, but I do not really know what they think about their own participation in the *Senior Choir*. This is what I wanted to learn more about when I decided to study this choir. Simultaneously, Solgunn Knardal, the conductor, decides that she wants to write her master's thesis about the choir and chooses to interview all the singers on their experience of singing together. We decide to establish a collaborative exploration, so that I may use the interviews as empirical material too, in ways supplementing her study. In addition I find out that I want to give the singers the "music sentence completion task" where they could produce multiple responses to statements such as "Music is ...," "For me, singing in a choir is ...," "When I sing, then ...," and "Without music ... ."

A few rehearsals later I give the singers the form I have created for this part of the investigation, and they fill it in after the break, just before they start singing. They are deep in concentration as they do it. Part of the time it's so silent that you could have heard a pin drop, the main exception from the silence being the conversation that develops between Solgunn and Lilly, the one member of this choir that has reached a severe stage of dementia due to Alzheimer's disease. She

---

[2]   The Norwegian word he used for this was *arbeidsfellesskap*, which we could translate to "fellowship-in-working," or, perhaps: "community of practice."

is not able to read or write, but when Solgunn reads the questions out loud she responds spontaneously and Solgunn writes down the responses for her.

The last to finish writing is the man that after a previous rehearsal told me about his childhood life on the farm. I can see that he has carefully filled in his responses to the open phrases given. When he delivers, he smiles at me and says:

I guess it's not going to be an A, but here it is…

This man is almost 40 years older than me, and as participant observer in the choir I have often felt like a pupil, eager to learn and understand. In his eyes, the fact that I deal with reading and writing may have put me in the category where teachers used to belong in his childhood, even though his smile at the delivery also reveals that categories are somewhat blurred in this case.

Once the writing is done, there is more singing. In this rehearsal too, I have been invited to sing in the men's group. We are still working on the wedding march and the melody and harmony continue to be difficult to deal with, but we are doing much better now.

After the rehearsal I am eager to read the responses given on the music sentence completion task, as I expect that they will give me new perspectives on the senior singers' perception of music and of singing in a choir. Back in my office I start reading the responses to the final phrase given, on the imagined situation "Without music …" Many of the responses to this go in the same direction, suggesting that life would be grey, dry, and boring. One singer even refutes the given phrase, stating: "It is not possible."

I then turn to the reading of responses to the phrase "For me, singing in a choir is …" The responses to this phrase are quite varied, but one strikes me as standing out, namely "… *singing in a choir is humane.*" At this point I don't know why this statement hooks me, but I feel that I need to find out.

Chapter 18

Reflection

Practicing Music as Mutual Care

Brynjulf Stige

What is this life if, full of care,
We have no time to stand and stare.

William Henry Davies

In caring for the other, in helping (her) grow, I actualize myself. The writer grows in caring for his ideas; the teacher grows in caring for his students; the parent grows in caring for his child. Or, put differently, by using powers like trust, understanding, courage, responsibility, devotion, and honesty I grow also; and I am able to bring such powers into play because my interest is focused on the other.

Milton Mayeroff

Participation "in Spite of"

What would I like to do when I get older? More and more people are asking themselves this question, even though in many cultures phrases such as "If health is with me" or "Tomorrow, God willing" traditionally would have been added to any speculation about the future. Standard phrases such as these, which may sound archaic for younger people today, could be interpreted as revealing at least two basic assumptions: Health is a gift of fortune, and the future is unpredictable. In many ways I find it hard to argue against these assumptions. They reflect central aspects of the human condition. Still, these very assumptions have been considerably modified among many people the last few years, partly in response to improved living conditions and health services. More than used to be the case people have started expecting to stay alive and healthy until older age. They have also started to think that health is not only fortune; it is performed process too. There is more than enough information around for people to realize that the activities and social networks they belong to contribute to shaping the complex web of influences on life and health.

There is much information on health and function as performed process already, and the interest is growing every day, not least among the older adults who now represent a large proportion of the population in many countries. I was reminded about this as I listened to the radio one April afternoon. The radio program was reporting from a fair in France, where new computer programs for older adults' cognitive training were being promoted. The radio reporter interviewed the Norwegian brain researcher Per Andersen, who commented upon this new trend. He suggested that the computer programs probably could be quite helpful for many people, since stimulation is essential for fine cognitive functions. Andersen added that such commercial products could have several "side effects," however, as they are available only for a certain segment of the older population and because they represent individualized solutions to shared problems. As an alternative to specialized computer programs for cognitive training he suggested the conscious use of everyday activities and situations that in various ways request the use of cognitive skills. In order for this to work, he added, you need *repetition* and *concentration*. This requires high *motivation*, which indeed means that it helps to take part in activities that you enjoy.[1]

In the small town of Sandane, in rural Western Norway, about 20 citizens aged 70–92 have chosen to become members of an activity they seem to enjoy, the *Senior Choir*. Every Thursday before noon the singers, who have an average age above 80, come together and practice collaborative singing for about two hours. Some of them have been singing in various choirs for decades, others are finding their voice as part of a singing group for the very first time in their life. Why do they join the choir and what do they get from it? Obviously they join because they like singing, but further elaboration of the question is adequate, because some of the members of the choir are investing quite some time and effort in order to be able to take part. They are, as music therapist Solgunn Knardal (2007) puts it, participating "in spite of;" for instance in spite of problems of transportation and in spite of various health concerns. Some of the members may have to drive 30–40 kilometers on winding roads before they get to town. Others are living closer but may be physically fragile so that they need to arrange some sort of transport. To join the choir and turn up every Thursday before noon is therefore quite an investment.

When there is participation "in spite of" there must be a strong "in order to." One aim of writing this essay is to understand more of the reasons why the pensioners make these efforts, the main focus of the study being to read and interpret the singers' own narratives on experiences and benefits of choir participation. The case study is based upon material from literature studies, fieldwork, a sentence completion task, and semi-structured interviews.[2] Interpretation and discussion of transcriptions of the sentence completion task and the interviews will represent the main bulk, while notes and reflections from the fieldwork represent a context for my reading of these transcriptions.

---

[1]   For more specific information on research and theories on memory and cognition, see Andersen et al. (2007).

[2]   I want to express my deep gratitude to the senior singers and to music therapist Solgunn Knardal for collaboration on this research project.

The Elderly, Music Therapy, and Choir Participation

Even though many elderly people in western countries today indeed live longer and are stronger than people of the same age of previous generations, there is also research evidence suggesting that as many as 80 per cent of this population have chronic ills of various sorts (see CDC and Merck Company Foundation, 2007). Some ills may require pills but there is an increasing understanding of the limitation of medication and the relevance and importance of focusing upon psychosocial approaches to prevention and health promotion. In relation to the issue of memory maintenance, for instance, Andersen et al. (2007) have documented that *participation in activities that motivate* may be a key, which indicates that music and choir participation may be quite interesting activities in the perspective of prevention and health promotion.

As the Finnish music therapist Kimmo Lehtonen has suggested, many elderly people have a strong interest in music:

> In Salminen's research project (1990) "the formation of musical tastes" it is stated that people in old age are very interested in music ... McCullough (1981) has also got similar results when examining over 65-year-old people living in the United States (276 persons). Of the old people examined, 31% considered music "important to some extent," 11% "important" and 29% "extremely important." Through music it was possible to reach vividly pleasure-giving memories and meaningful experiences connected with earlier phases of life, which could otherwise remain out of reach. This kind of experiences became all the more important, as the old person's earlier social relations decreased as his/her close circle got smaller. In McCullough's research (1981) half of the subjects reported that the meaning of music had increased with age and only one fifth reported that it had not increased. The examined persons said that music gave them new energy. Especially listening experiences were considered therapeutic. They also promoted common group discussions, which gave listeners feelings of unity in sharing experiences anchored in music. (Lehtonen, 2002)

Lehtonen gives special attention to listening experiences, but the music therapy literature also underlines the potentials of active participation in music (see e.g. Bright, 1981, 1997a, 1997b; Aldridge, 2000; Ridder, 2001a, 2001b, 2003; Myskja, 2006, Sæther Kvamme, 2006). Often, music therapy for the elderly focuses upon active participation in *groups,* for instance with open group sing-along where people may join in no matter if and how they sing. The group thus offers the possibility of being together with others in a musical situation, with spaciousness in relation to participation (see e.g. Forrest, 2002; Wigram, Pedersen and Bonde, 2002).

Participating in a choir may seem somewhat different, since there are more rules regulating what is adequate voicing etc. Nevertheless, the therapeutic value of choir participation has aroused some interest in the literature lately, within and without the discipline of music therapy. For instance, Bailey and Davidson (2003) discuss amateur group singing as a therapeutic instrument in a study of a group of Canadian homeless men. Neither the conductor of the choir studied nor the researchers investigating the case are music therapists, but music therapy theory is used in the interpretation and discussion of it. This is also the situation with Dorota Lindström's (2006) study of several Swedish choirs, which are investigated from music education perspectives where aspects of music therapy theory have been integrated also. Lindström describes choirs that in the Swedish context are called "health choirs" and "rehabilitation choirs."

While the general tendency when you ask people why they take part in choirs is that they have an interest in the joy of singing and in community, Lindström (2006, p. 38) suggests that these new types of choirs articulate and illuminate a third dimension (that may also be present to various degrees in other choirs), namely health promotion and therapeutic benefits. In an analysis of qualitative interviews with female participants in a rehabilitation choir, she summarizes the findings by stating that most participants find the atmosphere of the choir very positive and stimulating, which they also relate to the contribution of the conductor (choir leader) (Lindström, 2006, p. 94). Many participants describe the choir rehearsals as "energy kicks," which may be considered important in relation to their health problems, many of them suffering from "burnout syndromes" (Lindström, 2006, p. 115). Summing up her study, Lindström (2006, pp. 137–9) speculates on the value of the "third state" described by the Polish philosopher Tatarkiewicz, who took interest in the strong feeling of being alive that could be produced in people when work and play merge.

Within the music therapy literature there has been a renewed interest in community-based health promotion lately, which also has opened up the possibility of working with and studying community choirs such as senior choirs. Two recent examples of this include the studies of Brazilian music therapist Claudia Zanini (2006) and Norwegian music therapist Solgunn Knardal (2007). Zanini (2006) focuses upon singing as a means for self-expression and self-fulfillment, with implications for the participants' self-confidence and expectations about the future. Knardal (2007) focuses upon choir singing as a resource in relation to memory, physical functions, emotions, and community. The present study is therefore to be understood in the context of a small but growing tradition of choir studies focusing upon participation and health benefits.

"Singing in a Choir is Humane ..."

The Senior Choir to be studied here was established by music therapist Grete Skarpeid in 1992, as an expansion of the community-oriented music therapy projects that had been developed in Sandane during the 1980s (Kleive and Stige, 1988). At the time I did the fieldwork for this study (between 2005 and 2007)

Solgunn Knardal, another music therapist, conducted the choir, which she had been doing for a few years already.

As explained above, some of the choir members had been singing in various choirs for decades, others were singing in a choir for the first time. In both cases it is plausible to assume that the senior singers have sustained or increased their interest in music, as Lehtonen (2002) discussed. This strong interest in music must be seen in relation to the life situation of these elderly people. In senior choirs such as the one studied here, we are not talking about a client population as such. The choir members are not people we identify with reference to specific diagnoses.[3] They are people of older age, living at home, with the range of health problems that usually accompany high age even when people define themselves as healthy. In addition, most of them have to relate to a series of losses; they may feel that cognitive functions such as memory are challenged, they may experience loss of mobility or physical capacities, and usually they also encounter bereavement and reduction of their social networks.

At the personal level, current health problems and personal losses do not constitute the only horizon that may color the experience of participating in a senior choir. When you pass 70, 80 or 90 years, you indeed know that death or the need for professional health care services is a potential reality. "Tomorrow, God willing" or similar phrases are not empty sayings for most of the choir members. It is therefore relevant to expect that choir participation could be motivated by more than musical interest, for instance interest in keeping the doctor away.

When I started studying the choir I had been living in the town for more than 20 years and had had the pleasure of hearing the choir on several occasions. The liveliness of these performances and the energetic humor of the singers had struck me as fascinating, and – as described in the narrative preceding this essay – the experience of the fieldwork when I started studying the choir was one of becoming part of an atmosphere of hospitality. As a participant observer of the choir, one of the things I noted very early was the high degree of responsiveness to each member's needs. For instance, the conductor would swiftly hand out extra copies of the music sheets if she observed that someone had forgotten or lost their copies. And many singers would help each other in various ways; read the lyrics, repeat a melodic phrase, bring a chair, or whatever would be needed. Possibly, this sounds like something too good to be true, or at least too nice to be authentic. But such acts were common in the choir and my impression was that the atmosphere surrounding them was positive and genuine. I should not under-communicate, however, that tension and conflict also was part of what I observed, in relation to issues of collaboration (e.g. how the choir's expenses should be managed) or in

---

[3] Some singers may well have various diseases and diagnoses identified by the health care system, but these are of limited relevance for understanding their choir participation, as this is not established as therapy in the health care system, but as a leisure activity in which they have chosen to take part.

relation to various identity issues (such as choice of song material, language, and sites of performance).

In this section I will present and discuss the empirical material produced through use of the sentence completion task that the choir singers were invited to complete. I presented a sheet with four open phrases for the senior singers in one of my first visits as a field researcher. That day, 15 of the 20 members of the choir were present, and they all filled in the form. The one singer with Alzheimer's disease was given the necessary help by the conductor to be able to respond to the questions. The other singers filled in the forms themselves. In the following I will briefly report on the analysis of the statements given by the choir members.

Music is ...

Each of the 15 singers present in the rehearsal gave between one and four responses, altogether 43 responses to this first open phrase. When a person gave several responses, these were often linked together, either following up one theme (e.g. aspects of music as positive experience) or presenting contrasting perspectives (such as personal experience versus cultural value). One striking feature of the responses to this phrase was that most of the responses focused upon music in relation to the individual, or on more general and abstract qualities of music(s) and situations. Only three singers gave responses that underlined relationships between music and community. This could be related to the way the open phrase was created (possibly interpreted as mostly referring to music as an object).

Of the 15 singers, 14 reported on *positive* experiences and effects of music, the exception being one singer who gave more "neutral" descriptions, such as "music is song, waves on the beach, instruments, orchestra." Eleven of the 14 that reported positive experiences and effects used phrases such as "Music is encouraging" and "Music is ... an *experience*,[4] [it] gives me tranquility, happiness, and also harmony." The others used briefer and more robust statements, such as "Music is absolutely necessary" (two respondents), "Music is part of life," "Music is alive," and "Music is everything for me." One singer gave the explicit statement that "To sing in a choir is, without doubt, therapy." Three of the singers qualified their positive statements, requesting that the music should be of the right sort; "not too noisy," "not jazz," and "not black metal."

As stated above, only three singers gave responses focusing upon music as community. One of these was only implicitly focusing upon this: "Music is contributing to a positive atmosphere." The two other singers were more explicit, but rephrased the given statement in order to express their experience, one singer stating that "Music uplifts, loosens up, and connects" and another that "To perform is social and creates a sense of community."

---

[4]   The Norwegian term used here is "oppleving," comparable to the German "Erlebnis," which refers to experience in a given moment or brief period of time. The term is often used with positive connotations.

Figure 18.1   The *Senior Choir* in Sandane in concert. Photo: Rune Rolvsjord

For Me, Singing in a Choir is ...

The second open phrase, "For me, singing in a choir is ..." produced 39 statements. There was now more focus upon community and collaboration. Eleven out of 15 singers gave statements about this, compared to three out of 15 singers in the above section. Responses that expressed this included "... fellowship," "... nice to be part of," "social," "humane," and "to use your voice in community."

Most of the singers simultaneously gave responses that linked singing to positive personal experiences. They described singing in a choir as "... the best entertainment," "very nice" etc., with effects such as "good mood" and "joy," and gave valuations such as "something I'll never have enough of."

In addition, seven singers focused upon singing as aesthetic experience: "Nice to listen to," "Not possible to express in words," "If the choir is in tune and in balance and have some good voices, then it's very beautiful," and "I can express and use myself in different ways than in other situations."

Also, five singers described singing in a choir as cognitive engagement and stimulation, with statements such as: "Inspiration," "Concentration," and "Reminiscence."

When I Sing, Then ...

When the given phrase referred to the act of making music ("When I sing, then ...") the statements given were more personal, reflecting emotional experiences, contact with the body, and moments of identity and transcendence.

Fourteen of the 29 responses to the given phrase were statements on emotional experiences, including statements on positive emotions ("I have a good feeling," "I become happy and uplifted," etc.) and more painful emotions ("I feel a variety of emotions; grief, sadness," "I express frustration, sorrow"). Also there was a statement on more long-lasting moods with behavioral implications ("I am thriving in my work").

Emotional experiences imply contact with the body, and there were also a few statements that more or less explicitly mentioned the body: "I relax," "My breathing calms down," "I become quickened," "I become more balanced, so that I keep my voice in shape."

Five or six statements could be labeled statements on identity, with a touch of transcendence, e.g. "I am not so alone," "The sounds of the song carry me," "I am part of something that gives meaning to life," "I find my*self* (especially when we sing hymns)," "I dream," and "I am where I ought to be."

In addition there was a statement about personal responsibility ("As a choir member you need to sing"), while three statements were about the possibility of using and training cognitive functions ("I sharpen my memory," "I may use my thoughts, memories, and words," and "I may express emotions and thoughts").

Without Music …

When the given phrase referred to the imagined situation of music's disappearance ("Without music …"), 22 statements were produced in response. One singer refused to make a statement and another refuted the open phrase itself ("It is not possible").

Of the remaining statements, 18 focused upon the description of a flat, sad, and grey world, for instance "Everyday life would become deprived," "It would be so silent," "It would be empty." "It would be sad," "The world would become grey," and "Life would be cheerless." One statement described the unaccompanied state of being without music through the single word "Alone."

Two statements suggested countermeasures: "I would need to troll," "Music is a habit. When I have no music around, I sing, and then I can enjoy everyday life."

Summary and Reflection

Taken together, the statements produced in response to the three first phrases of the music sentence completion task suggest several themes worthy of closer consideration. The singers described their relationships to music, choir participation, and singing as characterized by:

- positive emotional experience;
- experience of community and collaboration;
- aesthetic experience;
- cognitive engagement and exercise;
- identity formation and confirmation;
- contact with and stimulation of the body;
- sensitivity to painful emotions.

These statements are put in context by the responses to the fourth phrase on the imagined situation of music's disappearance. The majority of these responses described a gloomy and colorless world, indicating that music is quite important for the participants' experience of wellbeing.

The sequence of the above list of themes is defined by the frequency of responses that relate to each theme. More specifically, the themes form two groups in relation to frequency: The first two themes are supported by more than 20 statements each, the latter five are supported by five to seven statements each. The themes produced do support and supplement findings in previous studies on choir participation, such as Lindström's (2006) investigation, where she suggests that the singers take part because of an interest in a) the joy of singing, b) community, and c) therapeutic effects.[5] Lindström, however, underlines one dimension that was not present in the

---

[5] Interestingly, this also resonates with an ethnographic study of HIV/AIDS and music/ dance/drama in Uganda, where one of the participants in a women's indemnity group

material produced by the present music sentence completion task, the importance of the role of the leader or conductor. According to her findings, singers ascribe much of the positive effects of choir participation to the contributions of the conductor. No statements in the sentence completion task pointed directly in this direction. As we will see, this theme was prominent, however, in the interview statements that the *Senior Choir* members made at a later stage in the research process.

Before proceeding, I find it necessary to comment upon the ordering of themes in relation to frequency of response. At one level, this obviously has some value. Themes that are supported by a large amount of statements are – in some way or another – important for a large amount of the participants. The picture produced is obviously not complete, however, since rarer statements are excluded. This incompleteness may be more substantial than suggested if we think of it in terms of "some details are lacking." Non-frequent responses may sometimes be of special interest. They could, for instance, have been formulated with special intentions, such as the intention of providing a specific interpretation of the phenomenon investigated (it is of course not only researchers that are interpreting). In this case the singers knew that they were being part of a research project and may have produced statements that are not "naïve" representations of their experience but appraisals intended to summarize their relationship to the phenomenon under investigation.

Several of the rarer statements given by the senior singers in the music sentence completion task may be interpreted in this direction, such as "Music is absolutely necessary," "Music is part of life," "Music is alive," and "Singing in a choir is humane." I will give special attention to the latter statement. When I studied the empirical material, something in this statement struck me as especially important and worthy of further consideration. It is quite possible that this in part is related to my own pre-understanding, but this is not the whole story. One of the reasons I took interest in this specific statement is that it seemed to capture a central aspect of my experience of being participant observer in the choir, namely the atmosphere of *hospitality*.

The word "humane" – and my preliminary translation of it – requires some comments. The Norwegian term used is the compound "medmenneskeleg." It is a term at some distance to everyday language, even though the components of it are rather ordinary words (referring to "being *with*" and to "what is *human*"). The compound is thus easily understood at one level but it also sounds somewhat solemn and therefore stands out among most of the other statements in the empirical material. The solemn quality in itself does not give the statement a specific value but does suggest that it may have been intended as a summary or general interpretation that requires further analysis and interpretation. *Humane* is one possible translation of the word used, but does not quite capture the "being-with-quality" that is implied in the Norwegian original. *Compassionate* and *caring*

---

explains: "These women come here for help, for community, and to dance" (Barz, 2006, p. 78).

are therefore supplementing translations that also need to be considered and in the following I will use the form "humane/caring" when referring to (the translation of) this singer's statement.

I will examine to which degree the statement "Singing in a choir is humane/caring" could function as a defendable précis of a central aspect of participation in this senior choir. I will do this through analysis of semi-structured interviews.

Figure 18.2   We came to sing and stayed to dance ... Photo: Rune Rolvsjord

Dimensions of Care

As described above, the music therapist conducting the *Senior Choir* in Sandane at the time I did my fieldwork has studied the singers' experiences through use of semi-structured qualitative interviews. Her study was informed by the following research question: "How does participation in a senior choir influence non-institutionalized elderly people's experience of health and quality of life?" Knardal's (2007) inquiry confirms suggestions made in previous research (e.g. Lindström, 2006): Choir participation is a holistic enterprise with effects that may range from physical to cognitive, emotional, and social domains. Knardal qualifies this claim in an important way, however, when she underlines that the narratives given by the senior singers vary substantially in relation to how this range is related to. Some singers concentrate on one or more concrete aspects, such as choir participation as a way of improving their breathing, while others are careful to describe their perceived benefits in a holistic way, where the emotional value of being part of a community is emphasized alongside more concrete benefits such as improved voice control.

My reading of Knardal's (2007) study also supports the relevance of exploring in further detail possible meanings of the specific statement that I highlighted from the sentence completion task: "Singing in a choir is humane/caring." More specifically, my reading of her study suggests that the latter translation – singing in a choir is caring – is especially relevant to explore, my preliminary understanding of care then being to *provide for needs and support growth.* Knardal describes choir participation as a way of providing for one's own needs, in relation to say physical limitations such as breathing problems. She also describes the choir as a mutually supportive milieu where the participants help each other to perform. This could be contextualized by some brief comments that Knardal herself makes on how she as a conductor needs to "read" each choir member carefully:

> Many of the members of the choir quite explicitly show that they need encouragement. On rehearsals I can see that they are responsive to whatever attention they may get, and they give a lot too. Others hide more and are more difficult to read, but it is equally important to reach them. (Knardal, 2007, p. 77)[6]

Knardal describes this kind of "reading-response" as part of the skills and the responsibilities of the professional.

In the following I will analyze the same interview material as Knardal analyzed, with the specific purpose of exploring various dimensions of *care* and the possible interplay between them. My intention is not to make a better interpretation of the material than that made by Knardal herself, but to produce a different reading by focusing upon one specific theme.[7]

Rereading and analyzing the transcripts in many ways confirmed Knardal's interpretations, which focus upon the singers' positive personal experiences and benefits in relation to areas such as memory, physical functions, and emotions. For most of the singers, this was linked to the experience of the choir as *community.* When the specific focus of examining statements on various dimensions of care is added, my analysis suggests that all singers made substantial statements on this and that these statements also represent a considerable portion of the total amount

---

[6]   My translation from Knardal's Norwegian original.

[7]   This is done with Knardal and the choir's kind permission. In collaboration with Knardal I decided that a second analysis of the same material was preferable to making new interviews, both in order to avoid stress and confusion for the singers and because the existing interview material was rich in detail (due to the singers' willingness to tell their story, related to Knardal's particular access as one who knew the singers very well).

of statements, in spite of the fact that none of the singers used the Norwegian term for care ("omsorg") explicitly.

In the following I will ground this claim, by explicating statements and patterns that could be related to various dimensions of care. The analysis of the interviews were performed through systematic identification of themes (Malterud, 2003), supplemented by an interpretive approach to analysis of these themes (Smith, 2008). My analysis and interpretation focus upon the three dimensions that were most prominent in the material; "self-care," "care for others," and "professional care."

Self-Care

Almost all of the singers framed their choir participation in terms that may be described as self-care, that is; attention to one's own needs and interests, nurturing of strengths, etc.

A few singers do this by explicit reference to physical needs and problems. They describe singing as a remedy, that is; they sing because they "need to do so," for instance because of asthma or other breathing problems. Others term their choir participation more in the direction of prophylactic self-care, for instance by contrasting it to the passivity of many other seniors, a passivity they tend to describe as a potential health threat:

> These things are so important! And I think that many people of old age they ... well ... they are not able to keep up in every respect ... If they are not given the possibility to take part, then they become more and more droopy. That happens to many; they are just sitting there, alone ... You know, to have something which you know you can go to and which you can look forward to ... I think it keeps us up and going. (female singer, 85 years old)

The above statement focuses upon the mobilization of resources through music and could be described as attention to one's own *needs*. Many statements also describe choir participation as attention to one's own *interests*. Some do this by referring to the *Senior Choir* as a welcome possibility to take care of a life-long interest in singing and music-making. One singer, for instance, emphasizes that he has been singing in choirs for more than six decades. Another singer emphasizes that he grew up in a "music world" and that singing is a vitalizing activity for him. Others describe the *Senior Choir* as an inclusive community which has given them the possibility to sing in a choir for the very first time in their life, which for some means the realization of an old dream of participation.

Four of the singers stress how important the choir is for them by emphasizing that choir participation is something which they give high priority. They tell their friends and family that *Thursdays are choir-days*; days when choir participation has precedence over other activities.

Care for Others

Care for others includes interactive events as well as more concrete acts such as driving fellow singers to rehearsals: Five of the 19 singers emphasize the care given by other singers who take passengers in their cars. This issue is important because of the long distances from where they live to the town where the rehearsals are. The rural context of this choir implies lack of public transportation. Part of the picture is also the fact that this is a choir in a northern country with plenty of bad weather, including snow and ice, which may make it difficult for older and more fragile people to leave their houses and go to town.

Another aspect of care for others in the choir is the way the singers relate to Lilly. She is the only member of the choir that is institutionalized, due to Alzheimer's disease and severe dementia. In the interviews, six of the singers initiate reflections on Lilly's participation. These singers do not only emphasize that choir participation seems to be important and helpful for Lilly, they also emphasize that they appreciate this, as fellow singers. They describe how they enjoy Lilly's participation:

> *And Lilly, and everything ... you know, it's splendid. She sits there, and she is so positive. She is ... well, I must admit, I'm almost as old as her ... And then sometimes it happens that she misses a note, and she ... she takes it with a sense of humor! Well ... and that's what she says herself too, she's so happy about this [the choir]: "This is the only thing I've got left." (female singer, 88 years old)*

This statement exemplifies tolerance for the fact that different people have different needs and illuminates how many of the singers encourage and support each other. Related to this is the fact that many singers talk about a strong sense of *community* and *friendship*. Choir singing, they claim, is *social*, but in a way which is quite different from just coming together over a cup of coffee. One singer that was quite new in town explains the intensity of the experience in the following way:

> *You know, when I came here to Sandane, I was a stranger, I had no ... I knew nobody. And then I read in the newspaper that this choir should start again with rehearsals after the summer vacation. Well, I was bold and decided to go ... and since then I've been part of it ...*
>
> *I used to be new here. ... I knew nobody else, but today I would say that I think of us as a really good group of friends. Or: we are siblings; singer-siblings ... (female singer, 79 years old)*

This particular singer discovered the choir through the local newspaper, while a large group of the singers explain how they have been personally recruited by friends and fellow singers. One male singer explains how he just dropped in once to observe a rehearsal, since he happened to be in town and "was a little curious."

He was very warmly welcomed by the choir-ladies: "I didn't know if they would ever let me go," he laughs, and explains how that motivated him to come back.

The friendship and sense of community was also explained in many other ways, such as when a non-believer explains how she works with herself in order to be able to deal with the majority's interest in performing in religious sites. She also talks about how much each and every one of the members are important to her and that she misses them if they for some reason do not turn up at a rehearsal. Another singer describes the choir as a *team* and emphasizes how much she enjoys being part of it:

> It's a nice group.[8] I really think so! And, well ... I don't know, but ... I'm part of the team now, so to say. ... I did know a few people here from before, but I try to get to know the others too. ... I enjoy that! (female singer, 74 years old)

In short, the positive experience of choir participation seems to relate to the positive experience of being with other singers. But the positive experience of others does not stop here; it includes experiences of the conductor, the music therapist.

Professional Care

The importance of the conductor is mentioned by most choir members, and the singers produce a range of statements on what her role and contribution is.

One of the more common remarks is that the conductor is a very positive person, encouraging them with humor, attention, and positive remarks but also providing relevant feedback when that is required. In other words, a high degree of *mutual trust* seems to be involved. The singers describe the conductor as having an engagement that goes beyond just conducting; there is an interest for each singer, they explain. The important function of the conductor is not limited to this aspect, however. How she influences each and every singer while working with the whole group is another aspect. Many singers use terms that could be translated as *quickening* when they try to explain how they experience this.[9]

Sometimes the gestures that the singers describe as encouraging and helpful are quite concrete, such as when the conductor writes the music notation in ways that are less demanding to read, speaks clearly so that it is easy to hear, or hands out new sheets of music to those who may have lost their copies. Other times the processes are much more subtle:

> It would have been strange to change the conductor ... and there is contact, you know. Well, think of just the eye contact. That's a very good thing for me,

---

[8] The Norwegian phrase used here was "triveleg gjeng," which may imply a pleasant and supportive group or (working) gang.

[9] See Ansdell (1995) for considerations on the term "quickening" in music therapy.

to be able to look the conductor into her eyes and things like that ... [laughs]...
(female singer, 79 years old)

It is noteworthy that many of the singers seem to experience the conductor's contributions as support of their own efforts of providing care for others, which they also may relate to self-care. One longer quote may exemplify this:

We are so different, so you need to be flexible. We talk to everybody, but, you know, it is not always as much ... I don't know; I talk to everybody, but...

The group is OK, however, and I try to help, in flexible ways, so that ... Most of the time things are OK. You know, some of us don't hear too well, so you never know if things said are actually being heard. That may be a problem, sometimes, and there may be some misunderstandings too, but ...

And then there is Anna, she asks me a lot of questions and it seems like her thoughts are somewhere else, like they are out for a walk on their own roads. And that's the thing, you know, the sheets of music and things like that. You [the conductor] are quite good at presenting extra copies in the right moment. You know, these sheets they tend to disappear, it is not so easy to be in control. One may put them in a special place and think that one knows where they are, but then they are gone! I think it's very good support that you're there with an extra copy when one needs it ...

You know, people get quite frustrated when they think they know where things are but can't find them. They may grow hectic and start looking around: "I put it here, didn't I?" I want to help, then, but I don't always know how, and when, and ... Maybe I'm too cautious. Well, with some of them, like John, you may have some fun joking with these kinds of problems, but with others, you really need to be careful. I think you [the conductor] read that, very well. I feel that you know them!

... [When we sing] it's not just myself standing there, it's my neighbors too: Will he be able to stand the whole time today, or ...? I mean, I'm not too curious, I hope, and we should mind our own business too, but ... [laughs] ... (female singer, 70 years old)

The professional care that this singer comments upon is differentiated care, then, the conductor being credited for sensitively reading the needs and interests of each individual singer. This seems to be experienced as support not only by the singers in need but also by the neighbors of those in need. It also seems to make the "intrapersonal negotiations" on how to balance self-care and care for others somewhat easier to handle.

Relating to Conflicts of Care

Based upon the above descriptions I will suggest that the conductor and the singers collaborate in building a *culture of care*. In this culture, self-care, care for others, and professional care seem to be linked in many ways. Examples of supportive interplay between professional care and the singers' care for each others were given in the previous section. Similarly, self-care and the singers' care for each other were often linked, as in the following quote on the pleasure of performing:

> *I like it [to perform]. I really enjoy it, and, you know, we are ... How should I say this? It's like ... doing good for others. (female singer, 78 years old)*

To invite new members to the choir could be considered care for the choir itself, which – given the singers' positive valuation of choir participation – is a type of self-care too:

> *Well, I don't know, but if this* Senior Choir *is to survive there should be some [fresh] water supplies. I mean; some new members ... And maybe they should not be quite as old as we are ... [laughs] ... (male singer, 85 years old)*

The fact that I suggest that a culture of care is being nurtured does not, however, mean that themes of conflict were absent in the *Senior Choir*. The diversity of values and goals represented among members combined with a range of personalities and communication styles made many situations quite tense and complex. I have described this a few times already, relating it to practical issues such as transport and economy and identity issues such as choice of repertoire, language, and sites of performance. In the interviews, several singers comment upon these conflicts and suggest that they would never have been able to function as a group if they did not have the singing to bring them together.

We may describe this as the group's interpersonal conflicts in spite of its culture of care. In the following I will discuss some other types of conflict that the singers talk about in the interviews. These also include intrapersonal conflicts, often expressed as ethical dilemmas, directly related to issues of care. For instance, some singers talk about the concern of being or becoming a burden for others:

> *I've become so ... You know, I may just take one step to the side and then I've already forgotten what I was about to do. That's how it is now. I haven't lost my memory completely yet, I hope not, but ... [laughs]...*
>
> *You know, one often carry within the music that one heard as a child. I really love choir music – that has been with me since I was a kid. But, I want to tell you, I think it's very nice to be part [of this choir], but I am concerned that I may be a burden, because I'm so old that I don't ... I think maybe I am too old now. (female singer, 90 years old)*

Such a statement could be mirrored by statements where singers feel a need to legitimatize their participation by suggesting that they are not a burden yet. The following statement is produced by a singer who feels that as a pensioner he may finally claim that he has time to sing. Previously in his life, hard work on the farm had taken all his time and resources and under these conditions he had been forced to think that "singing doesn't bake bread." But now he feels he can sing, as long as he is not a burden to others:

> *I have always liked singing, and now ... I have started to think that I do actually*
> *have time to do it. It's like, you know ... I may now sing without feeling that I'm*
> *neglecting something else that I rather ought to do. And it's a nice pastime and*
> *I need to go to town too, to buy food and things, and then I can do that on the*
> *rehearsal day and sort of combine things. And as long as I'm able to drive my*
> *own car without having to bother anybody I have been thinking that it doesn't do*
> *any harm ... (male singer, 85 years old)*

These statements exemplify perceived conflicts or tensions between self-care and care for others, a theme which was especially acute for one singer who described self-care-cum-singing as an activity stealing time from the duties that she felt she had in relation to a family member living at home in need of continuous care. None of the choir members did intimate any easy solutions to these kinds of dilemmas and conflicts, but several singers suggested that the conductor's encouragement, the joy of singing, and the other choir members' support made them come to rehearsals, in spite of conflicts and concerns such as the ones described here.

A different angle to the theme of how choir participation may relate to conflicts of care is suggested by one singer who contrasted the collaborative atmosphere of the choir to the more authoritarian atmosphere of the health care system, exemplifying the latter with a story of a friend living in a nursing home where she was not allowed to accept the gift of a bottle of brandy, except if it was defined as medicine ...

These descriptions give nuance to the rough "typology of care" that I suggested. Two central patterns could be identified: Sometimes there is confluence between various types of care, other times there are conflicts of care. In the interview material analyzed, most of the examples of the first pattern are from choir situations, while most of the examples of the second pattern are from everyday situations or from experiences of the health care system. This tendency should not lead to a simplified interpretation of the choir as a conflict free zone. The material presented in this case study includes descriptions of conflicts, for instance on choice of language. While some would suggest that conflicts about language are less important in relation to the issue of care, it could be argued that to care for language is to care for values that you value, in other words; it is related to self-care (see Manning, 1992/2001). If you care more for your values than for your neighbors, some dangers are involved, but the senior singers seem to manage – sometimes with the conductor's mediation – to avoid getting stuck in these conflicts, as explained by many singers who underline that singing requires and enables collaboration. The seniors' *care for music* is indeed helpful here.

In talking about how singing requires and enables collaboration, many of the singers underline the value of *responsiveness*, often mentioned in relation to the conductor, but not exclusively so. The conflicts of care described are often related to care as burden, or fear of becoming a burden, in other words; to issues on *responsibility*. In discussing the findings from this study, I will therefore concentrate on the issues of responsibility and responsiveness, with a specific focus upon how responsibilities seem to be shared and responsiveness nurtured in the *Senior Choir.*

Responsibility and Responsiveness

Some examples demonstrating that *responsibilities are being shared* at the group level were documented through the fieldwork. The singers themselves are responsible for the choir in that they run the board that make decisions on repertoire, finances, performance sites, etc. This function is performed in dialogue with the conductor. Similarly, the conductor is responsible for the rehearsals, in continuous dialogue with the singers. If we think of the moment-to-moment musical processes of each rehearsal, the interview material presented above also gives descriptions of how responsibilities are being shared. Several singers describe how singing in a choir is different from just standing there singing together with others; you have neighbors to think of and care for. They do describe, then, how this responsibility for the other is being checked against one's own needs, the specific interests and needs of the neighbor, and the observant contributions from the conductor.

There is a link here to the next theme, the *nurturing of responsiveness.* This is maybe most clearly described in relation to the music therapist, both in her own words on how she pays attention to each member's need for attention and in the singer's words on how she makes a difference by being welcoming, perceptive, and encouraging. But the responsiveness certainly does not stop with the conductor. The singers' descriptions of how they carefully monitor their concerns for their neighbors suggest responsiveness indeed. As participant observer in the choir I was repeatedly struck by how flexibly the singers were attentive to each other. The tradition of warmly inviting new members could also be an example of this, as explained by the male singer who just dropped in once in order to observe a rehearsal and then was welcomed so warmly by the ladies that it motivated him to come back.

A hypothesis generated by this study, then, is the following: Participation in a senior choir may be experienced as helpful in that it offers a *reduced level of conflicts of care*. This may be linked both to the choir being a context enabling *shared responsibility* so that burdens of care are bearable, and *enhanced responsiveness* so that capacities for care are being nurtured and sustained. I will put this proposal in the context of pertinent theory on care.

Knud Løgstrup (1956/1991), a Danish philosopher, has argued that the basic human condition is interdependence and he thus suggests that the ethical demand of caring for others is given; it is not something you could choose. The responsibility for the other is primary, not secondary, according to this way of thinking. Care is not something you do because you expect something back. In principle it could thus not be regulated by contract. The Norwegian philosopher Arne Johan Vetlesen (1994) demonstrates how these premises suggest that the human responsibility for others go beyond showing respect and "not doing harm." It implies active care for the other which requires empathy and capacity of communication.

In the philosophy of care that could be developed on the basis of the work of Løgstrup, responsibility and responsiveness are linked directly.[10] In relation to the *Senior Choir*, we have seen how this was exemplified in the conductor's efforts on being able to "read" each singer in order to see if he or she was in need of musical, practical, or emotional support of some sort. This illuminates how the reading (or understanding) of the other could not be separated from the responsiveness to his or her needs. For the music therapist this linking of responsibility and responsiveness may be described as part of the professional role, but this is a secondary description. According to this theoretical tradition, this link is primary for all human beings.[11]

This may give perspective to the many statements made by the singers emphasizing that they appreciate the conductor's "reading-responses" (observant attentiveness directly linked to some action of care). In the words of the English philosopher Peter F. Strawson (1974), we may argue that the conductor is demonstrating a *participant attitude*, that is; an attitude of involvement and participation in human relationships. In line with the thinking of Løgstrup, Strawson thinks of the participant attitude as basic to the human condition, in contrast to the "objective attitude" which would suggest that the other should be managed or cured or trained in some way. The objective attitude is quite necessary at times, as Strawson explains,[12] but only the participant attitude can nurture relationships.

If the basic perspective developed by philosophers such as Løgstrup and Strawson are taken into its extreme, it may become problematic to define any limits on any individual's responsibility. Feminist theories on care (see e.g. Manning, 1992/2001) have paid more attention to this mundane and in consequence humane issue. Various combinations of and alternations between participant and objective

---

[10] Another European philosopher with related ideas is Emmanuel Levinas (1972/1993), and there is also a growing body of literature exploring an ethics of care from feministic perspectives (e.g. Manning, 1992/2001) and from that of various health professions (e.g. Martinsen, 1989).

[11] A careful philosophical argument for this claim is given by Glendinning (1998), through a close reading of the works of Heidegger, Derrida, and Wittgenstein.

[12] "We have this resource and can sometimes use it; as a refuge, say, from the strains of involvement; or as an aid to policy; or simply out of intellectual curiosity" (Strawson, 1974).

attitudes may be required. It is for instance quite possible that the responsiveness of the music therapist nurtures the responsiveness of each singer through relieving their strains of involvement to a bearable level. In sum: For the singers, professional care may promote participant attitudes and at the same time reduce the strains of involvement so that self-care and care for the other could be balanced.

In the interview material, the experience of singing in the choir was sometimes contrasted with experiences from the health care system, where – with the terms introduced by Strawson – we could say that objective attitudes at times may dominate, as exemplified by the story given about a friend who was not allowed to accept the gift of a bottle of brandy. This little story may exemplify a more general problem in the health care system, where effective specialist interventions increasingly have become desired by those concerned with cost control. In consequence, the value of *attending* to a person in an emotional and "holistic" way may be challenged.

A senior choir, part of the cultural scene of its community, may be in a different place and position, with better conditions for cultivating care. As Christopher Small (1998) has argued, collaborative music-making may be capable of articulating and shaping human relationships in all their multilayered and multiordered complexity and changeability. The senior singers seem to have discovered this and to have taken advantage of it. I am thus proposing that *mutual care* could be descriptive for senior choir participation, if responsibilities are bearable and responsiveness to music, yourself, and others are nurtured. From the sentence completion task described in the first part of this essay, there were statements such as "When I sing, then the sounds of the song carry me." The analysis and interpretation of the interview material suggests that this statement could be linked to another statement made in the same sentence completion task: "When I sing, then I am not so alone."

Just Care?

Three variants of the question in the sub-heading above will frame problems that request reflection, namely: Care only?, Only care?, and Fair care?

First, to what degree could "music is caring" and "choir participation as mutual care" be considered a satisfactory interpretation of the original statement that initiated the exploration, namely "music is humane/caring"? Alternative readings could focus upon singing as interplay, interaction, communication, and contact. Possible theories for contextualization of such themes could be interaction theory (see e.g. Stern, 1985) and various music therapy theories on music as dialogue and communication (see e.g. Rolvsjord, 2002; Ansdell and Pavlicevic, 2005; Garred, 2006). To what degree such readings would deviate from the focus developed in this case study would depend upon the perspective taken on human nature. In conceptions focusing upon individualism, care would need to be defined more in the direction of duty or utility and could therefore be treated as an issue separate from situations of communication. In conceptions focusing upon human connectivity, the issues of care and communication will be interwoven. In the latter case, readings of "music is humane/caring" in the direction of mutual care and in the direction of musical communication would therefore be related.

This clarifies a premise for my understanding of the second question, why should we care about care? If we understand human nature as characterized by interdependence, then we will be able to understand the double origin of human care as concern for both weal and woe, that is; as consideration for a person's pleasures and resources as well as his or her sorrows and problems (Stige, 2006a). This idea puts the issue of care into the context of everyday life challenges as well as in the context of the philosophy of ethics. An "ethics of care" or an "ethics of being with the other" – inspired by the work of philosophers such as Heidegger, Derrida, Løgstrup, and Levinas – has been promoted as alternative to dominating traditions of ethics such as utilitarianism and Kantian ethics (see e.g. Martinsen, 1989; Manning, 1992/2001; Vetlesen, 1994; Vetlesen and Nortvedt, 2000).

One of the problems for an ethics of care is framed by our third question: Could care and justice be combined? As a philosophical question this relates to the particularity of situations of care as opposed to the universality implied in an ideal of justice (someone close to you could be in need of care, but the need of someone not so close could be even more severe). From the perspective of caregivers, feminist philosophers have focused upon the fact that caring in some cases may be a burden, which often has continued to be women's burden (Manning, 1992/2001). Various conflicts of care were also illuminated by some singers in the *Senior Choir.* This issue is not easily resolved, neither at a philosophical nor at a practical level. An "ethics of care" may run into problems of biased prioritization while an "ethics of rules and rights" may grow insensitive to the acute needs in specific situations. Some kind of "check and balance" between the two perspectives will therefore need to be cultivated (see Manning, 1992/2001; Vetlesen and Nortvedt, 2000).

In conclusion; mutual care as each person's interest for the other's weal and woe is particularly relevant for a senior choir where the singers have sustained a strong interest for music in spite of the fact that they may have taken "ills here and ills there." Mutual care is of course not all there is to a choir, but if we realize that mutual care is not necessarily separated from the pleasure of singing, then we may see how mutual care may imply caring for immediate needs but also cooperative political action, in this specific case through performances challenging attitudes in the larger community.

In Antiquity, choirs were not only belonging to the sphere of music, as we tend to think of it today, but to the broader practice of mousiké where singing was part of dance and drama. In contemporary society it may be that some choirs such as the *Senior Choir* studied here could be considered elements in the social drama of developing communities of care and justice.

PART X

Chapter 19

Conclusion

When Things Take Shape in Relation to Music: Towards an Ecological Perspective on Music's Help

Brynjulf Stige, Gary Ansdell, Cochavit Elefant and Mercédès Pavlicevic

> Music is constitutive of the social in so far as it may be seen to enter action, and/or conception when things take shape in relation to music.
>
> Tia DeNora

Introduction

This book has portrayed music's help in action within a broad range of contexts around the world; with individuals, groups and communities – all of whom have been challenged by illness or disability, social and cultural disadvantage, or injustice.

Music and musicing has helped people find their voice (literally and metaphorically); to be made welcome and to welcome others; to be accepted and to accept; to be together in different and better ways; to project alternative messages about themselves or their community; to feel respected and to give respect; to connect with others beyond their immediate environment; to make friendships and create supportive networks and social bridges; and, quite simply, to generate fun, joy, fellowship, and conviviality for themselves and their communities.

Should any of this seem surprising? Perhaps most of us, if asked why music is important in our lives, would explain that it has helped us in just these various ways. People often say these days that music is "therapeutic" for them. It is curious, then, that the profession of music therapy has to date largely resisted such a broad agenda for itself. Music therapy has mostly, for the last 30 years, been unduly modest in its aim and applications – restricting its area of help to cultivating intimate relationships with individuals medically classified as physically or mentally sick, and offering such help mostly within the privacy of a therapy room. The theories it has used to legitimate itself have been mostly medical and psychological – with the concurrent tendency to individualize both problems and solutions. The stories in this book have, on the contrary, shown just how much more music and music therapy is capable of doing – and how the professionally trained music therapist can assist in mobilizing music's help in a broader and more flexible way for people and communities, whilst ensuring the safety of often vulnerable people and sensitive situations.

The narratives and essays in this book have brought into relief how, for example, participation, performance, ritual, collaboration, and inter-group processes have been vital to the success of the projects. We have elaborated on these themes, drawing on a broad range of musical, psychological, socio-cultural, and anthropological literature. What we could learn from these projects is to a large degree contained in the case studies themselves. Readers are invited to explore to what degree one or more of these studies could serve as parallel cases to those that they encounter in their own work. The patterns that we have identified could then be examined and modified in new contexts. This suggests that there are limits to the merits of a synthesis, but we do find it meaningful to discuss the case studies in relation to each other. What follows is partly a meta-ethnography (Noblit and Hare, 1988), where we look at similarities and differences across the case studies, and partly a theoretical synthesis, where we look at relationships between themes developed here and current literature of relevance for an understanding of music and health in community.

In organizing this final part of the book, we return to the broad questions that we presented in the Introduction: "How can Community Music Therapy processes be described in relation to their specific social and cultural contexts?" "How do clients/participants participate in and experience Community Music Therapy projects?" "In what ways can Community Music Therapy promote health and change? Does it offer other cultural benefits?" These questions have not regulated the details of each case study, where foci and designs have been emergent, but contextualized explorations of the questions are found in the various chapters. What we could do here is to develop some general reflections on how to think about such questions in Community Music Therapy and to illuminate some aspects which may become clearer through comparison between cases.

In relation to the first question on how to describe Community Music Therapy, we will discuss some key features that may identify assumptions and values that inform the Community Music Therapy projects we have studied. In this way we hope to develop a better understanding of Community Music Therapy both as practice and academic field of study. In relation to the question on how participants participate in and experience Community Music Therapy projects, we will reflect upon music as identity, diversity and community and then discuss relationships to contemporary theories on social-musical processes. The final questions on the ways Community Music Therapy can promote health and other cultural benefits will be addressed through a discussion of an "ecology of outcomes," which we will then relate to the issues of professionalization and participation.

Key Features

The eight projects described in this book illuminate Community Music Therapy as the promotion of musical communication and community in the service of health, development, and social change. On the basis of these case studies we will propose some broad "key features" of Community Music Therapy practice. Our intention is not to present a definition, but to sensitize to Community Music Therapy as a broad (meta)theoretical perspective, along with the values-base that seems to inform practice. Hopefully, future research will modify or challenge our conclusions.[1]

The projects we have studied suggest that an *ecological* metaphor is at the heart of Community Music Therapy. They also suggest that Community Music Therapy practice is inherently *participatory*, *performative* (in a broad sense of this word), *resource-oriented*, and *actively reflective*. None of these features are necessarily unique to Community Music Therapy, but the combination of them may suggest a necessary revision of current music therapy thinking in relation to assumptions about people, music, and health.

This proposal requires a clarification of the relationship between this list of features and the various themes that have been developed in the essays of this volume. The fact that only some of these themes are included in the list of key features does not reflect an appraisal of which are the most important. It reflects how these themes have been developed from different perspectives and on different conceptual levels. For instance, the theme of *belonging* and the concepts of *community* that are developed in Part II constitute a context for reflection upon why Community Music Therapy is relevant in late modern societies. The concept of *collaborative musicing* explored in Part IV illuminates central processes in Community Music Therapy practice, while the notion of *mutual care* developed in Part IX clarifies one possible set of outcomes. The following is therefore *not* a list of the most central themes discussed in this book, but a list of features that may help identify the assumptions and values informing Community Music Therapy projects.

With these caveats in mind we will give a brief explication of each of the five key features, with reference to examples from the various case studies and with thoughts on how each feature may add to our understanding of Community Music Therapy more generally.

---

[1] The formulation of features brings to mind Wittgenstein's (1958/1969, p. 125; 1953/1967, § 67) famous notion of *family resemblances*; whilst no member necessarily shares all features, there is a certain distribution of key features within a given family, which somehow defines its identity.

Ecological

An ecological perspective is strongly implied in the Community Music Therapy projects that we have studied, and this finding resonates with recent literature on music studies. As Ansdell puts it in Part II, with reference to the work of Christopher Small: "the group is performing not just the music, or themselves, but their whole ecology of relationships: to each other, to their context, to their culture and its many complexities and conflicts." We are using "ecology" here in a quasi-metaphorical sense (as used by socio-cultural theorists), for description of transactions and processes involving partnerships and networks, diversity and dynamic balance.[2]

Various ecological conditions and processes are important to all the case studies of this volume, from *Musical Minds* in Part II to the *Senior Choir* in Part IX. In some of the case studies the ecological dimensions are apparent in that for instance mesosystem relationships are in focus. Other studies mostly focus upon microsystem processes and the use of the ecological metaphor may be less explicit. An example of the latter is Pavlicevic's discussion in Part IV of optimal moments of collaborative musicing in the Heideveld Children's Choir. But the ecological perspective is central even here; an ecology involving individuals and (sub)groups in the choir as well as in the broader community is essential to the process. One of the more explicit examples using the ecological metaphor is given by Elefant in Part III. She describes how two separate microsystems (two separate groups of children) can be linked through music and how this leads to inclusion in a broader community setting. The process she describes thus involves developments not only at the microsystem level but at the meso-, and exosystem levels as well, and it is influenced by the macrosystem. This case study also illuminates how various systems may be understood as nested. In various ways, the new microsystem created is embedded in and influenced by other ecological layers of the broader community. In return, the children are also able to influence the organizations and the locality that they belong to.

How could this add to our understanding of Community Music Therapy more generally, for instance compared to conventional individual or group music therapy? Conventional music therapy may of course also be interpreted or discussed with use of ecological metaphors.[3] If therapy leads to change, there may be a ripple effect in that the environment reacts – positively or negatively – to the changes in the individual. What characterizes the Community Music Therapy projects that we have tracked is that they reveal an *active* and consciously-directed multisystem approach. We will argue that most Community Music Therapy projects actively explore relationships between individuals, microsystems, organizations, localities,

---

[2]   Interestingly, similar principles are central to Capra's (2003) discussion of the scientific principles of ecology.

[3]   See e.g. Kenny (1985, 1989), who has developed a theory on music therapy processes that is informed by field theory and systems theory.

and macrosystems, and development of partnerships and networks is central to the process. Which levels and networks that are actively involved will vary, depending upon the needs and resources in each context.

Participatory

Several of the essays in this volume have underlined that Community Music Therapy is not just an expert-directed practice. Community Music Therapy is characterized by a *participatory ethos*. This involves a willingness to listen to each participant and to acknowledge his or her voice. Consequently, practice focuses upon enablement (working with personal and musical qualifications for participation) and empowerment (increased assertiveness and communicativeness in relation to the community) and may be supplemented by negotiations with other agents and communities concerning access to arenas and activities.

The participatory character of Community Music Therapy is explored most explicitly in Part V where Stige discusses the participatory creation of social space and in Part VII where Elefant discusses Participatory Action Research, but it is implied in all narratives and essays in this volume. For instance, in Part IV Pavlicevic discusses how music therapists generate optimal collaborative musicing and suggests that one strategy is "A Complex Attentiveness to the Moment – and 'Doing as Little as Possible.'" In Part VI Ansdell discusses how respect must be performed and suggests that musicing is exemplary of collaborative "respect-in-action." And in Part VIII Pavlicevic conveys an everyday practice that depends on the sharing of knowledge, skills, and expertise of all participants.

The examples demonstrate continuity in relation to conventional music therapy, where therapists also may cultivate respect, mutuality, and complex attentiveness to the moment. But the case studies of this book suggest that Community Music Therapy may be more radically democratic than conventional practice in a clinic allows for. Processes where participants and music therapists negotiate goals and roles are described and discussed in several of the case studies. This participatory feature also helps revealing a values-base that seems to be central to most Community Music Therapy projects. We may articulate this in relation to the ecological metaphors described above: At the individual and microsystem levels, the personal and interpersonal value of *mutual respect* seems to be central, while at levels such as organization, locality, and macrosystem social values with political implications are also involved, such as the values of *solidarity, equity,* and *diversity*.[4]

---

[4]   We will argue that if there is space for respect, solidarity, equity, and diversity there is also a fair amount of liberty. See Stige (2003) for further discussion of values in relation to Community Music Therapy.

Performative

The overall orientation of the work described in this book is often "outwards-and-around" (in contrast to conventional music therapy's typical concentration on working "down-and-within"). We have chosen to label this feature as performative, in the broad sociological meaning of that term. While concerts and gigs at times may be important, the performative character of Community Music Therapy suggests something much broader than this. It is based upon a *relational perspective* on human development and it also emphasizes the music-centered nature of Community Music Therapy in a way that suggests a concept of music which emphasizes its social character, as we will explore later on.

The idea of "musicing-as-performing" with potential for personal and social transformation is most explicitly discussed in Part VI, where Ansdell clarifies how the notion of performance has been "moved back to the center" from the margins of both music therapy and music studies more generally. Inspired by the work of Victor Turner and others, he illuminates how performances are *reflexive*. In performing the individual reveals herself to herself and to others, with the implication that communities may be performed too.

In employing a broad notion of performance, we acknowledge that presentation of self and the collaborative creation of groups are part of human everyday practice, as pioneers of sociology such as Goffman and Durkheim have suggested. In the case studies presented in this book, there are therefore many examples of musicing-as-performing in non-concert situations. One example of this is given in Part III, where Elefant describes the music meetings of a group of young children with severe special needs:

> Some staff members stay in the room, listen to our music making as a smile of pride appears at the corner of their mouths – just like a mother watching her child performs. The children glance back at them as if saying "did you hear me play? Aren't you proud of me?" The staff who know these children very well nod with contentment. (Elefant, Part III in this volume)

An important corollary of Community Music Therapy's performative character is that it could not be thought of as therapy in any individualized or curative sense. Community Music Therapy is primarily collaborative and proactive work in relation to health, development, and social change. The focus is upon promotion of health and prevention of problems rather than curative interventions. Community Music Therapy projects may at times collaborate with the health sector, but they are usually not oriented towards treatment and they may collaborate with or be part of other sectors in the society as well, such as education and social care.

Resource-oriented

The participants in the projects that have been studied here have all in various ways been challenged by problems, ranging from disease or disability to social disorder or disadvantage. Problems are important parts of the picture in these Community Music Therapy practices, but they are not the main focus of attention. Instead, mobilization of resources seems to be key. As was the case with the term "ecology," our use of the term "resources" is quasi-metaphorical. Resources may be tangible or intangible and may refer to both personal strengths and material goods as well as to symbolic artifacts and relational and social processes that may be appropriated by members of a community.

The projects described in this volume illuminate the acknowledgment of client/participant strengths (such as creativity and musical talents), of relational resources (such as trust and emotional support), and community resources (such as music organizations and musical traditions). So we may see variously the "re-cycling" of musical and social resources through performances and collaborations. For instance, Elefant explicitly refers to "resource-oriented music therapy" in both of her essays, focusing upon music as an individual and a communal resource, while Ansdell in Part II discusses how communities of musical practice may generate social and musical capital. In Part V Stige describes how non-conventional forms of participation such as silent participation or eccentric participation may be a resource in the process of building an inclusive social space. In Part VIII Pavlicevic describes the mobilizing of a network of hitherto hidden resources, creating pathways towards the Heideveld Community Concert.

The resource-oriented feature of Community Music Therapy may be quite close to characteristics of some other contemporary perspectives on music therapy, such as the approach to "resource-oriented music therapy" in mental health described by Randi Rolvsjord (Rolvsjord, 2004, 2006, 2007; Rolvsjord, Gold and Stige, 2005a, 2005b). Rolvsjord's approach to music therapy is informed by contextual perspectives and focuses upon personal strengths, collaboration, and mutual empowerment. We acknowledge these similarities and think that they demonstrate how Community Music Therapy may be developed in dialogue with other practices of and perspectives on music therapy. The resource-oriented feature of Community Music Therapy of course also resonates with developments in other related disciplines, such as recent research and theory on efficacy and positive emotions in psychology and on social capital in social studies.

Actively Reflective

The chapters in this book have been based upon a fairly formal research stance in relation to practice. This has served to balance the relative lack of research on Community Music Therapy until now. This is not to say that we expect all future Community Music Therapy projects to be research-driven, but it has become clear to us that underlying the overtly practical approach that most music therapists take there is in this tradition a strong investment in reflective and reflexive practice. This involves not just "clinical reflection" on the nature of the immediate music-therapeutic work (as is often the case in more conventional music therapy) but also "active reflection" in terms of the wider influence that Community Music Therapy practice has in the socio-cultural community. This implies a broadening of the concept of "reflective practice" – one which is more dialogic and collaborative.

This is demonstrated in the case studies in the current book, most explicitly perhaps in Part VII where Elefant discusses a Participatory Action Research project with the *Renamim* Choir, but it is equally central to several of the other cases. For instance, Ansdell in Part VI demonstrates and discusses performative aspects of reflection in relation to the study of *Musical Minds* and *Scrap Metal*. Pavlicevic in Part VIII describes the Heideveld Children's Concert as "the meeting place of secrets" and discusses the power of singing to communicate messages and initiate reflections and dialogues. Stige in Part IX discusses how the *Senior Choir* members negotiate on their values in order to be able to position themselves in relation to the broader community where they live.

As these examples reveal, the notion of reflection in Community Music Therapy must be a broad one, to include verbal and social-musical processes in context. This does not imply that we should downplay the importance of the theoretical and research-based knowledge that music therapists could bring into the various contexts where they work. If values such as respect, solidarity, equity, and diversity matter, then relationships between the social world and academic thinking become crucial. The ethos of reflection and research in Community Music Therapy thus can be likened to the practice ethos Pavlicevic described for the Music Therapy Community Clinic in Heideveld, South Africa:

> This social and territorial fluidity is reflected in the Music Therapy Community Clinic's ethos: disinterested in having a fixed base, the MTCC is a "traveling service," able to shift to and from whichever place and event asks for music therapy – and able to withdraw and move on, once no longer needed. (Pavlicevic, Part VIII, this volume)

Community, Identity, and Diversity

The key features described here may help us in recognizing the "family" of Community Music Therapy, but the features are characteristic only if and as they are linked to an exploration of *musical community*. We will try to clarify this through reflections upon how participants participate in and experience Community Music Therapy projects. The case studies demonstrate how community for the participants involves experiences of identity and diversity. We will start with reflections on this theme and then proceed to the more specific theme of social-musical processes.

Community Music Therapy projects involve groups, substantially albeit not exclusively. Due to the ecological and multisystem character of Community Music

Therapy there are not only processes within and between individuals in the groups involved, but also between various other systems, and there is usually some sort of "outreach" involved.[5] There is something more at stake, then, than just adding a little unity and fellowship to a standard conception of individual or group music therapy.

Several of the key features described in the beginning of this chapter provide us with tools for reflection upon the notion of *community* in Community Music Therapy. This notion, which obviously is central to Community Music Therapy, was discussed explicitly in Part II and implicitly in several of the other parts of this book. In Part II Ansdell suggests that:

> ... rather than just happening, contemporary community must be performed, it is something that we create, rather than somewhere we just are, or are "inside." This perspective emphasizes how contemporary community happens through its specific modes of communication, and relies less on traditional factors such as locality, fixed social structures, or ritual events. (Ansdell, Part II, this volume)

Ansdell developed this assumption in relation to *Musical Minds*, but it seems to be confirmed by the other cases in this book, where various forms of *community through communication* are portrayed. There are variations among cases and authors as to how this is described and interpreted. For instance, while Ansdell in the quote above describes ritual events as traditional factors contrasted to contemporary communication communities, Stige in Part V describes everyday interaction rituals as vehicles for the communication that may create and maintain community. In spite of these specific differences, we will argue that the idea of "communication communities" is a shared one in the case studies of this book. One way of explicating this could be to describe the interrelationships between *bonding* and *bridging* through music, that is; between relationships *within* a community and *between* communities.

Bonding and Bridging

Bonding is explicitly used as a metaphor for the process of developing interpersonal ties within a group in several of the case studies in this volume. For instance: In Part II Ansdell discusses the fostering of musical community and includes a reference to Buber's term *Verbundenheit*. In Part III Elefant suggests that "the group as a medium for help deals with cohesion and bonding around mutual purposes."

---

[5] Stuart Wood's work in southern England exemplifies this. Starting off with relatively conventional individual work with patients in a medical rehabilitation unit, "Stuart found himself challenged to deal with the changing needs of these people as they developed beyond the acute stages of their illness. Now the need was rather how to re-integrate people back again into their family and community life" (Ansdell, Part VI of this volume). See also Wood, Verney and Atkinson (2004) and Wood (2006).

In Part IV Pavlicevic discusses optimal moments of collaborative musicing and suggests that they may produce bonding almost too powerful to be sustained for long. There are also other texts in this volume that describe processes of bonding without using the metaphor, such as the essay in Part V, where Stige discusses the creation of group solidarity through interaction rituals in music.

Similarly, many of the case studies employ the metaphor of *bridging* for description of processes of outreach, where relationships between communities are developed: In Part II Ansdell touches upon this when he discusses musical community in light of the literature on communities of practice, where Wenger (1998, p. 277) talks about "the creation of connections across boundaries of practice: a frail bridge across the abyss." In Part III Elefant describes two groups of children that "were neighbors but lived in such dissimilation" and how the idea of bringing these two groups together was nurtured by the assumption that "music could become the connecting 'bridge' for the purpose of uniting the groups." Another example is given in Part VI, where Ansdell writes about Stuart Wood's work: "By nurturing these connections that musicing created ... something interesting was happening: a natural outward movement for people. As hoped, music was an ideal bridge-building activity, which helped people re-integrate back into the outside community once they were ready for this step." There are also examples in this volume that discuss bridging activities without using the metaphor. For instance, in Part VIII Pavlicevic describes the Heideveld Community Concert as "the meeting place of secrets." She underlines "how the concert brings together people who would otherwise have no reason to do so" and how it "enables the children to address their elders in a way that would be unthinkable in daily life."

While the case studies vary as to whether they have focused upon bonding or bridging or both, our claim is that usually Community Music Therapy projects carefully cultivate the *interplay of bonding and bridging*. We could exemplify this by revisiting the *Senior Choir* that Stige discusses in Part IX: The practice of performing publicly was part of this choir's identity. Most of the singers seemed to enjoy public performances, some thinking of it as a personal challenge, some as affirmative group experience, and others as "social action" challenging attitudes in the larger community. In this way, the singers may be said to be able to combine the strategies of bonding and bridging, that is; to build trust within the group (bonding) and to contribute to the inclusive building of social capital in the community (bridging), the latter through reaching out on public occasions, supplementing the bonding of immediate care with bridging to others not so close.[6]

The features of Community Music Therapy described above, such as the ecological, participatory, performative, and resource-oriented qualities, allow for

---

[6]   This suggests that theories of and research on social capital will be highly pertinent for Community Music Therapy, as has already been proposed by Simon Procter (2004, 2006). One important contribution to our understanding of social capital has been developed by Robert Putnam (2000) in his tome *Bowling Alone: The Collapse and Revival of American Community*.

developments in bonding and bridging that are different from and perhaps "go further" than what is typical in conventional music therapy. We will exemplify by a discussion of participation in Community Music Therapy leading to *friendships* and *activism*.

Bonding for Friendships

Most of us hope to make and keep friends: in the hope that we will do things together, look out for one another, have fun, have conflicts, get beyond them, share things that have happened to us, and help one another when need be. Music therapy is not usually associated with making friends (or at least, music therapists don't usually talk about this) – and yet this seems to be the experience of some of the participants in this book. The children in Heideveld have "made new friends in the choir." In Israel, children from different schools and with different abilities have come together through music therapy. They start attending one another's birthday parties and the children from the elementary school tell the music therapist that the special children are "their best friends." In Norway, the members of the *Senior Choir* look out for one another and help one another "with flexibility and humor." As one of the singers put it: "I used to be new here. ... I knew nobody else, but today I would say that I think of us as a really good group of friends. ... Or: we are siblings ... singer-siblings ..." In London, people with mental health problems come together and through singing together, experience the sense of familiarity and belonging together that is in contrast with the rest of their isolated lives "on the edge of society."

The participatory, performative, and resource-oriented features of the Community Music Therapy projects studied imply sharing and a leveling of roles and responsibilities which may nurture friendships. It is perhaps the ecological character of Community Music Therapy that enables the maintenance of these processes over time and also indicates their importance. The projects studied are not secluded therapy groups, but woven into social networks in broader communities. They are part of people's everyday life. This explains why friendships among participants may be very important in Community Music Therapy.[7]

The idea of friendships implies mutuality, while professional practice is characterized by certain responsibilities. There is a tension here which requires careful consideration of the roles, responsibilities, and relationships involved.

It may seem self evident that the music therapists, as "experts," carry "overall" responsibility for Community Music Therapy practice: They have training and

---

[7] A few music therapists, such as Curtis and Mercado (2004) have talked about friendship in relation to Community Music Therapy and a recent text discusses friendship in relation to music therapy more generally (Foster, 2007). The claim we made above that this theme is rarely discussed in the music therapy literature seems still to be warranted. Klefbeck and Ogden (2003) argue that this theme also by and large has been neglected in the literature on social networks and social support (surprising as this may sound).

skills, they are paid for their work; it is "their job" to make sure that things work. Within the musicing events that we have studied the music therapists' responsibilities can be summed up as enabling and facilitating optimal musicing, engagement, participation, and collaboration. This involves use of music therapy specific skills that witness and listen, adjust and correct, support and encourage. It would be a mistake, however, to think of the music therapists as the active agents and the clients or participants as recipients. The process is more mutual than that. In the Community Music Therapy projects that we have studied the mutual and collaborative dimension is sometimes especially strong.[8] There are also often many different agents involved. In other words: There are multiple axes of responsibility, some of which are shared and negotiated among all, also those who are not engaged directly in music-making (i.e., kitchen staff, carers, parents, teachers, drivers, festival organizers, etc.). All of these agents share responsibility for ensuring that events and processes run as smoothly as possible.

Equally, participants assume musical responsibility. In YDO, a young man has written a song and brings it to music therapy where its music is co-composed by the group. At the *Cultural Festival* workshop, a "musical mutiny" by participants changes the script and energy of the workshop, while in *Scrap Metal*, a woman with neurological disabilities brings to music therapy instruments made out of old things in her house, and an absent member of the group has composed a song, performed by all at the concert. In relation to such initiatives, we can think of the therapist's responsibilities in terms of "scaffolding" around and during the musicing events – whether a rehearsal, concert performance, or a group music therapy session. Solgunn ensures that there are extra copies of sheet music in large print for the *Senior Choir* members. At the *Cultural Festival*, the music therapists prepare the "ritual script," choosing songs for the structure and flexibility these provide for predictable and unexpected episodes. In preparing for the Heideveld Community Concert, the music therapists ask for help, calling on the local teachers when failing to secure a venue, while, the *Musical Minds* group discusses with Sarah the food and drink situation for their coming concert.

There are important nuances of having and assuming responsibility, giving responsibility, taking it, and sharing it – any one of which seems to be activated at different times, according to circumstances. Part of the music therapist's skill is in not being the sole expert, but in negotiating expertise and roles with others. Stuart, in the *Scrap Metal* concert, becomes the compère, managing the event while the "clients" perform – he emerges at the end of the concert and teaches the audience a round written by an absent member of the group. Sarah is accorded a rather different role and status, from being the musical director to becoming "the piano

[8]   This argument suggests that professional domination is unacceptable in Community Music Therapy but it does not exclude the possibility that music therapists at times may have "transformative power," that is; an unequal exercise of power aimed at a gradual transformation towards a more equal exercise (see e.g. Jerlang, 1988/1991, Wartenberg 1990, in Mattern, 1998, p. 151).

player" whose role is now to allow the performers to "shine." In the process of collaboration that grows out of the encounter between the two groups of children in Raanana it is the children who more and more start to produce the solutions of the problems they encounter and it is the children themselves who come up with the radical and inclusive idea of arranging a summer camp. The *Cultural Festival* in Norway includes examples when the music therapists let scripts go altogether, when need be.

The examples illuminate how there is trust in one another's expertise and skills, in one another's knowledge of the local networks, and a mutual according of roles and responsibilities. Would these processes nurture friendships between participants and therapists also? This is a more controversial idea than that of friendships among participants and it requires specific considerations on roles and interpersonal relationships in Community Music Therapy. The present case studies do not investigate this in any detail, but there are indications suggesting that there are friendship-like aspects in the participant-therapist relationships in several situations; when roles are redefined and scripts go, when mutual trust and empowerment is especially prominent, and when the therapist's engagement in the projects exceeds what would usually be expected (concerning when, where, and how to work, for instance). In the midst of these "violations" of standard professional norms, there is one norm which the therapists seem to be very concerned about *not* violating, namely the responsibility to ensure that the processes are safe and beneficial for participants.

It would not be precise, then, to think of these examples where roles are leveled and mutuality nurtured as situations when the music therapists are no longer professional. A redefinition of the professional role is involved. In relation to the projects that we have studied, the cultivation of *multiple roles and relationships* seems to be key. All eight projects demonstrate how the professional role becomes multi-layered and complex within an ecology of interpersonal processes and relationships. In some of the roles that the therapists take in the projects studied, such as that of being a co-musician or a community advocate, there may be more space for friendship-like dimensions than in some of the other roles.

All parties in the various projects need to handle a range of roles and relationships, then, often simultaneously or within short time spans. The importance of the *active reflection* that we described above is evident here. Not very many predefined rules about therapist roles could be established; they need to be collaboratively negotiated in relation to the multiplicity of roles and relationships that evolve in each context.

Beyond Bonding and Bridging: Social Activism through Music

In the narratives and essays of this volume, Community Music Therapy practice can often be thought of as "identity work" where identities are being generated and performed – with limited identities being extended, new identities being claimed, and negative identities being discarded and replaced. Through musicing, all kinds of identity shifts are affected – in some instances these change the lives of those whose individual identity risks being dominated by collective, public labeling (be it mental illness, physical disability, senior citizens, or young criminals).

In Part V, Stige refers to "cultural politics" – a theme that runs throughout the work – where collective musicing effects transformation that moves beyond the individual. This rippling effect of musicing together moves from the individual to the group and opens out towards society, through the rituals of musical performances, rehearsals, and concerts. It ripples inwards too from the public event towards the group and the individual. Identity work resonates with social activism: which in this book ranges from micro to macro. One of the (at times quiet) stances through most essays is one of social advocacy: whether to "give voice" or to change public attitudes (towards senior citizens, children with "little potential," disabled people, persons with mental health problems, etc.). The *Senior Choir* wants to be seen as having energy and vitality – to challenge social views of old people as less valued citizens – and this challenge happens in the act of singing with and to others, with vivacity. The Heideveld children are seen in a new way by their teachers, parents and families, resulting in a new social attitude towards them as children who can "do music" rather than children who will inevitably join the local gangs. These and similar public musicing acts may transform social attitudes within and also around the zone of performance with potential to change its musical and social ecology – thus rippling beyond the musicing event, both in time and place.

Bonding and bridging allows for experiences of unity and for the development of shared identities. But unity is always only partial. People and groups have various experiences, interests, and values and may differ in many respects, as all case studies in this volume exemplify. And as Ansdell in Part II suggests; participation in and experience of Community Music Therapy must be understood in the context of diversity and discrepancy. Communication communities are dynamic and sometimes conflictual and therefore involve active cultivation of such communicative competences as dialogue and negotiation:

> Consequently, participation in such communities can often seem both communal *and* "discrepant" at the same time, as people work to reconcile their equal, but sometimes conflicting, needs for autonomy and togetherness. (Ansdell, Part II, this volume)

Ansdell argues that community in Community Music Therapy could therefore not just be based upon tradition or the psychological need for fellowship. In order to be inclusive and allow for growth and change, communities must be able to handle diversity and dispute. The type of community that is cultivated in Community Music Therapy is *participatory*, and the proposed values-base of respect, solidarity, equity, and diversity also suggests that it is *democratic*. Such processes and values are strongly part of Sarah's thinking about her work with *Musical Minds,* for example. She sees herself as an advocate for the group (and for individuals within the group) and also as a mediator and negotiator in situations where there are conflicts of interest and disputes in the group.

Mark Mattern (1998) has previously discussed a democratic conception of community in relation to music, and described it as "community that is consistent with diversity, supports collective political action and a strong form of democracy, and potentially encompasses extensive populations and geographical regions as well as local settings" (Mattern, 1998, p. 10). His work includes case studies of Chilean, Cajun, and American Indian music and thus focuses more upon extensive populations and geographical regions than upon local settings, while the opposite is true of the case studies in this volume. Some notions that Mattern has developed for description of music as social and political action nevertheless could shed light on the case studies that we have presented, since all case studies in this volume thematize challenges of handling diversity within and between communities.

Mattern (1998) describes music as a communicative arena, which is an idea that is congruent with the ecological perspective that we have taken. He then launches the metaphor of "acting in concert" in order to describe social activism or community-based political action through music. Mattern suggests that there are three distinct forms of "acting in concert": confrontational, deliberative, and pragmatic. A confrontational form takes place when one community uses music to resist or oppose another community. In Mattern's work, the prominent case example of this is protest music, such as the Chilean "new song" movement. Before the military coup in 1973 singers such as Violetta Parra and Victor Jara contributed to the creation of a community of democratic socialists in clear confrontation with the right wing politicians in that country. In a democratic society, confrontational "acting in concert" may have positive effects such as publicizing a political issue and drawing citizens into active participation. Also, when there is massive repression, confrontational "acting in concert" may sometimes be experienced as the only possibility (there may be little space for deliberation with generals). But Mattern argues that there are limits to the effects of a confrontational approach, as it leads to polarization and thus may increase possibilities for use of violence in various forms. Mattern therefore suggests that deliberative and pragmatic forms of "acting in concert" many times are equally or more efficient. In deliberative forms – as in confrontational forms – the premise is divergent interests, but music becomes a framework for negotiation rather than either-or-struggle. In pragmatic forms of "acting in concert," the premise is that there may be some shared interests among people and the focus is thus upon mutual beneficial problem solving.

The story of *Renanim* (Part VII) includes this choir's experience of being dominated by another choir. "People need to get to know us in a better way." This voice belongs to a member of the *Renanim* choir, after a performance which the choir describes as an experience of being "swallowed up" by the other group. The music therapist's bringing together of *Renanim* and the more vocally powerful *Idud* choir in public performance to "give voice" to the *Renanim* group has gone "wrong" – and *Renanim* decides to do it alone: "people need to get to know us in a better way." The comment signals a collective reflexivity about being witnessed negatively and being accorded a negative identity. It also signals a desire for a better way of being witnessed, one more congruent with the group's own identity. *Renanim* did not choose to engage in confrontational actions towards *Idud*, even though this would have been a possibility. The Participatory Action Research process they engaged in enabled them to negotiate between their own need for identity and the shared need for community. This type of music work that affects identity shifts can be thought of as *deliberative* activism. In fact, the confrontational form is hardly present in any of the case studies of this volume. The deliberative and pragmatic forms of social activism seem to be more typical for the Community Music Therapy projects that we have studied.

The Heideveld Community Concert, as discussed in the narrative of Part IV and the essay of Part VIII, is a prime example of *pragmatic* social activism. The concert offered the neighborhood a chance to come together in a new way, and "the whole of Heideveld" seemed to come. They used the opportunity to build ties and develop pride in their children. They performed their community, so to say. In consequence, the event galvanized everyone and the music therapists experienced that the Heideveld community claimed the concert as theirs, with subsequent changes in the music therapists' roles. This example also illuminates how pragmatic and deliberative forms of "acting in concert" may develop into hybrid forms. While the concert focused upon shared concerns for the future of this community, the children also engaged in deliberative action by singing "what is unspeakable – what is generally hidden and silenced."

Orientation to Social-Musical Processes

We have discussed participation in and experience of Community Music Therapy in relation to community, identity, and diversity. An implicit aspect of this, which we here want to make more explicit and explore theoretically, is that we are talking about participation and experience in relation to music and music-making. One of the recurring themes in this volume is how musicing is understood as social-musical process (or musical-social process – you will find both terms in the various case studies). A summary of our "findings" in relation to this could be as follows: Music(ing) is never alone, never abstracted from either its immediate context of place or use, or separated out into just sound. This could be specified in the following ways:

- Musicing is always embodied and embedded, as "song-and-dance," somewhere and with someone else.
- Musicing is never just a personal or individual activity: it is always (however modestly) something social, cultural, and political within the context of its performance.
- Musical and social resources and responsibilities are always shared, distributed, and fluid.

- Musicing and music therapy is seldom (if ever) truly "contained" or confidential: it naturally links people into networks, and helps form bridges between people, groups, and communities.
- Musicing helps with seemingly "non-musical" personal and social problems.

One theoretical outlook on social-musical processes is offered by Ansdell and Pavlicevic who developed the notion of *collaborative musicing* (Ansdell and Pavlicevic, 2005; Pavlicevic and Ansdell, 2009). In Part IV of the present volume Pavlicevic explains this term and how it is based in an understanding of group music therapy as a complex social-musical event. Pavlicevic then describes an episode in the back-row of the choir rehearsing for the Heideveld Community Concert in the following way:

> I saw a social-musical improvisation in which musical space is generated, molded, occupied and dismissed with split-second precision and collective dexterity. This social-musical improvisation seemed to be known within and between all minds and bodies as one, complex, phenomenon. (Pavlicevic, Part IV, this volume)

In several other essays in this book, the term *social-musical* is employed to describe Community Music Therapy situations and processes. For instance, in Part V, Stige describes a musical greeting ritual in the *Cultural Festival* and portrays this as a social-musical process where the interest is not just the song and the person introduced, but the integrated experience of the person's participation in the musical activity. In some of the essays, the related term *musical-social* is employed, for instance by Ansdell in Part II when he discusses *participatory discrepancies* in music. In Part VI he also employs this term, now with reference to the social outreach of musical orchestras.

At one level our use of terms such as social-musical and musical-social denotes something rather obvious; when it comes to music there are usually people involved. We are, however, making claims that go beyond this and suggest that there is something inherently social in music. This is not to support an environmentalist doctrine where music is reduced to social stimulus. Music is always embodied and grounded in personal experience, but in musicing our experiential world is a shared world (Whitehead, 2001). So what we are suggesting is that music as an embodied and personal phenomenon is simultaneously, and in principle, a social phenomenon. This theme is probably key to an understanding of Community Music Therapy and we will give it some specific consideration here.

We will start with a brief clarification of the psychobiological foundation for musical participation – understood as part of a social-musical motivational system (Dissanayake, 2000a, 2000b, 2001; Trevarthen and Malloch, 2000; Trevarthen, 2000; Malloch and Trevarthen, 2009). We will then continue with an exploration of relationships between musical and socio-cultural processes. Our approach has been particularly stimulated by recent work in the anthropology, psychology, and sociology of music (Small, 1998; DeNora, 2000, 2001, 2003, 2005; Clarke, 2005; Martin, 2006), and from elaborations of this by music therapists testing these ideas in relation to their practical work.

We will attempt as we go further in this section to reflect more systematically on the ways in which the seemingly "specifically musical" phenomena entailed or afforded the various seemingly "extra-musical" personal, social, and political outcomes portrayed in the case studies. The perspective we take on this question will not, however, be a traditional one of suggesting that music is some kind of singular (and analytically extractable) "power" that has quasi-magical effects on people and situations. Neither will it be the related modern view that music can be a solution "prescribed" by experts (such as music therapists) in an instrumental way – where music becomes some targeted, evidence-based tool which will, if used effectively, achieve desired and predictable outcomes. We will instead try out a "third way" – an ecological perspective on musicing as song-and-dance in context and collaboration – whose help is real and potent only insofar as it manages to get within-and-amongst the perceptions, experiences, and actions of people-in-places, and to afford them varying possibilities and pleasures aligned with their local needs.

The Psychobiological Foundation for Musical Participation

Researchers studying infant communication have demonstrated how the newborn baby engages in interactions with other human beings in ways that are phrased, pitched, and regulated by a pulse. From birth the child seems to be biologically programmed to be directed to other humans (Dissanayake, 2000a; Trevarthen and Malloch, 2000). This psychobiological foundation enables the baby to enter in affiliate interaction with adults and start on a trajectory of cultural learning. Dissanayake (2000b) therefore argues that music must be considered an "evolved behavior" (in the ethology-sense of that term) and that participation in music is a human need related to the experience of meaning. She clarifies, however, that what we in any culture call "music" is an "artification" of the "protomusical components, including concurrent vocal, visual, and kinesic elements, whose effects encourage participation and positively affect the participant's sense of well-being" (Dissanayake, 2001, p. 165).

The basic psychobiological capacity for relating to sounds, rhythms, and movements that Dissanayake calls protomusicality is by Malloch and Trevarthen (2009) termed *communicative musicality*. The *cross-modal quality* of communicative musicality is central. Some of the biological reasons why this may be so are emerging in the developing picture of human (proto)musicality coming from various quarters. The psychobiologist theory of cross-modal communicative action (Trevarthen, 2001) links with recent discoveries in neuroscience of so-called "mirror neurons" which help us to read others' emotional and social intentions and to thus coordinate our actions empathically with others (Rizzolatti et al, 2006).

This discovery supports the assumption that musical sensitivity may have a cross-modal foundation. Scholars studying the origins of music through paleoanthropology (Cross, 2003; Dunbar, 2004; Mithen, 2005) tell us that *music and dance* were undoubtedly always paired in pre-history. The anthropological perspective comes to much the same conclusion (Blacking, 1973; Becker, 2004) through studies of different cultural manifestations of music and how these emphasize the essential embodiment of music through conjoint song and dance. Charles Whitehead (2001) suggests that we hyphenate *song-and-dance* as it is best considered a single phenomenon and a single coherent system at both psycho-physical and socio-cultural levels.

Implications of this type of psychobiological research and theory for music therapy needs to be explored in further detail, and it would be to generalize too much to claim that song and dance together are more therapeutically powerful than music with less focus upon movement. This depends upon context and use. But the fact that the researchers on music's psychobiological foundation have stressed the multi-modal character of music may suggest that song-and-dance as hyphenated phenomenon may be especially important in the creation of affiliate interaction and musical community. In the case studies of this volume there are many observations to support this suggestion.

One of the children in the Heideveld Children's Choir says: "Dancing helps you sing … singing helps you dance … singing without dance is boring!" The video of their rehearsal shows the reality of her statement, with a scene of vibrant musicing, where song and dance are indistinguishable. When Pavlicevic analyses one of the important micro-moments of collaborative musicing that happens during an in-between moment of the rehearsal with these children, this is how she describes it:

> Half the group taps the song's rhythm on the table, which tapping anchors and drives the continuing crescendo and tightening of the singing, towards a sudden sforzando of vocal and physical energy with exclamations of Ya-Ya-Ya!. Simultaneously, all jump backwards, away from the table, laughing, and almost immediately forming various looser pairs. (Pavlicevic, Part IV, this volume)

This is not dancing added to music, but dancing as the bodily *generation of* musicing, seen from our view that communicative musicality (with its cross-modal expressions) naturally prepares for collaborative musicing (with its negotiated timing and spacing in the service of social creativity). A similar scenario is seen in the Mountain song, where the young men in the Eersterust project are seen creating a song together. Pavlicevic describes:

> At one point, after someone else has said something, everyone exclaims "ja!, ja!" and "the leader" begins playing on the drums. This is interrupted by more animated discussion, until, without cueing, the young men begin drumming, dancing, and singing together. … The singing and dancing gathers intensity, and the tempo and dynamic level, as well as the body movement become tighter and

more energized. The entire group "grooves" and, just as suddenly, the singing
moves into laughter and exclamations, and a rapid diminuendo. (Pavlicevic, Part
VIII, this volume)

This description again characterizes the inability to separate out the music from
their dance, or their body movement from their creative musical collaboration.

It might of course be said that both of these examples are characteristic of
an embodied style of African musicing. In the Heideveld Community Concert,
for example, the music therapist Sunelle describes how if the children sang or
danced, the audience too would get up and clap and dance. Bodily participation
is quite natural within this culture, and affords a particular type of musical-social
experience. What then of more Western musical cultures, which have developed
in an arguably increasingly "dis-embodied" way? In the cases we studied in
Europe and Israel there was admittedly a more restrained and formal approach
to musicing and performance. But if we look more carefully then much the same
phenomenon is happening as with the African examples. In the *Musical Minds*
concert the audience participate in the same way – waving hands above their heads
and swaying to "You'll Never Walk Alone," albeit still keeping in their seats. On
the other contrary, the children Elefant worked with in the school in Israel often
found it difficult to keep in their seats as the music animated them. Dancing and
moving was part of their experience of music.

One of the first vignettes that Stige describes from the *Cultural Festival* in
Norway is of one of the participants "subverting" the therapists' movement warm-
up into his own dance:

> Gradually he transforms the movement activity into a dance. He snaps his
> fingers and starts moving his hips in a spectacular way before he grabs the
> first music therapist with his left hand and the other with his right, while he is
> smiling in a peculiarly charming way to the group. All of a sudden the situation
> is transformed. (Stige, Part V, this volume)

Later a man without words has his excitement translated by another participant.
"You may tell him" she says to the man (who's addressing Stige) "that you've
been dancing with me!" Clearly for these people, to music is also to dance, and the
social-musical rituals they develop within the festival are distinctly multi-modal.
Stige describes his reaction to the final concert, saying: "I'm moved by this music,
not only because of what I hear but because of moments of sound and gesture
linked to a shared history."

For two of the other groups – the *Senior Choir* in Norway and the *Scrap Metal*
project in the UK – the participants' physical limitations also limit the amount
of overt movement that is possible within their musicing. This is by no means to
say that their musicing is *not* embodied. Indeed, in the *Scrap Metal* project the
physicality of singing or playing the scrap metal instruments is key to the feelings
of wellbeing, empowerment and shift in identity that the participants report. Their

dance is just less visible. And for the senior singers, the dance tune of a fiddle could make them forget about their feeble and aching feet for a moment or two, as Figure 18.2 so clearly reveals.

All of these examples have confirmed for us the belief that music is both embodied and embedded. Music(ing) is never "just sound," never abstracted from either its producing bodies, or from its immediate context of place or "use." Rather, musicing is always *song-and-dance* in some way, somewhere, and with someone else. This all suggests that we are witnessing (in both theory and practice) a "re-embodiment" of music. When thinking of music's help for people and places we should perhaps always think not only of "musicing" instead of music, but also of musicing precisely as *song-and-dance* in context and collaboration.

How the Musical "Gets into" the Social

A conceptual problem remains however. Whilst attempting to keep this perspective of the "total event" of music-in-action, there is also the analytical dilemma of finding a convincing link between specifically musical action and the palpable but various "extra-musical" benefits it offers people and communities. Recent work from the so-called "new sociology" of music attempts to answer just this question: to explore exactly how music "gets into" action. The sociologist Tia DeNora suggests:

> Music comes to afford things when it is perceived as incorporating into itself and/or its performance some property of the extra-musical, so as to be perceived as "doing" the thing to which it points. Music is active, in other words, as and when its perception is acted upon, and this circularity is precisely the topic for socio-musical research into music's power. Thus, music is more than a structural "reflection" of the social. Music is constitutive of the social in so far as it may be seen to enter action and/or conception when things take shape in relation to music. (DeNora, 2003, p. 57)

Some examples: music seemingly "moves" you (physically or emotionally); it expresses your feelings; it connects you to someone else; it coordinates your marching feet, or swells your heart with national pride. In another passage, DeNora further clarifies:

> Music acts, albeit only "in concert" with the material, cultural and social environments in which it is located ... It is thus possible to speak of the ways that music is a medium within and with which being is performed. It is a medium, in other words, of action. Music gives us modes and instrumentalities for doing social life ... music is simply one way in which we do that which we end up calling social action. (DeNora, 2003, p. 157)

The ecological concept of "affordance" is key here. An affordance is more than a property of something in that its usefulness is reciprocal to the agent's engagement with it, which is in turn related to their current need or purpose. Your chair (and its very specific form and material qualities) variously affords your sitting relative to your desk in order to write something, or standing on to fix a lightbulb, or defending yourself when taming a lion.

In this way the affordances of something specifies its potential uses only in relation to your specific perceptions of it, your needs within a given context, and your active "appropriation" of what the thing affords. So the notion of a "musical affordance" conveys exactly how music is different from being a one-sided stimulus or effect, anytime, anywhere (which is what some accounts of, for example, music's "healing qualities" may lead us to believe). Just as in the various affordances of your chair, specific music in specific circumstances *can* variously afford emotional expression, identity clarification, communicative connection, social aggression, or coordinating material for marching feet. But it all depends on the *when*, *how*, and *with whom* of the given context. The meaning of music(ing) is reflexively dependent on our perceptions, experiences, and actions in relation to it.

Our various stories in this book have shown how it makes sense to adopt such a conception of music's action (and therefore of music's potential help). It is not enough to say "music does such-and-such" for people, without specifying the circumstances and meanings of such use. Equally, it is not enough to say that certain forms of music are a straightforward reflection of either the psychological or the social situations of those playing. This is, of course, not to retreat into formalism and pretend that music is just an abstract pattern of notes. Every single person in the Community Music Therapy projects we tracked demonstrates the concrete and living link between people and music. Our theoretical task is rather to find a formulation to account for this "living link" which does not either *reduce* the musical to the merely physical or psychological or social, or, alternatively, artificially separate out music into its own rarefied realm, of "music for music's sake." How are we, then, to think about the relationship between what seems to happen "inside" music(ing) (the "intra-musical") and what "outside" (the "extra-musical")? In fact, to what extent does it make sense to talk of an inside/outside dichotomy?

Let us look again at Tia DeNora's suggestion for how seemingly "non-musical things" (such as movements, emotions, communications, identities, and events) take shape in relation to seemingly "purely musical things" (sounds, forms, and their performances). First, we are going to suggest an alternative to the phrase "extra-musical," as this gives the wrong impression that things are either "totally musical" or *extra-* (that is, "outside") musical. Instead what we want to understand is the kind of relationship between those phenomena that we perceive as specifically "musical" and all of those actions and activities which "go-with" these. We will use the term *para-*musical" for this latter "go-with" class of phenomena – para-musical meaning the "more-than-musical" phenomena that have been documented throughout this book (and which are often justified as the therapeutic outcomes of these projects – be these individual, relational, social, or political phenomena).

DeNora (in the previously quoted passage) suggests a fundamental circular process, with music(ing) being perceived, experienced, and acted upon when (i) para-musical things are somehow incorporated into music(ing), and consequently (ii) the musical is subsequently seen to afford and entail the para-musical (see Figure 19.1).

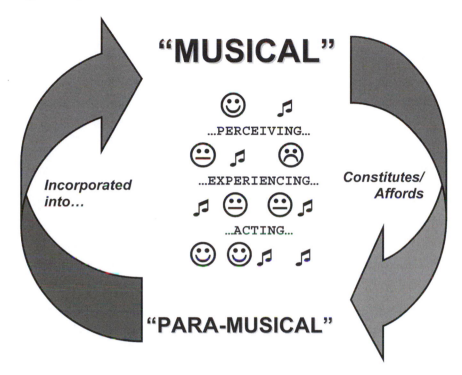

Figure 19.1   When the "para-musical" takes shape in relation to the "musical"

Cross-modal communication, as discussed in the previous section, could be understood as para-musical activity that in a given situation could be developed into musical activity. This, then, could generate the para-musical experience of musical community leading to new musical possibilities. We see that an endless circle or spiral is imaginable, where music is not a stimulus leading to certain outcomes, but an integrated element in an ecological process where the musical and para-musical could be separated only through analysis resting upon culture-specific conceptions. This illuminates how we must explore *where* music is performed, perceived, experienced, acted, and reflected upon in order to understand *how* it helps.

Community Music Therapy as Social-Musical Practice in Cultural Contexts

What any cultural group would call music (varied as this can be) is not something you could take part in without a history of learning. In line with Solli (2006) we could argue that the human psychobiological capacity for relating to sounds and rhythms is a "universal resource," but we need to consider how conditions for participation are contingent on cultural learning and cultural context. We are talking about processes and effects-in-context, but not about "context-dependent" effects narrowly conceived.

A central point in this argument is that what is musical is already personal and social. Personal and social participation is incorporated into musical structures and practices which then afford various para-musical outcomes. Participants are not just shaped in and by context, then; they are actively contributing to the shaping of these contexts also, for instance through musical performance and participation.[9]

Some sub-cultures of music – such as classical music – have developed sophisticated musical rules and ideals of perfection which make these musical cultures quite *exclusive* (Lubet, 2004). Also, the social aspects of say the performance of a symphony are so stylized that we at times may even forget that we observe a social process (except perhaps, in our observation of the embodied expressiveness of the conductor). In contrast, the events that have been described in this volume are all relatively inclusive and social:

> Within the ethnically diverse area they lived in, the members [of *Musical Minds*] were unusually homogeneous and historically rooted – all being white "East Enders" from a similar working-class background. Because of this they shared something in common from the traditional socio-cultural frame and history of the local East End culture – for example, its social-musical tradition of pub sing-songs, which was often reflected in the routine and style of their singing. Yet, to a varying extent all of the members were also living on the margins of society as a result of their long-term mental health problems. So there were varying senses of how they were both embedded *and* marginal to the so-called "local community." (Ansdell, Part II, this volume)

The cultivation of inclusive music cultures is central to Community Music Therapy. It would not be very accurate to suggest that Community Music Therapy is "all about reducing musical expectations," however. It is much more precise to say that it is about creating a better fit between participant, activity, and context.

> Sarah talked a lot about the relationship between individuality and togetherness in her work with *Musical Minds* – how the group had developed in the last few years from a rather individualistic "doing their own thing" style to, more

---

[9]   For a related discussion, focusing upon the contextual interplay of shared protomusical capacities and personal and cultural histories, see (Stige, 2007) on the "Grieg Effect."

recently, building both musical and organizational collaboration. Sarah has encouraged the group to listen more to each other's songs, and to join in and work on group numbers. Social collaboration seems to have followed musical collaboration. (Ansdell, Part VI, this volume)

That social collaboration sometimes follows musical collaboration could at times be experienced as the "magic" of music therapy. If we want to develop a different language for it, the term "social-musical process," as developed here, may be one place to start. For the members of *Musical Minds*, their love for music and their musical expectations (based upon their protomusicality *and* their learning of musical culture) led them to work together in order to get the music better. This, then, engaged them in a social-musical process that later entailed smoother social processes when language and not music was the medium of communication.

Sometimes music is a social resource that makes it relevant to claim that there are musical solutions to social problems, as *Musical Minds* and several of the other groups discussed in this volume experienced. Other times music is part of the problem. Orientation to social-musical processes involves musical and social possibilities, but also possible problems. This latter possibility is maybe not so clearly exemplified in the case studies of this book, but we can see glimpses of it when the *Senior Choir* disagree about musical repertoire and performing sites, when the *Renanim* members feel that the voices of the *Idud* choir were dominating, or when the children in Heideveld experience that some songs embody division and distance along linguistic fault lines. The case studies also elucidate how some of these musical-social problems could be negotiated, and we are again reminded about the importance of the *actively reflective* feature of Community Music Therapy projects.

An Ecology of Outcomes in Process

We are now turning to the final questions referred to in the opening of this chapter: "In what ways can Community Music Therapy promote health and change? Does it offer other cultural benefits?" It should be clear by now that it would be limiting to evaluate the effect of Community Music Therapy projects by just describing and/or measuring how individuals and groups develop during a certain course of music therapy sessions. Community Music Therapy practice accesses and also generates social networks and various ecological processes. Not just conventional music therapy sessions, but workshops, concerts, and various forms of collaborative projects are involved in the cases described in this book. Within an ecological framework it would make little sense to focus solely upon change in individuals and groups. Developments in the social and cultural context may be equally important. As described several places in this volume, there may be a *ripple effect* in that the environment reacts in relation to the changes in the individual or group.

We want to offer some thoughts on how the study of outcomes could be approached in future Community Music Therapy research. Our intention is not to present a comprehensive review of possible outcomes and approaches to the study of them. But the various case studies in this volume do offer some hints as to how we may think about outcomes in Community Music Therapy.

First, to the degree it makes sense to focus upon individual change, this would not be limited simply to reduction of symptoms or increase in wellbeing, but would involve those dimensions highlighted throughout this book: participation and performance; responsiveness and responsibility; relationship and belonging; enablement and empowerment. Second, outcomes may develop at any of the ecological levels (individual, microsystem, organization, locality, etc.) and to the degree each system is an open system, there will be reciprocal influences between systems, as Elefant demonstrates in Part III, for example, where the interaction between the children's initiatives and processes at the meso- and exosystem levels are described. Third, musical and therapeutic outcomes could often not be separated. In Part VI, for instance, Ansdell quotes Stuart Wood's observation that "the outcome of therapy [often] is as much in musical and social skills as it is in personal process" and he describes the *Scrap Metal* concert as the logical and practical outcome of a broader Community Music Therapy project.

Taken together, these three points illuminate that experimental research such as randomized controlled trials based upon the logic developed for medical studies will have limited relevance for the investigation of the outcomes of Community Music Therapy projects. This should not lead us to the conclusion that evidence is not of relevance, but that the *mode* of evidence is crucial. Participants come to Community Music Therapy because they love music and want community, but they usually also come because they think that music may help in some way in the particular and unique context in which they find themselves. There will be a continuous need for knowledge about when, where, and how music can help, but in contrast to the tradition of medical evidence, "local" evidence will mostly be more important than "distal" (DeNora, 2006).

One highly relevant trajectory is discussed in Part VII, where Elefant describes a Participatory Action Research project. This research tradition combines the quest for knowledge with the needs for action and reflection in context. Other paths may be taken in exploring research methods that so far have been less common in music therapy, such as qualitative approaches focusing upon evidence understood as "best explanation" (see e.g. Morse, Swanson and Kuzel, 2001) or quantitative surveys and statistical analyses of trends and developments in community resources, as has been developed in studies of "social capital" (see Putnam, 2000).

Whatever approach we take to the study of the outcomes of Community Music Therapy projects, we need to remember that we are studying the effects of contextualized collaboration rather than isolated interventions and that the usual music therapy logic of studying the outcomes of a specified number of sessions does not always apply. Sometimes we should study the ripple effects of a single event, such as a concert. And – as Stige discussed in Part V – Community Music

Therapy is not something that necessarily should be restricted to a limited period of time. Groups as diverse as *Musical Minds* and the *Senior Choir* may teach us that there is no reason to stop coming for music. They meet every week and their musical participation charges them with emotional energy and contributes to their ongoing feeling of agency and belonging.

This suggests that one of the cultural benefits of Community Music Therapy projects could be that they contribute to the generation of more inclusive musical activities in a given social and cultural context. This requires that music therapists see themselves as cultural workers, not just as health workers, and a benefit could in fact also be that Community Music Therapy contributes to changes in professional cultures.

Professional Participation

Community Music Therapy brings music therapy practices into interplay with other lay and professional practices. "Music and health" is a contemporary theme, flourishing in many contexts. This is therefore not a territory music therapists could or should claim exclusively for themselves. In the contemporary broader field of music and health there seems to be at least three types of practices that relate to each other in various ways; *popular practices*, *proprietary practices*, and *professional practices*. We will briefly examine characteristics of and relationships between these practices.

Popular practices of music and health include traditional practices, which are prominent in at least one of the four national contexts studied here, namely the South-African context (see e.g. Janzen, 2000). Currently, new popular practices are emerging in many societies, as more and more people have discovered that they can use music in their everyday efforts of promoting health and regulating health threats. These popular practices include "private" appropriations of music as a technology for health (DeNora, 2000, 2007; Ruud, 2002) as well as various collaborative enterprises (Bailey and Davidson, 2003; Batt-Rawden, DeNora and Ruud, 2005). Popular practices of music and health may of course operate in alliance with professional or semi-professional practices (Barz, 2006).

Growth in popular and proprietary practices tend to follow each others as object and shadow, and possibilities of music and health have not been lost on certain segments of the music business and health industry. One example could illuminate this trend: Recreational Music Making™ has been promoted recently by a group of music retailers in the USA, who offer recordings, instruments, and educational courses for people who would like to participate in drum circles or other activities that could promote health. For these retailers, music and health represents a vast untapped market (see e.g. Bittman and Bruhn, n.d.). Many people may use these services and find them helpful. There are, however, reasons to believe that those who would be most in need often would be those of least interest for such industry driven initiatives. The industry is in there for money, and many people are excluded for just this reason. Linked to the discussion of equity and social justice, there are therefore important values-based questions to examine in relation to proprietary initiatives for music and health.

In our judgment there are many reasons why there is a need for professional practices in addition to popular and proprietary practices of music and health. Professionals bring in a range of competencies that are not necessarily available in popular and proprietary practices and they may also bring in various sources of funding, including government funding. In relation to music and health, the discussion in this book focuses on the role of the music therapist, but this must be seen in relation to the work of other professionals. In the British context, for instance, many musicians who used to define their work as "community music" now increasingly define it as "music and health" (see Ansdell, 2002). Similarly, in the Scandinavian context the broader theme of culture and health has been in vogue with considerable government support for more than a decade now (see e.g. Hydle, 1991; Baklien and Carlsson, 2000; Festervoll, 2001; Bjørgan, 2007; Bjursell and Westerhäll, 2008). Similar developments exist in many countries.

We have argued that music therapists informed by the emerging movement of Community Music Therapy could be an important supplement in a broader field of popular, proprietary, and professional practices for music and health in and through community. This supplement would not achieve what it should without a serious rethinking of what it means to be professional, however. If there are limitations to the range of popular initiatives and to the industry's treatment of people as consumers, there may also be limitations to the professional's treatment of people as patients or clients. One problem of central concern here is that professionalization usually has been associated with specialization, protection of interests, and demand for professional authority and autonomy. This may create situations where priority is given to the outlook of the professional over that of the user of the services. If and when this is the case, there is an antagonism between professionalization and participation, that is, between the application of expert knowledge and the locally grounded knowledge of the participant. When possibilities and qualifications for participation in society is the goal of the process, the established modern role of the therapist as an expert could then be counterproductive (Knorth, van den Bergh and Verheij, 2002).

Partnership models may be proposed as a constructive alternative for Community Music Therapy. Here the roles and responsibilities of the professional and lay participants are negotiated in each situation, depending upon the problems and resources at hand. This suggestion resonates well with the case studies of this volume, where equality in the shape of participatory approaches have been key. In consequence, an openmindedness is suggested, where professionals could acknowledge the perspectives and situated knowledge of lay participants without loss of commitment to their own values and skills. This requires a sort of *polyphonic dialogue* with a shared willingness to construe knowledge and values from multiple perspectives, and it does *not* imply de-professionalization, rather what could be called *re-professionalization*.

Communicative competence and listening skills, attuned to the needs and resources of each particular situation, is asked for. This professional stance should not be an excuse for abdication of responsibility. It actually stresses the value of the professional as a *qualified* and *qualifying partner*. The Community Music Therapy projects described in this volume have exemplified a professional role focused upon enablement and empowerment – as working *with* people and situations, not "on" them. As we have seen, this could include the challenge of pragmatic and deliberative social activism; addressing repressive rationales and working with attitudes and assumptions in ways that may reduce social and cultural barriers for participation. In response to this, the role of the therapist may change in the direction of being a resourceful collaborator and moderator, rather than an autonomous expert.

As the eight case studies in this volume have exemplified; there are situations where the professional resourcefulness of the music therapist is required in order to establish helpful appropriation of music. This suggests that relationships between the quality of professional practice and the quality of participation need to be explored in future research. The implication we draw at this point is that a growing professionalization of Community Music Therapy is legitimate and necessary, if it is focused upon participatory processes and partnership models of practice.

Inconclusive Thoughts on Musical Conviviality and Hospitality

Cochavit: In one of the many cycles of action-reflection with the *Renanim* choir in Israel, one of the participants said: "We are here to sing, to have fun." This statement stood beside all of the problems and conflicts that the choir members also experienced. Their achievement was the pleasure of singing together and of giving equal pleasure to the audience. When I studied the video film of the event, I strongly felt that it communicates a communal and convivial atmosphere. I had the same experience when Gary shared the film of the *Musical Minds* concert. It shows tables cabaret-fashion, with food and drink. As well as being the setting for the evening concert, it conveys an informal party atmosphere designed to make people welcome and comfortable. This same atmosphere of conviviality has been witnessed many times by our research team as we studied the musical events of the various projects. An atmosphere being something collective, shared by all participants, having the qualities of friendliness, enjoyment, warmth, and closeness. Often such an atmosphere was cultivated by the combined pleasures of singing, dancing, eating and drinking – perhaps a basic need we all have for festivity and celebration together.

Brynjulf: Some of the events we studied were explicitly billed as a "festival," or taking place within some larger cultural event. This is true of the *Cultural Festival* in Norway – which is designed with festivity in mind. It is part of a long tradition of many of these people getting together each year, of all being included – singing and dancing and eating together. In her introduction to this festival the Director of Culture remarks that *joy* is a factor that shouldn't be underestimated as the basis of cultural activities. Whilst there are also more serious aims – *respect* for example, and *political awareness* of these people – the basic aim is to cultivate there the kind of convivial experiences most of us take for granted.

Gary: In a slightly different way, the *Scrap Metal* concert in the UK was part of an arts festival in the town, celebrating people and their artistic achievements. In one sense the *Scrap Metal* concert was unusual within this cultural frame, as by the end of the evening everyone has been included, welcomed into the event. Nobody has just been a spectator. The audience have been taught a round and sung it together with the participants. The *Scrap Metal* project reminded me somewhat of a *musical happening* by John Cage, and the words of his, that: "what will more and more come through is the expression of the pleasures of conviviality."

Brynjulf: "This is music as it should be" a member of the audience of the *Scrap Metal* concert says afterwards. Musical conviviality is based on inclusion, appreciation, and the warmth of nobody being left out: Community is *created* through musicing. We could ask: *How* is such musical conviviality created, often against many odds? When I studied the *Cultural Festival* I tried to develop one answer, focusing upon the importance of "everyday rituals" for both structuring and animating such festive events. Two ritual outcomes may be especially important when thinking of festivity and conviviality: *group solidarity* – a feeling of membership, and *emotional energy* – feelings of confidence, elation, strength, enthusiasm and initiative in taking action. In his ritual studies, Durkheim coined the term "collective effervescence," which Randall Collins lately has referred to as the formation of a collective consciousness and a condition of heightened intersubjectivity.

Mercédès: Another answer to this question deriving from our tracked projects might focus more on the role and actions of the music therapist in creating conditions for conviviality. Take music therapist Carol's work with the young men at YDO. What does she do there with them? What's her role there when the social-musical activity of collaborative musicing is happening? She retains her identity whilst not obviously "doing" much during the work on the Mountain Song. When we studied the video film of this event one of you commented upon her role and suggested: "She's clearing the floor … creates the space but still doesn't enter it … a gesture … that she is tidying up for them, serving them … Is she *hosting* them?" This is hospitality too; when you invite people into your space but remain the mistress of it …

there is a new set of social rules ... her as the hostess and [the man with] white hat as a potential dominant guest ... There is a retaining of external social rules and distance: male-female: younger men, older woman ... But there's a dual identity too: She is very clearly in her own identity – a middle-class woman ... and perhaps this even makes possible this collaborative event, even if she is the hostess ... She's a hostess-guest ...

Brynjulf: I remember the feeling of *hospitality* when I as a guest encountered the *Senior Choir* in Sandane; the friendliness when one of the old men asks me: "Do you want to sing with us?" Hospitality is something that characterizes the choir's activities, and one might say, *ethics*. In music they welcome all; the lady with dementia equal to the others, even though they in other activities and situations have plenty of differences. Solgunn, the music therapist, is also personally and musically hospitable. The choir is welcomed into the musical world she helps them create each week. She helps people with their music, but also members help each other, practically and musically. Again; not that there was not also tension, but that this was part of an overall atmosphere of welcome and mutual care. I'm reminded of something Sarah said about *Musical Minds:* "... at the end of the day they make music, and appreciate each others' music, and listen to each other. I usually try to move into doing music as quickly as possible ... otherwise they'll argue and row." She explains how they could even argue about how long they had argued for and not done any music ... So Sarah suggests that music is the common thing; they come back to sing and play and to talk about music.

Gary: Yes. The critics of the word and concept "community" – Derrida for instance – suggest "hospitality" is a better alternative – the welcoming of the other, the stranger, the sense of giving without losing. Instead of creating romantic notions of unity, dreaming of community, we should rather look at the situation we have: where people find it hard to be at home with themselves and at home with each other. "'We' are those who cannot completely say 'we,' who cannot settle into being *chez soi*, at home with themselves" writes Caputo in a commentary on Derrida's critique of community. What we *can* create is "an *open* quasi-community" which remains communicative and hospitable to difference, generous to the other, to different kinds of belonging, where "we do not have to choose between unity and multiplicity."

Mercédès: Could we see, then, that the kind of musicing promoted by Community Music Therapy is in some ways an alibi that enables people – in challenging and unlikely places – to get together, sing and dance and make friends and have fun together? As the sociologist Richard Sennett comments, you can't just respect people by saying "I respect you." You have to *perform* respect – and you have then to have some medium through which you do this performance of respect. Could it be the same for hospitality, for conviviality: You can't welcome people without a place and a genuine activity to welcome them *into*; you can't be together creatively without something genuine to do – something you want to do, something that's good to do. Music and musicing affords such hospitality, as welcoming in, such conviviality, as creating collective joy.

Cochavit: Why, then, does talk of hospitality and conviviality feel odd within therapeutic discourse, or even within contemporary thinking about social problems and their possible solutions? Probably because traditional therapeutic discourses have treated a group largely as a combination of individuals, a crowd as a threat, communal space as "unsafe," and the unexpected as intrusive. As for hospitality, food and drinking – and singing and dancing – are to be left outside of the therapeutic space; the therapist offers understanding and challenge, but certainly not hospitality, save for the symbolic milk of the therapist's nurture … And certainly not – even in groups – any notion of a party! Why?

Gary: Barbara Ehrenreich's recent book – *Dancing in the Streets: A History of Collective Joy* – gives some hints, as part of her thesis on the decline of the "festive tradition" and its accompaniments of hospitality and conviviality, which are techniques of "collective joy" in her words, shadowing the perceived and actual decline in community. If we naturally possess the capacities for collective joy, she asks, why do we so seldom put these to use now? One answer she gives is that hierarchical and authority structures actively work to repress them: "While hierarchy is about exclusion, festivity generates inclusiveness. The music invites everyone to the dance; shared food briefly undermines the privilege of class." And as she argues: At the height of festivity we may step outside of our assigned roles and statuses and into a brief utopia defined by egalitarianism, creativity, and mutual love. Community Music Therapy is perhaps serving as a reminder of the importance of this basic human festive tradition, and how it affords the vital practical and ethical virtues of hospitality and conviviality.

Brynjulf: "Convivio ergo sum"–

Mercédès: I party, therefore I am …

Cochavit: What happened to "argo ergo sum," I perform, therefore I am …?

Gary: Every party needs a performance!

Bibliography

Aasgaard, Trygve (2004). "A Pied Piper among White Coats and Infusion Pumps: Community Music Therapy in Paediatric Hospital Setting" in Pavlicevic, Mercédès and Gary Ansdell (eds), *Community Music Therapy*. London: Jessica Kingsley Publishers.

Aftret, Kari (2005). "'Samspill'. Om musikkterapeuten i kommunen" [Interaction in Music. On the Role of the Music Therapist in the Municipality]. Unpublished Master thesis in music therapy, Oslo, Norway: Norges musikkhøgskole.

Agawu, Kofi (2003). "Contesting Difference: A Critique of Africanist Ethnomusicology" in Clayton, Martin, Trevor Herbert and Richard Middleton (eds), *The Cultural Study of Music. A Critical Introduction.* New York: Routledge.

Aigen, Kenneth (2002). *Playin' in the Band: A Qualitative Study of Popular Music Styles as Clinical Improvisation.* New York: Nordoff-Robbins Center for Music Therapy, New York University.

Aigen, Kenneth (2004). "Conversations on Creating Community: Performance as Music Therapy in New York City" in Pavlicevic, Mercédès and Gary Ansdell (eds), *Community Music Therapy.* London: Jessica Kingsley Publications.

Aigen, Kenneth (2005). *Music-Centered Music Therapy.* Gilsum, NH: Barcelona Publishers.

Aldridge, David (1996). *Music Therapy Research and Practice in Medicine.* London: Jessica Kingsley Publishers.

Aldridge, David (ed.) (2000). *Music Therapy in Dementia Care: More New Voices.* London: Jessica Kingsley Publishers.

Aldridge, David (2004). *Health, the Individual and Integrated Medicine.* London: Jessica Kingsley Publishers.

Andersen, Per, Richard Morris, David Amaral, Tim Bliss and John O'Keefe (eds) (2007). *The Hippocampus Book.* Oxford: Oxford University Press.

Ansdell, Gary (1995). *Music for Life.* London: Jessica Kingsley Publishers.

Ansdell, Gary (1997). "Musical Elaborations. What Has the New Musicology to Say to Music Therapy?" *British Journal of Music Therapy, 11*(2), pp. 36–44.

Ansdell, Gary (2001). "Musicology: Misunderstood Guest at the Music Therapy Feast?" in Aldridge, David, Gianluigi DiFranco, Even Ruud and Tony Wigram (eds), *Music Therapy in Europe.* Rome: Ismez.

Ansdell, Gary (2002). "Community Music Therapy and the Winds of Change – A Discussion Paper." *Voices: A World Forum for Music Therapy*. Retrieved October 15, 2009, from http://www.voices.no/mainissues/Voices2(2)ansdell. html.

Ansdell Gary (2003). "The Stories We Tell: Some Metatheoretical Reflections on Music Therapy." *Nordic Journal of Music Therapy, 12*(2), pp. 152–9.

Ansdell, Gary (2004). "Rethinking Music and Community: Theoretical Perspectives in Support of Community Music Therapy" in Pavlicevic, Mercédès and Gary Ansdell (eds), *Community Music Therapy.* London: Jessica Kingsley Publishers.

Ansdell, Gary (2005a). "Community Music Therapy: A Plea for 'Fuzzy Recognition' instead of 'Final Definition'" [Contribution to Moderated Discussions]. *Voices: A World Forum for Music Therapy.* Retrieved October 28, 2005 from http:// voices.no/discussions/discm4_07.html.

Ansdell, Gary (2005b). "Musical Companionship, Musical Community: Music Therapy and the Process and Value of Musical Communication" in Miell, Dorothy, Raymond MacDonald and David Hargreaves (eds), *Musical Communication.* Oxford: Oxford University Press.

Ansdell, Gary (2005c). "Being Who You Aren't; Doing What You Can't: Community Music Therapy and the Paradoxes of Performance." *Voices: A World Forum for Music Therapy.* Retrieved September 14, 2008, from http:// www.voices.no/mainissues/mi40005000192.html.

Ansdell, Gary and Mercédès Pavlicevic (2005). "Musical Companionship, Musical Community: Music Therapy and the Process and Values of Musical Communication" in Miell, Dorothy, Raymond MacDonald and David Hargreaves (eds). *Musical Communication.* Oxford: Oxford University Press.

Association for the Study and Development of Community (July 2002). Retrieved July 7, 2006, from http://www.capablecommunity.com.

Atkinson, Paul (2006). *Everyday Arias: An Operatic Ethnography.* Oxford: AltaMira Press.

Bailey, Betty and Jane Davidson (2003). "Amateur Group Singing as a Therapeutic Instrument." *Nordic Journal of Music Therapy, 12*(1), pp. 18–32.

Baklien, Bergljot and Yngve Carlsson (2000). *Helse og kultur. Prosessevaluering av en nasjonal satsing på kultur som helsefremmende virkemiddel* [Health and Culture. Process Evaluation of National Action for Culture as a Health Promoting Tool]. Oslo, Norway: NIBR prosjektrapport 2000:11, Oslo.

Bar, Haviva and David Bargal (1995). *Living with the Conflict* (Hebrew). Jerusalem: Jerusalem Institute of Israel Research.

Barenboim, Daniel and Edward Said (2002). *Parallels and Paradoxes: Explorations in Music and Society.* New York: Pantheon Books.

Bargal, David and Haviva Bar (1992). "A Lewinian Approach to Intergroup Workshops for Arab-Palestinian and Jewish Youth." *Journal of Social Issues, 48*, pp. 139–54.

Barrett, Margaret (2005). "Musical Communication and Children's Communities of Musical Practice" in Miell, Dorothy, Raymond MacDonald and David Hargreaves (eds), *Musical Communication.* Oxford: Oxford University Press.

Barz, Gregory (2006). *Singing for Life. HIV/AIDS and Music in Uganda.* New York: Routledge.

Batt-Rawden, Kari Bjerke, Tia DeNora and Even Ruud (2005). "Music Listening and Empowerment in Health Promotion: A Study of the Role and Significance of Music in Everyday Life of the Long-term Ill." *Nordic Journal of Music Therapy, 14*(2), pp. 120–36.

Bauman, Zygmunt (2001). *Community: Seeking Safety in an Insecure World.* Cambridge: Polity Press.

Becker, Judith (2004). *Deep Listeners. Music, Emotion, and Trancing.* Bloomington, IN: Indiana University Press.

Benson, Bruce (2003). *The Improvisation of Musical Dialogue: A Phenomenology of Music.* Cambridge: Cambridge University Press.

Berkaak, Odd Are and Even Ruud (1992). *Den påbegynte virkelighet. Studier i samtidskultur* [Emerging Reality. Studies in Contemporary Culture]. Oslo, Norway: Universitetsforlaget.

Berkaak, Odd Are and Even Ruud (1994). *Sunwheels. Fortellinger om et rockeband* [Sunwheels. Stories about a Rock Band]. Oslo, Norway: Universitetsforlaget.

Bittman, Barry and Karl T. Bruhn (n.d.). Recreational Music Making. Retrieved January 15, 2006, from: http://www.namm.com/rmm/RMMOneSheets.pdf.

Bjørgan, Harald (ed.) (2007). *Kultur former framtida* [Culture Shapes our Future]. Oslo, Norway: Andrimne forlag.

Bjursell, Gunnar and Lotta Valhne Westerhäll (eds) (2008). *Kulturen och hälsan. Essäer om sambandet mellom kulturens ytringar og hälsans tillsånd* [Culture and Health. Essays on connections between cultural expressions and health conditions]. Stockholm: Santérua Forlag.

Blacking, John (1973). *How Musical is Man?* Seattle: University of Washington Press.

Bogdan, Robert and Steven Taylor (2001). "Building Stronger Communities for All: Thoughts About Community Participation for People with Developmental Disabilities" in Tymchuk, Alexander, K. Charlie Lakin and Ruth Luckasson (eds), *The Forgotten Generation: The Status and Challenges of Adults with Mild Cognitive Limitations.* Baltimore: Paul H. Brookes Publishing Co.

Bortoft, Henri (1996). *The Wholeness of Nature: Goethe's Way of Science.* Edinburgh, Scotland, UK: Floris Books.

Bradley, Benjamin (2005). *Psychology and Experience.* Cambridge: Cambridge University Press.

Bright, Ruth (1981). *Practical Planning in Music Therapy for the Aged.* New York: Musicgraphics.

Bright, Ruth (1997a). *Music Therapy and the Dementias.* St. Louis: MMB Horizon Series.

Bright, Ruth (1997b). *Wholeness in Later Life.* London: Jessica Kingsley Publishers.

Bronfenbrenner, Urie (1979). *The Ecology of Human Development. Experiments by Nature and Design.* Cambridge, MA: Harvard University Press.

Bruscia, Kenneth (1987). *Improvisational Models of Music Therapy.* Springfield, IL: Charles C. Thomas Publisher.

Buber, Martin (1947) (1947/2002). *Between Man and Man.* London: Routledge.

Bunt, Leslie and Mercédès Pavlicevic (2001). "Music and Emotion: Perspectives from Music Therapy" in Juslin, Patrik and John Sloboda (eds), *Music and Emotion: Theory and Research.* Oxford: Oxford University Press.

Cage, John (1980). "The Future of Music" in *Empty Words: Writings '73–'78 by John Cage.* London: Marion Boyars.

Capra, Fritjof (2003). *The Hidden Connections: A Science for Sustainable Living.* London: HarperCollins.

Caputo, John (1997). *Deconstruction in a Nutshell: A Conversation with Jacques Derrida.* New York: Fordham University Press.

CDC (Centers of Disease Control and Prevention) and Merck Company Foundation (2007). The State of Aging and Health in America 2007. Whitehouse Station, NJ: The Merck Company Foundation. Retrieved April 15, 2007, from: www.cdc.gov/aging/pdf/saha_exec_summary_2007.pdf.

Clarke, Eric F. (2003). "Music and Psychology" in Clayton, Martin, Trevor Herbert and Richard Middleton (eds), *The Cultural Study of Music. A Critical Introduction.* New York: Routledge.

Clarke, Eric F. (2005). *Ways of Listening: An Ecological Approach to the Perception of Musical Meaning.* Oxford: Oxford University Press.

Clarke, Eric F. and Nicholas Cook (eds) (2004). *Empirical Musicology: Aims, Methods, Prospects.* Oxford: Oxford University Press.

Clayton, Martin, Rebecca Sager and Udo Will (2003). "In Time With the Music: The Concept of Entrainment and its Significance for Ethnomusicology." ESEM CounterPoint, 1: XXX–XXX (Draft available from: http://www.ccs.fau.edu/~large/Publications/ClaytonSagerWill2004.pdf).

Clayton, Martin, Trevor Herbert and Richard Middleton (eds) (2003). *The Cultural Study of Music. A Critical Introduction.* New York and London: Routledge.

Clifford, James (1986). "Introduction: Partial Truths" in Clifford, James and George E. Marcus (eds). *Writing Culture. The Poetics and Politics of Ethnography.* Berkeley: University of California Press.

Cohen, Anthony (1985/1993). *The Symbolic Construction of Community.* London: Routledge.

Collins, Randall (2004). *Interaction Ritual Chains.* Princeton, NJ: Princeton University Press.

Condon, William and William D. Ogston (1966). "Sound Film Analysis of Normal and Pathological Behaviour Patterns." *Journal of Nervous and Mental Diseases, 143*(4), pp. 338–47.

Cook, Nicholas (1990). *Music, Imagination and Culture.* Oxford: Oxford University Press.

Cook, Nicholas (1998). *Music: A Very Short Introduction.* Oxford: Oxford University Press.

Cook, Nicholas (2001). *Analysing Musical Multimedia.* Oxford, UK: Oxford University Press.

Cook, Nicholas (2003). "Music as Performance" in Clayton, Martin, Trevor Herbert and Richard Middleton (eds), *The Cultural Study of Music. A Critical Introduction.* New York: Routledge.

Cook, Nicholas and Mark Everist (1999). *Rethinking Music.* Oxford: Oxford University Press.

Cross, Ian (2003). "Music and Biocultural Evolution" in Clayton, Martin, Trevor Herbert and Richard Middleton (eds), *The Cultural Study of Music. A Critical Introduction.* New York and London: Routledge.

Curtis, Sandra L. and Chesley Sigmon Mercado (2004). "Community Music Therapy for Citizens with Developmental Disabilities." *Voices: A World Forum for Music Therapy.* Retrieved January 13, 2006, from http://www.voices.no/mainissues/mi40004000162.html.

Dalton, James H., Maurice J. Elias and Abraham Wandersman (2007). *Community Psychology. Linking Individuals and Communities* (Second edition). London: Wadsworth (Thomson Learning).

Darnley-Smith, Rachel and Helen M. Patey (2003). *Music Therapy.* London: Sage.

Darrow, Alice-Ann (1999). "Music Educators' Perceptions Regarding the Inclusion of Students with Severe Disabilities in Music Classrooms." *Journal of Music Therapy, 36*(4), pp. 254–73.

Davidson, Jane (2001). "The Role of the Body in the Production and Perception of Solo Vocal Performance: A Case Study of Annie Lennox." *Musicae Scientiae,* Fall 2001, *V*(2), pp. 235–56.

Davidson, Jane (2002). "The Performer's Identity" in MacDonald, Raymond, Dorothy Miell and David Hargreaves (eds), *Musical Identities.* Oxford: Oxford University Press.

Davidson, Jane (2004). "What can the Social Psychology of Music Offer Community Music Therapy?" in Pavlicevic, Mercédès and Gary Ansdell (eds), *Community Music Therapy.* London: Jessica Kingsley Publishers.

Davidson, Jane (2005). "Bodily Communication in Musical Performance" in Miell, Dorothy, Raymond MacDonald and David Hargreaves (eds), *Musical Communication.* Oxford: Oxford University Press.

Davidson, Jane and James M. M. Good (2002). "Social and Musical Co-ordination between Members of a String Quartet: An Exploratory Study." *Psychology of Music, 30*, pp. 186–201.

Davies, Alison and Eleanor Richards (2002). *Music Therapy and Group Work: Sound Company.* London: Jessica Kingsley Publishers.

Davies, William H. (1911). Leisure (originally published in the collection *Songs of Joy*). Retrieved September 14, 2008, from http://www.poemhunter.com/poem/leisure/.

Delanty, Gerard (2003). *Community.* London: Routledge.

DeNora, Tia (2000). *Music in Everyday Life.* Cambridge: Cambridge University Press.

DeNora, Tia (2001) "Aesthetic Agency and Musical Practice: New Directions in the Sociology of Music and Emotion" in Juslin, Patrik and John Sloboda (eds), *Music and Emotion.* Oxford: Oxford University Press.

DeNora, Tia (2003). *After Adorno. Rethinking Music Sociology.* Cambridge: Cambridge University Press.

DeNora, Tia (2004). "Musical Practice and Social Structure: A Toolkit" in Clarke, Eric and Nicholas Cook (eds), *Empirical Musicology: Aims, Methods, Prospects.* Oxford: Oxford University Press.

DeNora, Tia (2005). "The Pebble in the Pond: Musicing, Therapy, Community." *Nordic Journal of Music Therapy, 14*(1), pp. 57–66.

DeNora, Tia (2007). "Health and Music in Everyday Life – A Theory of Practice." *Psyke and Logos, 28*(1), pp. 271–87.

Dissanayake, Ellen (1992/1995). *Homo Aestheticus. Where Art Comes From and Why.* Seattle: University of Washington Press.

Dissanayake, Ellen (2000a). "Antecedents of the Temporal Arts in Early Mother-Infant Interaction" in Wallin, Nils L., Björn Merker and Steven Brown (eds), *The Origins of Music.* Cambridge, MA: The MIT Press.

Dissanayake, Ellen (2000b). *Art and Intimacy: How the Arts Began.* Seattle: University of Washington Press.

Dissanayake, Ellen (2001). "An Ethological View of Music and its Relevance to Music Therapy." *Nordic Journal of Music Therapy, 10*(2), pp. 159–75.

Dovidio, John F., Samuel L. Gaertner and Kerry Kawakami (2003). "Intergroup Contact: The Past, Present, and the Future." *Group Processes and Intergroup Relations*, (6), pp. 5–21.

Dunbar, Robin (2004). *The Human Story: A New History of Mankind's Evolution.* London: Faber.

Durkheim, Emile (1912/1995). *The Elementary Forms of Religious Life* (Translated by Karen E. Fields). New York: The Free Press.

Ehrenreich, Barbara (2007). *Dancing in the Streets: A History of Collective Joy.* London: Granta.

Elefant, Cochavit and Anat Agami (2002*).* "Integration through Music of Children with and without Special Needs." Paper presented at the 10th Music Therapy World Congress, 24 July, Oxford, England.

Elliott, David J. (1995). *Music Matters. A New Philosophy of Music Education.* New York: Oxford University Press.

Elstad, Jon Ivar (2005). *Sosioøkonomiske ulikheter i helse: teorier og forklaringer* [Socioeconomic Differences in Health: Theories and Explanations]. Oslo, Norway: Sosial- og helsedirektoratet.

Evans, Ken and Maria Gilbert (2005). *An Introduction to Integrative Psychotherapy.* Basingstoke: Palgrave-Macmillan.

Everitt, Anthony (1997). *Joining In: An Investigation into Participatory Music.* London: Calouste Gulbenkian Foundation.

Falnes-Dalheim, Anders and Tove Irene Slaastad (2008). "Befolkning: Færre unge – flere eldre" [Population: Fewer Young People – More Old People]. *Samfunnsspeilet* [Reflections of Society]. Oslo, Norway: Statistisk sentralbyrå. Retrieved September 14, 2009, from http://www.ssb.no/-samfunnsspeilet/utg/200705/04/index.html.

Faulkner, Robert and Jane Davidson (2004). "Men's Vocal Behaviour and the Construction of Self." *Musicae Scientiae*, Fall 2004, VIII(2), pp. 231–55.

Festervoll, Åse Vigdis (2001). *Kultur og helse* [Culture and Health]. Oslo, Norway: Kommuneforlaget.

Fischlin, Daniel and Ajay Heble (eds) (2004). *The Other Side of Nowhere: Jazz, Improvisation, and Communities in Dialogue.* Middletown, CT: Wesleyan University Press.

Forrest, Lucy C. (2002). "Addressing Issues of Ethnicity and Identity in Palliative Care through Music Therapy Practice" in Kenny, Carolyn and Brynjulf Stige (eds), *Contemporary* Voices *in Music Therapy. Communication, Culture, and Community.* Oslo, Norway: Unipub.

Foster, Neil (2007). "'Why Can't We be Friends?' An Exploration of the Concept of 'Friendship' within Client–Music Therapist Relationships." *British Journal of Music Therapy, 21*(1), pp. 12–22.

Frith, Simon (1996). *Performing Rites: On the Value of Popular Music.* Oxford: Oxford University Press.

Furedi, Frank (2004). *Therapy Culture: Cultivating Vulnerability in an Uncertain Age.* London: Routledge.

Garred, Rudy (2005). "Fusing (or Confusing?) the Terms 'Music Therapy' and 'Community Music.' A Plea for Clarification." [Contribution to Moderated Discussions]. *Voices: A World Forum for Music Therapy.* Retrieved October 28, 2005 from http://voices.no/discussions/discm4_09.html.

Garred, Rudy (2006). *Music as Therapy: A Dialogical Perspective.* Gilsum, NH: Barcelona Publishers.

Gennep, Arnold van (1909/1999). *Rites de Passage. Overgangsriter* [Transitional Rites]. Oslo, Norway: Pax.

Gibson, James J. (1979/1986). *The Ecological Approach to Visual Perception.* Hillsdale, NJ: Lawrence Erlbaum Associates Publishers.

Gilroy, Paul (1987/2002). *"There Ain't no Black in the Union Jack": The Cultural Politics of Race and Nation.* London: Routledge.

Gilroy, Paul (1993). *The Black Atlantic: Modernity and Double-Consciousness.* Cambridge, MA: Harvard University Press.

Gilroy, Paul (2004). *After Empire: Multiculture or Postcolonial Melancholia.* London: Routledge.

Glendinning, Simon (1998). *On Being with Others. Heidegger – Derrida – Wittgenstein.* London: Routledge.

Godlovitch, Stan (1998). *Musical Performance: A Philosophical Study.* London: Routledge.

Goffman, Erving (1959/1990). *The Presentation of Self in Everyday Life.* London: Penguin Books Ltd.

Goffman, Erving (1955/1967). "On Face-Work. An Analysis of Ritual Elements in Social Interaction" in Goffman, Erving (1967). *Interaction Ritual. Essays on Face-to-Face Behavior.* New York: Anchor Books.

Goffman, Erving (1967). *Interaction Ritual. Essays on Face-to-Face Behavior.* New York: Anchor Books.

Goleman, Daniel (2006). *Social Intelligence: The New Science of Human Relationships.* London: Hutchinson.

Gorevitz, Zeli (2001). "The Fine Border between Identity and Otherness" in Deutch, Haim and Menachem Ben-Sasson (eds), *The Other between Man to Himself and to the Other* (Hebrew). Tel Aviv: Miskal.

Gouk, Penelope (ed.) (2000). *Musical Healing in Cultural Contexts.* Aldershot, UK: Ashgate Publishing Company.

Grinde, Bjørn (2000). "A Biological Perspective on Musical Appreciation." *Nordic Journal of Music Therapy, 9*(2), pp. 18–27.

Grogan, Katherine and Doris Knak (2002). "A Children's Group: An Exploration of the Framework Necessary for Therapeutic Work." in Davies, Alison and Eleanor Richards (eds), *Music Therapy and Group Work.* London: Jessica Kingsley Publishers.

Hastrup, Kirsten (1999). *Viljen til Viden. En humanistisk grundbog* [The Will for Knowledge. A Humanist Basic Text]. Copenhagen: Gyldendal.

Heidegger, Martin (1927/1962). *Being and Time.* San Francisco: Harper.

Heidegger, Martin (1969). *Identity and Difference.* New York: Harper and Row.

Hibben, Julie (1991). "Group Music Therapy with a Classroom of 6–8-Year-Old Hyperactive-Learning Disabled Children" in Bruscia, Kenneth (ed.), *Case Studies in Music Therapy.* Springfield, IL: Charles C. Thomas Publisher.

Holzman, Lois (1999). *Performing Psychology: A Postmodern Culture of the Mind.* London: Routledge.

Horden, Peregrin (ed.) (2000). *Music as Medicine: The History of Music Therapy since Antiquity.* Aldershot, UK: Ashgate Publishing Limited.

Hydle, Ida (1991). *Kultur og helse i et lokalsamfunn* [Culture and Health in a Local Community]. Oslo, Norway: Kommuneforlaget.

ICEVI (2002). Report from 3rd Workshop on Training of Teachers of the Visually Impaired in Europe. Warsaw, Poland. Retrieved September 14, 2008, from: http://www.icevi-europe.org/tt/ttw3/index.html.

Jampel, Peter (2006). "Performance in Music Therapy with Mentally Ill Adults." Unpublished Dr. Art Thesis. New York: New York University, The Steinhardt School of Education, Music Therapy Program, Department of Music and Performing Arts Professions.

Janzen, John M. (2000). "Theories of Music in African Ngoma Healing" in Gouk, Penelope (ed.), *Musical Healing in Cultural Contexts.* Aldershot, UK: Ashgate.

Jellison, Judith A. and Elisabeth W. Gainer (1995). "Into the Mainstream: A Case Study of a Child's Participation in Music Education and Music Therapy." *Journal of Music Therapy, 32*(4), pp. 228–47.

Jerlang, Espen (1988/1991). "Selvforvaltning – pædagogisk teori og praksis" [Enablement and Empowerment – Pedagogical Theory and Practice]. Copenhagen, Denmark: Munksgaard.

Jones, Lisa L. and Donald N. Cardinal (1998). "A Descriptive Analysis of Music Therapists' Perceptions of Delivering Services in Inclusive Settings: A Challenge to the Field." *Journal of Music Therapy, 35*(1), pp. 34–8.

Kacen, Lea (2002). "Bridging between Intergroups Facilitated by Simulations of Circular Dynamic" in Kacen, Lea and Rachel Lev-Wiesel (2002). *Group Work in a Multi Cultural Society* (Hebrew). Tel-Aviv: Cherikover Publishing Inc.

Kacen, Lea and Rachel Lev-Wiesel (eds) (2002). *Group Work in a Multi Cultural Society* (Hebrew). Tel-Aviv: Cherikover Publishing Inc.

Karolyi, Otto (1998). *Traditional African and Oriental Music.* Harmondsworht: Penguin.

Katz, Ya'akov and Mayah Kahanov (1990). "Reviewing Dilemmas in Facilitation of Meeting Groups between Meeting Groups of Arabs and Jews in Israel (Hebrew)." *Megamot Lamed Gimel (1)*, pp. 29–47.

Keil, Charles (1994). "Participatory Discrepancies and the Power of Music" in Keil, Charles and Steven Feld. *Music Grooves.* Chicago: The University of Chicago Press.

Kennair, Leif Edward Ottesen (2001). "Origins – Investigations into Biological Human Musical Nature." *Nordic Journal of Music Therapy, 10*(1), pp. 54–64.

Kenny, Carolyn B. (1982). *The Mythic Artery. The Magic of Music Therapy.* Atascadero, CA: Ridgeview Publishing Company.

Kenny, Carolyn B. (1985). "Music: A Whole Systems Approach." *Music Therapy, 5*(1), pp. 3–11.

Kenny, Carolyn B. (1989). *The Field of Play. A Guide for the Theory and Practice of Music Therapy.* Atascadero, CA: Ridgeview Publishing Company.

Kenny, Carolyn B. (1994/2006). "Our Legacy: Work and Play." Reprinted in Kenny, Carolyn, *Music and Life in the Field of Play: An Anthology.* Gilsum, NH: Barcelona Publishers.

Kenny, Carolyn B. (2002a). "Blue Wolf Says Goodbye for the Last Time." *American Behavioral Scientist,* Vol. 45, No. 8.

Kenny, Carolyn B. (2002b). "Keeping the World in Balance – Music Therapy in a Ritual Context" in Kenny, Carolyn B. and Brynjulf Stige (eds) (2002). *Contemporary* Voices *of Music Therapy: Communication, Culture, and Community.* Oslo, Norway: Unipub forlag.

Kenny, Carolyn B. and Brynjulf Stige (eds) (2002). *Contemporary* Voices *of Music Therapy: Communication, Culture, and Community.* Oslo, Norway: Unipub forlag.

Kerman, Joseph (1985). *Musicology.* London: Fontana.

Kern, Petra (2005). "The Use of Single Case Design in an Interactive Play Setting" in Aldridge, David (ed.), *Case Study Designs in Music Therapy.* London: Jessica Kingsley Publishers.

Klefbeck, Johan and Terje Ogden (2003). *Nettverk og økologi. Problemløsende arbeid med barn og unge.* [(Social) Networks and Ecology. Solving Problems with Children and Adolescents]. Oslo, Norway: Tano.

Kleive, Mette and Brynjulf Stige (1988). *Med lengting liv og song* [With Longing, Life, and Song]. Oslo, Norway: Samlaget.

Knardal, Solgunn (2007). "I songen vi møtest ... Ein tekst om pensjonistar som syng i kor, basert på medlemmene sine eigne forteljingar" [In Singing We're Relating ... A Text on Senior Choir Singers, Based Upon Their Own Words]. Unpublished master thesis. Oslo/Sandane, Norway: The National Academy of Music /Sogn og Fjordane University College.

Knorth, Erik J., Peter M. van den Bergh and Fop Verheij (2002). *Professionalization and Participation in Child and Youth Care.* Aldershot, UK: Ashgate.

Kramer, Kenneth P. (2003). *Martin Buber's I and Thou: Practicing Living Dialogue.* Mahwah, NJ: Paulist Press.

Kvamme, Tone Sæther (2006). "Musikk i arbeid med eldre. Musikk med pasienter med aldersdemens" [Working with Music and Elderly People. Music with Patients with Dementia] in: Aasgaard, Trygve (ed.), *Musikk og helse* [Music and Health]. Oslo, Norway: Cappelen akademiske forlag.

Law, Mary (1997). "Changing Disabling Environments through Participatory Action Research: A Canadian Experience" in Smith, Susan E., Dennis G. Willms and Nancy A. Johnson (eds), *Nurtured by Knowledge: Learning to do Participatory Action Research.* New York: Apex Press.

Ledwith, Margaret (2005). *Community Development. A Critical Approach.* Bristol, UK: The Policy Press.

Lehtonen, Kimmo (2002). "Some Ideas About Music Therapy for the Elderly." [online] *Voices: A World Forum for Music Therapy.* Retrieved March 18, 2007, from http://www.voices.no/mainissues/-Voices2(1)lehtonen.html.

Leppert, Richard and Susan McClary (eds) (1987). *Music and Society. The Politics of Composition, Performance and Reception.* Cambridge: Cambridge University Press.

Levinas, Emmanuel (1972/1993). *Den Annens humanisme* [Humanism of the Other. (Original title: Humanisme de l'autre home)] Translated by Asbjørn Aarnes. Oslo, Norway: Thorleif Dahls Kulturbibliotek, Aschehoug.

Lewin, Kurt (1948). *Resolving Social Conflicts: Selected Papers on Group Dynamics.* Edited by Weiss Lewin, Gertrude. New York: Harper.

Lifshitz, Hefziba and Joav Merrick (2004). "Aging among Persons with Intellectual Disability in Relation to Type of Residence, Age and Etiology." *Research in Developmental Disabilities, 25*, pp. 193–205.

Lindström, Dorota (2006). "Sjung, sjung för livet. En studie av körsång som pedagogisk verksamhet och av deltagarnas upplevelse av hälsa och livskvalitet" [Sing, Sing for Life. A Study of Choirs as Educational Activity and of Participants' Experience of Health and Quality of Life]. Piteå, Sweden: Musikhögskolan i Piteå, Institutionen för musik och medier.

Love, Andrew Cypian (2003). *Musical Improvisation, Heidegger, and the Liturgy: A Journey to the Heart of Hope.* Lewiston: Edwin Mellen Press.

Lubet, Alex J. (2004). "Tunes of Impairment: An Ethnomusicology of Disability." *Review of Disability Studies, (1)*1, pp. 133–55.

Løgstrup, Knud E. (1956/1991). *Den etiske fordring* [The Ethical Demand]. Copenhagen: Gyldendal.

Malloch, Stephen and Colwyn Trevarthen (eds) (2009). *Communicative Musicality.* Oxford: Oxford University Press.

Malterud, Kirsti (2003). *Kvalitative metoder i medisinsk forskning* [Qualitative Methods in Medical Research]. Oslo, Norway: Universitetsforlaget.

Manning, Rita (1992/2001). "Just Caring" in Kessler, Gary E. (ed.) (2001), *Voices of Wisdom. A Multicultural Philosophy Reader. Fourth Edition.* Belmont, CA: Wadsworth/Thomson Learning. [Originally published in Manning, Rita (1992). *Speaking from the Heart: A Feminist Perspective on Ethics.* Lanham, MD: Rowman and Littlefield.]

Martin, Pete J. (1995). *Sounds and Society,* Manchester University Press.

Martin, Pete J. (2006). *Music and the Sociological Gaze. Art Worlds and Cultural Production.* Manchester: Manchester University Press.

Martinsen, Kari (1989). *Omsorg, sykepleie og medisin. Historisk-filosofiske essays* [Care, Nursing, and Medicine. Historical-philosophical Essays]. Oslo, Norway: TANO.

Mattern, Mark (1998). *Acting in Concert: Music, Community, and Political Action.* New Brunswick, NJ: Rutgers University Press.

Mayeroff, Milton (1971). *On Caring.* New York: Harper and Row.

McAuley, Gay (1999). *Space in Performance. Making Meaning in Theatre.* Ann Arbor, MI: University of Michigan Press.

McEwan, Ian (2005). *Saturday.* London: Jonathan Cape.

McTaggart, Robin (1997). "Guiding Principles for Participatory Action Research." in McTaggart, Robin (ed.), *Participatory Action Research: International Context and Consequences.* Albany: State University of New York Press.

Mereni, Anthony-Ekemezie (1996). "'Kinesis and Katharsis.' The African Traditional Concept of Sound/motion or Music: Its Application in, and Implications for, Music Therapy – Part I." *British Journal of Music Therapy* *10*(1), pp. 17–23.

Mereni, Anthony-Ekemezie (1997). "'Kinesis and Katharsis.' The African Traditional Concept of Sound/motion or Music: Its Application in, and Implications for, Music Therapy – Part III." *British Journal of Music Therapy* *11*(1), pp. 20–23.

Merker, Björn (2000). "A New Theory of Music Origins. Comment on Grinde's Article." *Nordic Journal of Music Therapy, 9*(2), pp. 28–31.

Merriam, Alan P. (1964). *The Anthropology of Music.* Evanston, IL: Northwestern University Press.

Middleton, Richard (2003). "Introduction. Music Studies and the Idea of Culture" in Clayton, Martin, Trevor Herbert and Richard Middleton (eds), *The Cultural Study of Music. A Critical Introduction.* New York and London: Routledge.

Mithen, Steven (2005). *The Singing Neanderthals: The Origins of Music, Language, Mind and Body.* London: Phoenix.

Morse, Janice M., Janice M. Swanson and Anton J. Kuzel (eds) (2001). *The Nature of Qualitative Evidence.* Thousand Oaks, CA: Sage Publications.

Myskja, Audun (2006). *Den siste song – sang og musikk som støtte i rehabilitering og lindrende behandling* [The Last Song – Song and Music Supporting Rehabilitation and Palliative Care]. Bergen, Norway: Fagbokforlaget.

Newman, Fred and Lois Holzman (1997). *The End of Knowing: A New Developmental Way of Learning.* New York: Routledge.

Noblit, George W. and R. Dwight Hare (1988). *Meta-ethnography: Synthesizing Qualitative Studies.* Newbury Park, CA: Sage Publications.

Nordoff, Paul and Clive Robbins (1965/1971). *Therapy in Music for Handicapped Children.* London: Victor Gollancz, Ltd.

Nordoff, Paul and Clive Robbins (1977). *Creative Music Therapy. Individual Treatment for the Handicapped Child.* New York: John Day.

Northen, Helen and Roselle Kurland (2001). *Social Group Work.* New York: Columbia University Press.

O'Brien, Emma (2006). "Opera Therapy: Creating and Performing a New Work with Cancer Patients and Professional Singers." *Nordic Journal of Music Therapy, 15*(1), pp. 82–96.

O'Brien, John (1999). *Community Engagement: A Necessary Condition for Self-Determination and Individual Funding.* [Online] Lithonia GA: Responsive Systems Associates. Retrieved December 30, 2006 from http://thechp.syr.edu/ComEng.pdf.

O'Brien, John and Connie Lyle O'Brien (1993). "Unlikely Alliances: Friendships and People with Developmental Disabilities" in Amado, Angela R. Novak (ed.), *Friendships and Community Connections between People with and without Developmental Disabilities.* Baltimore: Paul H. Brookes Publishing Co.

Pavlicevic, Mercédès (1997). *Music Therapy in Context: Music, Meaning and Relationship.* London: Jessica Kingsley Publishers.

Pavlicevic, Mercédès (2003). *Groups in Music: Strategies from Music Therapy.* London: Jessica Kingsley Publishers.

Pavlicevic, Mercédès (2004). "Hearing African Voices: Music Therapy and the Polyphony of Near and Far …." *Voices: A World Forum for Music Therapy.* Retrieved October 26, 2009, from http://www.voices.no/mainissues/mi40004-000141.html.

Pavlicevic, Mercédès (2005). "Community Music Therapy: Anyone for Practice?" [Contribution to Moderated Discussions]. *Voices: A World Forum for Music Therapy.* Retrieved October 28, 2005 from http://voices.no/discussions/discm4_010.html.

Pavlicevic, Mercédès (2006a). "Music Performance as Social Action: A Case for Music Research" in Marcus, Tessa and Alexandra Hofmaenner (eds), *Shifting Boundaries of Knowledge: A View on Social Science, Law and Humanities in South Africa.* Durban: University of Kwa-Zulu Natal Press.

Pavlicevic, Mercédès (2006b). "Worksongs, Playsongs: Communication, Collaboration, Culture and Community." *Australian Journal of Music Therapy, 17*, 85–99.

Pavlicevic, Mercédès and Gary Ansdell (eds) (2004). *Community Music Therapy.* London: Jessica Kingsley Publishers.

Pavlicevic, Mercédès and Gary Ansdell (2009). "Between Communicative Musicality and Collaborative Musicing" in Malloch, Stephen and Colwyn Trevarthen (eds), *Communicative Musicality.* Oxford: Oxford University Press.

Pelach-Galil, Ricky, Frida Kaushinsky and David Bargal (2002). "Us and Them – Before we are Together: The Importance of the Process in Separate Groups Before the Intergroup Encounter" in Kacen, Lea and Rachel Lev-Wiesel (eds), *Group Work in a Multi Cultural Society* (Hebrew). Tel-Aviv: Cherikover Publishing Inc.

Poole, Steven (2006). *Unspeak: How Words Become Weapons, How Weapons Become a Message, and How That Message Becomes Reality.* London: Abacus.

Priestley, Mary (1975/1985). *Music Therapy in Action.* St. Louis, MO: MagnaMusic Baton.

Procter, Simon (2004). "Playing Politics: Community Music Therapy and the Therapeutic Redistribution of Music Capital for Mental Health" in Pavlicevic, Mercédès and Gary Ansdell (eds), *Community Music Therapy.* London: Jessica Kingsley Publishers.

Procter, Simon (2006). "What are we Playing at? Social Capital and Music Therapy" in Edwards, Rosalind, Jane Franklin and Janet Holland (eds), *Assessing Social Capital: Concept, Policy and Practice.* Cambridge: Scholars Press.

Putnam, Robert (2000). *Bowling Alone: The Collapse and Revival of American Community.* New York: Simon and Schuster.

Rappaport, Julian (1987). "Terms of Empowerment/Exemplars of Prevention: Toward a Theory of Community Psychology." *American Journal of Community Psychology, 15*, pp. 121–44.

Ridder, Hanne-Mette O. (2001a). *Musikk & Demens. Musikaktiviteter og musikterapi med demensramte* [Music & Dementia. Music Activities and Music Therapy with People Suffering from Dementia]. Aalborg, Denmark: FormidlingsCenter Nord.

Ridder, Hanne-Mette O. (2001b). "Musikterapi med ældre" [Music therapy with the Elderly] in Bonde, Lars Ole, Inge Nygaard Pedersen and Tony Wigram (eds), *Musikterapi: når ord ikke slår til* [Music Therapy: When Words are Not Enough]. Aarhus, Denmark: Forlaget Klim.

Ridder, Hanne-Mette O. (2003). "Singing Dialogue. Music Therapy with Persons in Advanced Stages of Dementia. A Case Study Research Design." PhD-dissertation. Aalborg, Denmark: University of Aalborg. Retrieved September

18, 2008, from http://www.musikterapi.aau.dk/forskerskolen_2006/-phd-ridder.htm.

Rizzolatti, Giacomo, Leonardo Fogassi and Vittorio Gallese (2006). "Mirrors in the Mind." *Scientific American,* November 2006, pp. 30–37.

Rolvsjord, Randi (2002). *Når musikken blir språk. Musikalsk kommunikasjon i musikkterapi – et dialektisk perspektiv* [When Music Becomes Language. Musical Communication in Music Therapy – A Dialectical Perspective]. Oslo, Norway: Unipub forlag.

Rolvsjord, Randi (2004). "Therapy as Empowerment: Clinical and Political Implications of Empowerment Philosophy in Mental Health Practices of Music Therapy." *Nordic Journal of Music Therapy, 13*(2), pp. 99–111.

Rolvsjord Randi (2006). "Whose Power of Music? A Discussion on Music and Power-relations in Music Therapy." *British Journal of Music Therapy, 20*(1), pp. 5–12.

Rolvsjord, Randi (2007). "'Blackbirds Singing': Explorations of Resource-oriented Music Therapy in Mental Health Care." Unpublished Doctoral Thesis. Aalborg, Denmark: Aalborg University, Institute for Psychology and Communication.

Rolvsjord, Randi, Christian Gold and Brynjulf Stige (2005a). "Research Rigour and Therapeutic Flexibility: Rationale for a Therapy Manual Developed for a Randomized Controlled Trial." *Nordic Journal of Music Therapy, 14*(1), pp. 15–32.

Rolvsjord, Randi, Christian Gold and Brynjulf Stige (2005b). "Therapeutic Principles for Resource-oriented Music Therapy: A Contextual Approach to the Field of Mental Health." *Nordic Journal of Music Therapy* [online]. Retrieved January 18, 2006, from http://www.hisf.no/njmt/appendrolvsjord141.html.

Ronen, Hannan (1997). "The Inclusion of Special Children in Mainstream Education (Hebrew)." *Issues in Special Education and Rehabilitation, 12*(2), pp. 21–9.

Rosenwasser, Nava (1997). "Group Work: A Means for Community Development" in Rosenwasser, Nava and Liron Nathan (eds), *Anthology of Group Training* (Hebrew). Jerusalem: Zippory Community Educational Center.

Rosenwasser, Nava and Liron Nathan (1997). "What is a Group – Basic Definitions in Social Psychology" in Rosenwasser, Nava and Liron Nathan (eds), *Anthology of Group Training* (Hebrew). Jerusalem: Zippory Community Educational Center.

Ruud, Even (1980a). *Music Therapy and its Relationship to Current Treatment Theories*. St Louis, MO: MagnaMusic-Baton.

Ruud, Even (1980b). *Hva er musikkterapi?* [What is Music Therapy?] Oslo, Norway: Gyldendal.

Ruud, Even (1987/1990). *Musikk som kommunikasjon og samhandling. Teoretiske perspektiv på musikkterapien.* [Music as Communication and Interaction. Theoretical Perspectives on Music Therapy.] Oslo, Norway: Solum.

Ruud, Even (1991). "Improvisasjon som liminal erfaring – om jazz og musikkterapi som overgangsritualer" [Improvisation as Liminal Experience – On Jazz and Music Therapy as Rites de Passage], in: Stige, Brynjulf and Bente Østergaard (eds), *Levande musikk. Foredrag og referat fra 1. nordiske musikkterapikonferanse* [Live Music. Proceedings from the First Nordic Music Therapy Conference]. Sandane, Norway: Høgskuleutdanninga på Sandane.

Ruud, Even (1995). "Jazz and Music Therapy as Modern 'Rites de Passage' in Kenny, Carolyn B. (ed.), *Listening, Playing, Creating. Essays on the Power of Sound.* Albany: State University of New York Press.

Ruud, Even (1996). *Musikk og verdier. Musikkpedagogiske essays* [Music and Values. Essays on Music Education]. Oslo, Norway: Universitetsforlaget.

Ruud, Even (1997a). "Music and the Quality of Life." *Nordic Journal of Music Therapy, 6*(2), pp. 86–97.

Ruud, Even (1997b). *Musikk og identitet* [Music and Identity]. Oslo, Norway: Universitetsforlaget.

Ruud, Even (1998). *Music Therapy: Improvisation, Communication and Culture.* Gilsum, NH: Barcelona Publishers.

Ruud, Even (2002). "Music as a Cultural Immunogen – Three Narratives on the Use of Music as a Technology of Health" in Hanken, Ingrid Maria, Siw Graabæk and Monika Nerland (eds), *Research in and for Higher Music Education. Festschrift for Harald Jørgensen.* Oslo, Norway: NMH-Publications, 2002:2.

Ruud, Even (2004a). "Foreword. Reclaiming Music" in Pavlicevic, Mercédès and Gary Ansdell (eds), *Community Music Therapy.* London: Jessica Kingsley Publishers.

Ruud, Even (2004b). "Defining Community Music Therapy" [Contribution to Moderated Discussions] *Voices: A World Forum for Music Therapy.* Retrieved October 21, 2005 from http://www.voices.-no/discussions/discm4_04.html.

Ruud, Even (2004c). "Systemisk og framføringsbasert musikkterapi" [Systemic and Performance-based Music Therapy]. *Musikkterapi,* 4-2004, pp. 28–34.

Ruud, Even (2005). "Community Music Therapy III" [Contribution to Moderated Discussions] [online]. *Voices: A World Forum for Music Therapy.* Retrieved October 21, 2005 from http://www.voices.-no/discussions/discm4_08.html.

Sacks, Oliver (2007). *Musicophilia.* London: Picador.

Said, Edward (1991). *Musical Elaborations.* London: Chatto & Windus.

Sawyer, R. Keith (2003). *Group Creativity: Music, Theater, Collaboration.* London: New Erlbaum.

Sawyer, R. Keith (2005). "Music and Conversation" in Miell, Dorothy, Raymond MacDonald and David Hargreaves (eds), *Musical Communication.* Oxford: Oxford University Press.

Schalkwijk, Frans W. (1987). *Music and People with Developmental Disabilities: Music Therapy, Remedial Music Making and Musical Activities.* London: Jessica Kingsley Publishers.

Schechner, Richard (2002). *Performance Studies: An Introduction.* London: Routledge.

Schutz, Alfred (1964). "Making Music Together: A Study in Social Relationship." in *Collected Papers, vol.2*. The Hague: Martinus Nijhoff.

Scott, Derek B. (ed.) (2000). *Music, Culture, and Society. A Reader.* Oxford: Oxford University Press.

Sennett, Richard (2004). *Respect: The Formation of Character in an Age of Inequality*. London: Allen Lane.

Smail, David 2005). *Power, Interest, and Psychology: Elements of a Social Materialist Understanding of Distress.* Ross-on-Wye, UK: PCCS Books.

Small, Christopher (1987). *Music of the Common Tongue. Survival and Celebration in African American Music.* Hanover, NH: Wesleyan University Press.

Small, Christopher (1998). *Musicking. The Meanings of Performing and Listening.* Hanover, NH: Wesleyan University Press.

Smith, Jonathan A. (2008). *Qualitative Psychology. A Practical Guide to Research Methods* (Second Edition). London and Thousand Oaks, CA: Sage Publications.

Smith, Linda Tuhiwai (1999). *Decolonizing Methodologies: Research and Indigenous Peoples.* London: Zed.

Smith, Susan E., Dennis G. Willms and Nancy A. Johnson (eds) (1997). *Nurtured by Knowledge: Learning to do Participatory Action Research.* New York: Apex Press.

Solli, Hans Petter (2006). "Aldri bare syk. Om ressursorientert musikkterapi for en mann med schizofreni" [Never Just Sick. On Resource-oriented Music Therapy for a Man with Schizophrenia]. Unpublished master thesis. Oslo, Norway: The National Academy of Music.

Steinberg, Jonny (2005). *The Number.* Johannesburg: Jonathan Ball.

Stern, Daniel (1985). *The Interpersonal World of the Infant.* New York, Basic Books.

Stern, Daniel (2004). *The Present Moment in Psychotherapy and Everyday Life.* New York: Norton.

Stewart, David (2004). "Narratives in a New Key: Transformational Contexts in Music Therapy" in Pavlicevic, Mercédès and Gary Ansdell (eds), *Community Music Therapy.* London: Jessica Kingsley Publications.

Stige, Brynjulf (1983). "Ngoma, musirør og anna rør" [Ngoma, Music, and Movement]. Unpublished thesis. Oslo, Norway: Østlandets musikkonservatorium.

Stige, Brynjulf (1993). "Endringar i det musikkterapeutiske 'rommet' – med kulturarbeid i lokalsamfunnet som eit eksempel" [Changes in the Music Therapy "Space" – With Cultural Engagement in the Local Community as an Example]. *Nordic Journal of Music Therapy, 2*(2), pp. 11–22.

Stige, Brynjulf (1995). *Samspel og relasjon. Perspektiv på ein inkluderande musikkpedagogikk* [Interaction and Relationship. Perspectives on Inclusive Music Education.] Oslo, Norway: Samlaget.

Stige, Brynjulf (2002). *Culture-Centered Music Therapy.* Gilsum, NH: Barcelona Publishers.

Stige, Brynjulf (2003). *Elaborations toward a Notion of Community Music Therapy.* Doctoral thesis, University of Oslo, Norway, published by: Unipub.

Stige, Brynjulf (2004a). "Community Music Therapy: Culture, Care and Welfare" in Pavlicevic, Mercédès and Gary Ansdell (eds), *Community Music Therapy.* London: Jessica Kingsley Publications.

Stige, Brynjulf (2004b). "On Defining Community Music Therapy" [Contribution to Moderated Discussions]. *Voices: A World Forum for Music Therapy.* Retrieved October 28, 2005 from http://voices.no/discussions/discm4_05.html.

Stige, Brynjulf (2005a). "Participatory Action Research" in Wheeler, Barbara (ed.), *Music Therapy Research.* Gilsum, NH: Barcelona Publishers.

Stige, Brynjulf (2005b). "Musikk som tilbud om deltakelse" [Music as a Possibility of Participation] in Säfvenbom, Reidar (ed.), *Fritidsaktiviteter i moderne oppvekst – grunnbok i aktivitetsfag* [Leisure Activities in Modern Adolescence]. Oslo, Norway: Universitetsforlaget.

Stige, Brynjulf (2006a). "The Problem of Pleasure in Music Therapy." *British Journal of Music Therapy, 20*(1), pp. 39–51.

Stige, Brynjulf (2006b). "Toward a Notion of Participation in Music Therapy." *Nordic Journal of Music Therapy, 15*(2), pp. 121–38.

Stige, Brynjulf (2007). "The Grieg Effect – On the Contextualized Effects of Music in Music Therapy." *Voices: A World Forum for Music Therapy.* Retrieved November 12, 2007, from http://www.voices.no/mainissues/mi40007000246.php.

Strawson, Peter F. (1974). *Freedom and Resentment* (excerpt retrieved April 14, 2007, from http://evans-experientialism.freewebspace.com/strawson_pf.htm). Original publisher: London: Methuen.

Streeter, Elaine (2006). "Response to 'Music Psychotherapy and Community Music Therapy: Questions and Considerations' by Alan Turry" [Contribution to Moderated Discussions] *Voices: A World Forum for Music Therapy.* Retrieved September 14, 2008, from http://www.voices.no/-discussions/discm42_04.html

Sydoriak, Diane (1996). "Defining Inclusion: How Do We Translate Words into Actions?" *Exceptional Parent, 26*(9), pp. 40–42.

Taylor, Charles (1985). "Language and Human Nature" in Taylor, Charles (ed.), *Human Agency and Language. Philosophical Papers 1.* Cambridge, UK: Cambridge University Press.

Thaut, Michael (2005). "Rhythm, Human Temporality and Brain Function" in Miell, Dorothy, Raymond MacDonald and David Hargreaves (eds), *Musical Communication.* Oxford: Oxford University Press.

Toynbee, Jason (2000). *Making Popular Music: Musician, Aesthetics and the Manufacture of Popular Music.* London: Hodder Arnold.

Trevarthen, Colwyn (2000). "Musicality and the Intrinsic Motive Pulse: Evidence from Human Psychobiology and Infant Communication." *Musicae Scientiae* (Special Issue 1999–2000), pp. 155–215.

Trevarthen, Colwyn (2001). "Intrinsic Motives for Companionship in Understanding: Their Origin, Development, and Significance for Infant Mental Health." *Infant Mental Health Journal, 22*(1–2), pp. 95–131.

Trevarthen, Colwyn and Stephen Malloch (2000). "The Dance of Wellbeing: Defining the Musical Therapeutic Effect." *Nordic Journal of Music Therapy, 9*(2), pp. 3–17.

Turner, Victor (1967a). "Betwixt and Between. The Liminal Period in Rites de Passage" in *The Forest of Symbols: Aspects of Ndembu Ritual.* Ithaca, NY: Cornell University Press.

Turner, Victor (1967b). "A Ndembu Doctor in Practice" in *The Forest of Symbols: Aspects of Ndembu Ritual.* Ithaca, NY: Cornell University Press.

Turner, Victor (1969). *The Ritual Process: Structure and Anti-Structure.* Chicago: Aldine.

Turner, Victor (1982). *From Ritual to Theatre: The Human Seriousness of Play.* New York: PAJ Publications.

Turner, Victor (1987). *The Anthropology of Performance.* New York: PAJ Publications.

Turry, Alan (2005). "Music Psychotherapy and Community Music Therapy: Questions and Considerations." *Voices: A World Forum for Music Therapy.* Retrieved October 28, 2005 from http://voices.no/-mainissues/mi40005000 171.html

Tyler, Helen (2000). "The Music Therapy Profession in Modern Britain" in Horden, Peregrine (ed.), *Music as Medicine.* Aldershot, UK: Ashgate.

Tyler, Helen (2002). "Working, Playing and Relating: Issues in Group Music Therapy for Children with Special Needs" in Davies, Alison and Eleanor Richards (eds), *Music Therapy and Group Work.* London: Jessica Kingsley Publishers.

Tyson, Florence (1968). "The Community Music Therapy Center" in Gaston, E. Thayer (ed.), *Music in Therapy.* New York: Macmillan Publishing.

Vetlesen, Arne Johan (1994). *Perception, Empathy, and Judgment. An Inquiry into the Preconditions of Mortal Performance.* University Park, PA: The Pennsylvania State University Press.

Vetlesen, Arne Johan and Per Nortvedt (2000). *Følelser og moral* [Emotions and Morality]. Oslo, Norway: AdNotam Gyldendal.

Wallin, Nils L., Björn Merker and Steven Brown (eds) (2000). *The Origins of Music.* Cambridge, MA: The MIT Press.

Walsh-Stewart, Ruth (2002). "Music Therapy Groups with Adults" in Davies, Alison and Eleanor Richards (eds), *Music Therapy and Group Work.* London: Jessica Kingsley Publishers.

Warner, Catherine (2005). "Music Therapy with Adults with Learning Difficulties and 'Severe Challenging Behaviour.' An Action Research Inquiry into the Benefits of Group Music Therapy within a Community Home." Unpublished Doctoral Dissertation, Bristol, UK: University of the West of England.

Wenger, Etienne (1998). *Communities of Practice: Learning, Meaning and Identity.* New York: Cambridge University Press.

Wenger, Etienne, Richard McDermott, and William M. Snyder (2002). *Cultivating Communities of Practice.* Boston, MA: Harvard Business School Press.

Whitaker, Dorothy S. (1985). *Using Groups to Help People.* London: Tavistock/ Routledge.

Whitehead, Charles (2001). "Social Mirrors and Shared Experiential Worlds." *Journal of Consciousness Studies, 8*(4), pp. 3–36.

Wigram, Tony, Inge Nygaard Pedersen and Lars Ole Bonde (2002). *A Comprehensive Guide to Music Therapy: Theory, Clinical Practice, Research and Training.* London: Jessica Kingsley Publishers.

Wigram, Tony and Cochavit Elefant (2009). "Nurturing Engagement with Music for People with PDD: Autistic Spectrum Disorder and Rett Syndrome" in Malloch, Stephen and Colwyn Trevarthen (eds), *Communicative Musicality.* Oxford: Oxford University Press.

Williams, Alastair (2001). *Constructing Musicology.* Aldershot, UK: Ashgate.

Williamon, Aaron and Jane Davidson (2002). "Exploring Co-performer Communication." *Musicae Scientiae, VI*(1), pp. 53–72.

Wilson, Brian L. (ed.) (1996). *Models of Music Therapy Interventions in School Settings: From Institution to Inclusion.* Silver Spring, MD: National Association for Music Therapy.

Wittgenstein, Ludwig (1953/1967). *Philosophical Investigations.* Oxford: Blackwell.

Wittgenstein, Ludwig (1958/1969). *The Blue and Brown Books* [preliminary studies for Philosophical Investigations.] Oxford: Blackwell.

Wood, Stuart, Rachel Verney and Jessica Atkinson (2004). "From Therapy to Community: Making Music in Neurological Rehabilitation" in Pavlicevic, Mercédès and Gary Ansdell (eds), *Community Music Therapy.* London: Jessica Kingsley Publishers.

Wood, Stuart (2006). "'The Matrix': A Model of Community Music Therapy Processes." *Voices: A World Forum for Music Therapy.* Retrieved September 14, 2008, from http://www.voices.no/mainissues/-mi40006000218.php.

Yalom, Irvin D. (1995). *The Theory and Practice of Group Psychotherapy* (4th edition). New York: Basic Books.

Zanini, Claudia Regina de Oliveira (2006). "Therapeutic Choir – A Music Therapist Looks at the New Millenium Elderly." *Voices: A World Forum for Music Therapy.* Retrieved April 9, 2007, from www.voices.no/mainissues/ mi40006000211.html.

Zharinova-Sanderson, Oksana (2004). "Promoting Integration and Socio-cultural Change: Community Music Therapy with Traumatised Refugees in Berlin" in Pavlicevic, Mercédès and Gary Ansdell (eds), *Community Music Therapy.* London: Jessica Kingsley Publishers.

Index